TREKS AND CLIMBS IN WADI RUM JORDAN

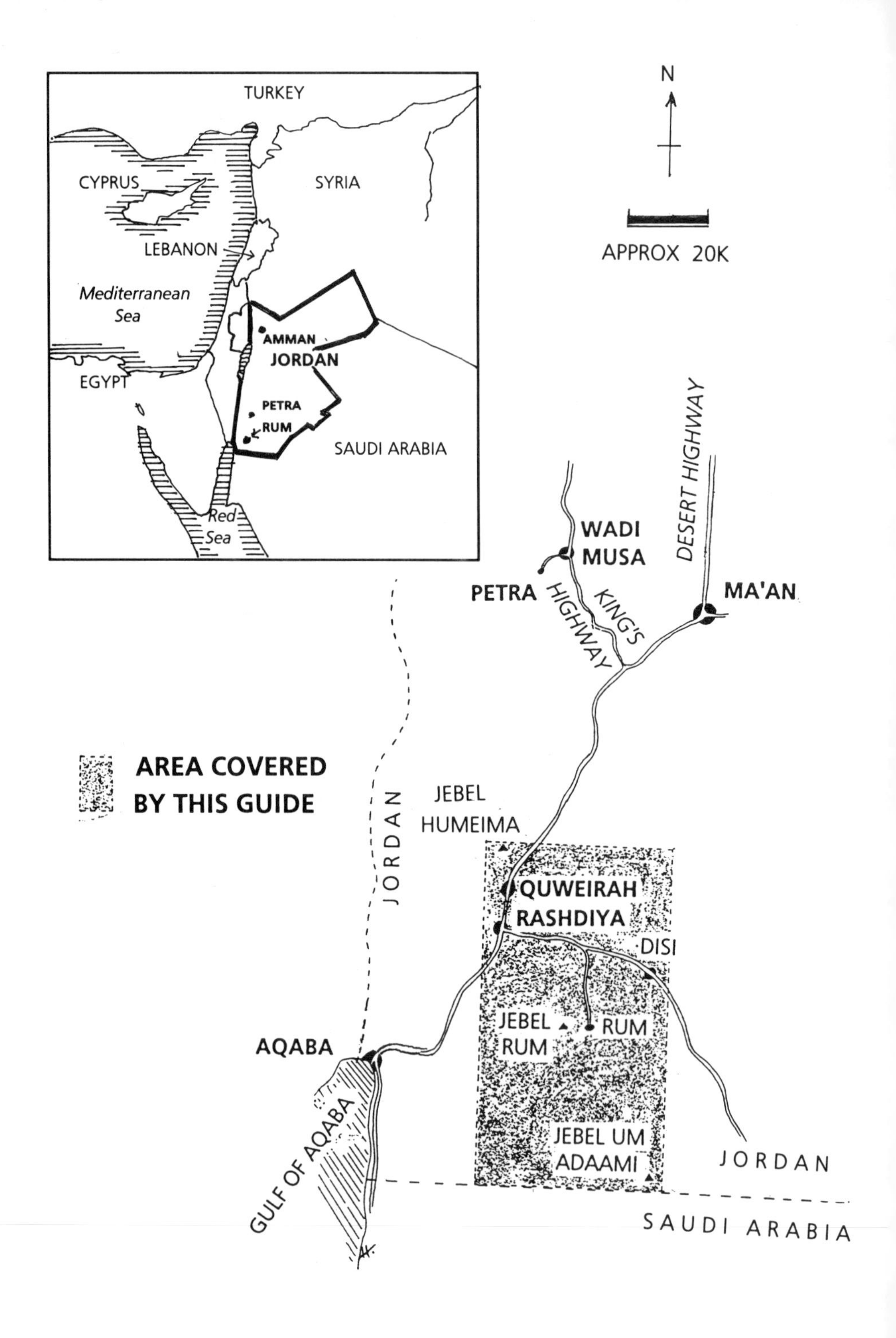
TURKEY
CYPRUS
SYRIA
LEBANON
Mediterranean Sea
AMMAN
JORDAN
EGYPT
PETRA
RUM
SAUDI ARABIA
Red Sea
N
APPROX 20K
DESERT HIGHWAY
WADI MUSA
PETRA
KING'S HIGHWAY
MA'AN
AREA COVERED BY THIS GUIDE
JORDAN
JEBEL HUMEIMA
QUWEIRAH
RASHDIYA
DISI
JEBEL RUM
RUM
AQABA
GULF OF AQABA
JEBEL UM ADAAMI
JORDAN
SAUDI ARABIA

TREKS AND CLIMBS IN WADI RUM

JORDAN

by
Tony Howard

Cicerone Press, Police Square, Milnthorpe, Cumbria, England

ISBN 1 85284 135 4

A catalogue record for this book is available from the British Library

1st Edition 1987
Revised 2nd Edition 1994
Revised 3rd Edition 1997

This Publication is sponsored by:
Ministry of Tourism
P.O. Box 224, Amman, Jordan
and was compiled under the auspices of
N.O.M.A.D.S.
(New Opportunities For Mountaineering, Adventure and Desert Sports)
An exploration group headed by the author, and Di Taylor

The author and publisher cannot accept any responsibility for loss, injury or inconvenience resulting from the use of information contained in this guide.

Readers are advised that whilst every effort is made to ensure the accuracy of this guidebook, changes can occur locally which may affect the contents.

The publisher would welcome notes of any changes.

Front cover: View across Wadi Rum to South Nassrani and Draif al Muragh, from Hammad's Route, Jebel Rum. Photo: Dawson

Back cover: The rock bridge of Burdah. Photo: Verin

CONTENTS

REGION OF WADI RUM

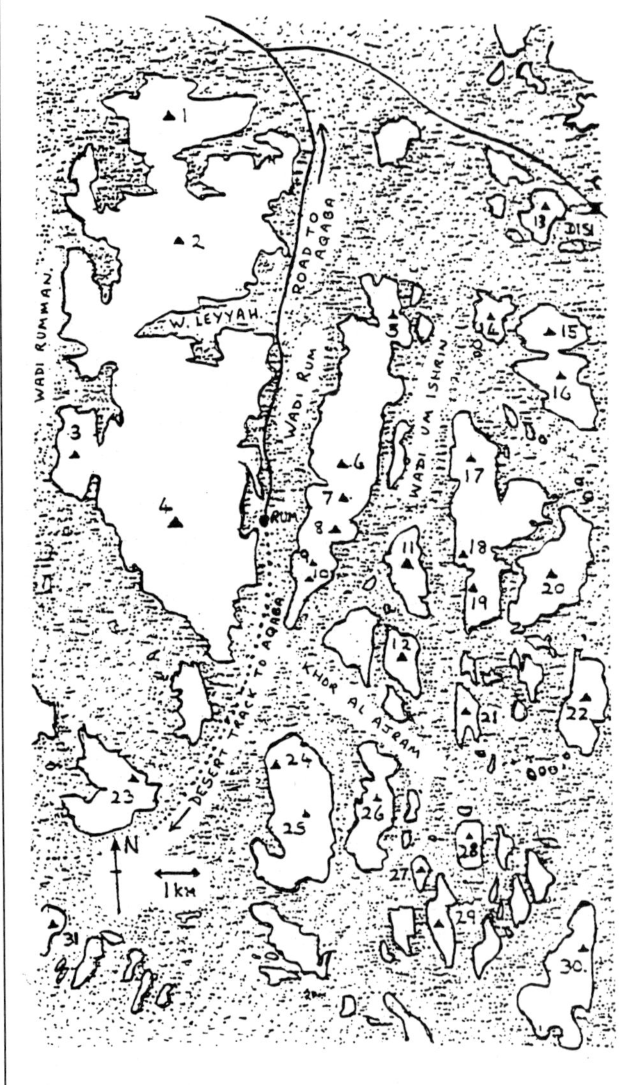

1 JEBEL HUBEIRA
2 JEBEL LEYYAH
3 JEBEL RUMMAN
4 JEBEL RUM
5 JEBEL MAKHRAS
6 JEBEL UM ISHRIN
7 JEBEL KHARAZEH
8 JEBEL UM EJIL
9 N. NASSRANI
10 S. NASSRANI
11 JEBEL ANNAFISHIYYAH
12 JEBEL UM KHARG
13 JEBEL UM ZERNOUK
14 JEBEL AL HASANI
15 JEBEL UM ANFUS
16 JEBEL ARASHRASHA
17 JEBEL BARRAH
18 AL RIDDAH AL BEIDAH
19 S. BARRAH
20 JEBEL ABU JUDAIDAH
21 JEBEL ER RAQA
22 JEBEL UM HARAG
23 JEBEL AL QATTAR
24 JEBEL KHAZALI
25 JEBEL KUSH KASHAH
26 JEBEL QABR AMRA
27 JEBEL IKHNAISSER
28 JEBEL ABU KASHABA
29 JEBEL ABU KHSHEIBAH
30 BURDAH
31 AL MAGHRAR

FOREWORD

"Rumm the magnificent... vast, echoing and godlike... a processional way greater than imagination... the crimson sunset burned on its stupendous cliffs and slanted ladders of hazy fire down its walled avenue."

T.E.Lawrence
Seven Pillars of Wisdom

We were indeed privileged to be the first climbing expedition to Wadi Rum in 1984 and over the following years to be able to prepare three editions of this guidebook to such a unique area described by a leading British climber as "one of the best desert climbing areas in the world".

No book of this nature is ever the work of one person: the author merely documents in hopefully understandable form the discoveries of those involved in the various treks and climbs. The first edition of this book was predominantly the outcome of the combined efforts of the author and four others: Alan Baker, Wilfried Colonna, Mick Shaw and Di Taylor, in later years aided by Bernard Domenech who became, like us, captivated by the area and its people. It must be said here that since inviting our friend Wilf Colonna to join us in Wadi Rum on our second visit, his annual contribution to the new route scene and his work on equipping descents, often with Bernard Domenech, has been outstanding.

Other climbers inevitably fell under its spell making major contributions to route development. First on the scene after us were the Remy brothers from Switzerland climbing a new route every day of their two visits in a frenzy of activity. Rowland Edwards and his son, Mark, also made a couple of early visits leaving some great classics. Precht and Haupolter and friends of Austria were soon on the scene, Precht returning annually to dominate the bold big wall activity, whilst Geoff Hornby and friends from England opened up, amongst other things, some excellent slab climbing on the eastern summits during their frequent visits. Other climbers from Italy, Spain, France, Britain and elsewhere in Europe made their mark with sport climbs and adventure climbs of all grades of difficulty rapidly putting each edition of this guide out of date. No doubt this issue will suffer the same fate as ever more climbers discover the delights of Rum: its desert canyons, its Bedouin classics and its big wall epics. I cannot resist a plea here that in doing so they will think very carefully before adding to the increasing amount of fixed and sometimes unsightly protection points that are remorselessly appearing throughout the area. The spirit of the Bedouin routes is pure adventure: let's keep it that way!

For us the Bedouin are the essence of Rum. They have become the closest of friends and continue to reveal ever more surprising climbs as well as treating us to their warm hospitality and roguish humour. The relationship between climbers and the local people has in fact generally been excellent, bringing both economic benefits to the community and unforgettable experiences to the visitor as well as allowing both to experience something of each other's culture: may it long continue to do so!

GENERAL ACKNOWLEDGEMENTS

I must first thank Mr M. Hamarneh and Mr El Bahri of the Jordanian Ministries of Information and Tourism without whose initial invitation and consequent sponsorship the first edition could not have been written. Also, Mr Nasri Atalla, for his continued support of subsequent editions - even into his retirement!

At the Royal Jordanian Society for the Conservation of Nature, I am grateful to Mr Omar Rahmad for his enthusiastic interest and his notes on wildlife of the region; also to Khalid Irani and Adnan Budieri for their advice, encouragement and efforts to protect the ibex, perhaps with the eventual creation of a National Park. For his Report on the ancient peoples of Rum I am indebted to M.C.A. McDonald.

I would also like to thank all those who sponsored, or in any way encouraged our first exploratory expeditions to Wadi Rum in 1984, '85 and '86 for the writing of the first edition of this guide. (In the early days, Wadi Rum was more of a Bedouin encampment than a village, approached by a pot-holed single track road which stopped just before the fort; the Rest House was an unused empty shell, there was no electricity in the village and what little water there was came from Lawrence's Well, so the term 'expedition' was rather more justified then than now!) In particular, I must thank Alia, the Royal Jordanian Airline, and Jasmin Tours for assistance with travel, and Wadi Rum Camel Corps and the Royal Jordanian Army for supplying maps and permits. For help with accommodation and general information, I am indebted to International Traders, Aqaba Hotel, Alcazar Hotel, Petra Forum Hotel and Sami Ajarmeh of the Aqaba Visitor Centre. Also, in recent years, to Samir Farouqa, the Tourism Ministry representative in Wadi Rum.

Once the Rest House came into use by the Tourism Ministry, we benefited greatly from the unique and often flamboyant management style of Jamal Ashab. I am happy to say this hospitality has continued to the present day, though the business is now in the very capable private hands of Mahmoud Hillawi and his son Ali. The excellent food of Ata the chef, (not to mention the beer), as well as all the other facilities have made this a great place to return to after a long hot day on the hill!

Thanks also to Jamal Ashab for writing the Arabic at the back of this book to thank the Bedouin for their invaluable contribution. In particular, I thank the late Mohammed Moussa and his son Salim for their friendship and the happy nights at their camp. Also Hammad Hamdan, Sheikh Kraim, Sabbah Eid and Atieeq Auda for some great days in the hills and warm nights by their fires and last but by no means least, Sheikh Atieeq and his family, particularly the brothers Mazied, Eid, Dayfallah, and Sabbah who have become our inseparable friends since 1984.

I also thank Christine Evans for help with translation and Linda Nelson and Tracey Morris of Troll Safety Equipt. Ltd., for having the patience to decode my notes and type this manuscript. Finally, a special thanks to Di Taylor without whose constant inspiration and encouragement none of this would have happened!

Tony Howard, January 1996

AHLAN WA SAHLAN, WELCOME TO JORDAN

MR N.ATALLA, DIRECTOR OF TOURISM

We hope your visit to Jordan will be a pleasurable one, and long enough to see all the unique and fascinating attractions the country has to offer. Jordan is a vacation land of surprising contrasts and variety, and there's something here for everyone to enjoy, a memorable wealth of ancient treasures and modern pleasures.

For the adventurous, there's an exciting trip to the long lost Nabataean city of Petra...scuba diving in the coral paradise beneath Aqaba's sparkling waters...bird watching at Azraq Oasis...and, of course rock climbing, para-gliding and camel riding in Wadi Rum desert where Lawrence of Arabia once rode.

If your interest is archaeology, you'll find ruins and digs in every corner of the land, some going back 10,000 years. For historians, there's the Graeco-Roman city of Jerash; for sensation seekers a swim in the Dead Sea, lowest spot on earth; for health addicts, the thermal springs where Herod bathed. Crusader buffs have the imposing castles at Kerak and Shoubak...Islamic students, the 8th century desert palaces of the Omayyad caliphs.

Add to that and more, the modern pleasures of Jordan - air conditioned hotels, restaurants that cater to every palate, from Arabic to American to Chinese...plus swimming pools, tennis courts, discotheques and, of course, souks, where gold bracelets are a real bargain.

And everywhere, there are the Jordanians. Each and every one is a self-appointed host and guide. Arab hospitality here is an imperative. From the first moment, you are made to feel at home. It's *Ahlan wa sahlan* from the heart. And when you leave, it will be *Ma'salami*.

Here's a mini-guide of what not to miss:

Amman

Amman's story goes back thousands of years, long before recorded history, to the Palaeolithic age. In Biblical times it was known as Rabbath Ammon and, under the Ptolemies, as Philadelphia. Today, Amman is Jordan's capital, a thoroughly modern, rapidly growing 20th-century city. It still sits splendidly on its traditional seven hills or jebels, has first rate hotels, provides restaurants for every sort of cuisine, and offers the visitor a variety of entertainment and sports. For camel-racing, it's the Amman Hippodrome, where you can also see fine Arab horses running in weekly meets.

Amman's most impressive monument is the huge Roman amphitheatre which dates to the 2nd century A.D. and stands in beautifully restored grandeur in the centre of the city. (And don't miss the Costume and Folklore Museums housed beneath its tiers.) Other sites of interest are the Roman ruins on Citadel Hill and the nearby Archaeological Museum, where there is a fine chronological display of Jordan's ancient treasures.

Jerash

This "Pompeii of the Middle East", is only a half-hour's drive north from Amman. Here are grand ruins - temples to Artemis and Zeus (listen to the Whisphering Columns), a vast Roman Forum, Hadrian's Triumphal Arch, and a mile-long street of Columns. Have lunch on the tree-shaded terrace of the attractive Government Rest House and look in at the Tourist Information Centre to learn more about the history of this second century Decapolis city. Take a short drive through the pine forests and olive groves of Debbin National Park to Ajlun and the Arab Castle of Crusader times, Qalat Er-Rabad, where you'll have a magnificent panoramic view of the entire Jordan valley.

Madaba, Mount Nebo, Dead Sea

Thirty kilometres south of Amman is Madaba where you'll see some of the finest Byzantine mosaics in the world. Most famous is the 6th-century mosaic map of Palestine, possibly the oldest map of the Holy Land in existence. Nearby is historic Mount Nebo, with a remarkable view of the Jordan Valley, The Dead Sea, and the spires of Jerusalem in the distance. On the summit at Siyagha in the ruins of a church are other rare and beautiful mosaics. Below Mount Nebo to the southwest lie the hot mineral springs of Zarka Ma'in, the Callirhoe of classical times used by Herod the Great to heal his afflicted body, now the site of a modern hotel and health spa. To the south is Moukawir, the site of Herod's palace, where tradition has it that Salome danced and John the Baptist was beheaded. A new road branching south from the Amman-Jerusalem highway leads to Suweimeh on the Dead Sea. Here you'll find a resort area with beach chalets, picnic areas, and an excellent restaurant. If you've never tried it, bathing in the Dead Sea is a unique and truly "unsinkable" experience.

Desert Castles

East of Amman and dotting the wide desert are a string of 8th century qasrs or castles built by the Omayyad caliphs of Damascus as hunting lodges. Best preserved of them and most interesting to visit are Qasr Kharaneh (the only one built for defence and not pleasure) and Qasr Amra, with its beautiful frescoes showing lively scenes of Omayyad times. Beyond the castles lies Azraq Oasis, the only permanent body of water in 12,000 square miles of desert, and a migratory path for hundreds of species of birds. Amid the many pools is Qasr Azraq, the black basalt fort originally built by Roman legionnaires that Lawrence of Arabia used as his headquarters during the Arab Revolt. There's a new government motel here offering excellent overnight accommodation.

The King's Highway, Kerak, Shoubak

One of the most historic and scenic roads in the world is the ancient King's Highway that runs from Amman to Aqaba. Motorists in a hurry take the modern Desert Highway, but leisurely travellers prefer the spectacular route down the Wadi Mujib past Madaba to Kerak and past Wadi Dana to Shoubak. About 125 kilometres from Amman along this highway is the Crusader castle at Kerak, imposing for its massive size and awesome location on the rim of a plateau 1000m above sea level. It was the most impregnable of the chain of fortresses built by the Crusaders in south Jordan. Within the remains of its ancient walls today lies a modern town whose inhabitants trace their ancestry back to the Knights of the Cross. Further south on the same road is another impressive Crusader fortress, Shoubak.

Petra

One of Jordan's most exciting and adventurous travel experiences is a trip to Petra, hidden away in the encircling craggy rock mountains south of the Dead Sea. Three hours by car over the Desert highway brings you to this "rose-red city half as old as time", carved from the living rock over 2,000 years ago by the Nabataeans. It is reached through a narrow defile or siq flanked by towering cliffs. The sudden view of Petra's most spectacular monument, the Khazneh or Treasury, at the end of the siq is a dramatic sight. Other unique monuments carved right into the vari-coloured mountains are the High Place, the gigantic Dier or Monastery, and the Roman-styled Palace Tomb. For accommodation, there is the Petra Hotel or the fine Government Rest House outside the siq. The nearby town of Wadi Musa has a number of good hotels of all grades, from Musa Spring and Al Anbat high above the town, to the Sunset Hotel, close to the Rest House.

Aqaba and Wadi Rum

Five hours by car or forty minutes by plane from Amman is Aqaba, Jordan's winter resort on the Red Sea. Here, fine sandy beaches, excellent all-year round bathing, water sports, deep-sea fishing, and a fabulous underwater world of coral reefs and tropical fish are the main attractions. Hotels are modern, air conditioned and three diving clubs offer excellent facilities for scuba divers. A day's excursion from Aqaba can be made into "Lawrence of Arabia" country, the desert of Wadi Rum, where weird, wind-sculpted hills stand like foreboding sentinels upon the pale sands. Camp at the Rest House, and enjoy the facilities of restaurant and bar, or have coffee at the Desert Police Post and ride a camel, and maybe have a 'mensef', that feast of Bedouin. Camp with them and climb amongst these spectacular mountains, even para-glide down again. It is an experience you will never forget.

INTRODUCTION

The scenic grandeur of Wadi Rum received its first accolade from Lawrence of Arabia in his Seven Pillars of Wisdom. His description of his entry into the Wadi is memorable:

"Day was still young as we rode between two great pikes of sandstone to the foot of a long, soft slope poured down from the domed hills in front of us. It was tamarisk-covered: the beginning of the Valley of Rumm, they said. We looked up to the left to a long wall of rock, sheering in like a thousand-foot wave towards the middle of the valley; whose other arc, to the right, was an opposing line of steep, red broken hills. We rode up the slope, crashing our way through the brittle undergrowth.

"As we went, the brushwood grouped itself into thickets whose massed leaves took on a stronger tint of green the purer for their contrasted setting in plots of open sand of a cheerful delicate pink. The ascent became gentle, till the valley was a confined tilted plain. The hills on the right grew taller and sharper, a fair counterpart of the other side which straightened itself to one massive rampart of redness. They drew together until only two miles divided them: and then, towering gradually till their parallel parapets must have been a thousand feet above us, ran forward in an avenue for miles.

"They were not unbroken walls of rock, but were built sectionally, in crags like gigantic buildings, along the two sides of their street. Deep alleys, fifty feet across, divided the crags, whose plans were smoothed by the weather into huge apses and bays, and enriched with surface fretting and fracture, like design. Caverns high up on the precipice were round like windows: others near the foot gaped like doors. Dark stains ran down the shadowed front for hundreds of feet, like accidents of use. The cliffs were striated vertically, in their granular rock; whose main order stood on two hundred feet of broken stone deeper in colour and harder in texture. This plinth did not, like the sandstone, hang in folds like cloth; but chipped itself into loose courses of scree, horizontal as the footing of a wall.

"The crags were capped in nests of domes, less hotly red than the body of the hill; rather grey and shallow. they gave the finishing semblance of Byzantine architecture to this irresistible place: this processional way greater than imagination. The Arab armies would have been lost in the length and breadth of it, and within the walls a squadron of aeroplanes could have wheeled in formation. Our little caravan grew self-conscious, and fell dead quiet, afraid and ashamed to flaunt its smallness in the presence of the stupendous hills.

"Landscapes, in childhood's dream, were so vast and silent. We looked backward through our memory for the prototype up which all men had walked between such walls toward such an open square as that in front where this road seemed to end. Later, when we were often riding inland, my mind used to turn me from the direct road, to clear my senses by a night in Rumm and by the ride down its dawn-lit valley towards the shining plains, or up its valley in the sunset towards that glowing square which my timid anticipation never let me reach. I would say, 'Shall I ride on this time, beyond the Khazail, and know it all? But in truth I liked Rumm too much."

Wadi Rum is a totally new area for rock-climbing and mountaineering and was first visited with these sports in mind as recently as October 1984 by a party of four English climbers (including myself), at the invitation of the Jordanian Ministry of Tourism. Apart from one climb made prior to this date only the Bedouin were familiar with the area and its mountains, including the top of Jebel Rum, which at 1,754m was Jordan's highest peak prior to changes in the Saudi/Jordan border to give increased coastal facilities to Aqaba. There is now a higher summit close to the new border in the south east of the Rum area, called Jebel um Adaami, 1,830m, which gives a nice scramble with amazing views.

Most of the peaks in the region have in fact been climbed by the Bedouin, often by more than one route, during hunting expeditions or whilst collecting edible or medicinal plants and herbs. Although originally climbed and reversed solo in barefeet and without any equipment, some of these routes are quite serious undertakings with complex route finding. The Bedouin are proud of them and rightly so! There are however a number of possibly unclimbed peaks in the area, as well as many new routes to be done on the various walls, ridges, slabs and crack systems, not to mention easier routes and scrambles through canyons with magnificent scenery.

Despite what at first may look to be horrendously soft and loose rock it will soon be found that excellent climbing is to be had here and that the quality of the rock adds a peculiar spice to the climbs rather than detracting from them. It is a remote and spectacular landscape, offering unlimited rock for the pioneer, as well as many superb existing routes of all grades of difficulty, whilst the desert and numerous "siqs" or canyons offer a wilderness experience not to be found elsewhere in the world. The wealth of this experience is further increased by the Bedouin whose homeland this is, and by the variety of wildlife to be found in the area. It is hoped that this book will allow others to savour the solitude and mystical magic of these deserts and mountains.

INTRODUCTION A L'ESCALADE DANS LE GRES JORDANIEN

WILFRIED COLONNA

Les parois du Massif de Rum sont uniques au monde. Les comparaisons sont impossibles, l'escalade présentant ici tout ce que le grès a d'original et de varié.

Les hauteurs et les formes des montagnes proposent un grand choix d'ascensions possibles; aussi bien dans la longueur, que dans le style (100 à 600 metres de dénivelé!) En généralisant, on distingue deux types de voies: les lignes "extérieures", empruntant plutôt les éperons, les dalles et les fissurages superficiels - les lignes "intérieures", qui remontent les immenses et logiques cheminées ou fissures, barrant les parois de haut en bas; l'escalade n'y est pas exclusivement intérieure, loin de là....!

Les marches d'approache sont courtes, voire inexistantes avec un véhicule tout terrain. Marcher une heure pour atteindres l'attaque d'une voie, parait être un maximum bien rare! Le choix des itineraries doit être etroitement lie a l'orientation. Une observation pertinente permettra d'utiliser au mieux les faces à l'ombre et d'éviter les chaleurs desséchantes. Par temps incertaink, se méfier sérieusement de tout ce qui ressemble à un canalisateur d'eau. Celle-ci, accumulée dans les gorges sommitales par la pluie, dévalera la montagne en trombes géantes avec une violence inouie et spontanée; les pluies étant très passageres et imprévisibles quant à leur importance. Les vents sont parfois très forts.

Le grès de Rum est sculpté avec extravagance par les humeurs de l'eau et du vent. Il est sournoisement abrasif, mais très adherent! Ses couleurs, changeantes aux différents éclairages du jour, varient du noir au rouge, passant par le pourpre et le blanc! Celles-ci indiquent souvent le caractère du rocher. Une savante observation, avec un peu d'expérience, pourra déterminer sa qualité. Les teintes foncées, telles le noir ou le rouge cuivré, indiquent en général un grès dur et de solides sculptures. Le jaune ou le rose font prevoir une matière plus tendre, parfois sablonneuse et fragile. Là où l'eau passe, le nettoyage s'est fait. Le rocher y est parfois poli à l'extrême et les reliefs fortement solidifiés. Ces parcours peuvent présenter des escalades d'une originalité criante! Mais aucune règle définitive n'existe; les surprises, mêlées aux incertitudes, apportent un piquant si particulier à ces escalades!

La stratification est horizontale. Alternance des couches, donc des couleurs. Présence de "vires-promenades" et de bourrelets surplombants, changement soudain du relief.

...Comparer paraît impossible, quoique l'amblance, doux mélange d'imprévisible et de malice rocheuse, rappelle cà et là, l'escalade dolomitique. Parfois on se croirait dans l'Utah.

...Sorti des fissures et des cheminées, l'absence de ligne naturelle, de cheminement évident et logique, amène la grimpeur à une constante improvisation, où la curiosité et une certaine audace seront la clé de la progression.

Nulle part ailleurs, autant de "Tafonis", de lunules géantes, de fines écailles dentelées ou de trous à gruyére! Gargouilees noueuses, polypes surdimensionnés d'où s'écoulent de minces filets rocheux, ressemblant à de la cire, dalles rougeoyantes criblées "d'oreilles de Mickey." Un relief extravagant, caricatures rocheuses de cathédrales gothiques, surmontées d'innombrables coupoles bysantines, où les pas se fatiguent, en marche pour un sommet lointain! Bizarre...

Un tel chaos de surface permet l'utilisation presque exclusive des moyens naturels de protection (coincurs, friends, sangles...). Méfiance pour les pitons classiques...Ils sont rarement très solides, et plutôt utilisés pour les rappels ou ancrages sans risque de choc. Les spits à expansion normale, eux, doivent être traités avec circonspection. Mis à part quelques exceptions, ils ne résisteront certainement pas à un grand choc ou à des chutes répétées. La texture sablonneuse du grès ne s'y prête guère.

La meilleur système utilisable dans les sections lisses, compactes, ou carrement torp tendres, semble être le "peg-bolt" (système "Carter" - trou sous-dimensionné et piton angle). Voir le chapitre en question.

Libre est l'escalade! Rares sont les points d'aide. Les styles sont varies. Grimper à Rum, e'est un certain engagement, une ambiance presque alpine. Peu ou pas de passages prééquipés, des protections parfois délicates (mentionnées dans les topos), de longues descentes en rappel ou en désescalade, rendues souvent difficiles par les caprices de ce rocher "papier de verre", des conditions climatiques particulieres...

L'autonomie du grimpeur, utilisant ici, plus ses qualités générales de "grimpeur-aventurier" que de pur acrobate.

Des voies de tous niveaux - des choix pour chacun. Mais ce qui domine, c'est bel et bien l'ambiance!

Voilà donc une succinte introduction à un fantastique terrain d'aventure.

Bonne grimpe,

Wilfried COLONNA, Samoens, le 2 juin 1986.

INFORMATION AND GENERAL ADVICE

Passports & Visas

To visit Jordan, travellers need a valid passport or a recognized travel document and a visa. These are issued by Jordanian Consulates abroad. Your visa application should be accompanied by one passport-sized photograph and a stamped self-addressed envelope. Tourists may also obtain visas upon arrival at Jordanian frontier posts and airports.This is far easier (and usually cheaper) than writing to a consulate. There may be a visa charge, dependent upon nationality (10.75 J.D. for U.K. citizens in 1992). A Group or Collective Visa is available for tour groups providing the group stays in Jordan two or more days. Visas last for one month and can be renewed at the police station in Amman or Aqaba a few days before expiry. It is a simple procedure, and is free.

Customs Formalities

Unless entering via Israel, there are no specific problems, but if carrying unusual items such as camping and climbing equipment, and medical provisions it is helpful and may prove useful to have these listed and the contents of each bag identifiable. This check list should be kept and up-dated for the return journey.

Medical Regulations and Recommendations

Anyone coming from epidemic areas is required to have a vaccination certificate for yellow fever. Although not required by Jordanian law, you may also want to be vaccinated against typhoid, paratyphoid, tetanus and cholera. Cholera vaccinations are required for travellers, except children under one year of age, coming from infected areas. Once in Wadi Rum, although there is a clinic for the Bedouin school children run by the Army, the nearest doctor is at Quweirah and the nearest hospital at Aqaba. It is therefore obviously advisable to take ones own medical supplies for minor cuts, bruises, burns, sprains, headaches and upset stomachs etc.. A strong pain-killer such as Fortral may also be worth having in case of accidents, and of course sun protection cream for lips and skin. In the unlikely event of scorpion or snake bite, make a mental note of size and colour, and any markings. Seek medical attention as soon as possible.

Travellers Health by Dr R.Dawood is worth having if you go abroad "off the beaten track" frequently.

Money

The monetary unit in Jordan is the Jordanian Dinar (JD), which is divided into 1000 fils. The exchange rate in Nov 1992 was approximately 1 JD to £1 sterling.

There are no regulations on the amount of Jordanian currency, foreign banknotes, or travellers' cheques, visitors may bring into or take out of the country.

Foreign currency, drafts and travellers' cheques, should be exchanged at banks or at authorised money changers. Exchange facilities are provided in the arrival lounge at the airport in Amman and at the border guard at Ramtha. In Amman and Aqaba, most banks and money changers are located centrally and near or in hotels. Hotels and merchants will accept travellers' cheques.

Credit cards are beginning to be used in Jordan but their acceptance is limited. Leading hotels and restaurants and a few merchants and travel agencies will accept the best-known ones, such as American Express, but do not expect to use them to cover your costs. Also, personal cheques are difficult to cash. To avoid problems, carry travellers' cheques. In out-of-the-way places, carry Jordanian currency in small denominations, as change may not always be available.

Tourist Information

For information on any aspect of travel to and in Jordan, the correct office to contact is: Ministry of Tourism, Jebel Amman, P.O. Box 224, Amman, Jordan. Tel: Amman 642311. Maps are not easy to obtain!

Travel to and in Jordan

Numerous international airlines fly into Jordan at Amman's Queen Alia International Airport. Costs vary from less than £400 to over £600 return from London dependent on choice of airline. For information on flights from Britain, contact Alia, 211 Regent Street, London or Jasmin Tours, High Street, Cookham, Maidenhead, Kent. Jasmin specialise in tours to Jordan and the Holy Land and can arrange flight, hotels and transport for groups or independent travellers.

Some travellers come to Jordan from Europe via Cairo, Sinai and the Red Sea ferry to Aqaba. This can be done for a similar cost to the direct flight, passes through an interesting part of the world and only takes two or three days. The ferry costs about 9 JD second class.

Once in Jordan, there are regular bus services between Amman and Aqaba (Jett Bus), costing only 3 JD (1992),and a rather less stylish local bus plies between Aqaba and Rashdiyah (at the Rum junction, just before Quweirah on the main Aqaba-Amman highway). If you are lucky enough to get a Disi bus, this will drop you at the Rum-Disi junction, 11 km from Rum village. The Aqaba bus station is 200m E of the market area, up the hill past a small park, and the fare to either destination is less than 0.5 JD. Either way, you will have to hitch-hike the remaining distance to Wadi Rum which is not too difficult but may take half an hour or so. The main difficulty is getting on the bus! They are quite small, almost always full, and don't run to any schedule. It is easier but considerably more expensive (15 JD) to get a taxi - they also depart from the bus station.

Leaving Wadi Rum poses similar problems in reverse, either you will have to hitch out to Rashdiyah, then wait for a bus (or hitch) to Aqaba, or make arrangements a couple of days earlier via the Rest House manager, for a taxi to come for you.

Having said all this, there is a plan to put the money earned at the Rest House toll gate towards the purchase of a bus for Wadi Rum, so you may be in luck!

Alternatively, you could hire a car. This costs from 20 - 40 JD per day and is only worthwhile if you intend doing a lot of travelling outside Wadi Rum. Inside Rum, you have to use Bedouin transport but it is worth noting here that over half the routes in this guide are within walking distance of the Rest House.

Fees for Travel and Accommodation in Wadi Rum

	JD
1. *Entry to Wadi Rum Desert* (40% is paid to the Rest House where you will be given a drink and 60% to the local community projects)	1
2. *Use of Tourist Campsites* (Rest House and Abu Aina Bedouin Camp). Tents and water are available at both sites. The Rest House site also has self-catering facilities, showers and toilets	2

3. Hire of camels or 4 wheel-drive vehicle and driver:

Destination	**CAMEL**	**4 W.D.**
Abu Aina Campsite	4	5
Khazali Canyon (rock inscriptions)	10	12
Sunset-site	12	14
W Side of Jebel Rum (for Sheikh Hamdam's Route)	-	12
Burdah (rock bridge) - includes waiting whilst climbing	-	25
Barrah Canyon - includes waiting whilst climbing	-	30
Jebel um Adaami (highest mountain) - includes waiting whilst climbing	-	30
Any area for full day	12	30

Transport in Wadi Rum

Obviously one can go virtually anywhere in Rum by 4 wheel-drive but in an effort to protect the fragile desert flora, the current policy is to restrict people from driving their own vehicles in the desert. This means you should use a Bedouin vehicle. The skill of the drivers is fortunately far superior to the apparent state of their vehicles, and of course their knowledge of the area is unsurpassable. Travelling with a Bedouin, you are also more likely to be asked into one of their camps for tea, and thereby learn something of their lifestyle.

Apart from travelling to the climbs, the best known 4 W.D. journey is the desert track to Aqaba, a distance of about 65 kilometres arriving either north of the town in Wadi Itm, or south, on the Red Sea coast just north of the Saudi border.

The alternative to 4 W.D. if you want to really savour the desert experience is to travel by camel! The following 1992 tariffs have been agreed with the Ministry of Tourism. If your driver insists on overcharging, you should complain to the Wadi Rum Tourism Manager and ask him to mediate. If you feel really strongly that you are being 'ripped-off' you can always take the problem to the police post!

Guided Holidays

Any of the following U.I.A.A. qualified Guides can be contacted for details of climbing and trekking holidays in the Rum and Petra areas:

Great Britain

Rowland Edwards, Compass West Adventure, Sennen, Nr. Land's End, Cornwall.
France
Bernard Domenech, 10 Rue Du Cazal, 13420 Gemenos, 13883 Cedex.
Claude Gardien and Wilfried Colonna, "Le Villars", Samoens, 74340 Haute Savoie.
In addition to climbing, Wilfried Colonna also takes horse treks from Rum to Petra.
Italy
Alberto Re, Les Arnauds, 10052 Bardonecchia, Casella Postale 27.

Additionally, visitors arriving in Rum and needing the services of a trekking guide should contact Dayfallah Atieeq or Sabbah Atieeq. Sabbah who is a naturally talented climber with a knowledge of all the Bedouin climbs in the guide as well as some of the 'modern' routes has also been on rock climbing and mountain rescue courses in Britain and is approved by the Ministry of Tourism as a climbing guide. The following is a quote from a French Guide: "We've seen Sabbah at work with clients - he is safe and sure. His rope technique is perfect and he is very patient with a completely natural authority." You may contact both Sabbah and Dayfallah at the Rest House.

Hotels

There are no hotels in Wadi Rum but the rest of Jordan is well serviced by hotels of all standards. In Amman, the cheapest hotels are down town not far from the King Hussein Mosque and will cost you about 3 JD. In the '3rd Circle' area where the tourism department and most of the embassies are, prices are around 15 JD and upwards.

In Petra, prices start at around 3 JD up above the town of Wadi Mousa, at the hotels of Musa Spring and Al Anbat where camping is possible. Down near the entrance to Petra, the Sunset is slightly dearer but very good value and the recently renovated Petra Rest House is dearer still at 19 JD per double, but much more up-market. There are good fixed price buffet meals here, as well as a bar.

Moving down to Aqaba, the cheapest hotels are in the market area (The Jordan Flower, Petra and Jerusalem) all at around 3 JD. There are of course many better quality hotels in Aqaba, not only the mid-range ones near the market but down by the coast. The Alcazar is good value and friendly, with a pool and there are numerous hotels along the beach. Take your pick. The Ministry of Tourism, P.O. Box 224, Amman will provide full information, or you should refer to the Lonely Planet guidebook *Jordan and Syria, A Travel Survival Kit.*

Swimming and Diving

For a small payment it is possible to swim in Aqaba's hotel pools or from private Red Sea beaches - try the Aqaba hotel or Hotel Alcazar. Alternatively, take the road out towards Saudi where there are public beaches with good snorkelling amongst the coral reefs, in particular, Yemenia Beach - an experience not be be missed.

If you have no snorkelling gear, get a taxi to the Royal Jordanian Diving Centre which is also out on this coast. They hire all the gear and the coral off this beach is outstanding. They also have a cafe, bar and pool and run diving courses. Some of the main hotels such as the Alcazar also provide diving courses.

Paragliding and Ballooning

Paragliding was first practised in Rum on the 9th October 1986 when Jean Phillipe "Dolby"

Monnet and Yves Duverney made the first flight from the summit of Jebel Rum's East Dome at 9.30 a.m. Since then quite a few flights have been made off this top, and Hammad's Domes. The huge dune south of Jebel Annafishiyyah and west of Jebel um Kharg, in Wadi um Ishrin has also been used as a practice area for both climbers and Bedouin!

The other high-flying sport which has been tried in Wadi Rum is ballooning. A mass flight was organised in November 1992 on the King's birthday when dozens of strange shaped balloons drifted up the valley. It is possible that this may become an annual event.

Wadi Rum Rest House

From a climber's point of view, the location of the Rest House could not be better and facilities have improved tremendously since our first visit in 1984 when there was not even any water! The business is now run privately by Mahmoud Hillawi who has been involved with tourism in Wadi Rum for many years and the Rest House now offers a Restaurant and Bar - what more could you want! For costs, see "Fees for Travel and Accommodation".

Camping

There is an official Ministry of Tourism campsite at the rear of the Rest House with a Bedouin tent and some two-man tents available for visitors as well as showers and toilets and a self-catering kitchen. The fee per night is 2 JD. (Many climbers prefer to camp 100m away, behind the rocks of the S ridge of Jebel Mayeen where the generator cannot be heard and there is peace and quiet, particularly if a tour group is visiting the Rest House for the evening.)

The water in both the Rest House and campsite facilities is drinkable (from Artesian Wells at Disi). You are, however, in a desert area so please use it sparingly even if others seem to be uncaring - Jordan's water-tables are dropping seriously. Also, the wash basins and toilets should be kept clean by those who use them so that the reputation of climbers does not become as soiled as day-trip tourists who sometimes leave the place in a disgusting state.

Regarding actual camping equipment, simple lightweight tents are adequate, to keep insects etc. out but remember that exposure to U.V. will damage lightweight tent fabrics.

Further afield, there is also a Bedouin tent at Abu Aina another 3km down the valley, for the use of visitors (2 JD): contact Dayfallah Atieeq who lives in the Bedouin camp just behind, by the spring. Otherwise, camping is possible just about anywhere in the desert, but beware of very low-lying ground which may be subject to flash-flooding. It is said more people die in the desert from drowning than thirst!

Wadi Rum Village

Just beyond the Rest House, and dominated by the small fort is the rapidly growing village, with a scattering of black Bedouin tents. Amongst the houses will be found a couple of small shops or 'dhokans' where basic necessities can be bought: tea, tinned milk, sardines, sugar etc., but no bread and rarely any fresh food. These must be obtained in Quweirah.

If you pay a visit to the 'Beau-Geste' style fort with its swaggering knife, gun and bandolier clad guards, you may well be offered tea or cardomum flavoured coffee: a pleasant custom, by the fireside in front of their tent.

Shopping and Post

As mentioned, very basic foods are available in Wadi Rum. Most foodstuffs including bread and fresh vegetables can be bought at Quweirah on the Amman road just north of its junction with the Wadi Rum track and about 30km from Wadi Rum. Quweirah is also the location of the nearest Post Office, but for collection Poste Restante, Aqaba Post Office is more reliable! There is also a small 'makram' (cafe) selling falafell sandwiches and drinks in Quweirah.

For higher living it is necessary to go 70 kilometres to Aqaba, and its shops, markets and numerous street cafes where a good meal can be had for just over 1 or 2 JD. Food prices in Aqaba tend to be slightly dearer than Quweirah and Wadi Rum, but camping gas canisters and some dehydrated foods can be bought here. The vegetable market is excellent with numerous small supermarkets nearby.

The Bedouin

The Bedouin are the inhabitants of Wadi Rum. They are members of the Howeitat tribe and are very proud and independent people, many still semi-nomadic, and possibly the most traditional of all Jordanian tribes since they claim to descend from the Prophet through his daughter Fatima. They also consider themselves to be descendents of the Nabataeans.

Most of the peaks have been climbed by the Bedouin on hunting trips and they took a particular interest in our climbs. If approached with the respect they deserve, those who can will be pleased to give information on routes, some of which bear their mark in the form of small cut holds and 'Bedouin steps' (rickety piles of stones, usually to pass overhangs), or 'Bedouin ladders' - branches jammed into cracks. There are also Bedouin cairns, but beware, some of them (usually large or wall-shaped) mean do not go this way!

The Bedouin are a very friendly people and if you are straight and open with them and respect their customs you will be welcomed as one of the family. At all times avoid appearing to them as a camera-clicking tourist. In particular do not photograph the women or approach groups of women either out in the desert or in the privacy of their camps. Never enter a Bedouin camp without permission. As one of our Bedouin friends said to us "If people are hard on us, we will break them, if they are soft with us we will squeeze them, if they respect us we will be their friends." Remember, Wadi Rum and its mountains are Bedouin territory - do not abuse their hospitality and you will have an unforgettable stay. Sitting around their camp fires under a starry desert sky, chatting and sipping tea or coffee is an opportunity not to be missed.

You may even be invited to a Bedouin wedding or other festive occasion, or be asked for a 'mensef', that feast of the Bedouin with the sacrificed sheep's head staring at you from a bed of rice, on a large round tray. Eat (as always) with your right hand and be prepared to savour the odd piece of meat that will be passed to you in the flickering firelight. It may be a choice morsel of liver or some such 'delicacy' or it could be a more unusual, or unpalatable portion of meat that's been given to you as a joke to watch your reaction! If you are vegetarian, don't worry, just eat the bread and rice. The meal, and the preceeding and succeeding teas and coffees are an opportunity for cultural exchange and 'Bonhomie' that should be savoured to full!

Whilst I hesitate to quote yet again from T.E.Lawrence, the following passage describes

the meal to perfection:
"...The bowl was now brim-full, ringed round its edge by white rice in an embankment a foot wide and six inches deep, filled with legs and ribs of mutton till they toppled over. It needed two or three victims to make in the centre a dressed pyramid of meat such as honour prescribed. The centre-pieces were the boiled, upturned heads, propped on their severed stumps of neck, so that the ears, brown like old leaves, flapped out on the rice surface. The jaws gaped emptily upward, pulled open to show the hollow throat with the tongue, still pink, clinging to the lower teeth; and the long incisors whitely crowned the pile, very prominent above the nostrils' pricking hair and the lips which sneered away blackly from them.

"This load was set down on the soil of the cleared space between us, where it steamed hotly, while a procession of minor helpers bore small cauldrons and copper vats in which the cooking had been done. From them, with much-bruised bowls of enamelled iron, they ladled out over the main dish all the inside and outside of the sheep; little bits of yellow intestine, the white tail-cushion fat, brown muscles and meat and bristly skin, all swimming in the liquid butter and grease of the seething. The bystanders watched anxiously, muttering satisfactions when a very juicy scrap plopped out.

"The fat was scalding. Every now and then a man would drop his baler with an exclamation and plunge his burnt fingers, not reluctantly, in his mouth to cool them: but they persevered till at last their scooping rang loudly on the bottoms of the pots: and, with a gesture of triumph, they fished out the intact livers from their hiding place in the gravy and topped the yawning jaws with them.

"Two raised each smaller cauldron and tilted it, letting the liquid splash down upon the meat till the rice-crater was full, and the loose grains at the edge swam in the abundance: and yet they poured, till, amid cries of astonishment from us, it was running over, and a little pool congealing in the dust. That was the final touch of splendour and the host called us to come and eat ...

"... Our host stood by the circle, encouraging the appetite with pious ejaculations. At top speed we twisted, tore, cut and stuffed: never speaking, since conversation would insult a meal's quality; though it was proper to smile thanks when an intimate guest passed a select fragment, or when Mohammed el Dheilan gravely handed over a huge barren bone with a blessing. On such occasions I would return the compliment with some hideous impossible lump of guts, a flippancy which rejoiced the Howeitat, but which the gracious, aristocratic Nasir saw with disapproval..."

Flora & Fauna

Without doubt the most talked about wild creature in Wadi Rum is not the Palestinian viper, sand snake or scorpion, but the ibex. This beautiful, if rarely seen animal inhabits the high jebels and is a protected species, though still sometimes hunted illegally. The other large mammal still reputedly to be found in the more distant jebels and wadis is the jackal, whilst the hyrax is still common as are the numerous smaller desert animals such as gerbils and jirds. The Arabian sand cat (*Felix margarita*) has also been seen in Wadi Rum and was reported by Guy Mountford whilst doing a survey for Jordan's Royal Society for the Conservation of Nature.

He also reported the black widow spider but was happy not to have seen the famous horned cerastes snake, "the terror of the Bedouin." In actual fact all snakes and scorpions as well as the disturbingly large and long-legged "camel spider" are treated as highly dangerous by the Bedouin, although the camel spider (which is not a spider but a selifugae) whilst having a powerful bite is not dangerous to man. There are of course numerous lizards and skinks, in particular the agama and fringe fingered lizard and gold skink. Some of the agamids are quite large, the orange spotted starred agama reaching 60cms. The beautifully coloured blue Sinai lizard seems only to be found around Petra. The ghecko is however quite common in Rum and can even be found in the Rest House. Birdlife too is quite abundant and a list of birds seen in Rum would fill this page. The largest are the various vultures, buzzards and eagles often seen circling the high domes on the thermals. The lammegeier has been seen here in the act of dropping bones to break them on the rocks below.

Ravens, partridges, pigeons, martins and sparrows are frequently seen as are the wheatear and various finches, larks and warblers. This list is long and anyone with special interest should contact Jordan's Royal Society for the Conservation of Nature, P.O. Box 6354, Amman. Guy Mountford's Book *Portrait of a Desert* is recommended reading. These sources also have all the relevant information on the flora of the area which includes the wild water-melon and the toadstool Podaxis Pistillaris known to the Bedouin as 'Banouq' and used as a wool dye. The water-melon supposedly relieves constipation! The Bedouin also make great use of the numbers of small plants and herbs found in the desert and mountains and whatever your ailment they seem to have a cure for it. There are also of course numerous desert bushes including the tamarisk, artemesan and others whilst on the higher mountains beautiful old juniper trees (called Aral by the Bedouin) are found, their gnarled roots extending many metres across the stony ground.

Weather

We have been to Wadi Rum numerous times in the autumn, arriving at the end of September and found that until October it was very hot - sometimes around 40°C, but climbing was still possible and enjoyable. In mid October there was quite an abrupt change, the mid-afternoon temperature dropping down to the 30°C mark and often strong cold winds in the morning and particularly evening and sometimes cool breezes through the day. Much more amenable for climbing! Apparently this is the norm, 17th October being reckoned as the start of winter. By early November there was often considerable cloud and even a couple of thunder storms with flash floods.

In the hotter months, allow a few days for acclimatisation so that the body can adapt slightly and will lose less moisture during climbing, otherwise if plenty of water is not carried, dehydration can be a serious problem.

During acclimatisation go for easier, shorter routes, as much as possible in the shade. This should also give an opportunity to familiarise oneself with the unusual complexity of the mountains and the peculiar nature of the rock!

December, January, February and early March are a little cooler but should still be fine for climbing although possible brief rain storms can be expected and there may even be snow falls on the summits, though melting quickly. The days are also rather short. Additionally, Christmas-time also poses its own peculiar problems, when, we are informed "the Rest House is Bedlam, with too many visitors."

WEATHER TABLES

Wadi Rum 29° 34'N 35° 25'E Elevation: 952m Period 1967/74

	Jan	Feb	Mar	Apr	May	June	July	Aug	Sept	Oct	Nov	Dec
Air Temperature °C												
Mean Monthly	9.6	11.9	15.0	18.4	22.5	25.1	26.9	26.5	25.0	21.0	15.2	10.6
Mean Max	14.6	17.7	21.1	25.1	29.9	32.9	34.6	34.3	32.9	28.6	21.1	16.1
Mean Min	4.6	5.9	9.0	11.8	15.0	17.2	19.3	18.7	17.0	13.4	9.2	5.1
Absolute Max	24.8	28.2	33.3	36.4	40.1	38.2	41.3	40.4	39.8	38.4	31.4	25.1
Absolute Min	-1.5	-2.1	-1.2	5.5	7.9	12.5	13.8	15.0	11.2	7.4	1.4	-3.3
Rainfall Amount (mm)												
Mean Monthly	19.2	9.6	18.4	6.7	3.2	0	0	0	0	2.4	6.3	9.4
Max Amount in Month	33.6	28.0	67.3	27.9	21.6	0	0	0	0	16.6	39.2	46.9
Max Amount in 24 Hrs	15.2	17.0	34.5	18.0	17.2	0	0	0	0	16.4	29.7	13.5
Relative Humidity %												
Mean Monthly	54	44	38	33	28	26	29	32	35	40	52	53
Wind Speed (Knots)												
Mean Monthly	2.4	2.1	2.8	2.1	2.9	2.5	2.5	2.3	2.1	2.0	1.9	2.0

We have also visited the area frequently in spring and found that April and part of May are similar to the late September, October, November period and are equally good for climbing. There may be some rain in April and quite a few cloudy days. This is however the end of the rainy season, water is more abundant than in the autumn and the desert is wonderfully green and carpeted with flowers. Another advantage of the spring season is the longer days with daylight from 5.00 a.m. to 7.30 p.m.

Mid-summer is far too hot for climbing. Rumour has it that "Birds fall out of the sky" with heat exhaustion!

Bivouacs

It is possible, of course, to sleep anywhere in the desert, but even on the mountains, good bivouac sites are common and a night out is a pleasure to be savoured. Water however is an obvious problem and on the hotter days at least 2 litres per person should be carried for each day. Also allow for long nights and 12 hour bivouacs: 5.30 p.m. to 5.30 a.m. in late October with temperatures fairly low (possibly freezing in December/January/February/March). A 1kg sleeping bag is about right.

Hazards

Flash floods are a possibility, particularly from the end of October to early April when short heavy rainstorms may flood the gullies some distance away from actual storm centres. Twenty Bedouin were reputedly killed in this way in the ravines of Jebel um Ishrin (hence the name - Mother of Twenty). We ourselves witnessed a one hour storm on Jebel Rum in late October 1985, when giant waterfalls cascaded almost instantly down slabs and out of concealed canyons all along five kilometres of the East Face, sending raging torrents a kilometre out into the desert.

As many of the routes involve ravines at some stage or other, this danger should be borne in mind if stormy weather is imminent. Rain also seems to soften the rock and extra care should be taken with small flaky holds and abseil pegs, after rain.

Snakes (in particular the Palestinian viper - brown and red markings) and scorpions are also a possible danger. Our party met one such snake in a bushy canyon almost stepping on it and snake tracks on sandy bivouac ledges were common! The three worst scorpion incidents we had involved one in some dead wood we had gathered for a fire whilst camping with Bedouin, one scuttling from a handhold whilst climbing and another walking up someone's arm whilst sleeping in a desert bivouac! It should however be said that the Bedouin know of few incidents where anyone has actually been stung or bitten by these creatures.

Dress (Clothing)

The question of what to wear must be considered not only from the point of view of what is best for the climate, but also bearing in mind the traditions of the Bedouin and the fact that certain styles of dress may be offensive to them.

In particular, women should not be seen around the Bedouin camps, wearing shorts or sleeveless vests. Legs and shoulders should be covered at all times. Ideally this applies to both sexes if one is not to alienate or offend the Bedouin in any way. Whilst around one's own campsite, however, this code of ethics can be relaxed but even there it may be bad taste not to change into more discreet clothing if Bedouin are visiting. For desert travel, walking and climbing, lightweight loose-fitting clothing is ideal. If you chose to wear tights for climbing, don't be surprised if you get some strange looks from the Bedouin! Obviously, good quality sunglasses are useful if not essential, and some form of hat will also be found necessary to keep the sun out of the eyes and off the head. Whilst climbing, some may prefer to use safety helmets, probably of lightweight design and in some instances it is probably recommendable, though we chose to do without. If it is intended to do a lot of desert travel by either four-wheel drive, or camel then the Bedouin "khafiya" head-dress will be found the most useful and versatile. Due to the extreme range of temperatures from day to night, varying from about 40°C down to freezing in October it is also advisable to carry lightweight underwear (we used Helly Hansen Lifa) or a thin sweater to wear in the long desert night. For actual bivouacs a 1kg down sleeping bag is ideal. The problem of heavy (albeit brief) rain falls must also be considered in spring and autumn and on occasions we carried lightweight waterproofs but never had to use them although violent thunder storms twice passed within a few kilometres of us and once we were actually in a storm for about half an hour. These storms can be of such a ferocity that all one can realistically do is seek quick shelter until they have passed. It is really not worth carrying waterproof gear, and any wet clothing dries quickly again.

Moving on to footwear, sandals are ideal around camp, and for desert travel a pair of inexpensive lightweight trainers are adequate. These can also be used for climbing on routes of lower grades. For higher grade routes, modern light rock boots should be used, with emphasis on flexibility and above all comfort - some of the routes especially on Jebel Rum are extremely long and cover a lot of easy ground to reach the summit, so that tight fitting footwear is out of the question. Alternatively, trainers could be carried in the sack for use on the summit plateau and rock boots used only for climbing but that of course, means extra weight.

Tourist Code

- Limit desertification - make no open fires and discourage others from doing so on your behalf. If you have no alternative to cooking with wood, use only the smallest of dead twigs, Bedouin style, and use the minimum necessary. Remember, even dead wood plays a role in the desert's ecosystem.
- Remove litter, burn and bury paper. (Toilet paper should also be burned before burying with wastes)
- Keep spring water clean
- Plants should be left to flourish in their natural environment
- Wildlife should not be disturbed
- Do not inscribe the rocks with names or graffiti
- If necessary, show your driver or guide that you are concerned about the environment. Wadi Rum may change you - please do not change it. As a guest, respect local traditions and cultures. Maintain local pride.
- When taking photos, respect privacy - ask permission and use restraint
- Giving anything to children encourages begging. A donation to a village project is a better way to help.
- You will be accepted and welcomed if you follow local customs. Use only your right hand for eating and greeting
- Respect for local etiquette earns you respect - when in the desert, loose lightweight clothes are preferable to revealing shorts, skimpy tops and tight fitting action wear. Hand-holding between opposite sexes or kissing in public are disliked by local people
- Observe standard charges for food, accommodation, travel and souvenirs and remember that any bargains you strike may only be possible because of low income to others
- Visitors who value local traditions encourage local pride and maintain local cultures. Please help local people gain a realistic view of life in Western Countries
- Be patient, friendly and sensitive. Remember you are a guest

The above advice is a modification of the Himalayan Tourist Code, published by Tourism Concern, sponsored by *The Independent* and The Rough Guides publications.

By following these simple guidelines you can help preserve the unique environment and culture of Wadi Rum.

Equipment for Climbing

The standard rack of gear used in the U.K. is ideal for Wadi Rum, i.e. a full set of wires and some hexagons and camming chocks. Cams and larger chocks tend to predominate in usefulness on medium grade routes and small wires are only required on harder climbs. For abseiling, many long lengths of tape or cord are necessary as abseil points are frequently quite a distance from the ideal place and need extending. Any abseil slings found in place should be mistrusted as they are almost certainly damaged by abrasion from abseil ropes and U.V. degradation from the intense sunlight. Tests at Troll on actual abseil tapes retrieved from Wadi Rum, indicate strength losses of up to 30% in six months and 60% in eighteen months. You have been warned!

Pegs

So far, apart from a few routes, pegs have only been required for abseils and belays, though obvious possibilities for aid-climbing exist. Long angles and thick blades seem to be the most useful although even secure sounding placements cannot be trusted automatically. Four of the abseil pegs we placed were later pulled out by hand! Beware! (Another actually fell out whilst someone was stood on a ledge sorting the ropes, half way down an abseil.) Unless intending to do any aid climbing (when a full rack of pegs will be necessary) probably half a dozen pegs will suffice for descent of any particular route. In-situ pegs should not automatically be relied upon and should always be tested.

Bolts

Bolts present two problems, ethical and physical. With regard to the latter, the self-drilling type of expansion bolt does not appear to work very well except in the hardest rocks, where some 10mm bolts have been fixed. The sandstone tends to disintegrate around the anchor as the hole is drilled, making it impossible to fix. It may be possible to use the Rawl type system, drilling an undersize hole to place the bolt in. This has not been tried, but 10mm holes have been drilled which hold small short angles well. These have been used for abseils and belays, and seem very reliable. Most recently, power drills have been used to place resin-glued bolts which are 'bomb-proof'.

Abseil Rings

In recent years, some of the most frequently used descents as well as many of the 'sport climbs' have been fitted with abseil rings and chains. The bolts are 10cm long, and fixed with resin. The work was done under the supervision of Wilf Colonna, a French Guide, at the request of the Ministry of Tourism. Some of them have safety warnings on, to stop the Army or the Bedouin trying to remove them!

Where there are no rings in-situ, you should take great care when abseiling from sandstone 'threads'. They are not always as solid as they might appear, and you should always try to have a 'back-up' sling. Also remember that after rain, the sandstone seems to be weaker.

To Bolt or Not To Bolt

Whilst I have no wish to be contentious, as one of the original activists in Rum, I am deeply concerned that its unique rock climbing should not be destroyed by over-bolting of new routes, or retro-bolting of existing ones.

Wadi Rum is first and foremost an 'adventure climber's' playground offering as a bonus some technically challenging 'sports climbs'. The vast majority of routes are protected by traditional means and in almost every instance when bolts have been placed it is to provide safe belays or abseil points, though even this may be considered reprehensible by some. In mitigation, the fixing of bolts on popular descents has allowed a lot of unsightly and dangerous slings and pegs to be removed, leaving the mountains cleaner and safer. The same 'clean' philosophy led to the fixing of protection bolts on Hammad's Route, to replace the ugly array of large and suspect pegs put there by the Jordanian Army in recent years.

Conversely, I am not too happy about the fixing of protection and belay rings at some points on Sabbah's Route on Jebel Rum, though Sabbah himself approves. I was involved with this action in the hope that the partial 'sacrifice' of the pure wilderness aspect of one of the best Bedouin climbs for the safety of guided parties would preserve other routes of this calibre for future climbers to experience in their original state. However, I do feel the route has lost a little of its essential spirit of exploration and adventure.

In fact, at the risk of upsetting some of my climbing friends with whom I have hotly debated the issue over many years, I feel a code of ethics should be established for Wadi Rum. In my opinion, during the last year or two the rock has, on occasion been excessively drilled and bolted either for aid purposes to allow routes to be climbed that would otherwise have been much harder, (or maybe impossible?), or, for protection where the route would have required greater commitment or could not have been climbed in safety.

To give two examples, I personally feel that both the drilling and placing by hand of thirty-nine bolts on 'Revienta o Burila', and the machine-gun slaughter by power-drill of the fine potential line of 'Al Uzza' are both open to ethical debate, as also is the placing of bolts on Musa's Slab (a 20m granite slab that can easily be protected by top-rope for bouldering). Despite the fact that the above routes undoubtedly give excellent climbing, I feel that excessive bolting is out of place in a wilderness area, and removes the challenge for future generations, putting 'nails' in the coffin of adventure climbing. Indeed, I would venture to suggest that over-use of bolts is yet another example of man's imposition on, and lack of harmony with, nature.

In May 1992, the British Mountaineering Council held an International Meet to demonstrate its concern for "the destruction of adventure climbing and the invasion of mountain crags by bolts." Perhaps it is not yet too late to think that Wadi Rum can be developed in as clean a style as possible: the sign at Wadi Rum Rest House which reads "Keep Wadi Rum Clean" applies to the cliffs as well as the desert!

Mountain Rescue Facilities

Obviously none exist since the sport is relatively new in Jordan. The Army may be able to assist in emergency and helicopters could get in to many of the routes. A successful helicopter rescue was carried out by the Jordanian R.A.F. from Rijm Assaf in January 1993. The climber had fallen when abseiling from a sandstone thread which snapped.

Some of the Bedouin may be able to help, particularly Sabbah Atieeq or Hammad Hamdan. Obviously the Police Post would be the first place to contact. There is an ambulance at Quweirah and the nearest hospital is at Aqaba. Someone should be informed if leaving camp for a few days, so that no-one raises any unnecessary alarm.

As Bedouin women and children have to move around the whole area with their goats, people should not shout unnecessarily when in the mountains. On at least one occasion, this has led to Bedouin men from the village driving all the way round into Wadi um Ishrin, believing their family had been shouting for assistance through the canyons of Rakabat um Ejil. Remember these are not empty mountains - people live here.

Maps, Guides and Information

For general travel in Jordan, the most useful map is the Oxford map of Jordan, published by Geoprojects, scale 1:730,000 (approximately 12 miles to the inch, not 120 as stated on the map!). This map also gives various items of information on Jordan together with large scale maps of Amman, Aqaba, Jerash and Petra. This, and the map of Wadi Rum are available from the Jordanian Ministry of Tourism, P.O. Box 224, Amman, (just off 3rd circle). Alternatively, try The Geographical Centre, P.O. Box 20214, Ali Jbeha, Amman. (Tel: 845188). They have the 1:50,000 maps of Jordan but you will need an 'official' letter before standing even a remote chance of buying any!

The Wadi Rum map (title Jebel um Ishrin) is a fairly accurate large scale map but does not in fact cover the whole area, missing off the peaks in the far west and south. The only well-known mountain in this guide that is not on the map is Burdah, but due to its unique rock arch it should be located without difficulty. It is, in any case, well known to all the Bedouin. There are in fact plans to produce a map specifically for tourism in Wadi Rum which will cover all possible climbing areas, meanwhile the map to this region is: Jebel um Ishrin, Sheet 3049-11, Series K737, Edition 1-AMS, scale 1:50,000.

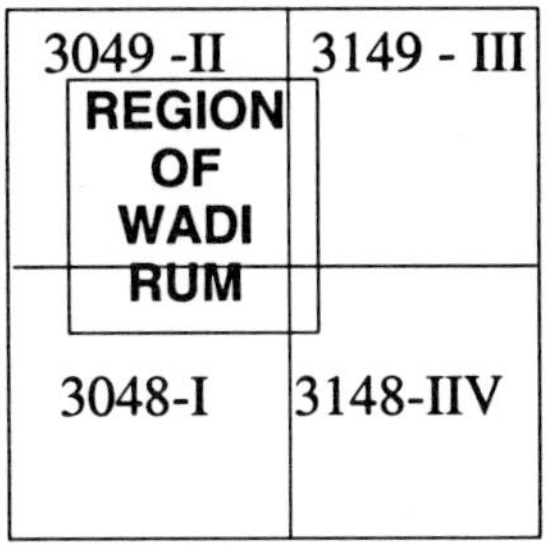

3049 -II	3149 - III
REGION OF WADI RUM	
3048-I	3148-IIV

Maps covering the region of Wadi Rum (scale 1:50,000).

The map references given in route descriptions are taken from this map, as are summit heights only a few of which have been trigonometrically verified.

The map was compiled in 1959 by the U.S. Army and has not been field checked. Apart from lacking nomenclature (and getting some wrong), it is mostly accurate and only the finer details such as the numerous narrow transverse ravines on Jebel Rum are omitted. As a consequence what may appear on the map to be easily crossable plateaus are sometimes quite impassable - you have been warned! The other maps to the Rum area that may be of use are 3149-111 (east of Rum; includes part of Jebel Abu Judaidah): 3148-IV (SE of Rum, includes the East Face of Burdah) and 3048-1 (south of Rum, includes Burdah, the southern end of Khazali, Al Maghrar, etc.). This set of maps are displayed in the Rest House.

For general information on Wadi Rum and other tourist areas, the Ministry of Tourism publish a number of leaflets which are available from them or the offices of Alia, Royal Jordanian Airlines in Europe and America. For background literature or travel in Jordan, Kay Showker's book *Jordan and the Holy Land* published by Fodor's Travel Guides, New York and available from any large book shop is well worth reading and in 1987 Lonely Planet published their guide *Jordan and Syria, A Travel Survival Kit* with indispensable information for any traveller on what to see, how best to travel and where to stay. Also recommended for anyone intending to visit Wadi Rum is T.E.Lawrence's *Seven Pillars of Wisdom* - wonderful reading with some superbly eloquent passages describing the area and its people.

Pre-Historical Sites

(Thamudic & Nabataean drawings, inscriptions and constructions)

These are found throughout the Wadi Rum area and date back to approximately 1,500 to 3,000 years ago. Indeed the valley of Wadi Rum and the surrounding area has sites of antiquity almost too numerous to mention. Inscriptions and small stone enclosures of various shapes and sizes are found at the foot of the cliffs on both sides of the main valley.

The largest group of Nabataean buildings are just west of the Rest House, below the East Face of Jebel Rum. There is also a building near the south end of Wadi um Ishrin at ref:383693 overlooking three major wadi systems. this is probably the ruins of the Nabataean building known as Um el Quseir. Just to its north at ref: 382699 is an ancient dam at the mouth of a siq. A similar dam exists on the west side of Jebel Abu Judaidah, in the Barrah Canyon, known as Um Sidd. Two more impressive Nabataean dam sites have been found in the Rum area, one on the eastern side of Jebel um Harag, east of Abu Judaidah, (at ref: 428685) and one on the eastern side of Wadi Rumman, just south of the Quweirah road. In Wadi um 'Ishrin there are some splendid Nabataean steps hewn into the rock and leading to a hidden valley where there are a series of deep water basins in the rock bed of the siq (ref: 378771). The occasional piece of pottery may also be found simply lying in the desert, and in the southern part of the region a village has been excavated and dated to about 4500 BC.

Regarding inscriptions and rock drawings of Thamudic and Kufic origin, these are to be found in a number of places, notably the entrance to the large siq at Khaza'li (ref: 349682) where various drawings are found on both walls. Also at the foot of the south west face of a small rocky outcrop at the north east entrance to Wadi um 'Ishrin (ref: 403793), and to the west side of Annafishiyyah (named Jebel er Rak'a on the map), ref: 376726. We also noted small inscriptions at the entrances to the El Kharazah canyon, ref: 362744, and the canyon of Al Makhman, ref: 360753, and also at the north end of the Um Ishrin Massif, ref: 372808. Two other unusual and interesting sites are to be found south of Khor al Ajram. the first is on the east side of Wadi Khush Khashah, at the foot of the west face of Qabr Amra, 2km into the first Wadi south of the Khor. There are numerous inscriptions here, including two large 'lions' and some curious whale shapes on legs! (Ref: 363666). Just to the east, 1km down the second big Wadi as you go SE down Khor al Ajram will be found a big boulder on a flat rock platform in the centre of the valley. There are many inscriptions on the boulder, and the flat rock below, which is a good vantage point round the valley, has small holes cut in it, making squares, seven to each side, for the movement of stone pieces. The Bedouin say that these are very old games and people would sit here playing games and watching their livestock in the surrounding Wadi. The place is known to them as Aerayq Asseja "Rock of Games" (Ref: 385659).

The huge inscriptions at Abu El Hawil 7km north of the Rum-Disi road junction are also worth visiting, and there are many other interesting sites of antiquity, adding another unusual aspect to travel in these mountains. The following article will help with identification.

Recommended reading: *Hasma* by Sir A.S.Kirkbride and Lankester Harding, Palestine Exploration Quarterly, 1947, and *Some Thamudic inscriptions from the Hashemite Kingdom of Jordan*, by Lankester Harding with the collaboration of E.Litlmann, 1952.

Prof. E.Borzatti is currently working on a book which will fully detail the immense wealth of antiquity to be found in the Rum area.

The Nabataeans: by M.C.A.MacDonald

The Nabataeans were originally Arabic-speaking tribesmen who, in the late 4th century B.C., settled in southern Jordan and made their capital at Petra. From this vantage point they controlled the great trade-routes of western Arabia - the myrrh and frankincense coming north from Yemen, spices from the Indies landed in the Arabian Gulf and brought westward overland, and the famous purple cloth coming south from Phoenicia. Thus they

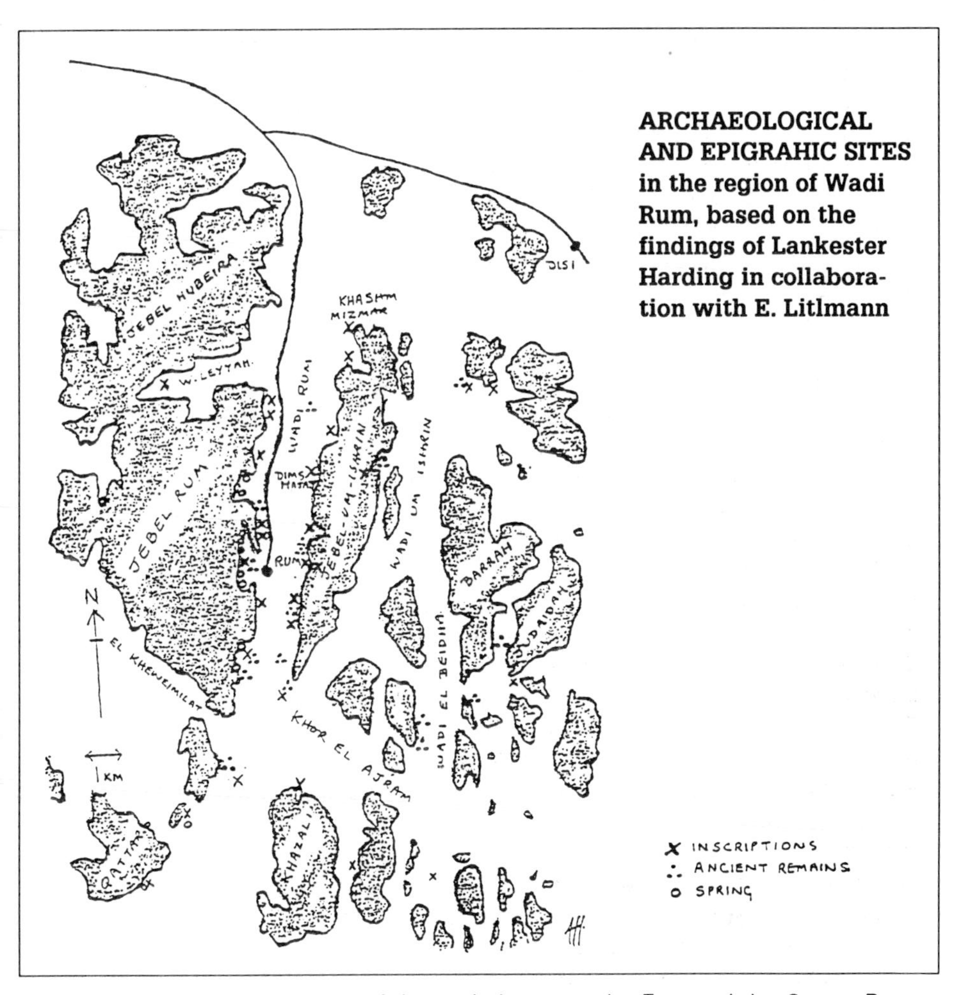

ARCHAEOLOGICAL AND EPIGRAHIC SITES in the region of Wadi Rum, based on the findings of Lankester Harding in collaboration with E. Litlmann

quickly came to dominate most of the trade between the East and the Graeco-Roman world. Gradually they extended their dominion south to the oases of the northern Hejaz (and, in particular, to the city of Meda'in Salih, the ruins of which are very similar to those at Petra) and northwards up into southern Syria to such sites as Bosra and the basalt cities of the Hauran. They also spread west into the Negev, dominating the trade-routes to the Mediterranean port of Gaza. The Nabataean kingdom was eventually annexed by Rome in 106 A.D. and declared part of the Roman Province of Arabia. However, Nabataean language and culture continued to flourish for many years after this.

The culture was extremely sophisticated, as can be seen from the surviving monuments at Petra and the eggshell-thin Nabataean pottery which is of a delicacy unrivalled in the ancient Near East. Since they lived, for the most part, in or on the edge of desert areas, water-conservation was of prime importance to the Nabataeans and in almost every part of their domain the remains of their elaborate water-catchment and management systems can still be seen such as the steps on Jebel um Ishrin. Wherever they settled they hewed out cisterns and pools and built dams and water-channels. The remains of an enormous dam some 50 metres long and 1.6 metres wide are visible at Bir Rumm al'Atiq. Another, smaller one (Um Sidd) is to be found in the west face of Jebel Abu Judaidah, and a further superb example can be seen on the east side of Jebel um Harag. There are numerous springs in the Rumm area most of which show signs of having been used by the Nabataeans. At Abu Aimeh, for instance, water channels are cut in the rock, at Sabagh a stone aqueduct leads to a masonry cistern, while at Ain Shelaali (close to the fort) there are the remains of a small sanctuary with carved betyls or idols. These almost always take the form of extremely stylised faces or simple pillars.

Indeed, Wadi Rumm was the site of an important Nabataean temple dedicated to Allat, whose name means "The goddess" (par excellence) and who is referred to in inscriptions as "Allat who is at Iram" (the ancient name for Rumm). The temple, which is very ruined, is to be found at the foot of Jebal Rumm not far from the Rest House.

Although they almost certainly spoke Arabic, the Nabataeans wrote in Aramaic (an ancient language of Syria which from the 6th century B.C. spread to become the lingua franca of the Near East and which therefore enjoyed enormous prestige, rather like Latin in Mediaeval Europe). Many of their inscriptions in a distinctive form of the Aramaic script can be found in Wadi Rumm area. Most of them are short graffiti, wishing peace on the writer or hoping that he would be remembered. They can easily be distinguished from the other ancient inscriptions (Greek, Minaean or Thamudic) because many of the letters are joined up, whereas in the other scrips each letter is separate.

There are a small number of Greek inscriptions in the Wadi Rumm area. Greek began to be used in Syria and Jordan in the years after Alexander the Great's conquest of the Near East in 332 B.C. and continued throughout the Roman and Byzantine periods. The Minaean inscriptions, in a very square monumental script, were written by South Arabian merchants and travellers from the state of Ma'in in Yemen. They established colonies in the oases of North Arabia to control the northern end of the incense trade, but were eventually supplanted by the Nabataeans. There is a good example of one of these inscriptions on a rock face to the east of the temple.

By far the most common inscriptions are the Thamudic (so named by Western scholars after the ancient Arabian tribe of Thamud, though there is no evidence that the two were connected). By chance some of the letters look like Greek, though they represent quite different sounds. The inscriptions are often written vertically and are sometimes accompanied by drawings. This was the script of the Arabian bedouin in the last few centuries B.C. and the first two or three centuries A.D. (it is impossible to be more precise since they are not dated). These bedouin, like their contemporaries the Nabataeans and Romans, must have been attracted to the Rumm area by the presence of perpetual springs and the seasonal grazing for their flocks and herds. They may also have come to worship at the temple, for Allat was the principle goddess of the North Arabian nomads. Their inscriptions can be found in almost every part of the area. they are all graffiti consisting mostly of the author's name ("Kilroy was here"), sometimes as the "signature" to a drawing ("so-and-so son of so-and-so drew this camel"). There are also short prayers ("May Allat remember so-and-so") and cries from the heart ("so-and-so loves so-and-so" or "By so-and-so as he grieved for his father", etc.).

Although some of the rock drawings are associated with these inscriptions many are

Bedouin Scenes in Wadi Rum

Sheikh Atieeq - photo: Howard

Camel Trek - photo: Taylor

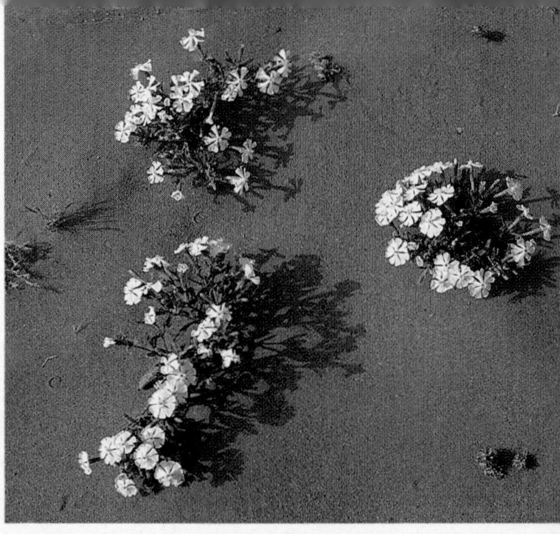

Flora, fauna and inscriptions. Photos Taylor & Howard

From left to right, top to bottom:

Orange tree, Rum village. Dune flora.

Horned viper. Inscriptions near Um Tawagi.

Inscriptions at Abu el Hawil (Note large inscribed figures at extreme left and right). Advice for visitors.

probably much older, though it is impossible to date them accurately. Some of them are extremely fine. The Siq, or cleft, of Khaz 'Ali has some particularly interesting examples, including elongated figures in tunics one of whom is apparently giving birth. Hands and feet are also favourite subjects, though it is not known why, as are hunting scenes. A wide variety of the ancient animal life of the area is represented including many species now extinct such as the Arabian lion, wild ass, adax, ostrich, etc.

There are also a number of early Arabic inscriptions in a stylised and rather beautiful form of the Arabic script known as Kufic. These were written mainly by pilgrims on their way to or from the Holy cities of Mecca and Medina, as well as by merchants and travellers. They mostly date from the early centuries of Islam (7th, 8th and 9th centuries A.D.) and are almost always of a religious nature. They can easily be distinguished from the other inscriptions because almost every letter is joined to its neighbours, either to the right or the left or both, and the text appears to be resting on a horizontal line.

Nomenclature

Wherever known, the Bedouin names for the mountains, canyons and wadis have been used together with their own translations of the meanings of these names in English. Spellings of Arabic words are phonetic and should not be considered definitive as, for instance, Lawrence refers to Rum as Rumm whilst the map says Ram and it may also be spelt Ramm or Rhumm.

Indeed, a young Bedouin boy suggested to us that the name derives from the chapter entitled 'The Dawn' in the Koran, N.J.Dawood's translation reads as follows:

"Have you not heard how Allah dealt with Aad? The people of the many columned city of Iram, whose like has never been built in the whole land?"

"And with Thamoud, who hewed out their dwellings among the rocks of the valley."

According to our Bedouin friend the 'many columned city of Iram' is nothing other than the mountains of Rum.

I include this colourful idea simply to indicate the reverence with which the Howeitat Bedu hold their homeland. Historians place the Iram referred to much further to the SE in Saudi Arabia in the territory of the Adites, or at Ubar, a recently discovered site in Oman's Empty Quarter. However, Rum was undoubtedly also known as Iram.

The medieval Arab geographer, Yaqut, was amongst the first to describe its location, adding that "the inhabitants of the wilderness stated that in Iram there were vineyards and pine-trees." Given the extensive water-management of the Nabataeans such a thing would certainly have been possible in antiquity and a memory of it, at least, may have persisted up to Yaqut's day (he died in A.D. 1229).

Ptolemy of Alexandria (the greatest of the ancient geographers and astronomers who lived in the first century A.D.) mentions the area under the Greek form of the name Aramaua and Nabataean inscriptions found there call it Aram or Iram.

The Rock

The mountains stand on a base of igneous rocks, predominantly granite and basalt. Above are sandstones, with narrow bands of quartzite, shales, grits and conglomerates. (The Quwerah Series.) Higher still are massive and thick bedded sandstones, (Rum and Um Sahn series) weathering respectively grey-white and purple, pink, white. The grey-white

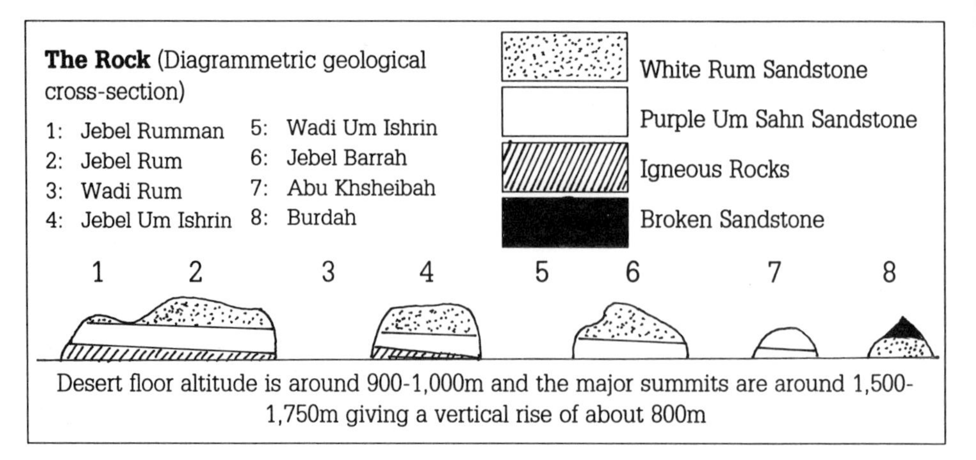

Rum sandstone forms most of the summit domes and gives smooth slabs of all angles and holdless cracks, whilst the Um Sahn series below gives steeper walls. The steepest walls (usually between 300 - 400m) are often festooned with overlaps like melted candles or bracket fungi. They have a most peculiar appearance, full of twists, whorls, pockets, holes and hanging slabs melting out into space, with the flamboyant exuberance of a Gaudi cathedral.

The rock strata itself dips from west to east so that the west peaks (Jebel Rumman) have a thick broken igneous base about 150 - 200m thick, diminishing to around 100m on the east side of Jebel Rum and the west side of Jebel Um Ishrin and vanishing altogether on the east side of Um Ishrin. This gives rise to a number of permanent water sources along the east side of Jebel Rum where the water, having percolated through the upper sandstones seeps out at the sandstone-granite junction. The series of sandstones immediately above the granitic rocks is about 300m thick and tends to be disappearing on the east side of the Barrahs so that the area to the far east is almost totally white Rum sandstone and much lower in altitude, giving towers varying from 10m to 200m or so. Beyond this area is the peak of Burdah with its huge natural arch high on the ridge. This peak, and those of Abu Judaidah to its north are capped with another series of more broken sandstone.

Further east still, the lower sandstone series fade out, being replaced completely by broken slopes of poorer quality sandstones and shales with no interest to the climber. Similarly, west of Jebel Rumman the mountains are rubble sided granites and basalts again with very limited opportunities for climbing.

Description and Grading of Routes

Even after eight years, not many routes have had more than a handful of ascents. In fact, many have not had a second ascent! This means I have had to rely almost completely on descriptions from first ascentionists with little or no feed back from other climbers. If many of the descriptions say "good rock" or "enjoyable climbing" this is because first ascentionists are invariably pleased with their creation and where there is no evidence to the contrary I have used the first ascent notes. If you form another opinion, please let me

UIAA - COMPARISON TABLE: RATING OF CLIMBING DIFFICULTIES
TABLE DE COMPARAISON UIAA DES ECHELLES DE DIFFICULTE EN ESCALADE
UIAA - VERGLEICHSTABELLE DER KLETTERSCHWIERIGKEITEN
TABLA DE COMPARACION UIAA DE LOS GRADOS DE DIFICULTAD DE ESCALADA

OVERALL ROUTE GRADE	TECHNICAL PITCH GRADE		
FRENCH	FRENCH	UIAA	BRITISH
F. - FACILE	1	I	1
	2	II	2
P.D. - PEV DIFFICILE	3 -/+	III	3
A.D. - ASSEZ DIFFICILE	4 -/+	IV -/+	4a
	5 -	V -	4b
D. - DIFFICILE	5	V	4c
		V +	
T.D. - TRES DIFFICILE	5 +	VI -	5a
	6 a	VI	5b
	6 a+	VI +	
	6 b	VII -	5c
	6 b+	VII	
E.D. - EXTREME	6 c	VII +	6a
	6 c+	VIII -	
	7 a		
	7 a+	VIII	
	7 b	VIII +	6b
ABO - ABOMINABLE!	7 b+		
	7 c	IX -	6c
	7 c+	IX	
	8 a	IX +	7a
	8 a+	X -	
	8 b 8 b+	X	
	8 c	X+	7b

N.B. FRENCH GRADES ARE USED THROUGHOUT THIS GUIDE, EXCEPT FOR THE 'HAUPOLTER' CLIMBS WHERE UIAA GRADES ARE USED AND INDICATED AS SUCH ON THE TOPO

know! Remember "good rock" does not mean you can expect the quality of Buoux, or Cornish granite: it's sandstone we are talking about here, and the terms are relative!

Where feed-back has been forthcoming, I have (if necessary) modified the notes accordingly. I have also endeavoured to provide a 'star-list' at the back of this book based on my own knowledge and the comments of others. The list is not in any way all-encompassing since there is insufficient information but I hope it will give newcomers to 'The Valley' not only a starting-pack from which to select their initial routes, but also some major objectives on the 'Big Walls'.

All major rock routes in this guide are given an overall grade using the modern French alpine system and a pitch grade also using the modern French system. However, there are two exceptions to this rule: the shorter 'sports' climbs have no overall grade as having comparatively easy access and descent they are considered to be less serious; more importantly, the climbs of Haupolter and Precht are graded by using the U.I.A.A. system. As few have been repeated, it was felt better to leave these routes as graded on their first ascent rather than attempt to convert them to the French system. For what it's worth, Muezzin given a U.I.A.A. tech. grade of V1+ was described as "at least English E3.5c" on its second ascent. This does *not* correlate with the comparative grading chart. Obviously the notes on the grades of the Haupolter-Precht routes (see Styles of Route) are not to be taken lightly!

A comparison of French, U.I.A.A. and English technical grades and the appropriate overall grade is given in the chart. As these grades and the climbing times for the routes and their descents are mainly based on first ascent experiences of different climbers, with few second opinions, there will almost certainly be discrepancies in both. (See 'Times Allowed')

After the name of each climb, are listed the names of the first ascentionists, and the date. If it is believed that the route had been climbed earlier by the Bedouin, then the named climbers are simply credited with "the first recorded ascent."

The character of the route is then described, followed by the vertical height of the route. (Actual route length is usually considerably greater). The overall grade is then given and the time required, with a list of relevant maps and topos. On short climbs (150 metres or less) having easy access and retreat, and good rock, only the pitch grades are given, with no overall route grade, since they give purely technical climbing with none of the hazards associated with longer more remote routes. The approach and descent descriptions follow, with times needed, where necessary. On the actual topos, pitch by pitch grades are given using the modern French grading system, unless marked 'U.I.A.A. grades'.

Other symbols used on the topos include the following:

R1, R2, R3 etc. Belay (French: relais) points are numbered on some of the topos.

(Exp) After the pitch grade, denotes exposed and unprotected.

(4 pts) After the pitch grade, indicates 4 points of aid (for example) are required on that pitch at the given grade. A harder free climbing grade is also given if the pitch has also been climbed without aid.

Pendulum — Pendulum required during the ascent.

Abseil used on descent route (sometimes the length of the abseil is given, but no abseils in this guide are longer than 45m unless marked otherwise).

The easier journeys and walks or canyon treks are given written descriptions and maps whereas the rock climbs are described by topographical diagrams only.

I hope the topos will reveal something of the complexity of peaks such as Jebel Rum, where I would not be too surprised if the over-enthusiastic climber arriving on the brim of the summit plateau for the first time, still experienced some difficulty in unravelling its mysteries: a mouse in a field full of bowler hats would be similarly confused! For aid climbing, the usual system of A0, A1, A2, A3, A4 is used to denote increasing difficulty and the number of pegs required is also given for example A0 means pegs (or chocks) may be needed for hand-holds or tension, whilst A1 (4 pts) indicates easy artificial, with four aid points. Due to the nature of the rock, it is likely that any aid sections which, at the moment require blade pegs, will, after a few ascents take nuts or even become free!

A list of routes to be found at each grade in each area will be found at the back of this book.

Times Allowed for Climbs

I have always endeavoured to give times that are realistic for a competent party of two. Nevertheless, general opinion seems to indicate that few of the times in this book are generous. Indeed, with regard to the Remy routes, there are few who can improve on their times for ascent or descent and the Haupolter times are equally fast, if not faster! Allow yourself some margin for error. Some very experienced rock climbers, alpinists and even Himalayan climbers have been caught out by the sunshine and relaxed atmosphere of Wadi Rum, and had to make forced bivouacs which can be a lot colder and more unpleasant than you might imagine!

Styles of Route

Over the past eight years, a lot of climbers have added to the wealth and variety of routes in Rum. However, it is worth noting the styles of routes by the main contributors and the trends in development:

1. *The Bedouin Routes.* Long routes often with complex route finding through and up natural features and almost always in magnificent scenery. Probably discovered by following or searching for ibex, and the knowledge passed down from father to son. The real adventure classics of the area demanding Grade 3 soloing capability. Maximum difficulty, 5. Descents similar.

2. *The Howard and Colonna Routes.* The first wave of European exploration, these climbs are wherever possible on open faces or, failing this in classical diedres or hand-cracks, with intriguing or attractive lines. The objective was always to find a classical route of interest and character. Descents are usually good.

3. *Duvernet-Monnet Climbs.* Good lines in the style of the original pioneers with a quest for adventure on classic features.

4. *The Remy Routes.* A rock invasion! Searching for steep rock, usually climbed by obvious crack-chimney lines with little choice of line, but powerful climbing. Exceptions are climbs such as 'Neige Dans Le Desert' and 'Merci Allah'. Abseil descents may need treating carefully!

5. *The Haupolter - Precht Routes.* Another rock invasion with a very pure 'no-bolts' ethic. Imaginative concepts, with bold, fast and committing climbing generally out in the open

on big walls - the most serious routes in this guide. Descents, "can be frightening!"

Following are some important points supplied by Wolfgang Haupolter, concerning their climbs and topos:

- the U.I.A.A. scale is used but the grading is severe
- usually one set of stoppers and one set of friends, including half size has been used
- 45-metre ropes have been used. The abseil points are most times slings on rock-holes. Sometimes there are really frightening rappels!
- no bolts have been used
- "SU" in the topos means small rock hole with a sling left
- "KS" in the topos also means fixed (knotted) slings

I think I should also point out that the descriptions of the rock quality on some of the Haupolter and Remy climbs are thought by subsequent ascentionists to be often over-enthusiastic!

Climbing History

There is almost no need for a historical review of the climbing activities in the mountains of Rum for apart from one route, no recorded climbs were made there until 1984 when we visited the area as "the first climbing expedition."

Nevertheless, it should be said that pre-historic man lived here over 200,000 years ago. The Thamuds and Nabataeans also lived here 2,000 years ago and certainly went up the lower canyons and maybe to some of the summits on hunting trips. The Bedouin certainly have known climbs to the summits of these mountains for many generations and took a survey party to the top of some including Jebel Rum when the first maps were made. The only other early reported ascent of Jebel Rum was by Charmian Longstaff and Sylvia Branford in 1952 with Sheikh Hamdan, the man who had lead the map-makers to the summit.

No other reported climbs were known to us prior to our first expedition in 1984. Countless other routes of all grades await the climber and the area should continue to provide mountain adventures far into the future.

Chronology of Mountain Exploration in Jordan

Pre-historic	Early Thamudic and Nabataean ways into the mountains. Bedouin routes for hunting, eventually to most summits climbable at grade 4 and below.
- 1949	Sheikh Hamdan took cartographers to summit of Jebel Rum and other peaks in the area.
November 1952	First recorded European ascent of Jebel Rum by mountain climbers, for sport. Charmian Longstaff and Sylvia Branford guided by Sheikh Hamdan.
1970 - 1980	Hammad Hamdan (son of Sheikh Hamdan) repeats harder Bedouin routes with other Bedouin on Jebel Rum and other peaks in the area, for pleasure and challenge! All climbed without equipment, including some grade 5 moves.
Oct - Nov 1984	Exploration of Jebel Rum's Bedouin routes by an English team of climbers (Baker, Shaw, Taylor and Howard) invited by the Ministry of Tourism, in co-operation with the local Bedouin "climbers" and hunters. Examples: Eye of Allah A.D. Sup Al Thalamiyyah A.D. Sup

Hammad's Route A.D. Sup

Oct - Nov 1984 Exploration of the whole Rum area by the same group, aided by the Bedouin to identify and evaluate the climbing potential: Burdah, Barrah, um Ishrin Massif, etc.

19 October 1984 Jebel Kharazeh "Vanishing Pillar" T.D. Inf. First ascent of an unclimbed summit by a modern climb, by the same team.

September 1985 First attempt to search for trekking and climbing potential outside the Rum area by the same team plus W.Colonna (French guide).

28 September 1985 Trek through Dana Canyon to Wadi Araba.

29 September 1985 Trek up the 'secret' Lower Petra Canyon, jealously guarded by the Saidi Yin Bedouin, from Wadi Araba (Bir Madhkhur) to Petra. Some climbing potential noted in both valleys.

October 1985 The same team begin ascents of the 'modern' classics of the Rum area, mainly face climbing of standards between French 4+ to 6A.

Examples:

10 October 1985 The Beauty T.D.

14 October 1985 Purple Haze D

24 October 1985 The Perverse Frog T.D. Sup

Rediscovery of two more Bedouin classics by the same group:

12 October 1985 Rijm Assaf A.D.

2 November 1985 Hunter's Slabs A.D.

April - May 1986 Many major crack-chimney lines climbed by Claude and Yves Remy, from Switzerland, also the first ascents of two major unclimbed summits:

21 April 1986 N.Nassrani "L'Autre Dimension" T.D.

7 May 1986 S.Nassrani. "Merci Allah" T.D. Sup

April - May 1986 The English/French group continue their explorations for classic lines at all standards, including the rediscovery of Sabbah's Route on Jebel Rum and the first route on Jebel Rum's important East Dome Wall:

27 April 1986 Inshallah Factor T.D. Sup

Oct - Nov 1986 The valley's first real climbing invasion with teams from the U.K. and all European alpine countries and another rise in climbing standards, especially on wall climbing:

Towering Inferno E.D. inf

The Star of Abu Judaidah E.D. inf

9 Oct 1986 A new sport introduced to Jordan with the first jump off the top of East Dome's East Face with paragliders by Jean-Philippe "Dolby" Monnet and Yves Duverney from France, at 9.30 a.m.

Oct - Nov 1986 International Guides Meet hosted by the Ministry of Tourism

Oct - Nov 1986 The appearance of short difficult routes in the modern style particularly along the foot of the East Face and the Barrah Canyon. Another increase in the technical level of climbing by two English guides, Rowland Edwards and Brede Arkless making an 'on-sight' ascent:

26 Oct 1986 Ziggurat 7A

15 March 1987 Rowland Edwards returns with his son Mark to produce another technical test piece, Sandstorm. 7A+.

This is immediately followed by two major classics:

19 March 1987 Lionheart E.D. Inf.

22 March 1987 Warriors of the Wastelands. E.D. The first route with full E.D. status and the hardest pitch to date in the valley, at 7B.

26 - 29 April 1987 A big mixed aid and free route on Jebel Rum's East Wall - The Red Sea - by Spanish climbers.

March 1988 Haupolter and Precht begin their explorations with numerous classics on Jebel Rum and Jebel um Ishrin massif setting a style for fast, imaginative and clean climbing.

Sept 1988 Renshaw and Green climb their splendid 'Siege of Jericho' at 7A.

21 - 23 April 1989 — Colonna and team still exploring for good new lines climb Al Uzza at E.D.Sup. 7A. The power-drill raises its ugly head for the first time on a new route in Wadi Rum. (About 20 holes drilled, to assist in the placing of 10 bolts for aid.)

April 1989 — Haupolter and Precht return and crank up the difficulty and commitment of their routes with:

2 May 1989 — No Way for Ibex, ED with pitches of UIAA V11-, (FR 6B or maybe 6C).

April 1990 — Back with a vengeance, Haupolter and Precht add to their quota of high standard routes particularly on Nassrani, setting the style for the future, with climbs such as:

8 April 1990	Never say Never.	E.D. Sup.
16 April 1990	Jolly Joker	E.D. Sup.
18 April 1990	Corner Line.	E.D. Sup
26 April 1990	Incredible Possibility	E.D. Sup., UIAA V111- (FR 7A or maybe 7B).

1991 — The valley is quiet as the 'Gulf War' stops play.

March 1992 — Spanish climbers add another mixed aid and free line up a blank section of Jebel Rum's East Face:
Revienta o Burila ED (7A). This required hand drilling of 39 bolts. Is bolted climbing the way for the future, or should bolts be used only for main belays and abseils? Keep Wadi Rum clean!

May 1992 — W.Colonna completes Mano Negra (7A+) adding another typical top quality contribution to the East Face climbs. This was followed later in the year by another top quality sports climb:

November 1992 — Cat-fish Corner (6c).

New Climbs

Amongst the route descriptions will be found some details of potential new routes of all grades from walks to big walls. Anyone making an ascent of any of these routes, or discovering a previously unrecorded walk or canyon trek, or a camel journey or desert drive of unusual interest should send details to me for inclusion in any future re-prints of this book, care of the following address: Troll Safety Equipment Limited, Spring Mill, Uppermill, Oldham, OL3 6AA, England.

There is also a New Routes book kept at the Rest House in which any new route information should be entered. As it now goes back quite a few years, it is beginning to make interesting reading with the usual strong comments from various climbers!

* * *

JEBEL RUM MASSIF

This huge massif extends for over 15km down the W side of Wadi Rum, though the northern third beyond Wadi Leyyah has so far proved of no interest for climbers or walkers. The main massif however has a vast selection of routes of all lengths and difficulties, most of which are easily accessible from the Rest House.

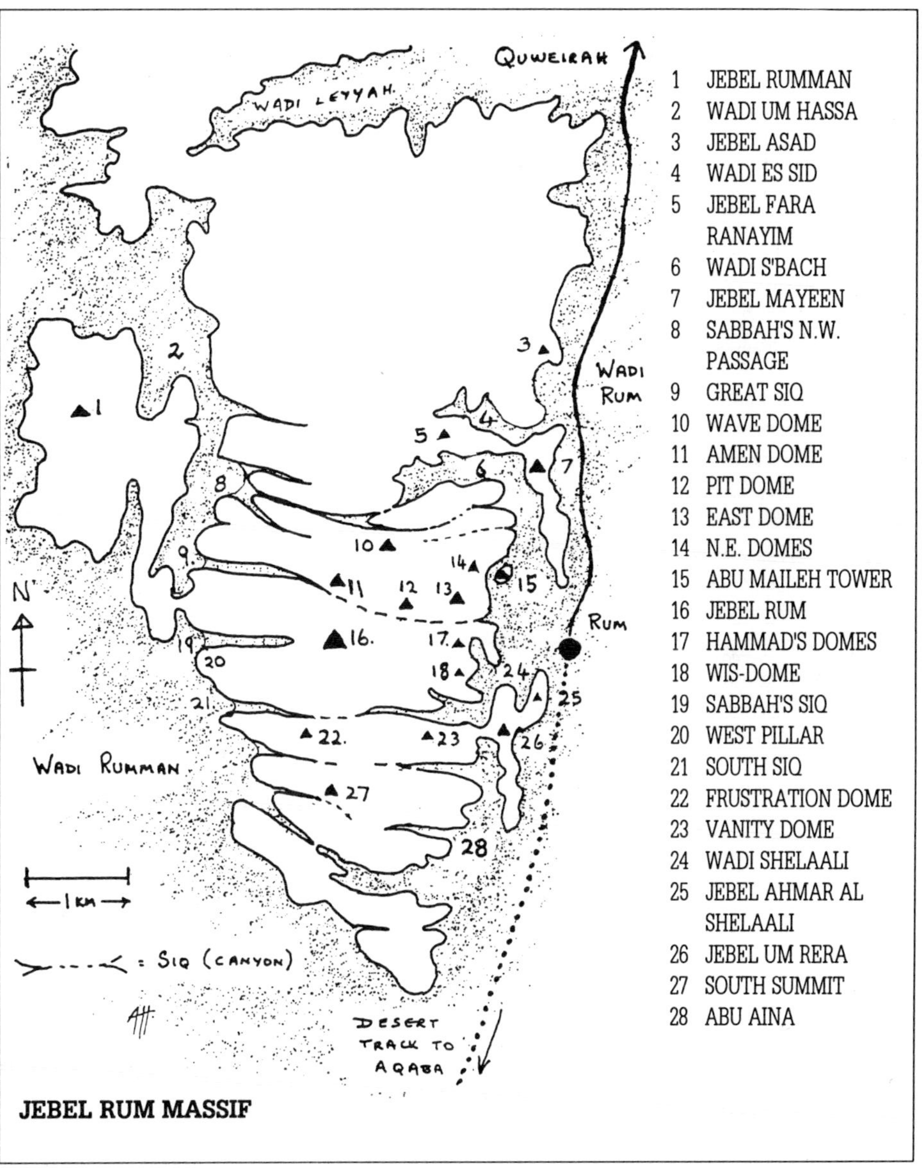

JEBEL RUM MASSIF

Major features of Jebel Rum (1,754m)

To facilitate understanding of the route descriptions on this complex massif, it is first of all necessary to appreciate the topography of the mountain and to identify the various features.

The Great Siq

The giant ravine which is visible from Wadi Rum village as the gully defining the left (south) edge of the East Face of East Dome, behind the Rest House, cleaves the mountain in half, right through to Wadi Rumman. Apart from it being a unique mountain feature in itself it also contains some amazing features of its own. In parts about 100 metres deep it varies from a few metres wide to over a 100 metres and, near the plateau area, contains a giant hole we named "The Pit" whose only water exit is an equally giant archway through which the sunlight streams in the early morning.

The North Plateau

This is the high desert area of the Summit Plateau of Jebel Rum, immediately north of the Great Siq. It is concealed from view from Wadi Rum by the 400-metre walls which make access to it both complex and difficult. It is a wild and strangely beautiful place - a natural reserve for the rare ibex.

There are numerous domes rising from this plateau, many unclimbed, and mostly un-named. The four peaks so far named are Wave Dome (ref: 326752), Amen Dome (ref: 322748) above the west end of Great Siq, Pit Dome (ref: 328746), above The Pit, and East Dome (ref: 333748) above the Rest House.

The Hidden Siq drains the south east corner of this plateau and forms the right (north) edge of the east face of East Dome. To its right are the North East Domes, then the Dark Tower and finally the amazing couloir of Al Thalamiyyah, which gives access to the plateau.

Juniper Flats

This black stony plateau harbouring large and ancient juniper trees at the foot of large white domes, rises above the south west corner of the North Plateau and has an excellent bivouac site beneath an east facing overhang.

It is possible to descend partway into The Pit from here, by an easy sloping corridor about 2 metres wide going straight down from near the south east end of Juniper Flats for about 200 metres. Awesome views of The Pit, The Archway and The Great Siq.

The Central Plateau

This is the area of the high plateau on which the summit is located, immediately south of the Great Siq. It is a rather complex area of domes and ridges, with its own small desert, with trees and bivouac sites. It is defined to its south by the canyon and siq of Wadi Shelaali which again appears to completely bisect the mountain.

The Southern Siq

South of the Central Plateau is another huge canyon again bisecting the mountain from east to west. There may in fact be more than one of these, since this part of the mountain was not explored fully by us. The Southern Siq referred to is the first major barrier reached when ascending from the south end of the massif. There seems to be at least one other, extending west from Wadi Shelaali, though these may in fact be different arms of the same canyon!

The Southern Plateau

This is the area of high ground south of the Southern Siq, extending to the southern end of the massif and fairly easily accessible from the Bedouin camp of Abu Aina.

* * *

1. Round Jebel Rum Trek *P.J.Lange, G.Fontaine 9th October 1986*

A very worthwhile, interesting and beautiful trek that can be completed in one day (9 hours including rests) with an early start from the Rest House in a clockwise direction round Jebel Rum.

Follow the track south to Abu Aina springs and Bedouin camp (3 kilometres). Here there are two possibilities: easiest, but longest, continue south 2 kilometres more, then round the end of the massif, and north west into Wadi el Khweimelat which leads eventually to Wadi Rumman.

Alternatively take the valley just south west of the Bedouin Camp (Rakabat Abu Aina) follow it over the col pleasantly into the descent valley ('Khmeileh - small place of trees) and so to Wadi el Khweimelat, on the west side of Jebel Rum. Follow the edge of the desert and go north below the west face screes, where there may be some Bedouin camps, into a cirque leading to the col between Jebel Rum and Jebel Rumman on the north west. (The big valley above on the east is the one taken by Sabbah's Route to the summit.)

Here it is best to keep close to the side of Jebel Rum up granite scree to a small pass (not in the larger valley which is immediately west). (3 hours of walking from the Rest House.) From the pass descend into Wadi um Hassa to where a big valley enters from the right (east). (This is the west entrance to the Great Siq, up which Sheikh Hamdan's route ascends.) Here there is a well and springs (1 hour from the pass). At this point the valley narrows through a polished granite river bed which is descended with some scrambling. Where the valley eventually opens there is a stone with some Thamudic inscriptions. There may also be a Bedouin camp.

Go north along the east side of the cirque until in the N end where three valleys enter; take the central (east) one and follow this up to a pass with a huge cairn, with a mountain basin just ahead. (1 1/2 hours from the spring in Wadi um Hassa.)

Go along the right side of the basin ascending a little until a big valley is seen going down, and winding left into Wadi Leyyah, through bushes and trees (1 hour to descend). Follow this wide valley east for 2 kilometres to the road and down the Wadi Rum road back to the Rest House (1 1/2 hours).

Jebel Asad. 1280m

This subsidiary peak stands above the small valley immediately N of Wadi es Sid.

2. South Face Divers-tissement *C.&Y.Remy 4 Nov 1986*

Some initial passages of doubtful rock lead to superb climbing in the obvious diedres. T.D. Sup 4 hours..

3. South Face. Boules brunes *C.&Y.Remy 4 Nov. 1986*

Interesting climbing with a splendid fifth pitch.T. D. INF. 3 hours.

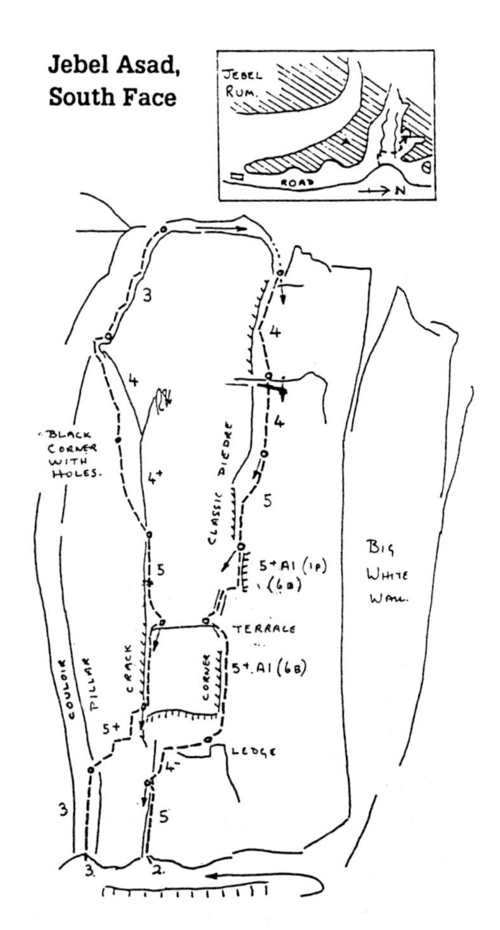

Approach: Both routes are easily reached by leaving the road at the big bend about 2km N of the Rest House and walking west towards the valley of Wadi es Sid. The cliff will be seen to the right (N) and the climbs are to the left of the big white wall, about 20 minutes from the road. *Descent:* By rappel down Boules brunes.

Jebel El Mayeen 1,100m (ref: 342760)

4. From the south *First recorded ascent D.Taylor, A.Howard 29th Oct. 1985.*

This small peak is immediately north of the Rest House and provides a pleasant excursion with good views of the Rum Valley and the walls of Rum and um Ishrin. Grade F. Allow 2 - 3 hours for the return journey which is described ascending the S Ridge, but may be made in either direction. Maps pages 44, 48.

Jebel Mayeen, South Ridge

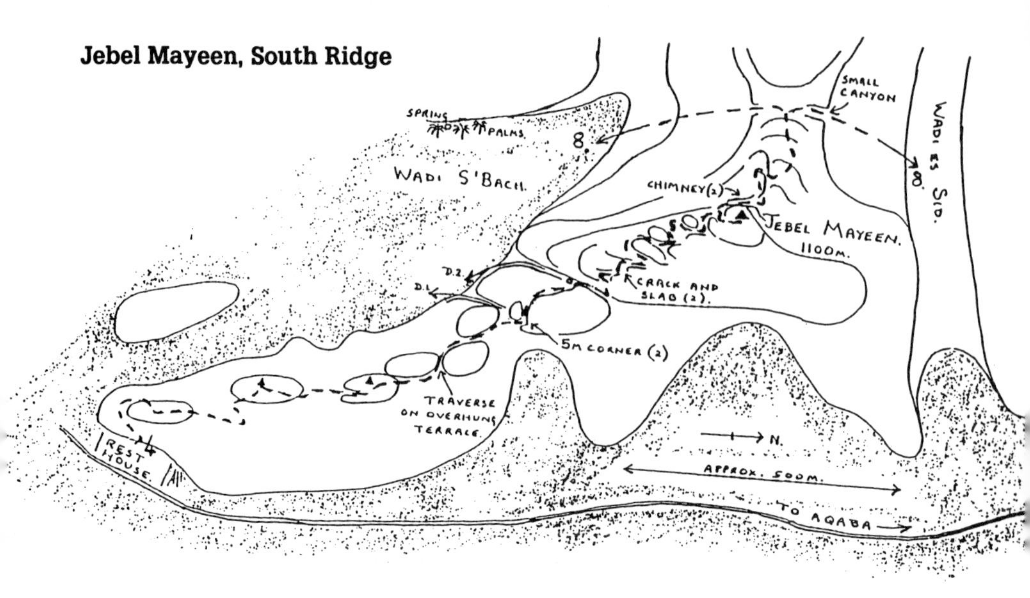

From the Rest House car park, scramble leftwards up the hillside to the end of the S ridge where there is a flat rock ledge and some burial mounds. Go N along the ridge, rising up the right side of the next top to more cairns and mounds and good views. Descend again to the right, to the second ledge down and walk round to the ridge beyond (more graves). Descend to a col and up a bushy gully to the right side of the next top.

Cross this plateau (more mounds), curving left to just below the next top. Do not go up. Instead descend a short bushy gully on the right and contour round left on a rock ledge under overhangs to the next col.

Pass through this and walk along below the left side of the next top and scramble down to a saddle. From here, go up a little slab and traverse along on ledges again, now on the right side of the mountain, to the next col. There are good views from all of these tops and the Dark Tower is immediately opposite to the W, across Wadi S'Bach.

Beyond here the way starts to become steeper and, for walkers, a descent can be made left (W) into Wadi S'Bach, down the gully (D.1.). (Keep left at the bottom to avoid overhangs above the valley floor.)

To reach the summit of Jebel El Mayeen, continue along on the right side then up rock steps and a steep V-groove (2) to a col below a tower on the ridge. Contour round onto its left side and descend to scree ledges. Walk along these, rising up slabs where easily possible to enter the next gully, near a flat rock with camel inscriptions. (Possible descent from here to Wadi S'Bach, again keeping left just above the valley floor, to avoid overhangs.) (D.2.).

Above, the gully goes up a little ravine to the col. From here, cross slabs leftwards, round a nose of rock and up the slabby ridge above it (1). Carry on up to a tree on the skyline. Here, go left, all the way round to the next tower, to reach the next saddle. Go straight up a bushy gully then pass the next rock bulge up cracks on its left (2). From the ledge at the top go right (not up the gully ahead) onto knobbly slabs and up to a ledge with boulders. Go left through these, to the left side of the mountain again where there is a little corner with a fallen block below. This leads abruptly to the top. Excellent view. (The summit boulder can be climbed - grade 3.)

Descent: Either return the same way, perhaps descending into Wadi S'Bach by the descent gully with the camel inscriptions, or take the N ridge:-

Go down the little fallen block corner then right to a bushy hollow with a col just beyond. Continue in the same direction, (easiest on the left, down slabs) to the top of a steep section. Descend a chimney (2) to a ledge, and down it again, under a boulder to the next ledge and down again to a third ledge above a juniper tree.

Go down behind this and left behind a boulder, then W along humpback slabs, on the left side of a gully which is gained by descending a little wall (1). From its foot, zig-zag right to the next ledge and walk W along this and down a little wall (1) to the shoulder above the saddle between Wadi S'bach and Wadi es Sid ($^1/_2$ hour from summit).

Return to the Rest House by either of these valleys. (See R.8 for the walk through Wadi es Sid.)

East Face

5. Jack Daniels *G.Claye and P.Languet. 13 Oct. 1986*

An enjoyable climb for an afternoon up slabs and strenuous cracks with an exposed but easy traverse on the third pitch. 180m A.D. Sup. 2 hours. Map page48.
Approach: Go N up the road from the Rest House for 1.2km, when the face will be seen on the left, with two trees at its bottom right. 20 minutes from Rest House to the foot of the climb.

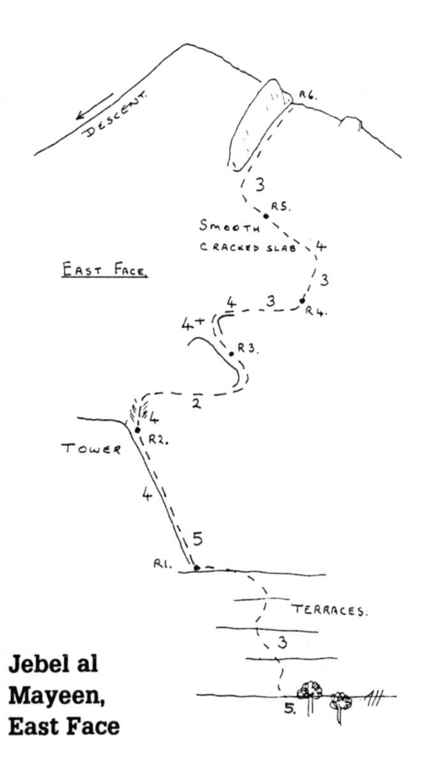

Jebel al Mayeen, East Face

Descent: By the S ridge to the Rest House, with some steps of 2, or the N ridge to Wadi S'Bach. $^3/_4$ hour.

The only other recorded route on this face is BODY ABUSE which trends left below the tower on R.5, to finish at the col with bad rock at Grade 3 and 4 "carries a Government Health Warning"!

West Face

6. Voie Laurianne *Yves Astier & Olivier Greber 3 Oct. 1987*

Takes the centre of the face, up the only obvious line, entering from the left above sandy overhangs and passing the bulge above with two pegs (4+), above which another pitch of 4+ leads to easier ground and the summit. 150m.

South West Face

7. Scots On The Rocks *A.Ghilchrist & D.Brown 10 April 1990*

An enjoyable though very short route giving a pleasant evening scramble to the S ridge, and thence the top of Jebel Mayeen, up the SW side of the mountain, climbing its main feature which is a Grade 3 chimney-crack, and the groove above (3+), or a variation finish which traverses right at the same grade. 100m.
Descent: By the S Ridge, $^1/_2$ - $^3/_4$ hour.

The Eastern Ravines of Jebel Rum

There are two wadis going NW and SW from the Rest House and curving like horns into the East Walls of Jebel Rum, where they eventually end as box canyons. They are respectively Wadi S'Bach and Wadi Shelaali. Both have numerous sweet-water springs and between them, immediately behind the Rest House are Nabataean ruins.

The springs below the East Face are listed by Lankester Harding and Sir A.S.Kirkbride as follows, from north to south:-

Sabagh	Stone aqueduct leads to a masonry cistern
Mugheireh	Stone troughs near two springs
Abu Remeileh	Consists of three springs. On the rock terraces above the main spring are the remains of walls and buildings and quantities of sherds; a rock-cut channel

	leads from this spring to a ruined masonry cistern
El Wujeihat	There are four small springs of this name
Abu Shleilieh	Nothing to note at the two springs
Ain Shellaleh	Nabataean inscriptions and buildings, 'Lawrence's Well.'

Both the valleys offer pleasant and interesting walks, Wadi S'Bach providing the start of a short trek:

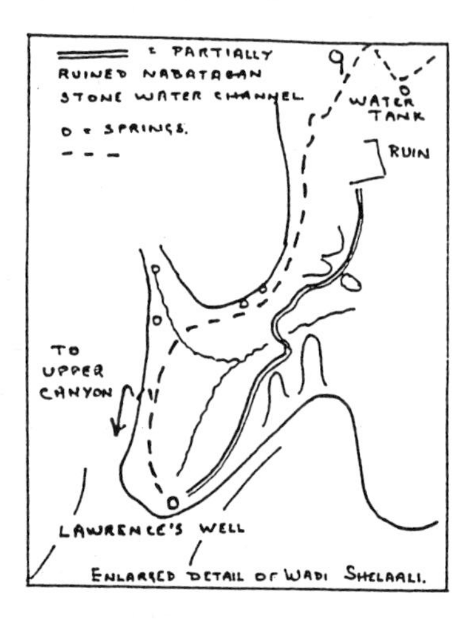

8. Wadi S'Bach to Wadi Es Sid

A pleasant scramble of about 6 kilometres up Wadi S'Bach, north west of the Rest House and over a col to its north, then through a cleft in cliffs into the pleasant narrow valley of Wadi es Sid which leads east to the road in Wadi Rum. Allow 2½ hours. Map page 44.

From the Rest House, walk up Wadi S'Bach with the big cliffs of Jebel Rum's E face on the left. The valley becomes increasingly green, with palm trees at spring locations on its W side, then after passing large boulders, the stream bed (quite often with a trickle of water) turns to the W.

Here continue N rising up to a col in the ridge at the head of the valley. To descend, it is essential to go down through a little ravine for 100m, otherwise cliffs will be met. Once through this, scramble easily down into Wadi es Sid. Go E down the stream bed to a narrowing where there are often pools. Pass these (some rock scrambling may be necessary) and descend a little cliff (1) to the desert.

Walk out E to reach the road, and follow it back to the Rest House.

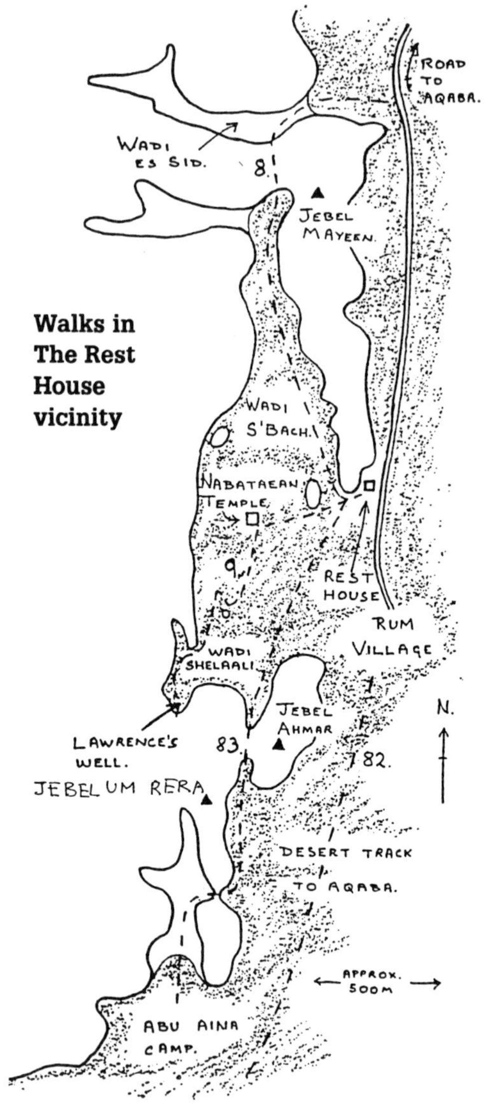

Walks in The Rest House vicinity

The other more famous valley is:

9. Wadi Shelaali (Valley of the Waterfall) - Lawrence's Well

An easy walk of 2.5 kilometres with a wealth of historical sites.

Allow 1 - 1½ hours for the return journey.

This valley is 1 kilometre SW of the Rest House and

makes a pleasant short walk that may also be combined with a visit to the Nabataean temple immediately W of the Rest House. It is the site of Lawrence's Well about which he wrote so evocatively in "The Seven Pillars of Wisdom", and also has a Nabataean rock water channel much of which is in place, from the spring down to an old Nabataean site just S of the temple. The spring is in the shade much of the day and is surrounded by greenery; here is an extract from Lawrence's description, of his visit on the 11th September 1917:

"The sun had sunk behind the western wall leaving the pit in shadow; but its dying glare flooded with startling red the wings each side of the entry, and the fiery bulk of the further wall across the great valley. The pit-floor was of damp sand, darkly wooded with shrubs; while about the feet of all the cliffs lay boulders greater than houses, sometimes, indeed, like fortresses which had crashed down from the heights above. In front of us a path, pale with use, zigzagged up the cliff-plinth to the point from which the main face rose and there it turned precariously southward along a shallow ledge outlined by occasional leafy trees. From between these trees, in hidden crannies of the rock, issued strange cries; the echoes, turned into music, of the voices of the Arabs watering camels at the springs which there flowed out three hundred feet above ground."

On another visit, Lawrence bathed in one of these springs which he described eloquently:

"Its rushing noise came from my left, by a jutting bastion of cliff over whose crimson face trailed long falling runners of green leaves. The path skirted it in an undercut ledge. On the rock-bulge above were clear-cut Nabataean inscriptions and a sunk panel incised with a monogram or symbol. Around and about were Arab scratches, including tribe-marks, some of which were witnesses of forgotten migrations: but my attention was only for the splashing of water in a crevice under the shadow of the overhanging rock.

"From this rock a silver runlet issued into the sunlight. I looked in to see the spout, a little thinner than my wrist, jetting out firmly from a fissure in the roof and falling with that clean sound into a shallow, frothing pool, behind the step which served as entrance. The walls and roof of the crevice dripped with moisture. Thick ferns and grasses of the finest green made it a paradise just 5ft square.

"Upon the water-cleansed and fragrant ledge I undressed my soiled body, and stepped onto the little basin, to taste at last the freshness of moving air and water against my tired skin. It was deliciously cool. I lay there quietly letting the clear, dark red water run over me in a ribbly stream, and rub the travel-dirt away."

To visit the spring, cross the desert either directly, towards a white water tank right of the valley entrance or, first, visit the Nabataean temple behind the Rest House.

From the tank, a well used track zig-zags up the hillside to a little flat plateau above the valley entrance. From here the path contours round above the valley and just below the cliffs, past the green minty springs of Abu Shleilieh to arrive at 'Lawrences Well'.

(The canyon of Wadi Shelaali - valley of the waterfall - is just above and can be entered from 200m right, up easy ledges. It is blocked after a few hundred metres by the steep cliffs of Jebel Rum.)

Around the area of the well will be seen the ancient 'tribal markings' described by Lawrence. From here, along the right (E) side of the valley will also be found the beginning of the Nabataean stone water channel. This can be followed back with care, down the right side of the valley, across the wadi bed above some smooth granite slabs, then along the other side of the wadi, to the valley floor. Or, of course, one can return by the same route.

Jebel Fara Ranayim 1460m

Situated at the head of the narrow ridge dividing the valleys of Wadi es Sid and Wadi S'Bach with good views.

10. East Ridge of Ranayim *D.Taylor, A.Howard 20th April 1988*

Nice open climbing on good rock in beautiful surroundings. A quick and enjoyable way to reach the domes. Almost a kilometre in length, but with less than 200 metres of actual climbing. A.D. SUP 2½ hours from Rest House. Maps and topos pages 48 and 49.

Approach: ¾ - 1 hour from Rest House to foot of climb. Up R.8 to the col between the two wadies, then east along ridge over small tops with one difficult overhang just right of crest passed using 'Bedouin steps'. Descend to final gap, then contour right and move up to foot of

Climbs in the Rest House Vicinity

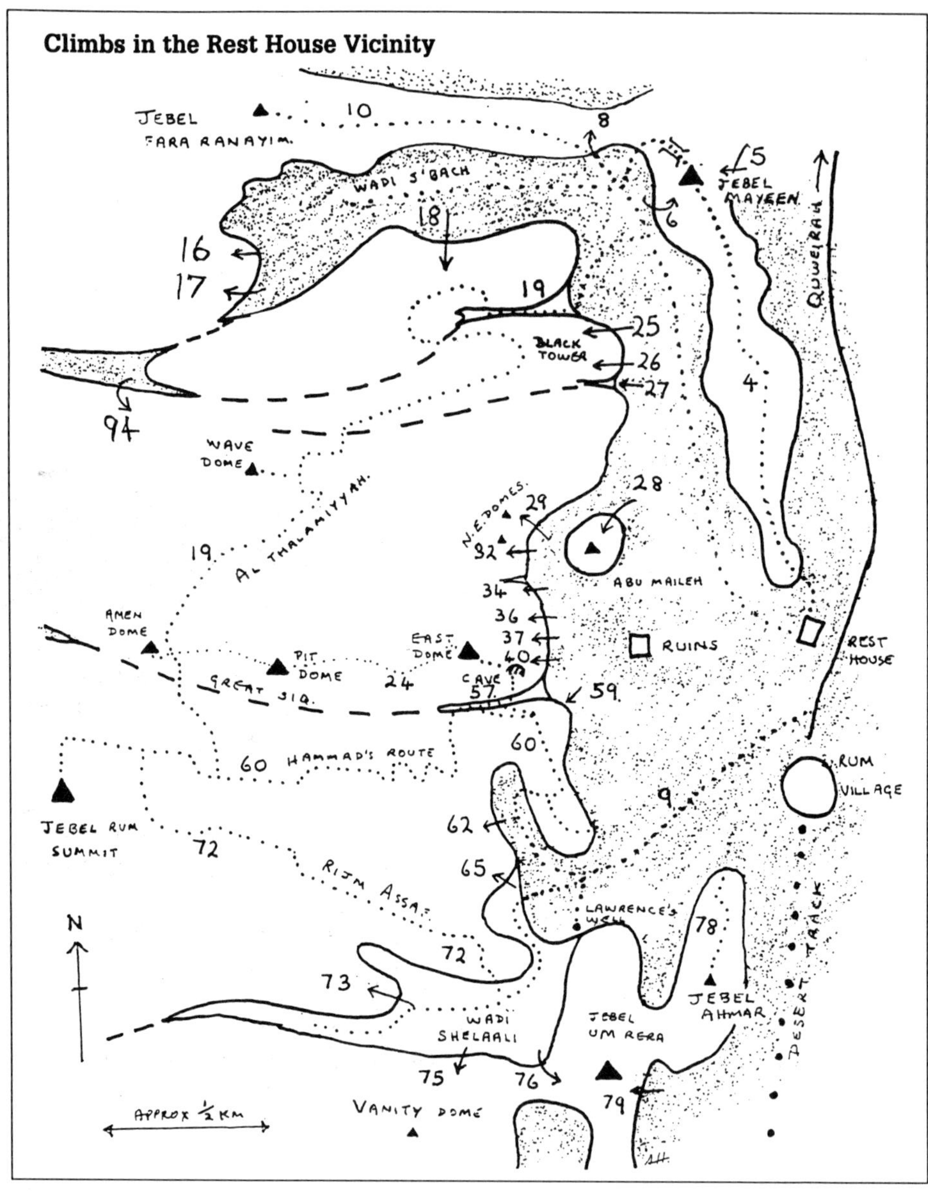

climb proper, at a groove bearing right in a smooth slab. *Descent:* Reverse the route, with two 20-metre abseils at the end. The first in a chimney left (S) of the route, the next down a chimney immediately above the start. From the col at the foot of the route, go east about 100 metres then zig-zag down into the gully (cairns) into Wadi S'Bach. Time from summit to Rest House approximately 2 hours.

Above:
Sunrise over Abu Judaidah from Khor al Ajram - photo Domenech

Left:
Sunset over Al Maghrar from Jebel Khazali - photo Howard

Moonrise over Um Ishrin - photo Remy

Below:
Storm over Nassrani - photo Shaw

Climbs on Jebel Rum's East Dome Wall
Above: Aquarius, pitch 1 - photo Howard
Below: Towering Inferno, pitch 6, first ascent - photo Howard

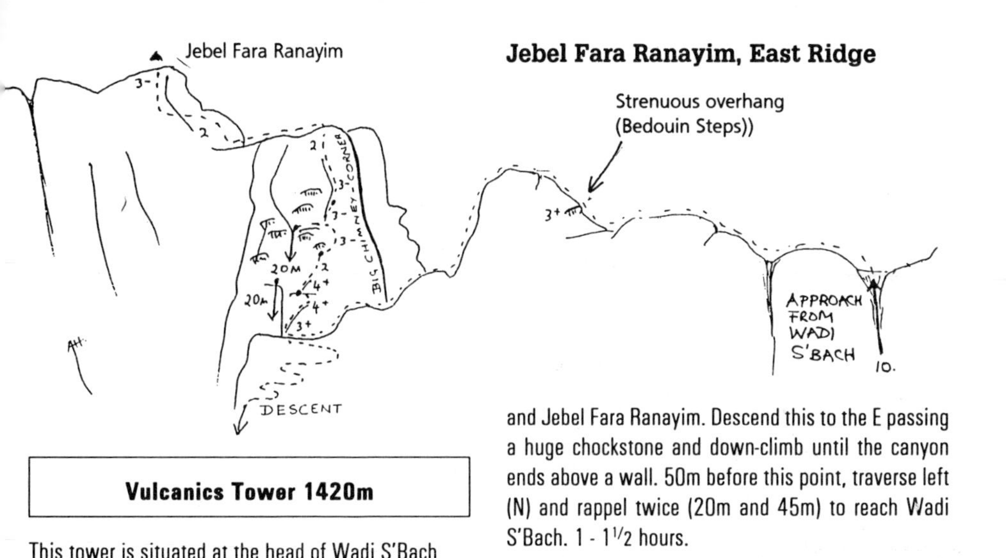

Jebel Fara Ranayim, East Ridge

Vulcanics Tower 1420m

This tower is situated at the head of Wadi S'Bach

11. East Face Route *W.Bogensberger, W.Haupolter, A.Precht March 1988.*

A nice introductory climb on generally good rock. 300m D. 2 hours.

Approach: Up Wadi S'Bach and the screes, to the foot of the route where a stepped crack leads to a corner. 1/2 hour.

Descent: Go NW into a small canyon between this top and Jebel Fara Ranayim. Descend this to the E passing a huge chockstone and down-climb until the canyon ends above a wall. 50m before this point, traverse left (N) and rappel twice (20m and 45m) to reach Wadi S'Bach. 1 - 1 1/2 hours.

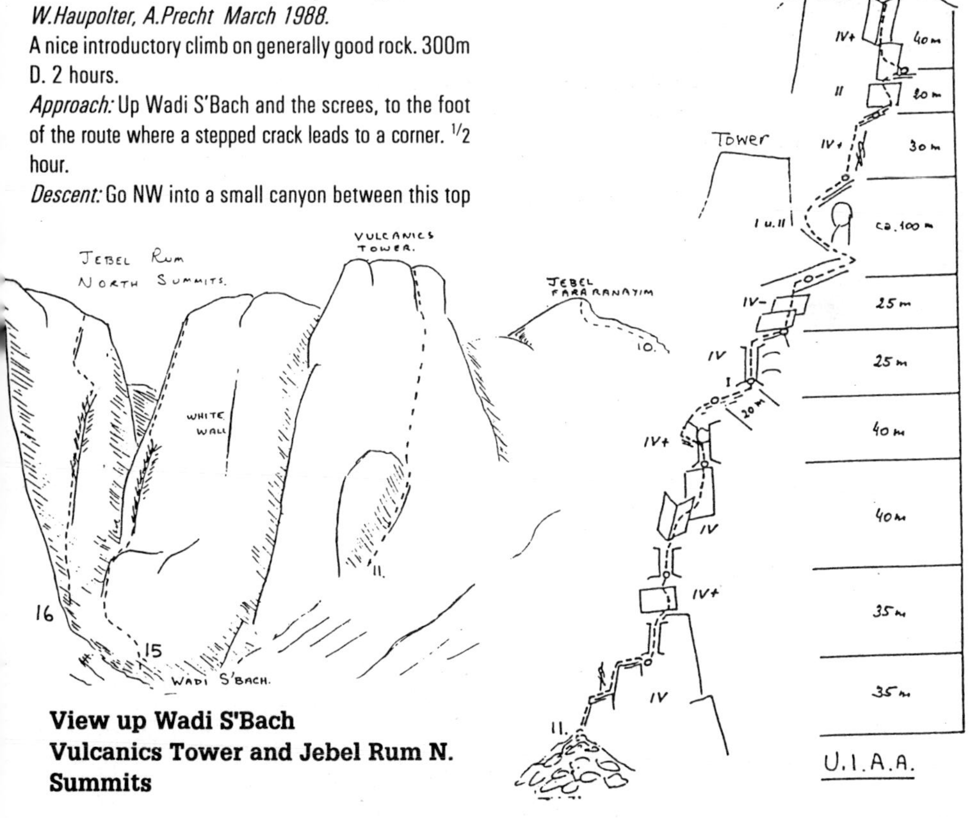

View up Wadi S'Bach Vulcanics Tower and Jebel Rum N. Summits

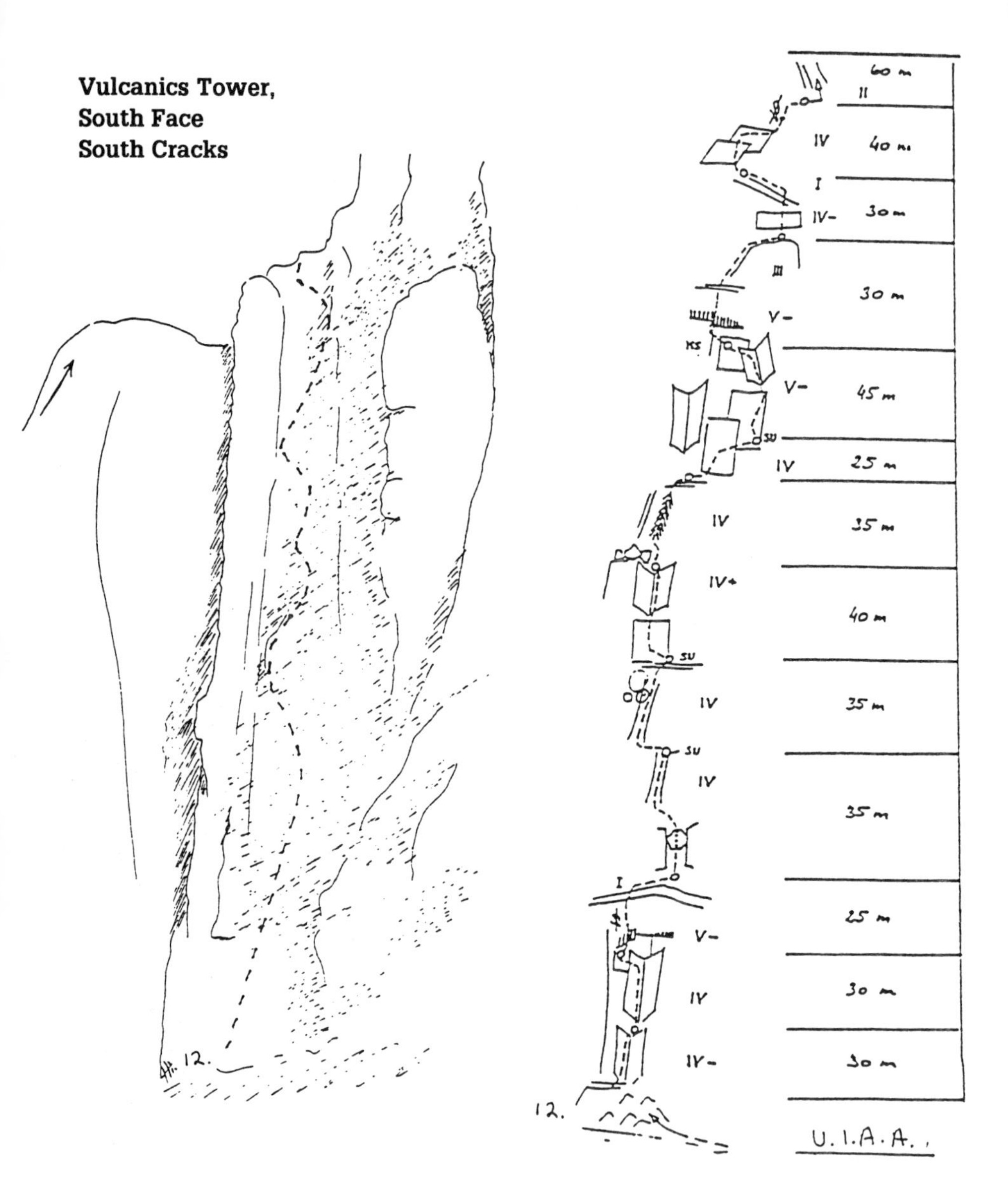

12. South Cracks *W.Haupolter & A.Precht March 1988.*

Good climbing up cracks 300m. T.D. Inf. 2 hours.

Approach: As R.11 to below two obvious crack systems in the S Face. 40 mins.

Descent: As R.11.

13. First Road *A.Precht, W.Aschauer, S.Inhoger, W.Haupolter 31st March 1990.*

Enjoyable and sustained on excellent rock up the S Face of Vulcanics Tower. Left of 'South Cracks', the face is marked by two corner-crack systems. The route takes the slabs between them. 300m T.D. 3 hours. Topo p. 51.

Approach & Descent: As for R.11.

Vulcanics Tower, South Face
First Road

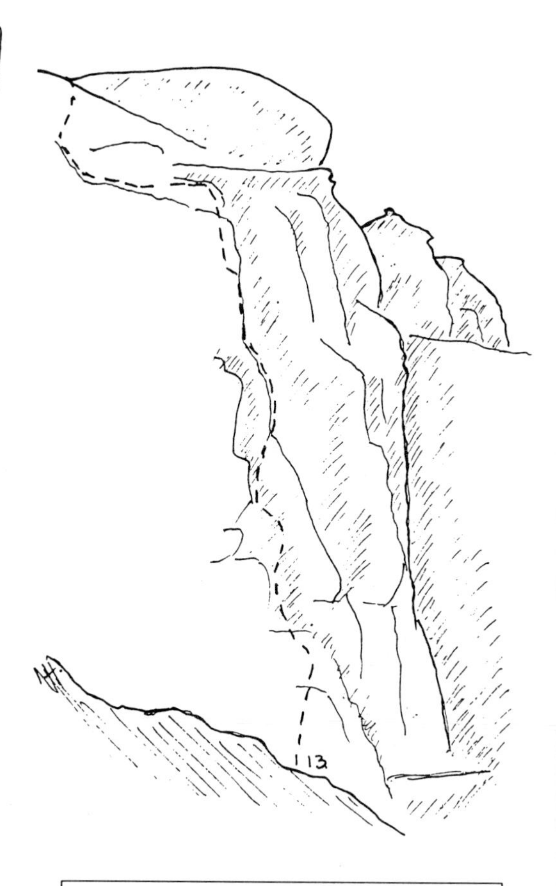

Jebel Rum, North Summit 1480m

This area of domes stands above the inner recesses of Wadi S'Bach and is divided into a number of cliffs, the most northerly of which looks very attractive with plenty of clean cut cracks in a smooth wall, to the left of First Road.

14. E. Face - Le Jardin du Prophéte

Yves Duverney & J.P. "Dolby" Monnet October 1986.
Unfortunately the cracks are often sandy and the climb is not recommended by the first ascentionists. Good belays but the protection is not always good, in sandy and broken rock. 200 metres. T.D. Inf. 3 hours.

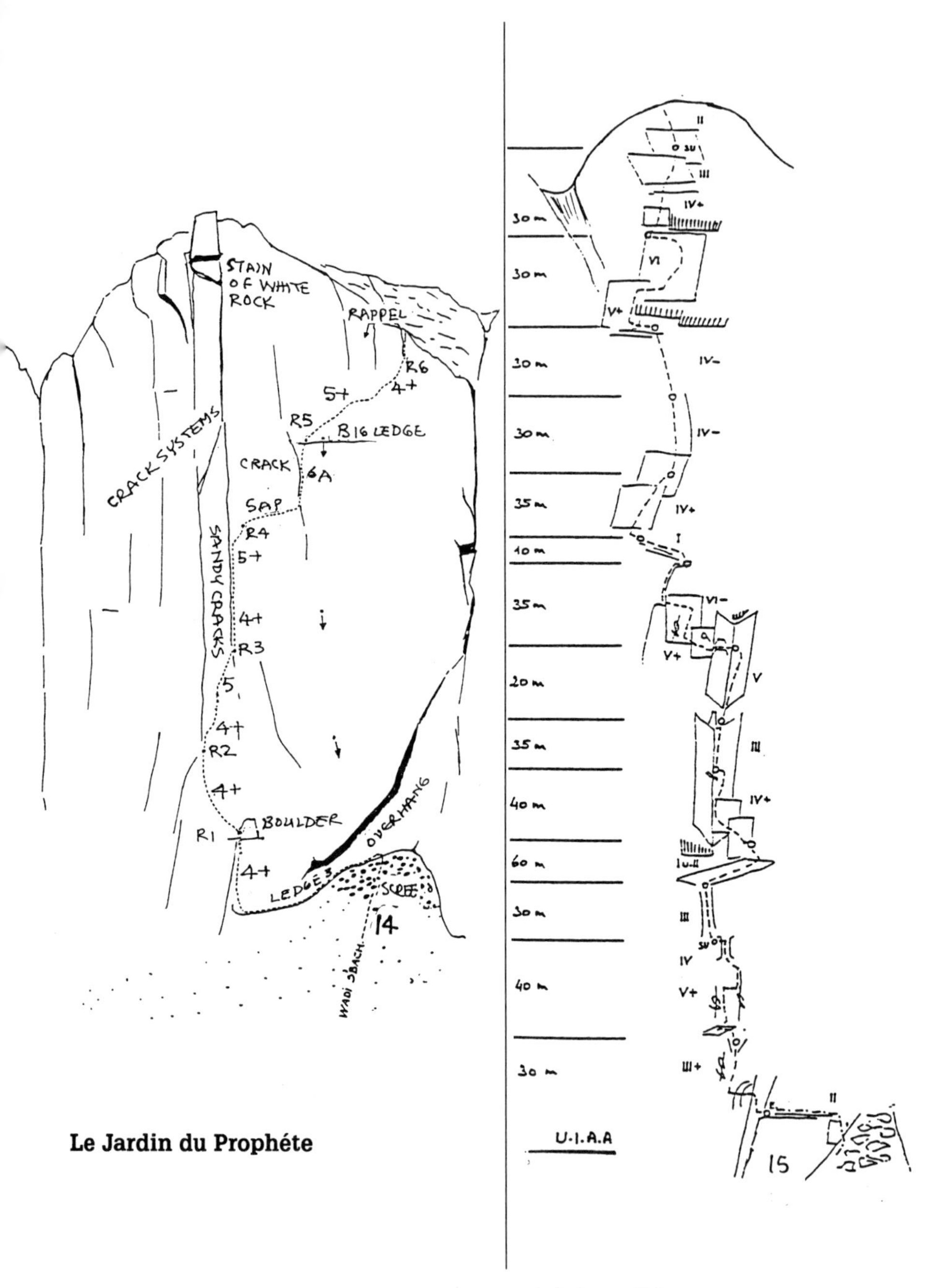

Le Jardin du Prophéte

Rainbow Edge

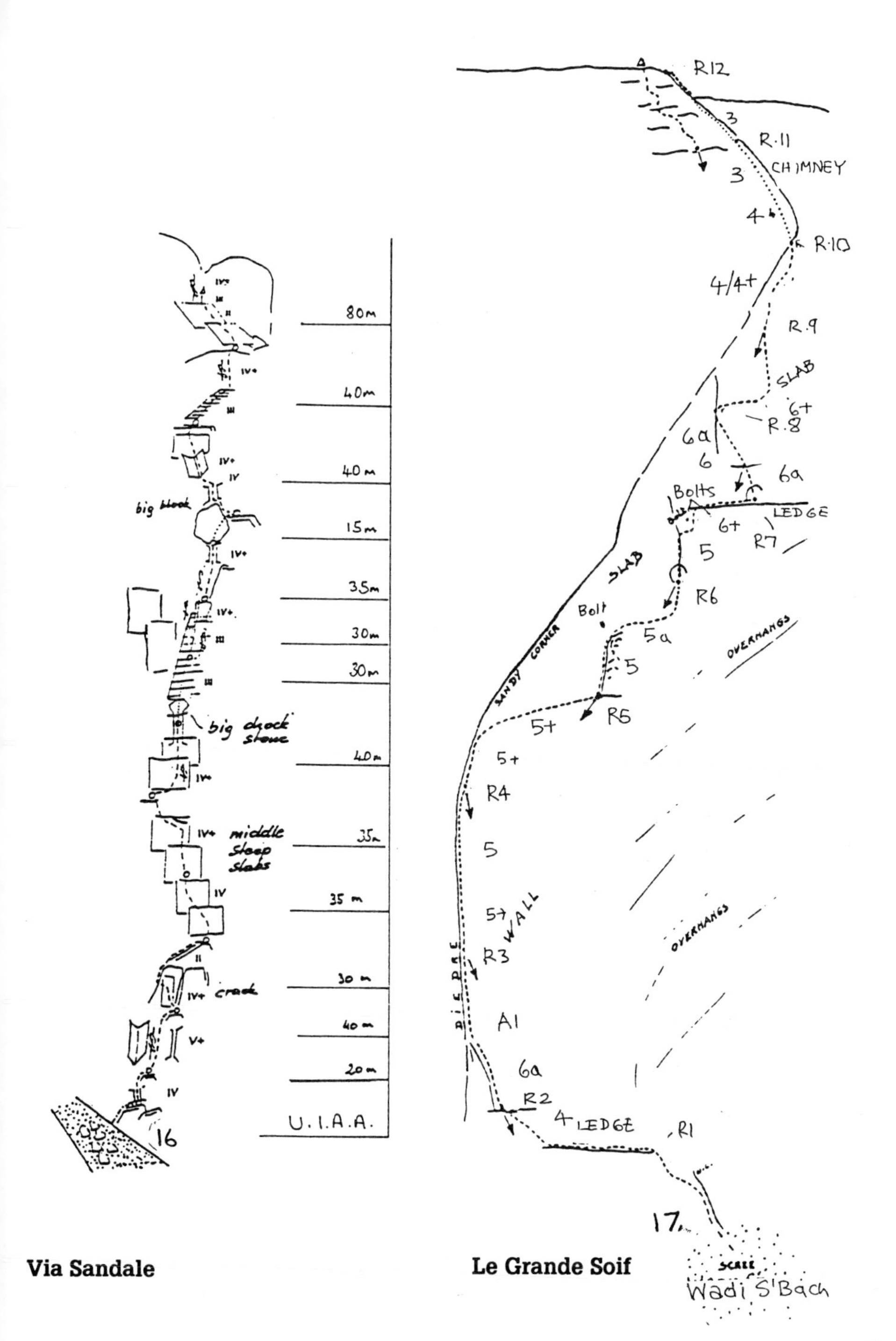

Via Sandale

Le Grande Soif

Topo, page 52.
Approach: As for First Road (3/4 hour) up Wadi S'Bach, the climb being located on the right side at the bend of the Wadi.
Descent: 1 hour, 4 abseils in place.

Left of here is a very striking grooved arête projecting SE into the valley.

15. Rainbow Edge *A.Precht, W.Haupolter, W.Bogensberger March 1988.*
Varied climbing, with the crux high on the route. 300m T.D. 4 hours. Maps and topos pages 49 and 52
Approach: Up Wadi S'Bach to below the obvious ridge with its big corner system at half height 1/2 - 3/4 hour.
Descent: Take a big loop right (NW) past a canyon to the top of Vulcanics Tower, and down as for R.11.

Immediately south of the previous route and across a siq is another ridge:

16. The East Pillar. Via Sandale
W.Haupolter, A.Precht, H.Gufler 21 April 1989
A recommended climb on good rock, first up slabs and cracks just left on the edge, then up obvious ramps. 300m D. Sup. 3 1/2 hours. Maps and topos pages 48, 49 53 and 56.
Approach: Up Wadi S'Bach to reach the bottom of the pillar by climbing over some boulders. The route starts at a chimney which leads to three cracks: take the middle one. 3/4 hour.
Descent: By great and interesting abseils down the siq north of the pillar 1 1/2 hours.

Left again, at the very inner end of the wadi in a remote and isolated location yet easily accessible is the fine hidden ramp of:

17. E. Face - La Grande Soif *Y.Duverney & J.P.Monnet October 1986*
Varied climbing on good rock, first in the obvious corner and then in the large system of slabs and walls with some exposed passages, in the heart of the Jebel Rum Massif! Superb atmosphere. All the belays are in-situ, also the abseil points (bolts or pegs). Also, two bolts in place for protection. For the A1 pitch, take some angle pegs and a few blades (15 pegs). 300 metres. T.D. Sup. 5 hours. Maps and topos, pages48, 49, 53 and 56.
Approach: From the Rest House follow Wadi S'Bach

Al Thalamiyyah Plateau, North Face
Captain Morgan

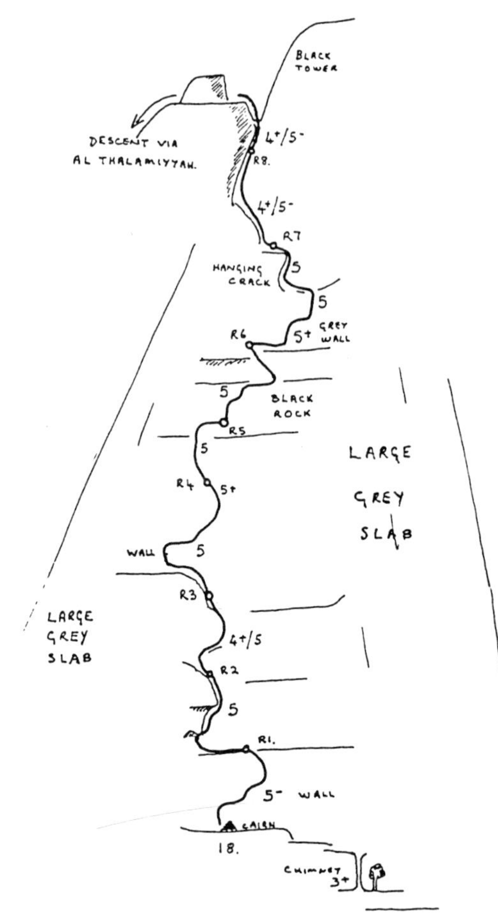

almost to its end. First to the north, under the east walls of Jebel Rum and then to the west to penetrate into the heart of the massif. La Grande Soif and its obvious corner is on the west side of the end of the Wadi. (3/4 hour)
Descent: 8 abseils. 1 1/2 hours.

Al Thalamiyyah, N Face

18. Captain Morgan *First Ascent W.Colonna, A.Howard 1st May 1986*

Entry Couloir of Al Thalamiyyah

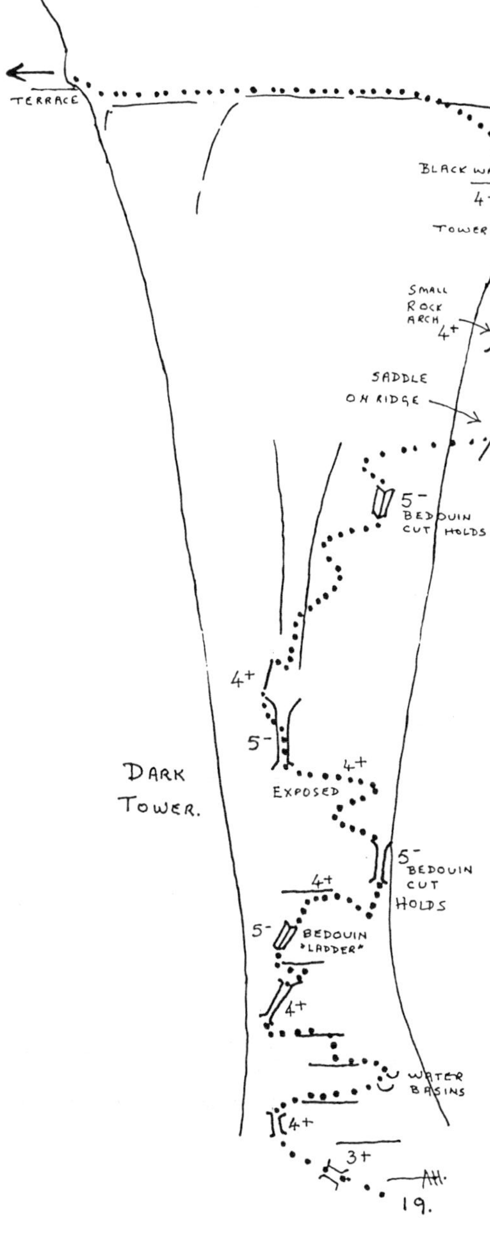

A steep and interesting climb up the huge grey slab which drops down from the top of Al Thalamiyyah into the upper valley of Wadi S'Bach. The climb is fairly unique in that most of the route is delicate wall climbing. Protection is sparse. Approximately 300 metres. About 3 - 4 hours. Overall Grade T.D. Inf. Maps pages 48, 54 and 56.

Approach: Follow Wadi S'Bach up, passing the springs at the foot of Al Thalamiyyah and continue up the valley until the huge sweep of the Grey Slab becomes obvious on the left. Scramble up to the bottom right edge and ascend easily leftwards up a chimney with a thin grey tree at its foot (3+) eventually reaching a platform at the bottom centre of the slab (1½ hours).

Descent: The best and fastest descent would be to fix an 'abseil piste'. Otherwise the route of Al Thalamiyyah must be followed down to the valley. The way is not always obvious though cairns mark most of the route. Approximately 1½ - 2 hours.

Jebel Rum North Plateau and Summit

19. Al Thalamiyyah (The Dark One - The Place of the Djinn) *First recorded ascent. A.Howard, D.Taylor, M.Shaw, A.Baker 23rd October 1984, as far as "Juniper Flats." Full route to the summit, crossing the Great Siq, A.Howard, M.Shaw 4th November 1985.*

Originally explored by the Bedouin, this continuously interesting, unusual, extremely long and complex route gains the north east rim of the plateau via the deep ravine above the well and palm tree in Wadi S'Bach. The way up the ravine is not always obvious, and once on

North Plateau of Jebel Rum

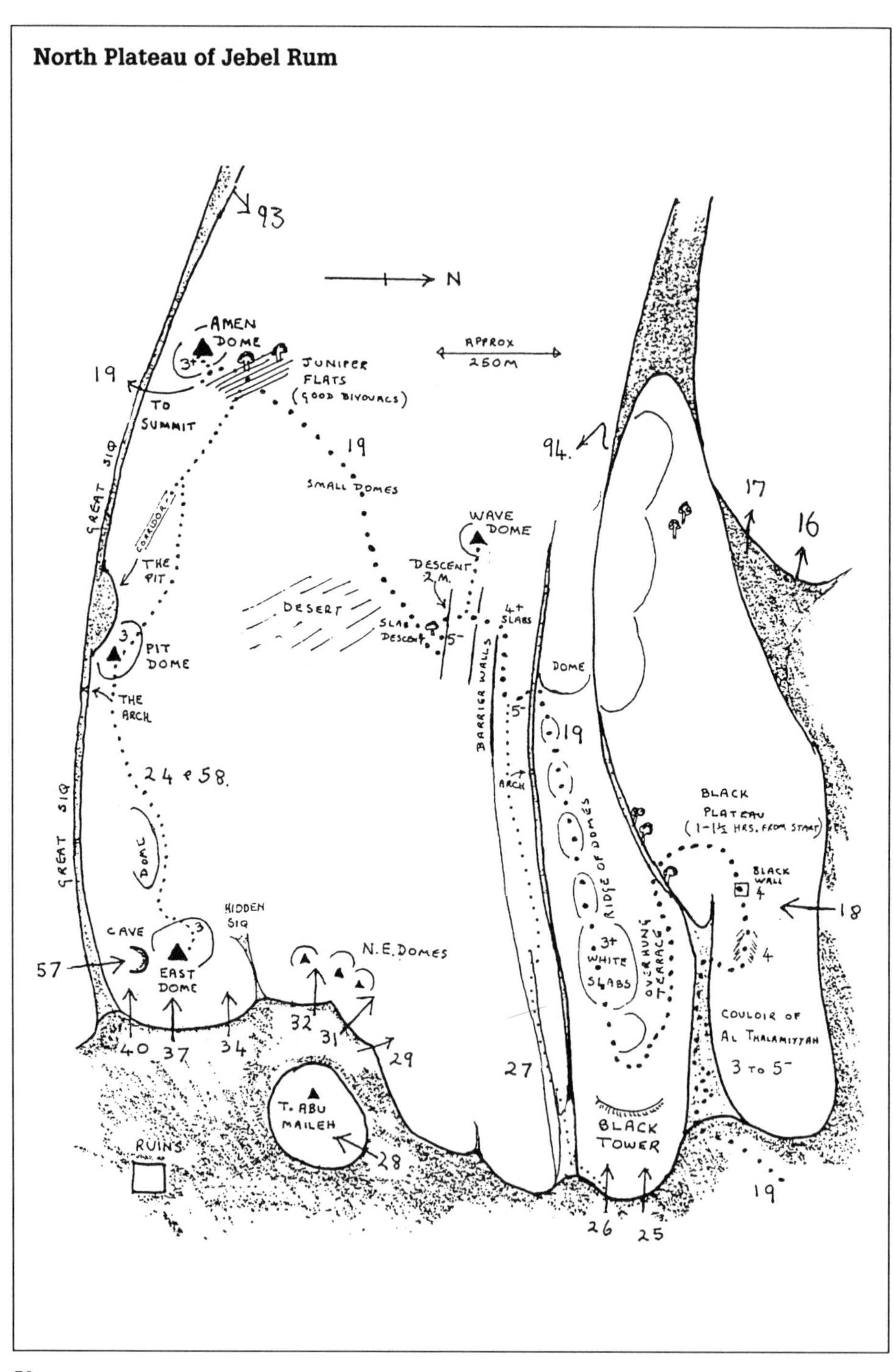

the plateau care must still be taken with route finding. Total distance to the summit is about 3 kilometres with perhaps 500 metres of climbing involved, mostly in the ravine. Allow about 4 - 4½ hours assuming no major route finding problems. Overall Grade A.D. Sup. Maps and topos pages 48, 55, 56, 74.

Approach: Follow the wadi north west of Rest House for just over 1 kilometre, to a pleasant area of bushes, vegetation, palm trees and well. Directly above here the ravine of Al Thalamiyyah cuts west into the mountain wall. (The main wadi actually continues a little further, also curving west.) To the left of the ravine is the Dark Tower.

Descent: From the summit, descend by Hammad's Route to complete a superb round-trip, or from Amen Dome bivouac site, via Pit Dome and East Dome (Routes 23 and 24, then down The Eye of Allah. Allow 2½ - 3 hours, taking care with route finding.

Wave Dome 1,560m (ref: 326752)

20. Eastern Slabs *First recorded ascent. A.Howard, D.Taylor, M.Shaw, A.Baker 28th October 1984.*

Climbed en route to North Plateau via Al Thalamiyyah. (1). Map page 56.

Amen Dome 1,640m (ref: 322748)

21. Eastern Slabs *First recorded ascent. A.Howard, D.Taylor, A.Baker, M.Shaw, 28th October 1984.*

From the bivy site at south east end of Juniper Flats it is possible to ascend small domes (3+, 2) trending north west above the Great Siq to the final dome on the ridge beyond which it does not appear possible to go. Good views of Wadi Rumman. Map page 56.

The route Simsalabim ascends the south face of this peak, from the western end of the Great Siq, to arrive on its west shoulder.

The Great Siq, The Pit and The Archway

It is possible to descend partway into the Pit from the north side by an easy sloping corridor about 2 metres wide straight down from near the south east end of Juniper Flats for about 200 metres. Awesome views of The Pit, The Great Siq and The Archway.

The Siq can be crossed from north to south at a number of points by abseil (the only one actually done so far being on the Al Thalamiyyah Route), with an easy climb out to the south. At this same point, it is also possible to cross the siq from south to north by climbing from below the abseil point diagonally to the right (4+) to gain the stream bed right of the abseil. It is also very likely that the Siq can be crossed via the Archway. The Arch itself has been gained from the south (5-), but the actual gap between the Arch and the North Side was not crossed, as we were short of time, though difficulties did not look insuperable. Maps pages 56, 74.

The Pit

There is one climb out of this impressive hole:

22. The Empty Quarter *R.M.Austin, A.O.Erskine 8th April, 1988*

Bizarre surroundings and a remote situation give this climb a serious atmosphere out of proportion to its length 80m 4+/6A.

Approach: Abseil into The Pit from a large thread just E of Pit Dome. The climb ascends the SW side of The Pit up the groove-crack to the obvious right facing corner which is gained by a delicate traverse and climbed by strenuous jamming with a close-up view of The Archway.

Pit Dome 1,560m (ref: 328746)

23. Western Slabs *First recorded ascent, M.Shaw, A.Baker, A.Howard, D.Taylor 29th October, 1984.*

From Juniper Flats descend slightly to the desert area to the east, and then go south until above The Pit. From here it is possible to climb pleasantly (3) to the summit of the highest dome above the north east edge of the Pit. Map page 56.

Jebel Rum, East Face
The Dark Tower

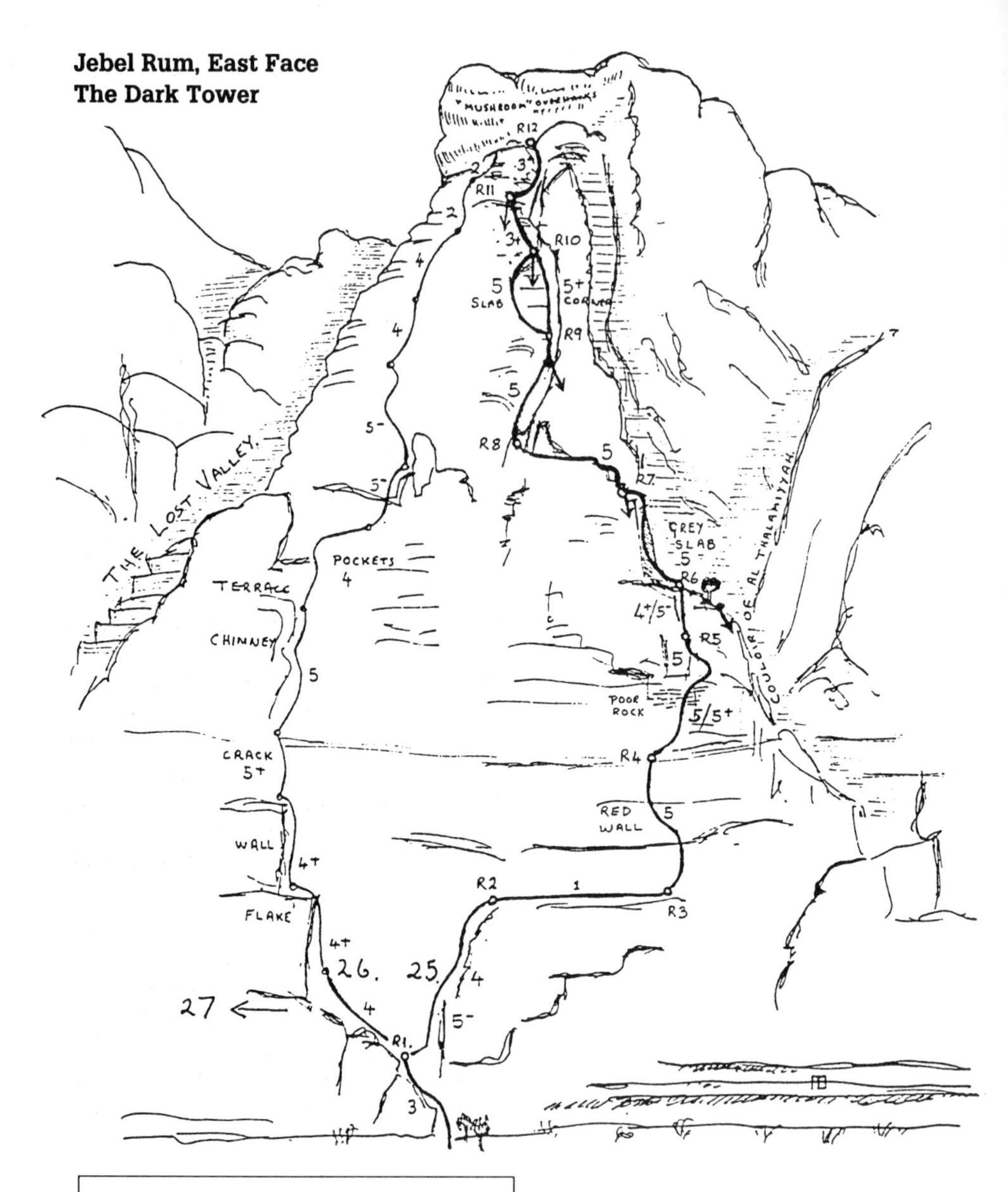

East Dome 1,560m (ref: 333747)

24. North Western Slabs *First recorded ascent. A.Howard, D.Taylor, A.Baker, M.Shaw 29th October, 1984.*

From Juniper Flats, ascend Pit Dome and then work round to the east, over some small domes and eventually down to a winding sandy wadi which leads to an impassable siq just north of the East Dome. This is Hidden Siq. From this point or 50 metres back, ascend the north west side of the dome by fairly easy slabs (3 and 4) to its top. (Junction with Eye of Allah Route).

Time from Juniper Flats, about 1/2 hour. Distance about 1 kilometre. Time from start of Al Thalamiyyah about 3 hours. Map page 56.

Descent from North Plateau

From the area of Juniper Flats, and the North Plateau, the easiest descents are down Al Thalamiyyah, about 2½ - 3 hours, or better, abseil across the Siq following Al Thalamiyyah to Hammad's bivouac and down Hammad's Route 2½ - 3 hours.

It is of course also possible to descend through The Eye of Allah which also takes about 3 hours from this point.

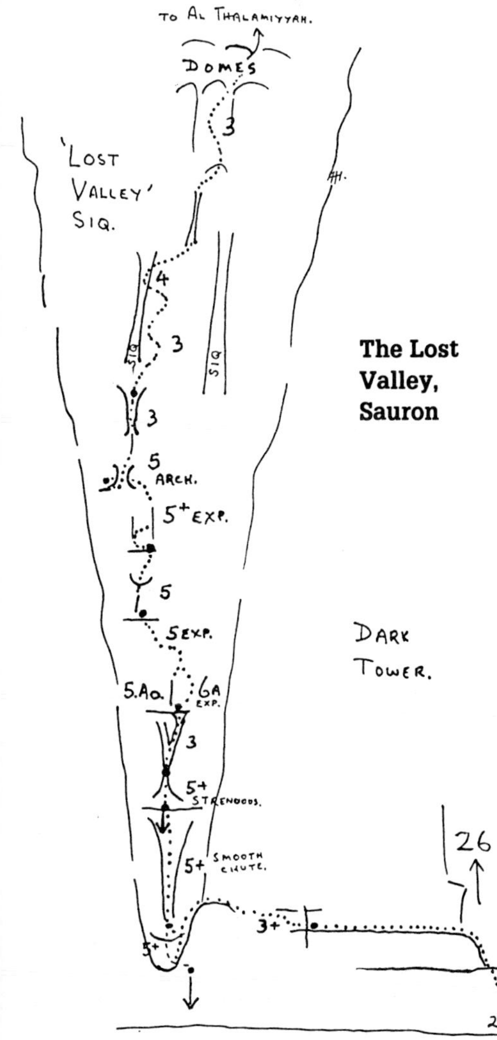

The Lost Valley, Sauron

The Dark Tower 1,300m (ref: 338754)

The excellent looking steep smooth East Face of this tower is just left of the ravine of Al Thalamiyyah. The face itself gives two excellent routes:-

25. Black Magic *W.Colonna, A.Howard, D.Taylor, A.Baker, M.Shaw. 17th October 1985.*
The approach is as for Al Thalamiyyah, leaving the wadi at the first area of trees known as El M'rera, to scramble up left to a pedestal just left of centre (½ hour). The route gives sustained climbing mostly on good rock and is very enjoyable, finishing on a ledge below the final 50m sandy and overhanging headwall. 3½ hours, 300 metres. Overall grade D. Sup. Maps and topos, pages 48, 56, 58.
Descent: Scramble down the last pitch to the ledge above the 100 Metre Corner, then five 40 metre abseils, the last from a tree below the Grey Slab, into the couloir of Al Thalamiyyah. Follow that route down. 1½ hours.

26. Mira Khoury *C.&Y.Remy 14th May 1986.*
Enjoyable and varied climbing and not too sustained, up the left side of the 'Dark Tower'. 300 metres. D. Sup. 3½ hours. Maps and topos, pages 48, 56, 58.
Direct Finish: A pitch of 6A goes up the head wall to the summit (C.&Y.Remy 1987). No details.
Descent: By Black Magic into the Siq of Al Thalamiyyah. 1½ hours.

The Lost Valley

This is the huge canyon left of the Dark Tower, with no obvious entry point. It is gained from the start of R.26, and once entered gives climbing on a variety of rock types with an adventurous feel akin to the Bedouin Routes:

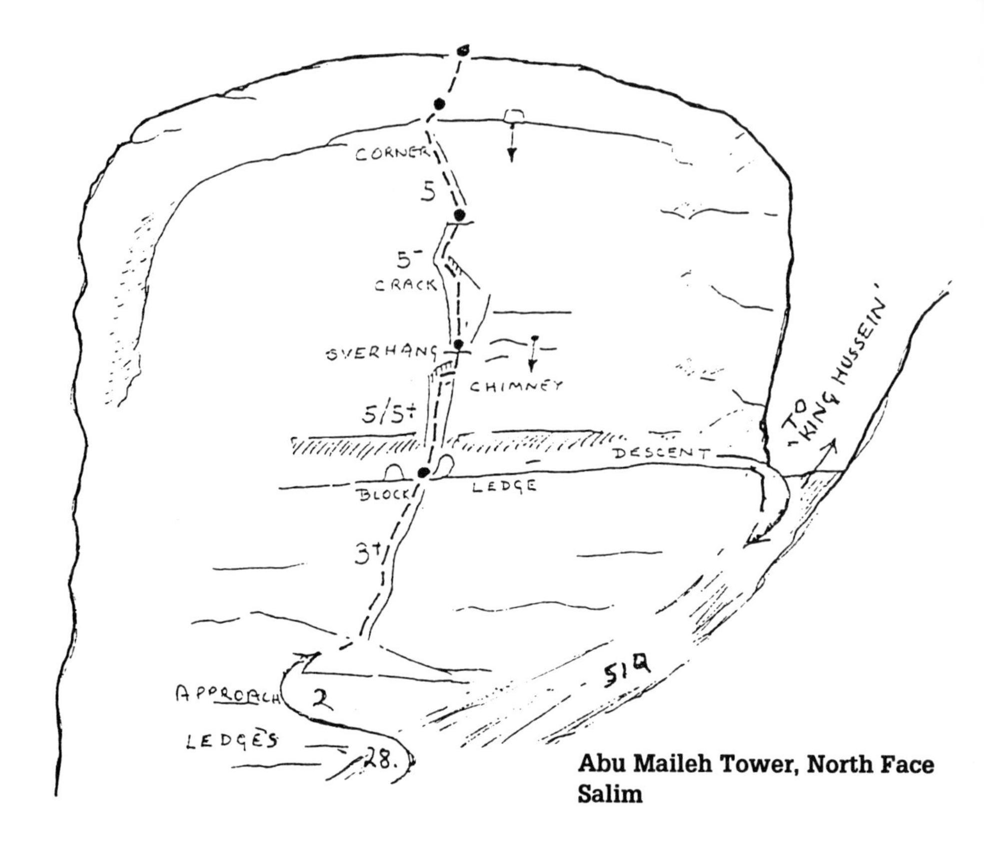

Abu Maileh Tower, North Face
Salim

27. Sauron (Lord of the Dark Tower - Tolkein) *Initial exploration, A.Howard, B.Vinton, D.Taylor 26 October 1991. Completion of route, W.Colonna, A.Howard 21 April 1992*
An interesting and unusual climb for a hot day, mostly in the shade, with a possible descent by 5 abseils (lower 3 in place) from the end of the hard climbing, otherwise, carry on up the siq, mostly on domes and ledges on its right, then in it, up a black chimney and right and through a corridor to the domes.

200m to the end of difficulties (3½ hours). T.D. 350m to the domes and Al Thalamiyyah (4½ hours). Maps and topos, pages 48, 56, 58 and 59.
Approach: As for Dark Tower climbs 20 - 30 mins.
Descent: By abseil 1½ hours from the end of the difficult climbing, or continue to the domes and descend via Al Thalamiyyah, 2½ hours (Al Thalamiyyah is joined where it crosses the siq after the 'ridge of domes')

Abu Maileh Tower

28. North Side. Salim *C.&Y.Remy with Salim Mohammed Mosa 16th May 1986.*
Enjoyable climbing up the only obvious line on the north side, with obvious belays and protection. 100 metres. 5+/5-/5. Ascent 1½ hours. Maps pages 48, 56.
Approach: From the Rest House, north west and up the siq below the north side of the Tower until directly under the line of the route (15 minutes).
Descent: By two rappels and then along the ledge to the right to enter the siq. ½ hour.

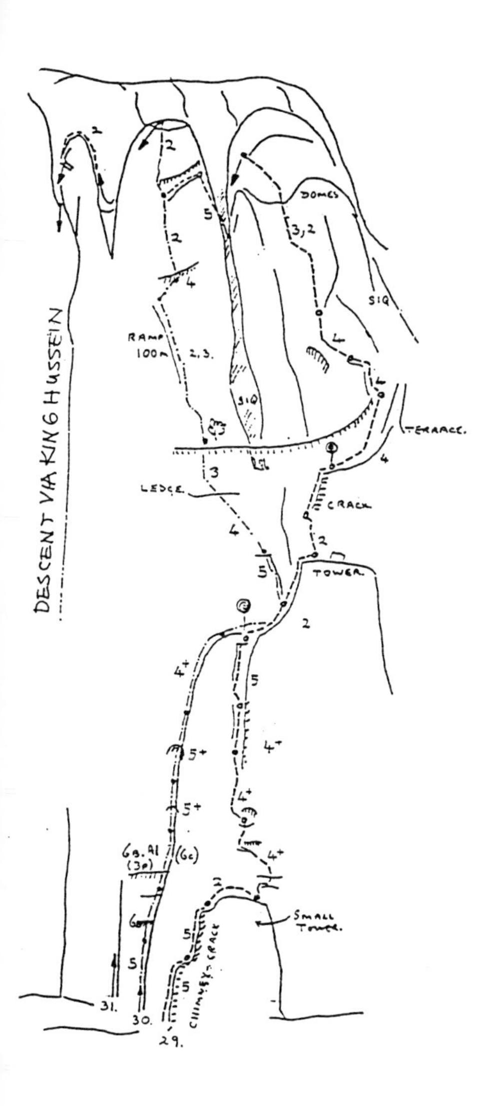

Jebel Rum, N.E. Domes, East Face Right-Hand Section

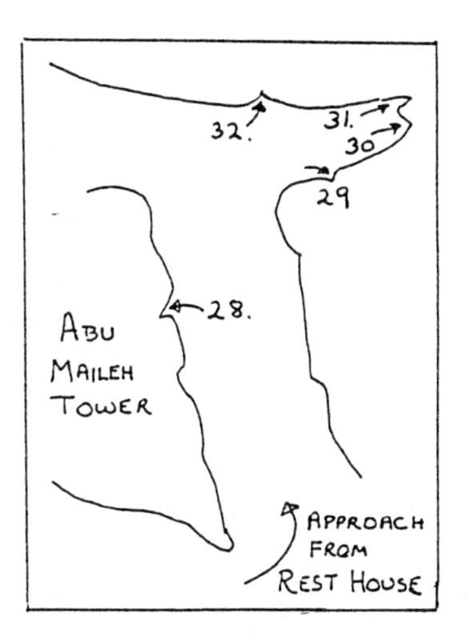

North East Domes. South East Face

The following routes are on the extensive multi-domed walls between the East Dome of Jebel Rum, and the couloir of The Lost Valley.

29. Grey Poupon *C.&Y.Remy 7th November 1986.*

A varied and pleasant climb. 300m D. Sup. 3 hours. Maps and topos 48 and 56.

Approach: Go NW across Wadi S'Bach and up the gully below the N Side of Abu Maileh Tower to find the chimney/cracks hidden on the right, 15 mins.

Descent: Cross the domes with a pitch of 5 to reach R.30 and continue to the abseils down King Hussein. 1½ hours.

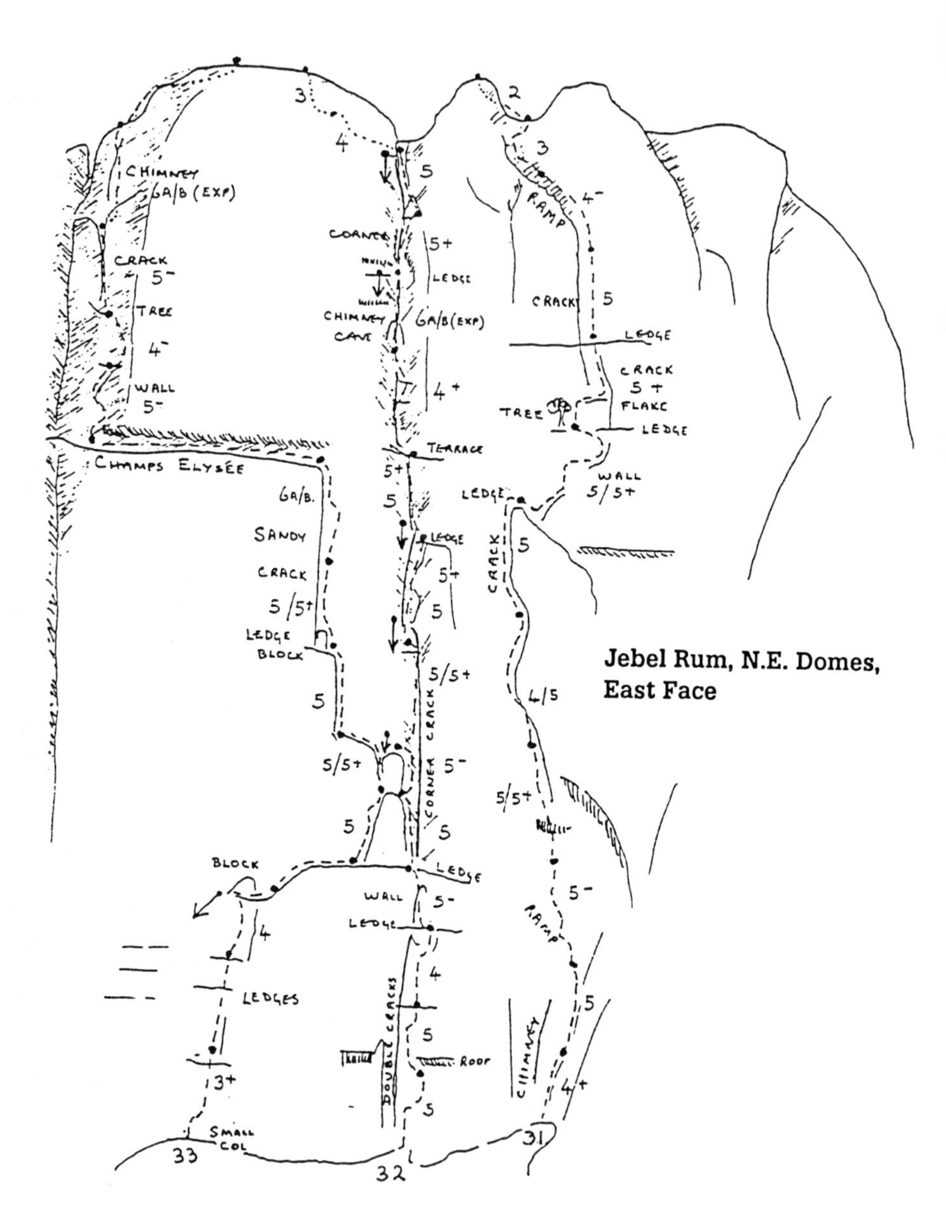

Jebel Rum, N.E. Domes, East Face

30. Expect No Mercy *C.&Y.Remy 2nd November 1986.*

Sustained crack climbing, leading to easier ground. 300m T.D. 4 hours. Map and topos pages 48, 56 and 61.

Approach: As R.29, the climb starting in the back of the bay on the right.

Descent: Go S across a siq and dome, and abseil down King Hussein 1 - 1½ hours.

31. Renee Van Hasselt *C.&Y.Remy 17th May 1986.*
Very enjoyable climbing in a magnificent setting, up an obvious line, with good belays and protection, 300 metres. T.D. Inf. Ascent 5 hours. Maps and topos, pages 48, 56, 61 and 62.
Approach: North west from the Rest House, and up the siq below the north side of Abu Maileh Tower. At the end, go to the right until directly below crack-chimneys. 15 mins.
Descent: By the route of King Hussein, by abseil. 1 hour.

East Face

32. King Hussein *C.&Y.Remy. 5th May 1986.*
Good climbing up a straight line of cracks, corners and chimneys. Described by the Remy's as one of the best of their climbs in Rum though conversely subsequent descriptions have varied from "some poor rock in the upper pitches" to "frightening, with vertical sand." The route defines the right side of the Dome, right of the East Dome, well seen from the Rest House. Good belays and protection except for a few exposed metres in the 6A/B chimney. (Friends necessary). 300 metres. T.D. Sup. Ascent 5 hours. Maps and topos, pages 48, 56, 61 & 62.
Approach: As route 29 north west from the Rest House to below the north side of Abu Maileh Tower, and up the siq to the foot of the cracks (15 minutes).
Descent is by abseil down the route. 1 hour.

33. Ramedame *C.&Y.Remy. 9th May 1986.*
Varied climbing in beautiful surroundings just to the left of King Hussein, up to the big terrace of the Champs Elysee, from where the route continues up the left side of the south east ridge of this dome. Good belays and protection, except for the exposed exit chimneys. In addition there is also a zone of sandy and soft rock halfway up the route. 300 metres. T.D. Sup. Ascent 4 hours. Maps and topos, pages 48, 56, 62 & 64.
Approach: From the Rest House go west to the foot of the right side of the East Face (spring). Continue up the gully (Bedouin Steps) to behind the Tower of Abu Maileh, 20 minutes.
Descent: By abseil down King Hussein. 1½ hours.

East Face

This is the obvious vertical wall of rock 15 minutes west of the Rest House defined by the mouth of the Great Siq to its left and the Hidden Siq to its right, into which Aquarius ascends. On it are a great collection of climbs from atmospheric serious big wall aid and free routes, to short sports climbs with fixed abseil pistes.

34. Aquarius. *W.Colonna, A.Howard. Original route 5th May 1986. Direct start 7th May 1986.*
An unusual route with a variety of technically interesting and sustained climbing up the right side of the East Face of East Dome, following the line of a waterfall, which cascades down this section of the wall from the upper Hidden Siq, after heavy storms. The rock is consequently clean and excellent almost throughout, though the route is not one to choose if heavy rain clouds are on the horizon! 300 metres, to the Big Terrace of the Champs Elysee at the foot of the headwall, where the route finishes, though it is possible to gain the top via the final pitches of Atalla, or Ramedame. T.D. Sup. Approximately 5 hours. Maps and topos, pages 48, 56, 64, 67.

The route starts in a sandy bay at the bottom right side of the East Face of East Dome below a steep black wall with parallel cracks, about 50 metres above the spring.

Descent: To descend from the Champs Elysee, follow the route back down to the top of the Polished Chimney. Abseil, then scramble down to above the 15-metre chimney, before going easily right to a position above the 100 metre crack. Abseil from good thread down to the top of the second pitch in the 100 metre crack. Abseil pegs in place here, for a diagonal rappel left down the rainbow coloured slab, to boulders. Descend the boulders easily to the juniper tree where another diagonal rappel from a bolt leads to the belay at the end of the first pitch of the Original Route. Three abseils straight down from here lead to the foot of the wall. 2 - 2½ hours.

35. Atalla *C.&Y.Remy. 15th May 1986.*
This route was first climbed starting up the line later to become Ziggurat, but used 3 points of aid on the first

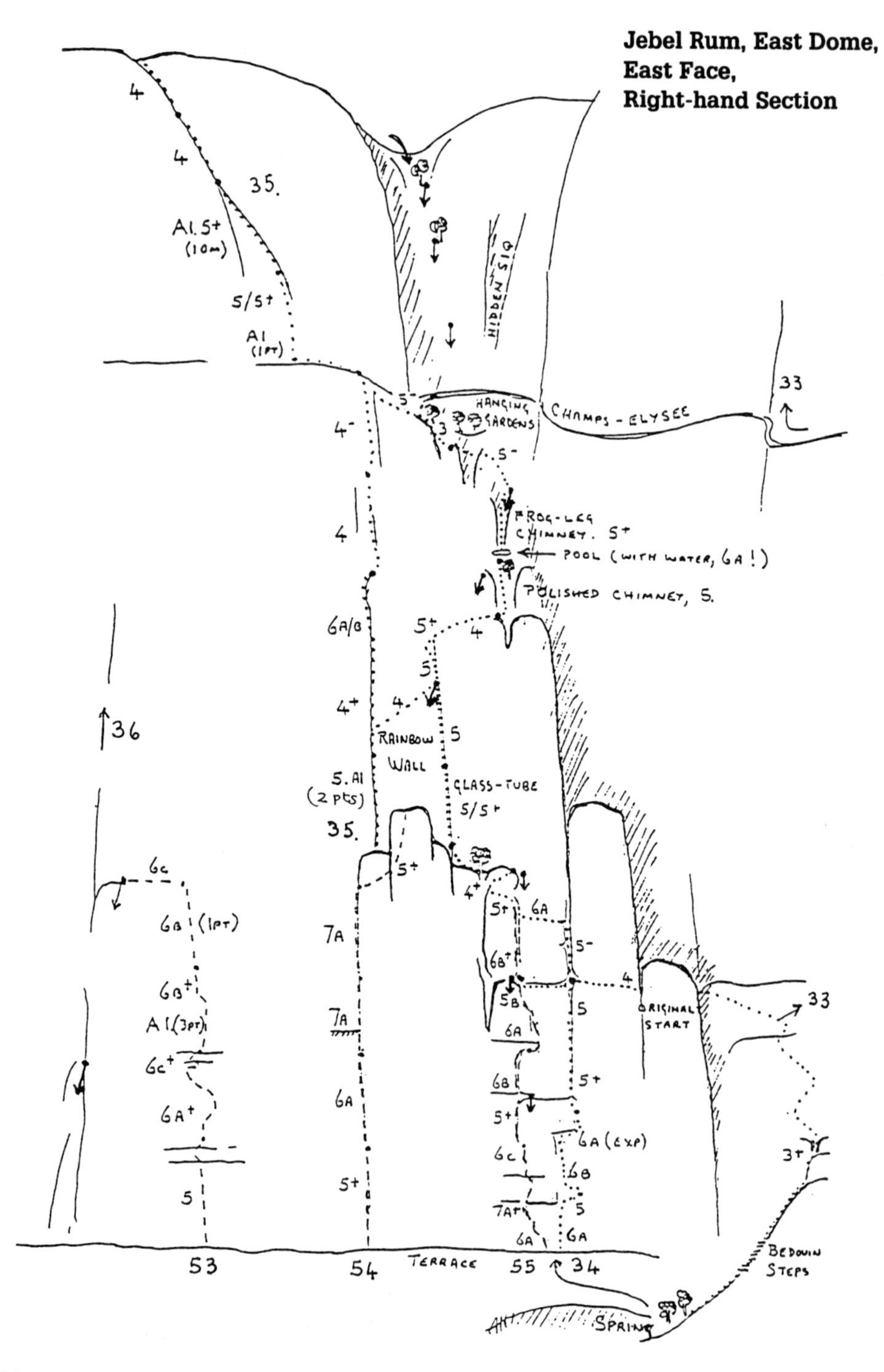

Jebel Rum, East Dome, East Face, Right-hand Section

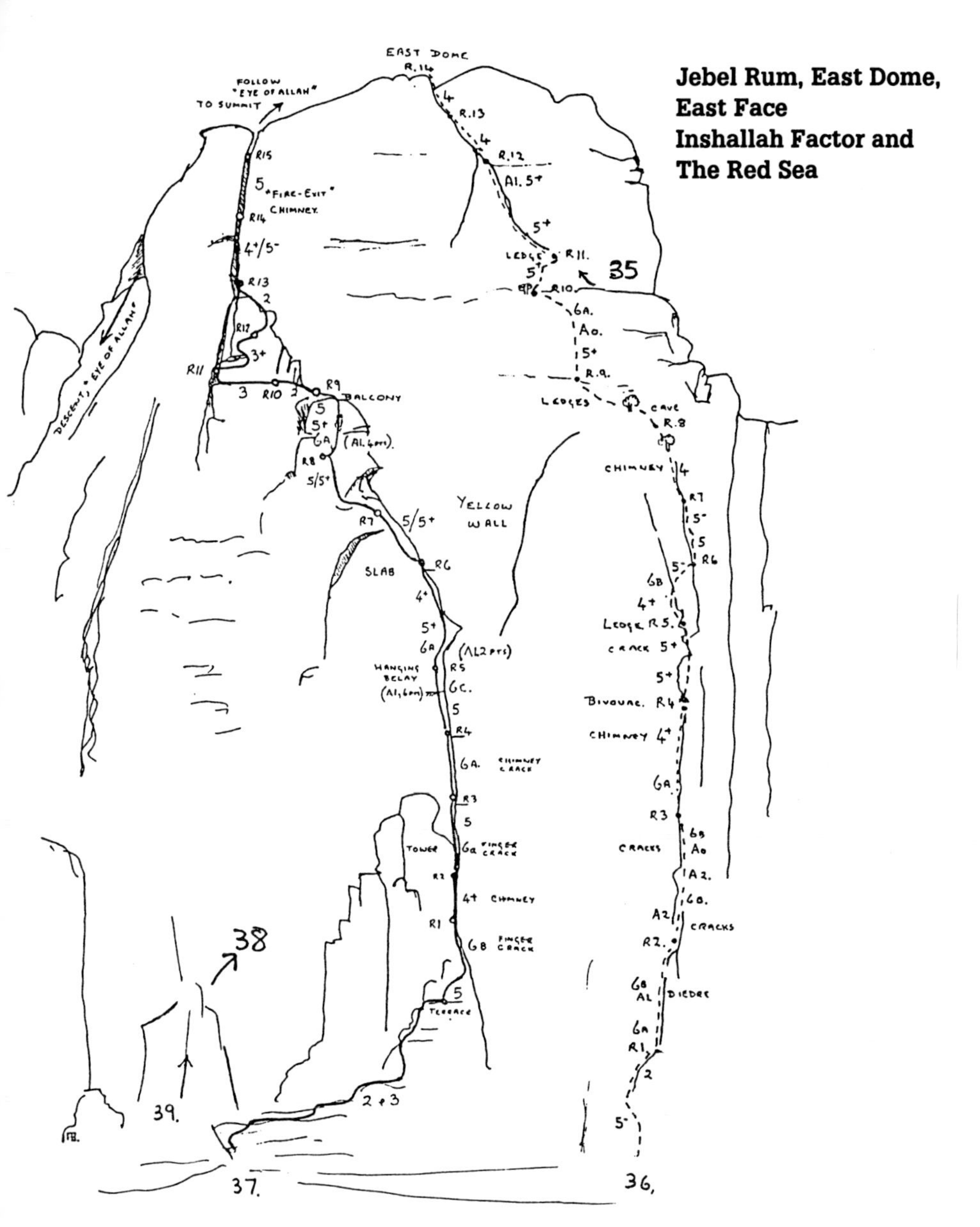

Jebel Rum, East Dome, East Face Inshallah Factor and The Red Sea

pitch (now free), and avoided the 4th pitch by traversing right, to the towers. From there it goes up the left side of Rainbow Wall, Aquarius, with 2 aid points, and some mediocre rock. (The left side of Rainbow Wall had been climbed previously by Colonna, Shaw and Howard, but was abandoned by them in favour of Aquarius which is excellent rock.)

The climb now therefore starts up the lower pitches of Ziggurat, or Aquarius to reach Rainbow Wall where two options are available to reach the headwall. This gives an excellent finish in a fine situation, the whole route being about 450 metres T.D. Sup. 7½ hours. With the Ziggurat start, the route would be E.D. and may take longer. Maps and topos, pages 48, 64 and 67.

Jebel Rum, East Dome, East Face Towering Inferno and Revienta o Burila

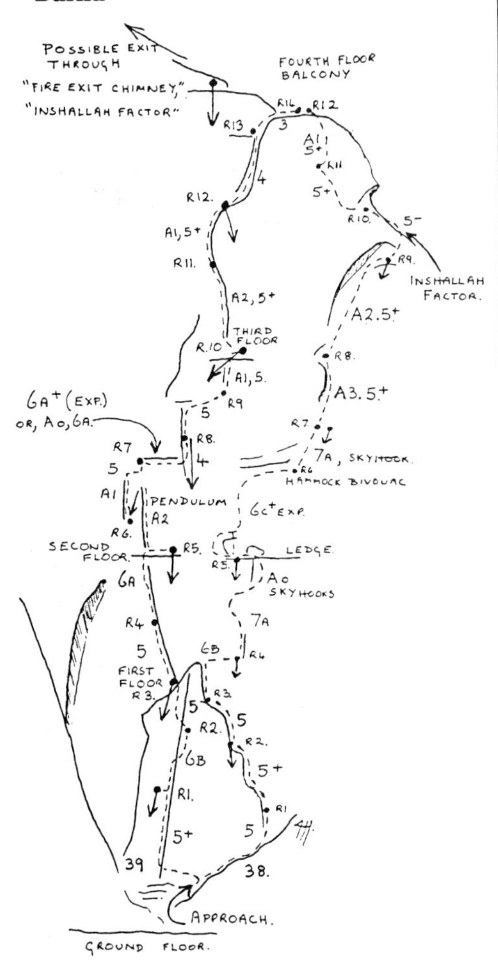

Descent: Fairly obvious, down the right (north) side of the wall. Scramble down to a tree, then 3 abseils and some down-climbing (3) to reach the abseils of Aquarius. Allow $2^{1}/2$ hours to the foot of the face.

36. The Red Sea *M.A. and J. Gallego 26 - 29 April 1987.*

Ascends prominent vertical chimney-cracks with some areas of bad rock to finish up the Atalla headwall. A mixture of fairly hard aid and free climbing giving a good and very sustained route. 50m ropes necessary. 450m

Jebel Rum, East Dome, East Face I.B.M.

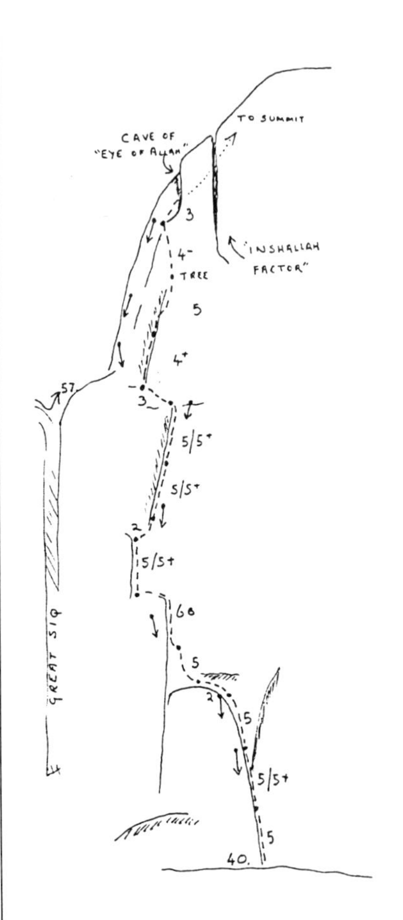

E.D. Originally climbed in two days after a day of preparation. Topos pages 64, 65 and 67.
Descent: Via Eye of Allah (R.57) 2 - 3 hours.

37. The Inshallah Factor *W.Colonna, M.Shaw, A.Howard, 27 April 1986. First free ascent W.Colonna, B.Domenech 16 April 1989.*

The first line to catch the eye, going straight up the centre of the East Wall, then winding left to exit through deep chimneys in the headwall. Originally climbed with aid, and later done free, both grades are given here

Jebel Rum, East Face

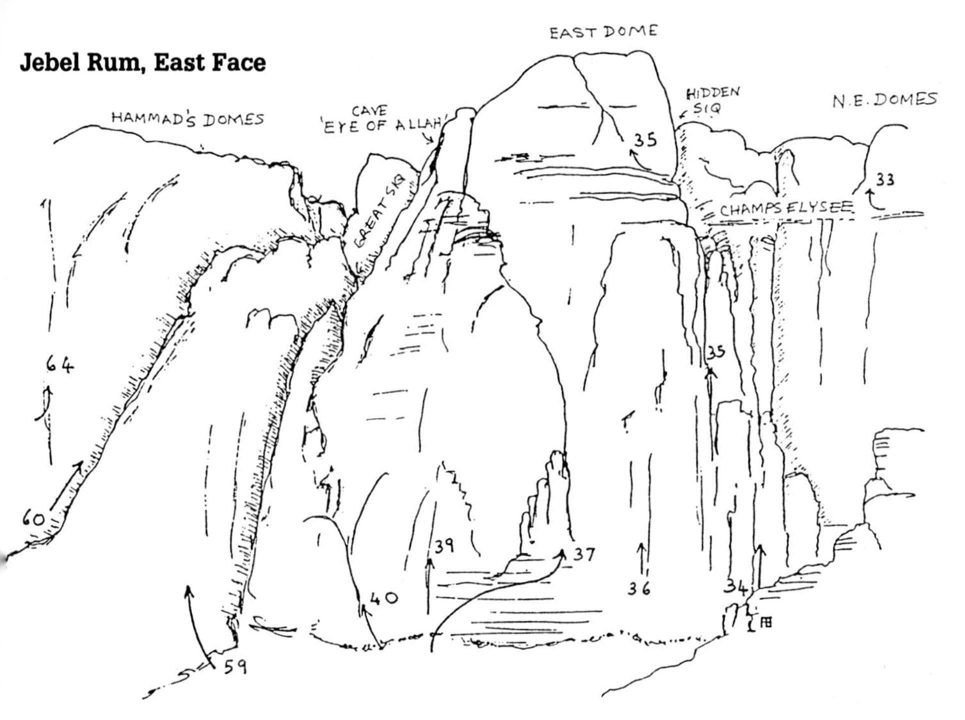

though pitch 5 is then serious with poor protection. All main belays are in place and a dozen pegs should be taken alongside the usual rack, if aid climbing. (Include blades, king pins and angles). The route has become a classic. 450m, 300m of which is sustained at a high standard. T.D. Sup. with aid, E.D. Inf. climbed free. 6 - 8 hours. Maps and topos pages 48, 65.
Descent: Via "Eye of Allah" (R.57). 2 - 3 hours.

38. Revienta o Burila *A.D. Asaho, M.A. Hernandez, J.M. Jimeno March 1992.*

A very sustained and technical climb mostly on steep black friction slabs, crossing the centre of the East Wall from The Mummy, to reach Inshallah Factor. The necessary bolts are in place (all 39 hand drilled on the first ascent). Carry 2 or 3 small pegs in case of necessity on the last two pitches; also a rack of friends from micro to No.4., as well as skyhooks, nuts, quickdraws and slings. 300m. E.D. Climbed over 4 days on the first ascent but should be possible in one, now the bolts are in place. Maps and topos pages 48, 65 and 66.
Descent: Abseil down the route.

39. Towering Inferno *W.Colonna, A.Howard 13th October 1986.*

The route was prepared by climbing to the "Second Floor" ledge on 10th October 1986, then to R. 8 on 11th October 1986 and returning by prusik to this point on 13th October 1986.

Delightful and exposed climbing up vague crack and groove systems on the left centre of the East Face, finishing on the 'Balcony' of Inshallah Factor. The first five pitches are excellent free climbing, with four aid pitches on the upper wall connected by a pendulum and an exciting traverse. The last aid pitch ascends thin sandy flakes to the exit chimney. Carry a full selection of about 25 pegs, from thin blades to wide angles, of all lengths. Also take a full set of Friends and a full rack of wires, although in the future it should be possible to reduce the mount of aid to one or two short sections. Allow a full day for ascent. 300 metres. E.D. Inf. Maps and topos, pages 48, 65, 66.
Descent: Finish by Inshallah Factor and descend Eye of Allah (3 hours), or abseil down the line of the route (abseil points in place), seven abseils, the third being very diagonal. 1½ hours.

40. I.B.M. (Inshallah, Bokra, Mumkin - God willing, tomorrow, possibly) *C.&Y.Remy 6th May 1986.*

Interesting climbing except for some passages of doubtful rock, but good belays and protection. The route finishes in the big cave at the top of The Eye of Allah. 400m. T.D. Ascent 4 hours. Maps and topos, pages 48, 56, 66, 67. Descent is down The Eye of Allah. 1½ to 2 hours.

The East Face Towers

In addition to the previous seven routes, this wall also offers a superb selection of short climbs along its base, all of which can be reached in fifteen minutes from the Rest House and are in the shade after midday. Good abseil pistes of 2-4 rope lengths will be found down all routes, and all but four are described in the topo below.

1. Route 41. Great Siq Route *5-/5+/5- D.Taylor, A.Howard 24th April, 1988*

Varied and enjoyable climbing to deep water basins in the bottom of the Great Siq chimneys, which are still unclimbed.

2. Route 42. Mumkin *5+/5/5-5+/5 C.&Y.Remy. 6th May 1986.*

First 4 pitches of I.B.M.

3. Route 43. Flight of Fancy *5+/5-/6A/6B/5+/5+. R.Edwards, B.Arkless. 23rd October 1986.*

Superb diedres and an exposed traverse.

4. Route 44. Mad Frogs and Englishman *5-/5-/6A,B W.Colonna, A.Howard, B.Domenech 11th April 1987*

A delightful corner with a delicate and exposed finish, wires needed for protection.

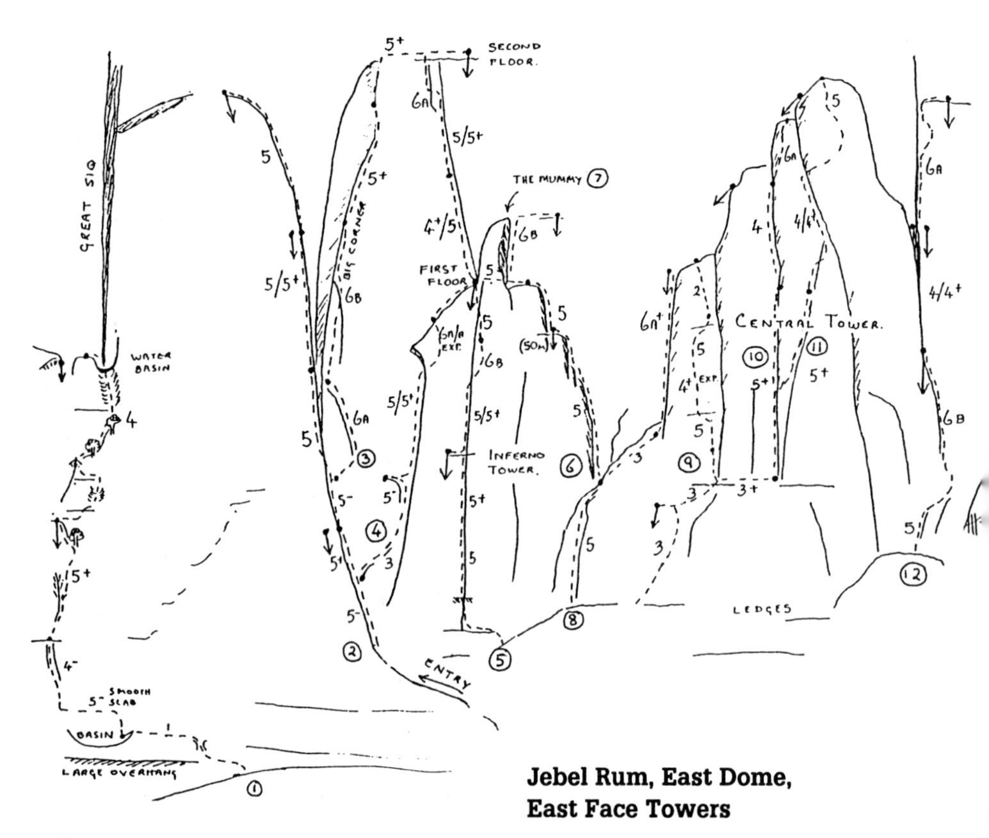

Jebel Rum, East Dome, East Face Towers

5. Route 45. Inferno *5+/6B/5/4+5/6A A.Howard, W.Colonna, D.Taylor. 10th October 1986.*
First 5 pitches of Towering Inferno.

6. Route 46. Walk Like an Egyptian *4+/5/5. W.Colonna, G.Claye 23rd October 1986.*
Strenuous cracks and corners with a nicely exposed traverse across the bottom of the Mummy.

7. Route 47. The Mummy *6B A.D.Abajo, M.A.Hernandez, J.Jimeno March 1992.*
A technical finish to the previous route, up the final pedestal, traversing right to the abseil point.

8. Route 48. Troubador *5/6A+ W.Colonna. A.Howard 4th October 1986.*
Powerful, archetypal laybacking and jamming.

9. Route 49. Wall of Lace *3/3/5 W.Colonna, A.Howard D.Taylor 13th April 1987.*
Bizarre climbing on filigree rock. Take plenty of threads for runners!

10. Route 50. Live and Let Die *3/4/5+/4/6A J.Dawson, I.Henderson 30th March 1992. (The middle pitches had been climbed by Laver and Pearce, 6 October 1988.)*
The obvious crack with resting places leads to a strenuous upper pitch right of the abseils.

11. Route 51. Goldfinger *3/4/5+/5 W.Colonna, G.Claye 23rd October 1986.*
Superb crack climbing up the front of the Central Tower, sharing a start with the previous route.

12. Route 52. Inshallah *6B/4/4+/6A M.Shaw, A.Howard November 1985.*
First 4 pitches of Inshallah Factor.

A brilliant finger crack followed by a chimney and a difficult corner to a good ledge. The first route on this wall.

13. Route 53. Arthur's Hammer *5/6C+/A1.6B+/6B/6C A.Donson, C.Mallen 19 - 21st May 1992.*
Climbs the fine groove in the centre of the big smooth pillar between Red Sea and Ziggurat. Traverse left at its top. Excellent climbing with a bold second pitch which had been previously climbed by W.Colonna. Take R.P.'s and Friends from $^1/_2$ - 3. Abseil down Red Sea. Topo, page 64.

14. Route 54. Ziggurat. *6A/7A/7A/5+ R.Edwards, B.Arkless 26th October 1986.*
Chimneys, and a ferocious corner crack to the top of the towers below Rainbow Wall. Descend by Aquarius. Topo page 64.

15. Route 55. Mano Negra *7A+/6B/6A/6B W.Colonna, E.Lancon May 1992.*
Fine technical climbing with bolt protection on pitch 2. Friends size 3 and 4 needed, and wires. Starts a few metres left of Aquarius and joins it at the top of pitch 4. Abseil chains and belays in situ. Topo page 64.

16. Route 56. Rainbow Warrior *6A/6B/5+/6A First 4 pitches of Aquarius. W.Colonna, A.Howard. 7th May 1986.*
Excellent and varied crack climbing with two exposed and poorly protected traverses, to reach the obvious tree, and the towers of Ziggurat. Topo page 64.

Jebel Rum, East Dome

South Face

57. The Eye of Allah *First recorded ascent M.Shaw, A.Baker, A.Howard, D.Taylor 9th October 1984.*
First climbed by the Bedouin, this is a very worthwhile route, passing through varied and incomparable rock scenery, and deserves to become a classic. The route is long and complex, and ascends a south facing ridge from sweet-water wells used by Lawrence, crosses the east end of the Great Siq and finally gains access to the summit via a tremendous cave we termed The Eye of Allah, with a view of the infinite desert beyond. The rock is good and the route covers almost a kilometre. 400 metres. Overall grade A.D. Sup. Allow $2^1/_2$ - 3 hours. Maps and topos, pages 48, 67, 70, 71.
Approach: From the Rest House cross the desert for about 1 kilometre to south west, to the base of a long ridge which goes up north in the direction of the East

Jebel Rum Massif, Hammad's Domes and East Dome

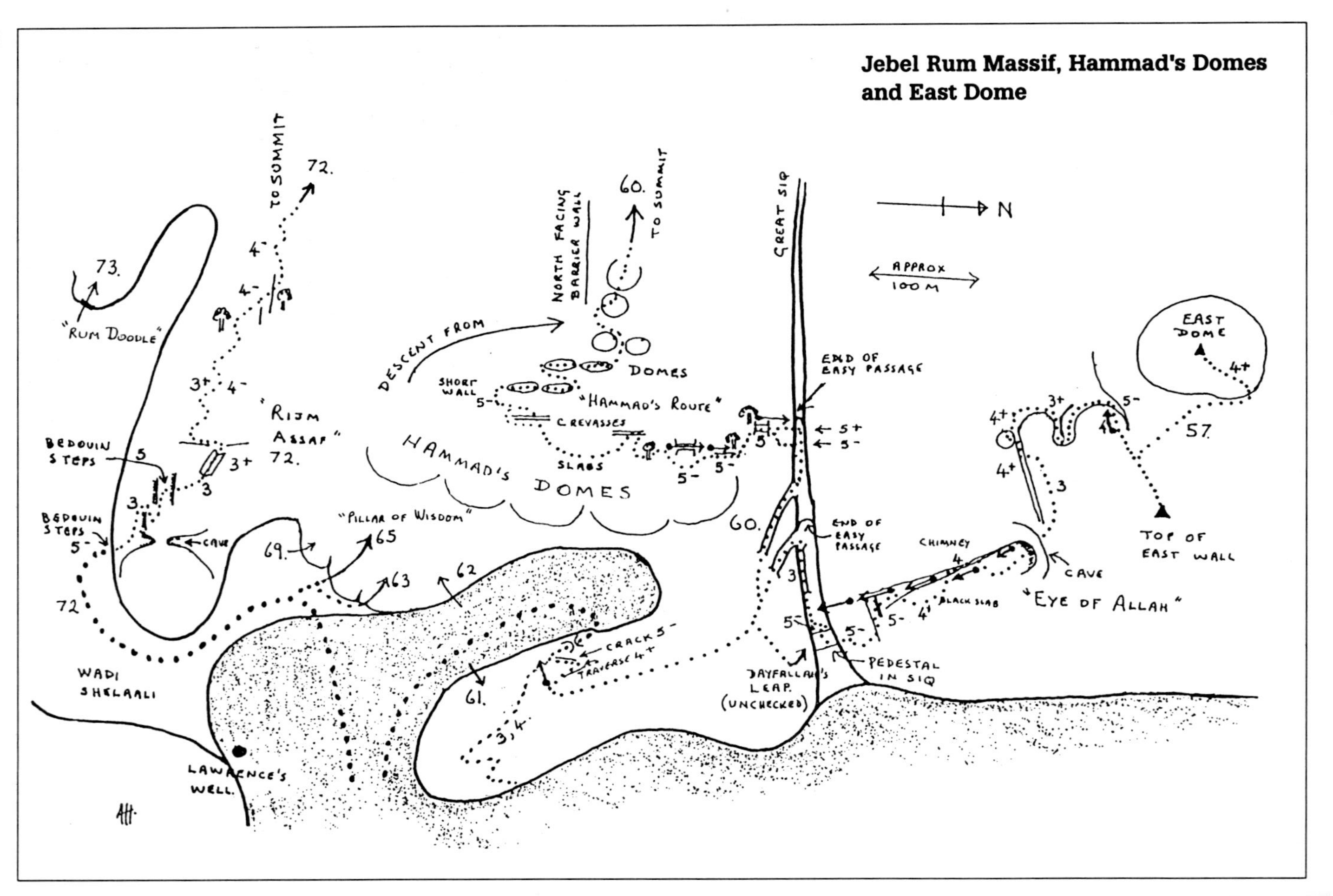

Jebel Rum, East Face, Left-hand Section

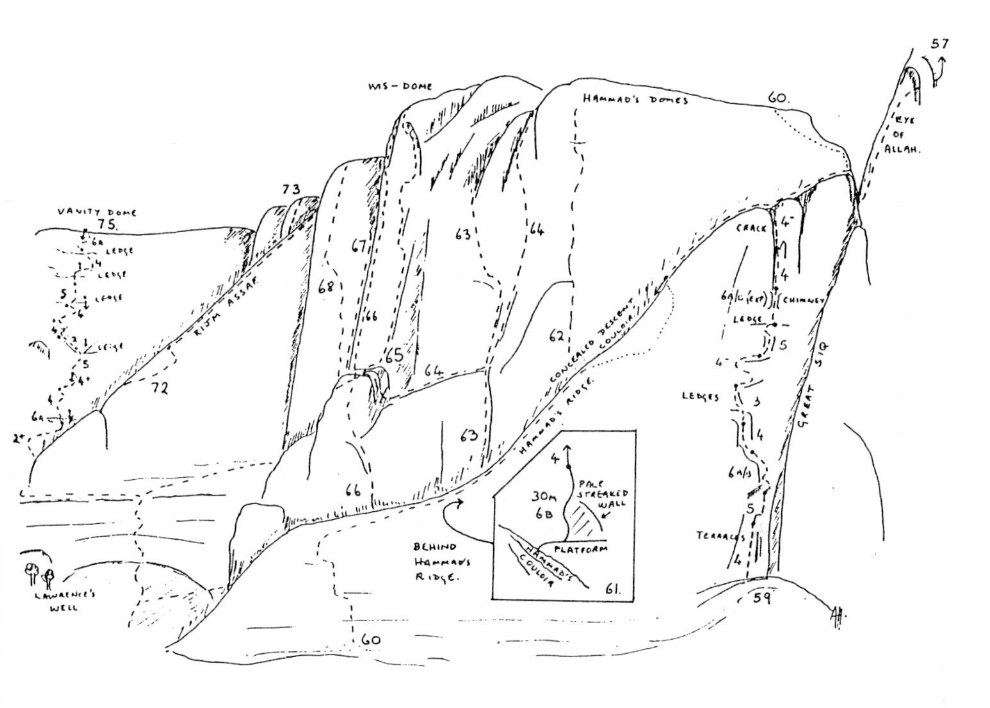

Dome summit. Either climb onto, and ascend the ridge (200 metres 3, 4-,4+) or continue round, passing one of Lawrence's Wells (sweet water in a green minty gully) and scramble up the gully parallel to and west of the ridge. At the head of the gully go across its true left wall up an easy ramp (3) and past some large precarious blocks to join the ridge route at a shoulder with some large boulders (cairn). The route commences up a diagonal crack in a steep slab.

58. Access to Jebel Rum Summit from East Dome

It is possible to reach the actual summit of Jebel Rum, by reversing route 24 back to the bivouac site at Juniper Flats ($^1/2$ hour), then continuing up the final section of Al Thalamiyyah across the Great Siq, joining Hammad's Route to the summit. Allow 1$^1/2$ - 2$^1/2$ hours from the summit of East Dome. Maps pages 48, 56, and 74.

If this route is followed, descend by Hammad's Route to the valley. If not, descent from the East Dome is as follows:-

Descent from the East Dome

Ideally, the best descent is to reverse the Eye of Allah (allow 2-3 hours). There are however other alternatives. It is of course possible to connect with Hammad's Route via the Juniper Flats bivouac site. If descending via the Eye of Allah, there is an abseil point to descend from the platform above the East Face, down the slab and crack of the last pitch. From here, reverse the route to the cave where a series of five abseils will be found, starting from the front right corner, and finishing in the Siq. From there, reverse the route to the end of the ridge crest where an abseil goes west down slabs to boulders. Descend these to the north, reversing the initial two pitches into the gully.

Jebel Rum, Hammad's Ridge North East Facet

59. Les Premices *C.&Y.Remy 8th May 1986.*

Interesting climbing but not too sustained, finishing on

the entry ridge of Hammad's Route, above the east exit of the Great Siq. Belays and protection are good, except in the exposed grade 6A/B chimney on the upper wall. 200 metres. T.D. Ascent 3 hours. Maps and topos, pages 48, 71, 74.
Approach: 15 minutes from the Rest House to the foot of the chimney below the Great Siq marking the left side of the East Face of East Dome.
Descent: Down south, on Hammad's Ridge (cairns), to the abseil point, and down the west side into the scree-couloir. 1 hour.

Jebel Rum Summit 1,754m (ref: 322743)

60. Hammad's Route *First recorded ascent, A.Baker, M.Shaw, A.Howard, D. Taylor 3rd November 1984.*

An enjoyable and direct route to the summit with few technical problems. The route passes through some very unusual mountain scenery and can be done in a day without problem. There are however, numerous good bivouac sites on the upper desert plateau and it is worth spending a night up there exploring some of the unique features of this mountain, in particular its numerous easy domes and the strange gash of the Great Siq. The rock is good throughout except for a short passage through fallen blocks, 50m from the start at the head of the couloir. From the Great Siq onwards, the rock is excellent, and as always on this mountain, the route is long. Much of it is however quite easy, with the serious climbing over once the walls of the Great Siq have been overcome. The climb follows the route of the Eye of Allah as far as the Great Siq which it then climbs by its north facing wall before heading for the summit. The distance involved is about 2 kilometres, only 250 metres of that being serious climbing. Overall grade A.D. Sup. Allow 4 hours. Maps and topos, pages 48, 67,70, 71 and 74.
Approach: Cross the desert south west of the Rest House and ascend the gully or ridge, as for the Eye of Allah until on the subsidiary summit above the east exit of the Great Siq. From here, go horizontally west and enter the Great Siq. (Do NOT descend the long narrow chimney of the Eye of Allah route.)

Follow the Siq back past water bowls in the bed (can be tricky if full of water) until an impasse is reached. here there are two options (see topos).
Descent: Follow the same route back with no problems (other than route-finding), descending the East Face until above the wall of the Great Siq. Enter this with three abseils.

The rest of the route can be followed back down, joining the Eye of Allah route, with a final abseil off the ridge to the boulders at the top of the passage of the jammed blocks, a rope-length above the scree slopes of the approach gully. All abseil rings in place. 2½ - 3 hours from the summit.

Part way up the approach couloir of Hammad's Route, on the right wall (going up), is a 30m technical corner crack above a platform, with a pale streaked wall on its right.

61. Egg Line *60m. 6B/4 A.Donson, C.Mallen 22nd May 1992.* Maps and topo pages 70, 71.

Hammad's Domes

These are the Domes of Hammad's Route, situated between the Great Siq and the canyon of Wadi Shelaali.

East Face

The wall drops steeply into the approach couloir of Hammad's Route, and is climbed by three routes:

62. Les Ripoux Sont Parmi Nous
C.&Y.Remy, 25th October 1986
Rather sustained with good exposed and varied climbing. Take a couple of blade pegs as well as the usual rack. 320m. T.D. Sup. 5 hours. Maps and topos 48, 70, 71, 73, and 74.
Approach: The climb starts on the right flank of the pillar which descends from the East face into Hammad's Couloir. Approach by R.60, ½ - ¾ hour.
Descent: Cross the domes to join Hammad's Route (cairns) above the abseils into the Great Siq, and follow this route down. 1½ hours.

63. Firestone *C.&Y.Remy 30th October 1986.*
Good sustained climbing in steep cracks and corners. 300m. T.D. 5 hours. Maps and topos 48, 70, 71, 73 & 74.
Approach: Just beyond the springs at the foot of Hammad's Couloir, a steep fissure blatantly splits the

Hammad's Domes, East Face

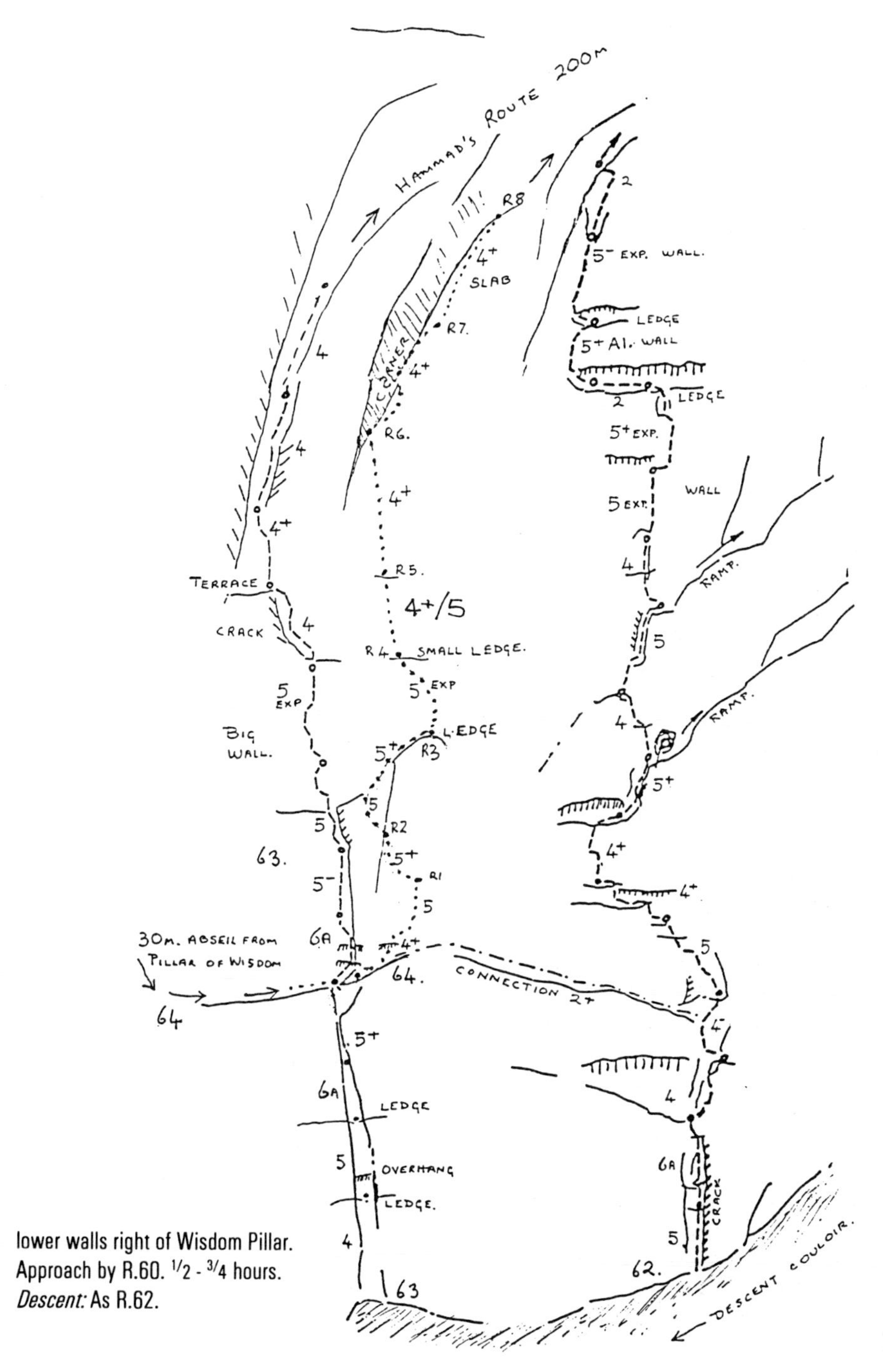

lower walls right of Wisdom Pillar.
Approach by R.60. 1/2 - 3/4 hours.
Descent: As R.62.

Jebel Rum, Central Plateau

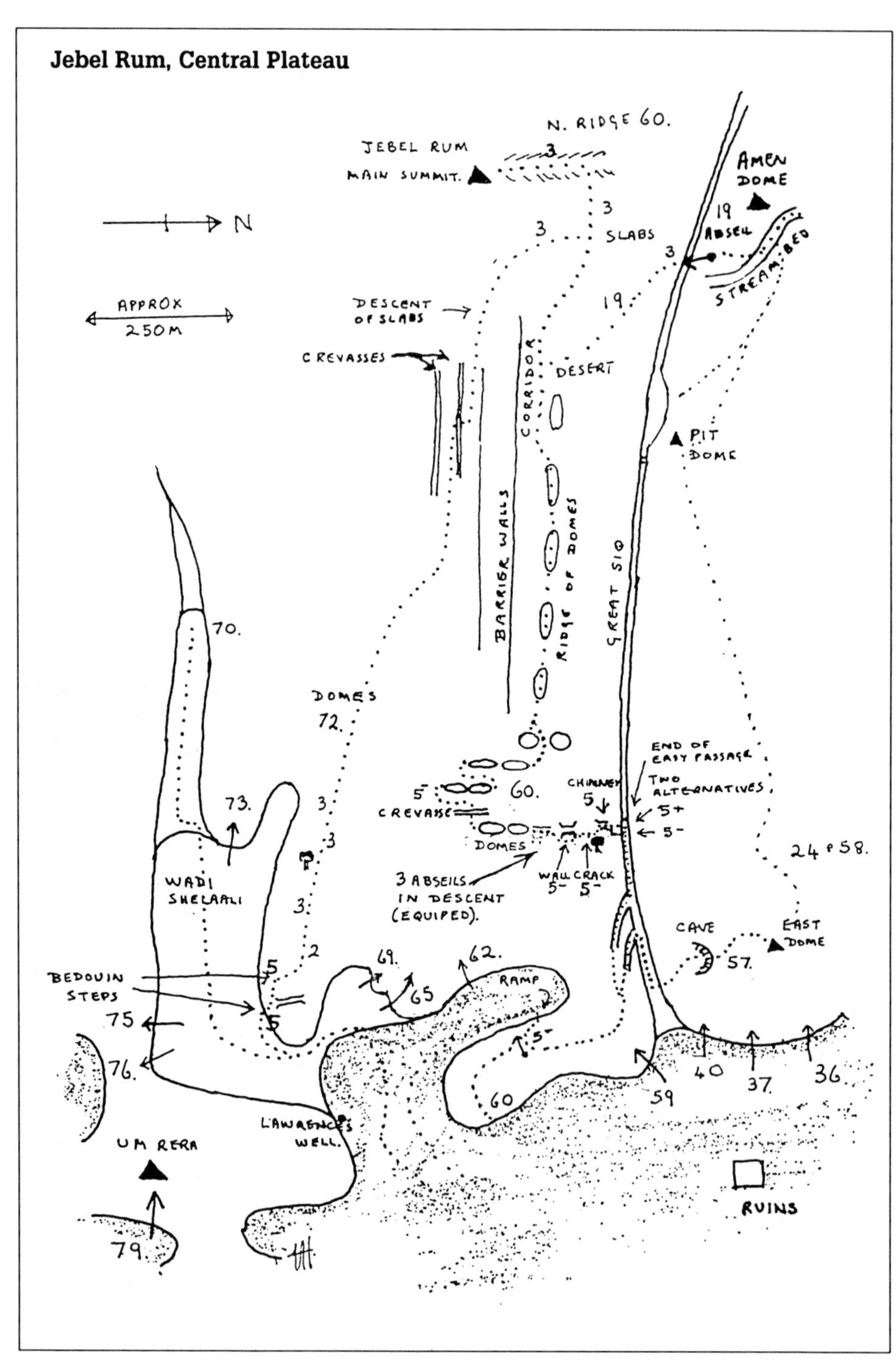

Hammad's Domes, Wisdom Pillar

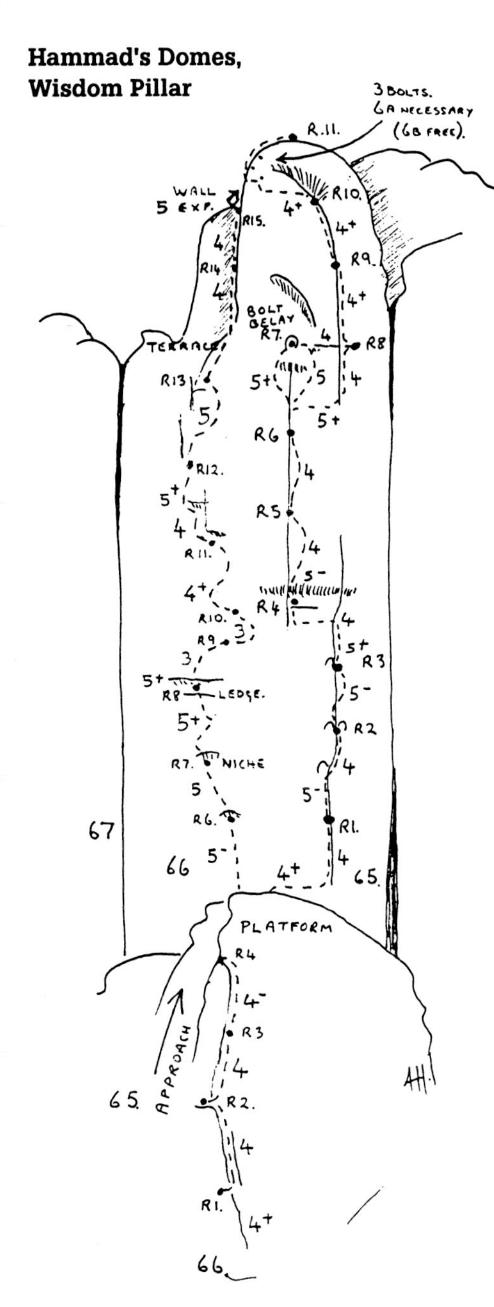

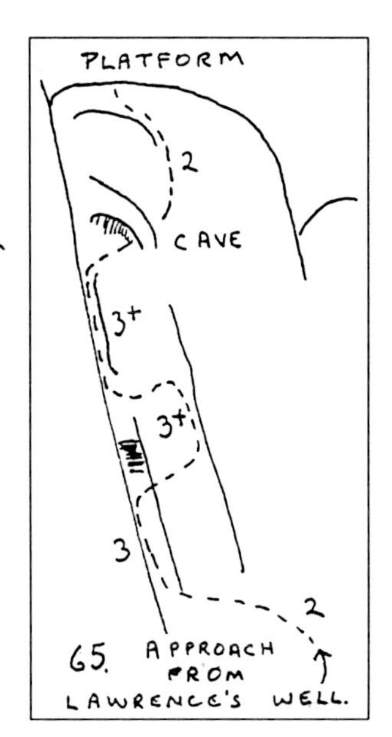

The next route ascends the wall between the previous two routes, but approaches from Pillar of Wisdom:

64. Mur de L'Allegresse *Y.Duverney and J.P.Monnet October 1986.*

A fantastic climb on an impressive open face, taking an improbable line on very fine rock sculptures, not difficult but very exposed! Protection is not obvious. Friends are necessary for good belays. 250 metres. T.D. Inf. 3 hours. Maps and topos, pages 67, 71 and 73.

Approach: Start up the lower four pitches of Firestone or, as on the first ascent, follow Pillar of Wisdom to reach the top of the pedestal at the foot of the Pillar (1 hour). Down-climb five metres in a little chimney (N). Then to the left and up to a small ledge. An abseil (30 metres) leads into a cirque. The start of the climb is on the right side of a huge wall, 5 - 10 metres right of and below a double crack system.

Descent: Hammad's Route, with 4 abseils. 1½ hours.

65. The Pillar of Wisdom *First ascent W.Colonna, A.Howard, D.Taylor 3rd October 1986.*

A superb route on good rock giving open and continuously enjoyable climbing and saving the crux for the very last moves. 350 metres in total, with 250 metres on the pillar. Verdict of subsequent ascentionist, "worth three stars." T.D. Inf. 3½ - 4 hours. Maps and topos, pages 48, 70, 71 and 74.

Approach: Cross the desert to the south west, to Wadi

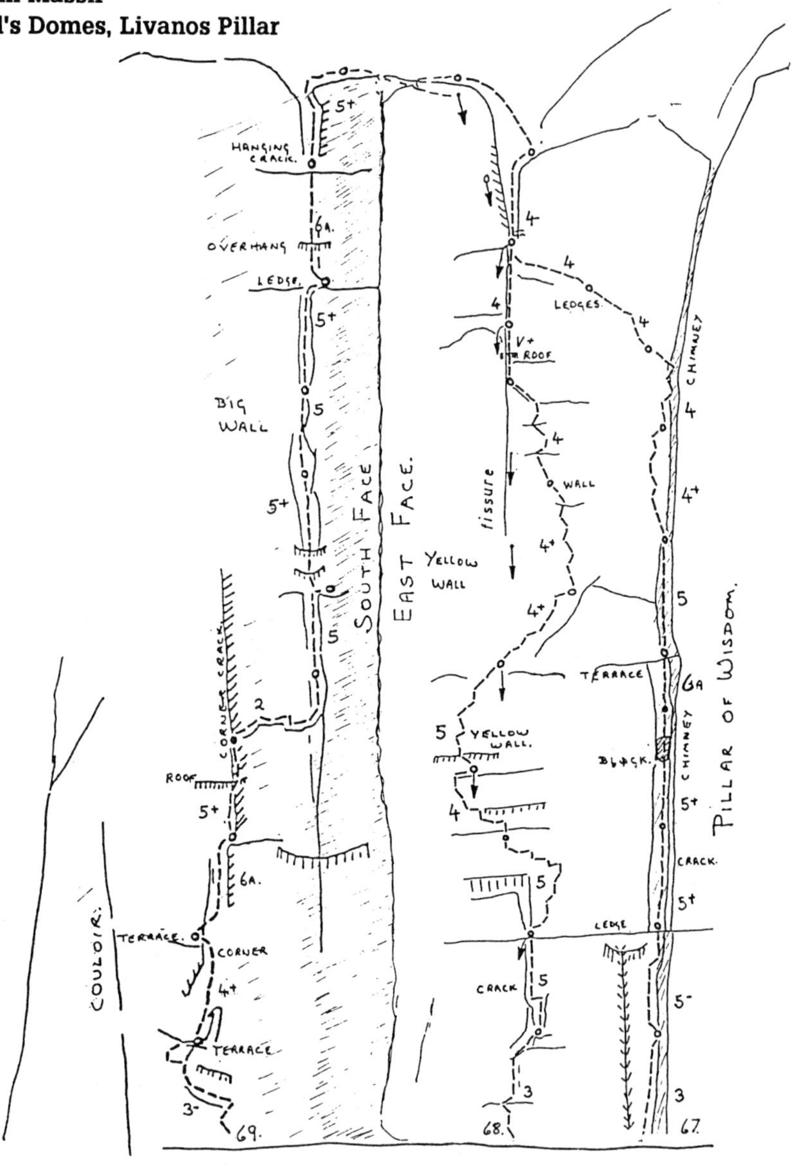

Jebel Rum Massif
Hammad's Domes, Livanos Pillar

Shelaali and move up to terraces in a bowl between this pillar (obvious by two huge vertical chimneys on either side), and the easier angled pillar of Rijm Assaf to its south. The route starts to the right of chimneys which lead to a platform at the base of the pillar, from the back of the basin. The line is very obvious from the Rest House.

Descent: From the top of the pillar go up the right hand dome and continue approximately north west along domes, past a hollow with two juniper trees then left round a final dome and down it, to a big sandy basin where it meets Hammad's Route. Cairns will be found from here, marking the descent which goes first north, before passing through a narrow gap and zig-zagging down to the abseils into the Great Siq and down Hammad's Route. $2^1/_2$ hours.

The next route parallels Pillar of Wisdom on its left, but has an independent direct start:

66. Coup Par Coup *N.Christie, C.&Y.Remy 26th October, 1986.*

Good climbing up a less obvious line to Wisdom. T.D. 350m. 5 hours. Map and topo 71and 75.

Approach: Up Wadi Shelaali to directly below Wisdom Pillar, where chimneys and corners lead up to the pedestal at the foot of the route proper.

Descent: As for Pillar of Wisdom.

The chimney left of Wisdom Pillar gives the line of:

67. Le Sourire De La Vengeance

C.&Y.Remy Nov. 1986

Steep and strenuous climbing T.D. 250m. 4 hours. Maps and topos 71, 75 and 76.

Approach: $^1/_2$ hour up the Wadi Shelaali path towards Lawrence's Well, and scramble up to the rock basin.

Descent: By abseil down La Fureur De Vivre, $1^1/_2$ hours, or it should be possible to join Hammad's Route and descend this.

68. La Fureure De Vivre *C.&Y.Remy 28th October 1986.*

Good steep climbing up the impressive tower left of Wisdom Pillar. T.D. 250m. 4 hours. Maps and topos 71 and 76.

Approach & Descent: as R.67.

On the S wall of the same tower is:

69. Le Grec *(Dedicated to George Livanos) C.&Y.Remy 6th November 1986.*

Beautiful sustained climbing in grand atmosphere. 250m T.D. 4 hours. Maps and topos 70, 74 and 76.

Approach & Descent: as R.67.

70. The Canyon of Wadi Shelaali (Valley of the Waterfall) *First recorded ascent: 28th October 1985 M.Shaw, A.Howard.*

This canyon is immediately above the springs of Lawrence, 1 kilometre south-west of the Rest House. It is entered by scrambling up terraces 200 metres right of the waterfall and then walking in left along the highest terrace; easy to reach. This comes into the upper valley just a few metres above its floor. The valley can then be followed back westwards for about $^1/_4$ kilometre, until it ends in a steep smooth chimney on the left.

To enter the next upper valley, climb about 50 metres right of the watercourse, up cracks (4) or a chimney (4+) to the right, for 50 metres and then walk in along terraces to the left. Here, the watercourse is followed directly up smooth chimneys (sometimes 4) until the valley widens out again. It soon closes but can be followed westwards towards the heart of Jebel Rum on either the left side (5-) or the right (4+).

Eventually the ravine opens again into a small sandy floored area with fig trees before the walls close in completely and become impassable, although the canyon does continue above if the next section could be climbed. Time to this point from Rest House 2 hours. D. Inf. Map page 74.

Descent: Simply reverse the route, if necessary abseiling from a good thread down the initial entry wall to the lower wadi.

71. Wadi Shelaali, Bedouin Route *Sheikh Kraim, Sabbah Eed, Atieeq Auda, W.Colonna and party November 1992.*

This recently re-discovered route follows an old and long forgotten Bedouin climb to the domes. Occasional Bedouin steps mark the way and moves of 5+ are obligatory! No precise details but 6 hours to the domes. D.

Jebel Rum Summit 1754m

72. Rijm Assaf (The Steps of Assaf) *First recorded ascent, W.Colonna, M.Shaw, A.Howard. 12th October, 1985.*

This is an excellent, classic and fairly straightforward Bedouin route, sustained at a fairly easy standard provided thought is given to choosing the easiest way. The route takes a fairly direct line from the upper hanging valley of Wadi Shelaali, south west of the Rest House, from where the line of the route up the narrow projecting east south east ridge of Jebel Rum can be seen. The only difficulties are at "Bedouin Steps", the second set of which has to be seen to be believed! Over $1^1/_2$ kilometres of rock, with 250 metres mostly grade

Rum Doodle Pillar

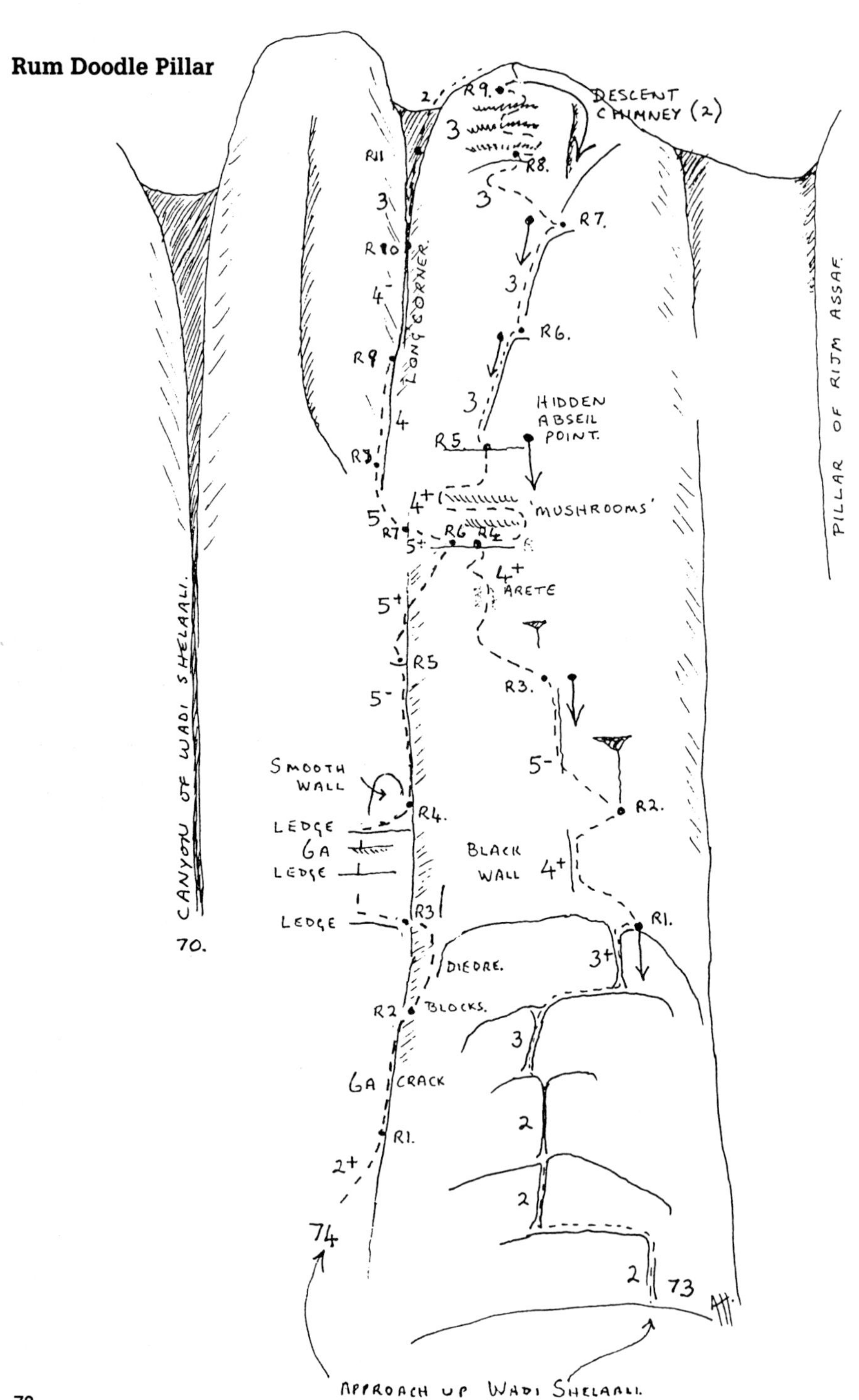

3 and 4. Overall grade A.D. Sup. Allow 3 - 5 hours. Maps and topos, pages 48, 70, 71, 74.

Approach: Cross the desert for about 1 kilometre, south west of the Rest House taking R.9. towards Lawrence's Well, scrambling up easy terraces about 200 metres right of the main watercourse and Lawrence's Well, which is beneath the entrance to the upper ravine of Wadi Shelaali (Valley of the Waterfall). Walk left to enter the upper valley along the highest easily accessible terrace. About 1/2 - 3/4 hour. The East South East Ridge is on the right. Contour round the foot of it and once round inside the mouth of the upper canyon, scramble up a 20 metre slope to the first set of "Bedouin Steps" below a short hanging crack.

Descent: As for Hammad's Route, taking care with route finding. 4 abseils 2 1/2 - 3 hours.

Alternative Exit onto Pillar of Wisdom

G.Claye, P.J.Lange 6th October 1986.

From the top of the main pillar, near a cairn, between trees, ascend the purple wall for two rope lengths (5), then left (4), then easier across domes to Wisdom Dome. This enables Hammad's Route to be gained quickly, for descent.

73. Rum Doodle *W.Colonna, A.Howard 8th October 1986.*

Enjoyable, open and surprising climbing on 'crisps' up the front of the right hand of two hidden pillars in Wadi Shelaali. Protection is somewhat curious! The route finishes on the domes, which should give access to the summit. 250 metres. D. 3 hours. Maps and topos, pages 48, 70, 71, 74, 78.

Approach: Up into Wadi Shelaali as for Rijm Assaf and up the right branch of the wadi, or the central dividing ridge to the foot of the first tower. Continue by scrambling up, starting at a corner 50 metres right of the ridge, below a big chimney. A ledge goes almost immediately left, then chimneys and cracks (2 with some moves of 3) up the front left side of the tower lead to the start of the route. (3/4 hour).

Descent is straightforward, first down a hidden chimney a few metres north of the finish then four abseils down the pillar and one more to the foot of the climb. 1 - 1 1/2 hours. Take care with the ropes on the many rock 'crisps'.

The tower south of and adjacent to Rum Doodle gives:-

74. Decapolis *C.&Y.Remy 8th November 1988*

Pleasant and varied climbing with a number of slings in place, marking the route which passes through some steep rock to reach the obvious upper diedre. T.D. 250m 4 hours. Topo page 74.

Approach: As for R.73, but continue round the foot of the Rum Doodle ridge and up the main valley of Wadi Shelaali a short way to the foot of a fissure in the left side of this ridge. 1/2 hour.

Descent: Cross to the top of Rum Doodle, and descend by the abseils of that route. (Take care with the ropes on the many rock 'crisps') 1 1/2 hours.

Immediately opposite this route, on the S side of Wadi Shelaali, above and behind the well, and obvious from the Rest House is:-

Vanity Dome 1480m

North Face

This face has been climbed by Bedouin, though the exact line is not known. However, there is a route up the centre of the wall:-

75. L'O mine rale *N.Christie, C.&Y.Remy 24th October 1986.*

Mostly Grade 4, it has some hard starting moves (6A) to pass the overhang above the lower ledges, and a similarly difficult finish. 300m T.D. 4 hours. Maps and topos, pages 48, 71, 83.

Descent is by abseil down the route.

Jebel Um Rera 1250m

This summit is east of and below Vanity Dome, and can be climbed either from Lawrence's Well on its NW side, or from Wadi Rum, on its E side. The easiest ascent, which is also useful as a descent route is:-

West Face

76. Voie Normale *First recorded ascent, B.Vinton, A.Howard, D.Taylor October 1991.*

A pleasant scramble up what at first appears to be a deep unpleasant gully/chimney but which actually gives an easy and enjoyable way to the top, in the shade. The route ascends the right hand of the two massive chimneys above and behind Lawrence's Well. A short distance up, a couple of short pitches of 3 zig-zag up the right wall. The chimney splits at the top and the dividing ridge is climbed (2) to the col above the valley of Abu Aina down to the S, before going left up a crack (2+) to reach the broken rocks of the summit ridge 200m A.D. Inf. 1 - 1½ hours. Maps pages 48, 74.

Approach: Up the Wadi Shelaali path to the upper valley above Lawrence's Well ½ hour.

Descent: Reverse the route with one abseil down the pitches of 3.

North West Face

A route has been recorded on this wall, starting 100 m left of the Well:

77. Lawrence's Well Crack *R.Feichter, H.Baldinger 28th April 1989.*

The route goes almost directly up crack and chimney systems to the N Summit with four pitches of climbing to easier ground 4+/4+/5+/4.

Descent: 3 abseils down the route, then W on ledges into Wadi Shelaali.

Before reaching the E Face climbs on Jebel um Rera, one passes by a subsidiary summit, which flings down a ridge of rock almost into the village:

Jebel Ahmar Al Shelaali (also known as Jebel Athab) 1125m

This top has been climbed by a route on its West Face, starting from the col. The route takes the shortest way up the cliff and is described by its first ascentionists as a climb "on fine quality sand - the first shower of winter should obliterate it entirely."

Much better is a really enjoyable scramble up its N ridge to reach the summit - an excellent viewpoint over the village and valley of Rum.

78. The N Ridge *First recorded ascent A.Howard, D.Taylor October 1991.*

A pleasant way to a good viewpoint situated directly above the S end of the village, and E of the entrance to the valley of Wadi Shelaali.

Walking and easy scrambling, apart from the summit rocks which are grade 2 (safety rope advised if not familiar with rock climbing). F. Allow 2 hours for the return journey from the Rest House. Map page 48.

Cross the desert directly towards the mountain, to a ridge of granite boulders which extends a short way northwards into the wadi.

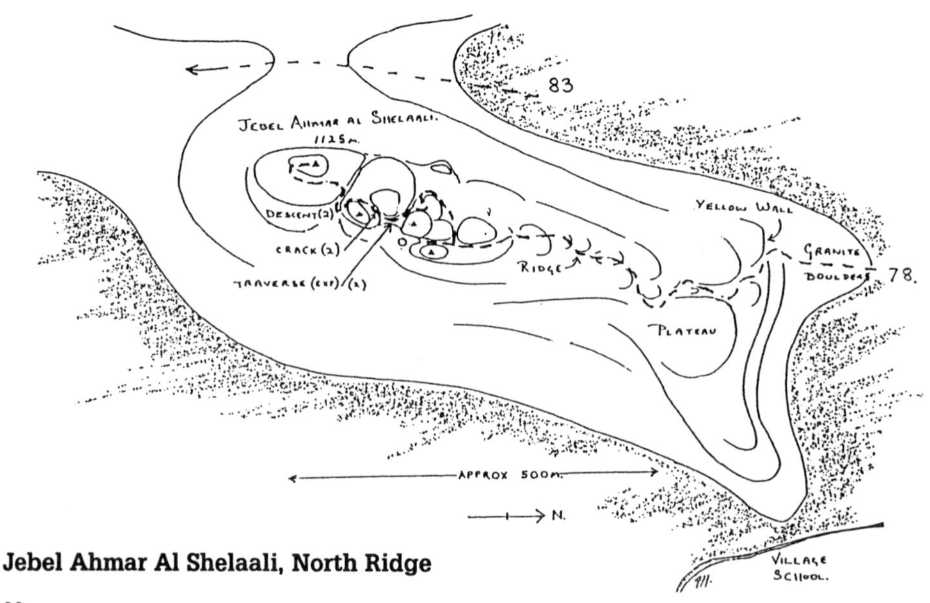

Jebel Ahmar Al Shelaali, North Ridge

Go up this and trend right, towards the right side of a large smooth yellow cliff. (There is a flat-topped boulder with inscriptions about 30m below the right end of the wall.) Go up left from here, to the left edge of the yellow wall and up 3m to a flat ledge (cairn).

Go left, and trend up left for about 50m into an easy angled bushy gully. Scramble up past a split then walk right below a sandy overhang, out of the gully and up left onto a plateau. Good view (20 mins from Rest House).

Walk S along the ledge a little way, then up rocks on the right, to cross the rounded ridge and walk along its right side a short way. Gain the ridge again, and follow its top to the next little plateau and walk S, to a prominent gap between the mountain and a tower on the skyline. Through the gap, there are good views S down the desert to Khazali.

To continue to the top, go back a few metres and scramble through a little gully, crossing the ridge to its W side, then walk along to the furthest gully. (Across Wadi Shelaali, W of here, the rock climbs of Pillar of Wisdom and Eye of Allah and many others are easily seen.)

Go up the gully, then almost immediately left up a slab to avoid vegetation and a steep section of rock. Step onto the next slab and make an exposed traverse left (1) to a corner which is followed easily back right to regain the top of the gully.

Here, go through a slot onto the E. side of the mountain and traverse a ledge (exposed, 1), to a bush in a recess. From here it is possible to reach the top by some very exposed moves (2), after going right along the ledge but it is better to go directly up the leaning chimney and crack above (also 2) to the top of the North Summit.

To reach the South Summit which is marginally

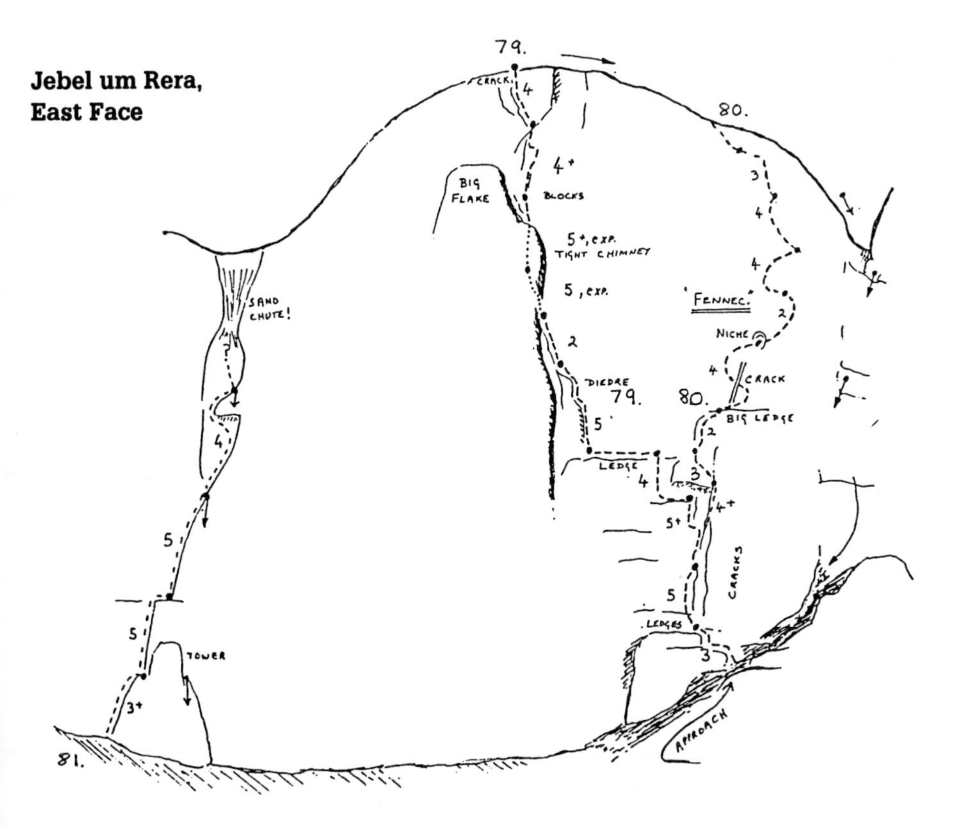

Jebel um Rera, East Face

higher, go S to the edge of the little ravine which separates the tops. Walk left 10 m on a flat black ledge. Descend 2m (exposed, 1) and scramble back right into the ravine, climbing up easily to the next top and the summit rock which is just beyond. Excellent views.
Descent: return by the same route.

Moving south down the valley, we once again come to:

Jebel um Rera 1250 metres (Ref: 337736)

This is a small peak just south of Rum village, above the Aqaba track.

79. Les Freres Mousson *C.&Y.Remy 22nd April, 1986.*
An interesting climb with a very tight chimney pitch and a splendid pitch at the start of the corner. Good belays but the protection is not always obvious, with some exposed sections. 200 metres. T.D. Inf. Ascent 3 hours. Maps and topos, pages 48, 74, 81, 83.
Approach: From the village walk 10 minutes to the south and 10 minutes up scree to ledges below the right side of the obvious corner.
Descent is by the north ridge, and by a short rappel gain the breche from where the descent goes down the East Face with two rappels. 1 hour. (Or, see Fennec).

80. Fennec *Francois Lenfant and Gilles Claye 24th October 1986.*
A pleasant route starting as for Les Freres Mousson and trending right up the wall. 200 metres. D. Inf. 3 hours. Maps and topos, pages 48, 81, 83.
Descent: Down R.76, follow the ridge south-south-west and descend broken rock until the couloir is visible. Down this for about 150 metres to an abseil point on the left, down a chimney to reach Wadi Shelaali above Lawrence's Spring. 3/4 hour.

The left side of the east wall is split by a big chimney-line:
81. Sandeman *A.Howard, M.Carr 18th April 1987.*
Three strenuous crack pitches in a good corner and a final chimney in a massive but masochistically dusty cave pitch lead into a horrendous sand chute! 3+/5/5/4. Topo page 81.
Descent: 3 abseils, finishing north of the tower.

Um Rera. South Buttress
Short sports climbs on steep walls of around 50 - 100 metres have been done on the walls overlooking the Bedouin camp of Abu Aina.

Abu Aina Camp
This traditional Bedouin campsite is concealed in a hollow at the SE end of Jebel Rum. There are permanent springs in the cliffs above the camp and if you ask for Lawrence's Well you will no doubt be directed here by the Bedouins. He would almost certainly have used these springs but the one specifically referred to in *Seven Pillars of Wisdom* is in Wadi Shelaali (R.9.).

There is also usually an extra Bedouin tent here, provided for the use of tourists as a campsite. Ask at the Bedouin Camp behind if you wish to use it. Dayfallah Atieeq lives here and speaks good English. He is in charge of this tourist camp.

82. The Desert Track to Abu Aina
Simply walk down the desert track S from the village, below the cliffs of Jebel Rum, turning right on tracks into a bay below the mountain, where the black tents will soon be seen. 3 kilometres. 3/4 hour. Maps pages 48, 83.

83. High level route to Abu Aina
Cross the desert SW towards Wadi Shelaali, then go up the little valley W of Jebel Ahmar al Shelaali to the pass. Continue S above the desert track and below the steep east facing cliffs of Jebel um Rera until another pass is found on the right. Go through this to a parallel valley which is then followed S to Abu Aina. A pleasant scramble 3 kilometres, 1 - 1 1/2 hours. Map page 80.

84. South South East Route

A reported Bedouin route taking the valley north then west from the wells of Abu Aina (ref: 335725). After about 1 kilometre, the route reputedly goes north west to the summit of Jebel Rum, crossing the domes and ridges of the South Plateau. Total distance about 2½ kilometres. Supposedly fairly easy, but unchecked. In fact, this way, like the next route, is likely to be blocked by big siqs!

85. South Siq and South Summits from Abu N'Khala (Place of the Palm Trees)

First recorded ascent 6/7th October 1985 (summits climbed on 6th October) W.Colonna, A.Baker, M.Shaw, D.Taylor, A.Howard.

An enjoyable and easy way meandering up the gully of Abu N'Khala and then northwards to the barrier of the South Siq. Good rock throughout and good views of the southern desert and west down impressive canyons into Wadi Rumman. 2 kilometres, gaining 400 metres in height. 3 - 4 hours. Grade A.D. Inf.

Approach: From the Bedouin camps at the well of Abu Aina and Abu N'Khala, follow the wide Hanging Valley with a palm tree left of its entrance, passing an area of trees and mint higher up, before working up the left side of the ravine to terraces at its head. These are followed north, along the SE side of the mountain, before contouring round to gain the south plateau and its summits.

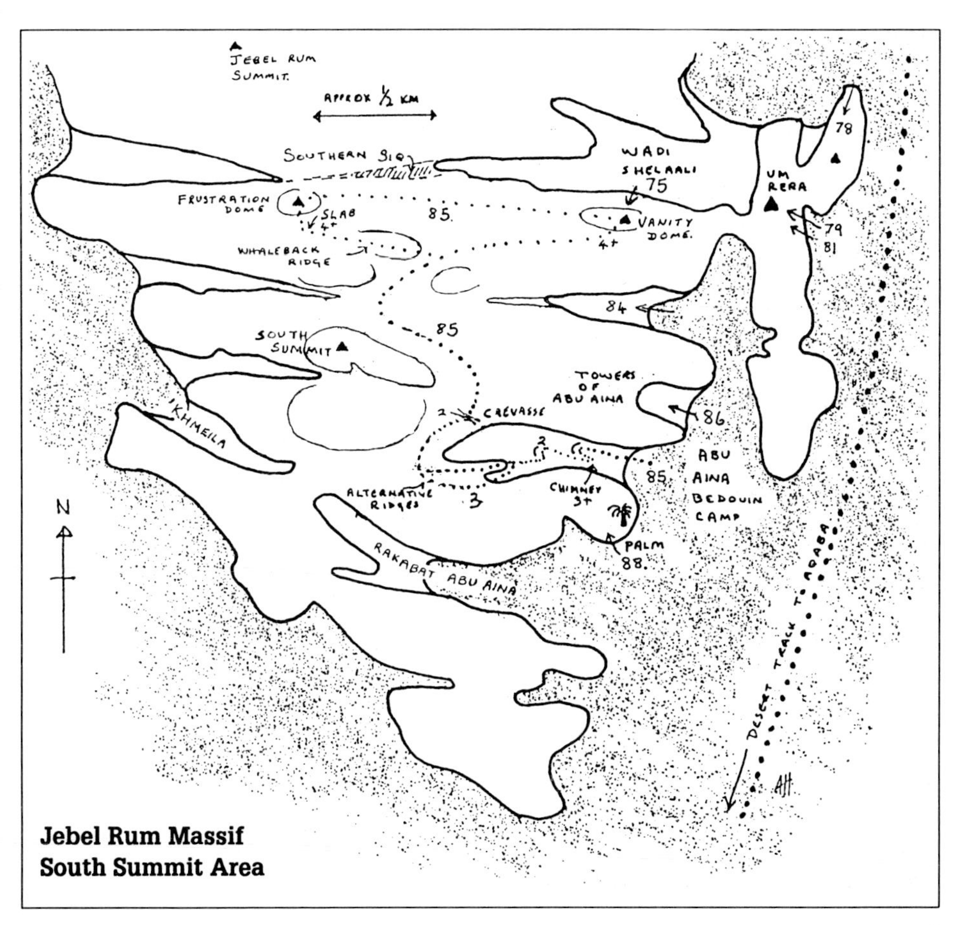

Jebel Rum Massif
South Summit Area

Jebel Rum Massif
Abu Aina Towers, Lionheart

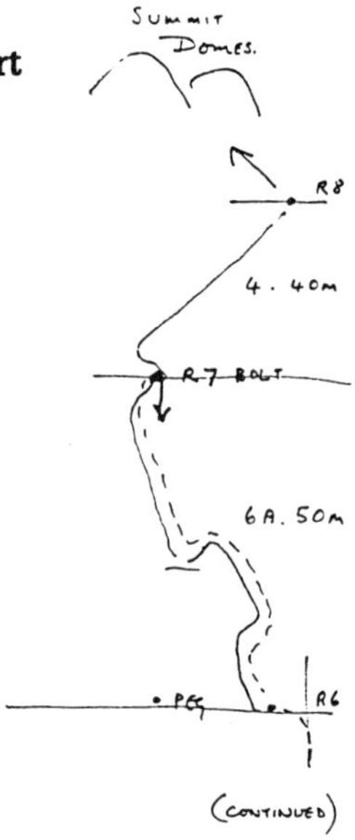

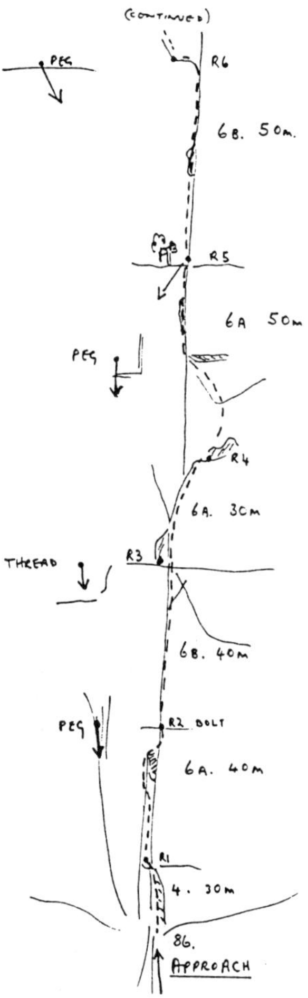

86. Lionheart. *R.&M.Edwards 19th March 1987*

Described by the first ascent team as "one of the best new routes we have ever done, with superb crack and groove climbing."

This excellent and very sustained route takes a direct line up four magnificent corners, passing an overhanging jamming crack to finish by a superb steep slab on the left wall of the big cleft. 350m. E.D. Inf. 5 hours. Map page 83.

Approach: Scramble up the hillside from the water tanks to a spring by some trees. Just left, a short climb behind a huge chockstone brings one into the hanging valley. Go up to below the big central tower and belay below the first chimney. $\frac{1}{2}$ - $\frac{3}{4}$ hour.

Descent: By abseil down the route $1\frac{1}{2}$ hours.

Descent: Is by the same route. Approximately $2\frac{1}{4}$ - 3 hours from the summits, or 2 - $2\frac{1}{2}$ hours from the bivouac area.

Abu Aina Towers

These towers present the last big eastern face of the Jebel Rum massif, and rise from a hanging basin above the well and water tanks of Abu Aina, from where they present an impressive vertical cracked wall. The left-hand crack finishes in a giant roofed-in cleft:

Abu N'Khala Towers

The towers immediately behind the palm give the following routes:-

SE Face

87. Sabbah's Number Two *F.Lenfant and Simone Badier 21st April 1987.*

A pleasant climb for the afternoon up the right-hand tower, with easy access and descent, just above the Bedouin camps of Abu Aina and Abu N'Khala. No. 4 Friend required for protection. 200 metres. A.D. Sup. $2\frac{1}{2}$ hours. Maps and topos pages 83, 85.

Descent: By ledges to the north east into the hanging valley of Abu N'Khala. 20 minutes.

88. Gulab Tower. Skyline Buttress *Sharu Prabhu, Doug Scott 12th April, 1987.*

The left-hand tower. A pleasant varied climb on good rock, after a shaky start up the left side of the obvious square-cut slab. Two short pitches up a chimney-crack (5) are followed by a traverse right to the centre of the buttress. Continue past an overhang (5+) and up the red buttress to the summit (5-) 200m. D. Sup. $2\frac{1}{2}$ hours. Map page 83.

Descent: Down the back of the mountain. $\frac{1}{2}$ hour.

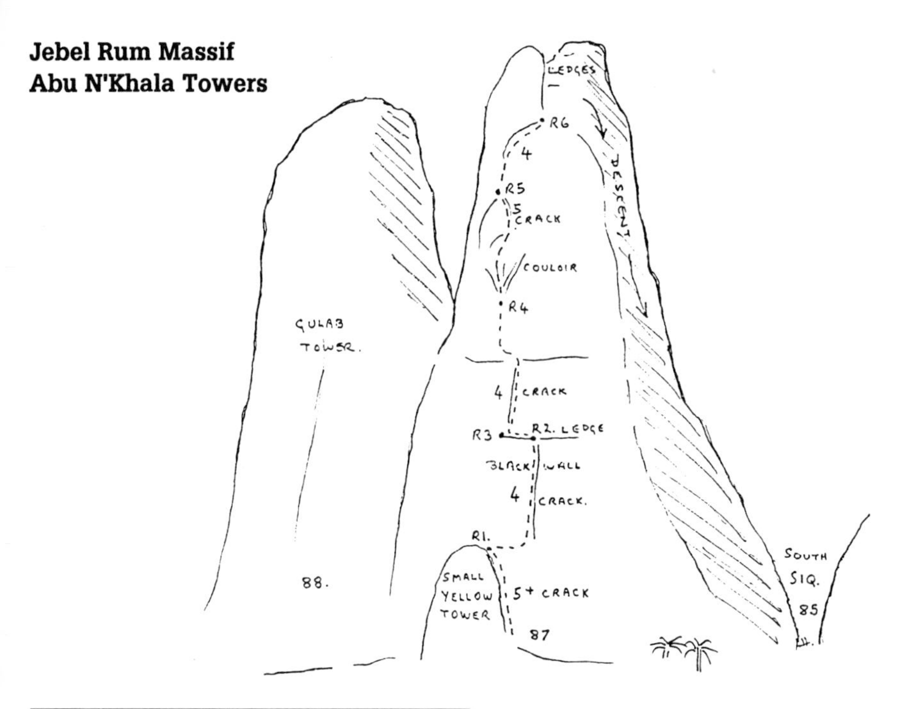

Jebel Rum, West Face

89. West Pillar *W.Haupolter, S.Inhoger, A.Precht 12th April, 1990.*

This is the sentinel-like tower standing guard at the SW entrance to the huge siq of Sabbah's Route, directly W of the summit of Jebel Rum.

An interesting and amazing route on good rock up obvious crack systems in the red slabs and then right of the pillar in a chimney. 300m. T.D. Sup. 4 hours. Maps and topos pages 86, 87.

Approach: By Bedouin taxi round Jebel Rum (10km) and walk up the screes to the granite ledges (1/2 hour).

Descent: Walk towards the top of Jebel Rum (10 min) and then turn to the north and down climb easily into the valley north of the Pillar. Continue on Sabbah's route down to the start of the climb (1 1/2 hours)

90. Sabbah's Route *First recorded ascent W.Colonna, D.Taylor, A.Howard 3rd May 1986.*

This magnificent route takes the true left side (right, facing in) of the huge hanging valley directly west of the summit of Jebel Rum, starting from Wadi Rumman at map ref: 305740, about 5 kilometres north west of the southern tip of the mountain. (Accessible by four-wheel drive, about 10 kilometres from the Rest House.) The way is fairly straightforward and direct, with few difficulties, covering about 1 1/2 kilometres. Allow 2 1/2 - 3 hours from Wadi Rumman. Excellent climbing on good rock. A Bedouin classic - one of Sabbah's masterpieces! P.D. Sup. Maps and topos, 86, 87. Also, see R.91.

91. Jebel Rum West-East Traverse

W.Colonna, D.Taylor, A.Howard, 3rd May, 1986.

Gives a classic traverse of the mountain, linking Sabbah's Route with a descent of Hammad's Route. About 3 kilometres long in total, and fairly serious for its grade. A.D. Allow 5 - 8 hours. Maps and topos, 86, 87.

The hanging valley is easily identified by the steep West Pillar on its right (south) with its huge open diedre. Scramble up right of the stream bed on scree and polished granite slabs, to gain a terrace between the foot of the pillar, and the stream bed. Do NOT enter the canyon bed proper, but wind up the right (south) side of the canyon taking slabs, chimneys and terraces (cairns) always keeping as high as easily possible (some 2), the next identifying feature being a huge cave recess.

Continue east still zig-zagging up the right side until a way is found (2) up slabs left of a 50 metre cleft. The cleft itself can also be climbed (3). Still in the same direction a long terrace is reached, eventually leading to a juniper tree below a hanging crack with a Bedouin step at its base. Go up this (3) and traverse immediately back right (3) and up easily to the next terrace with red rock below and the white domes above. Follow this all the way along right (cairns), and back left at the end, up a gully with a tree into the domes.

Alternatively, from the Bedouin step, there is another way going left and back up right to reach the same point. Slightly harder (3+) very exposed but with bolt protection and well worth doing.

Jebel Rum, West Pillar

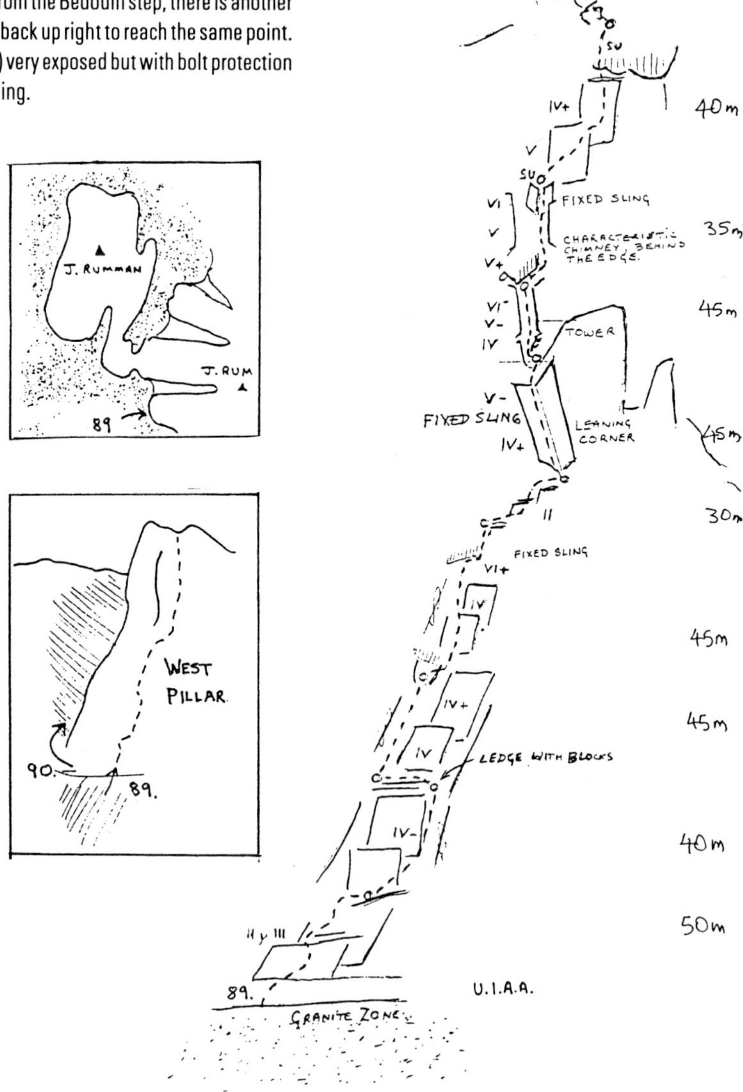

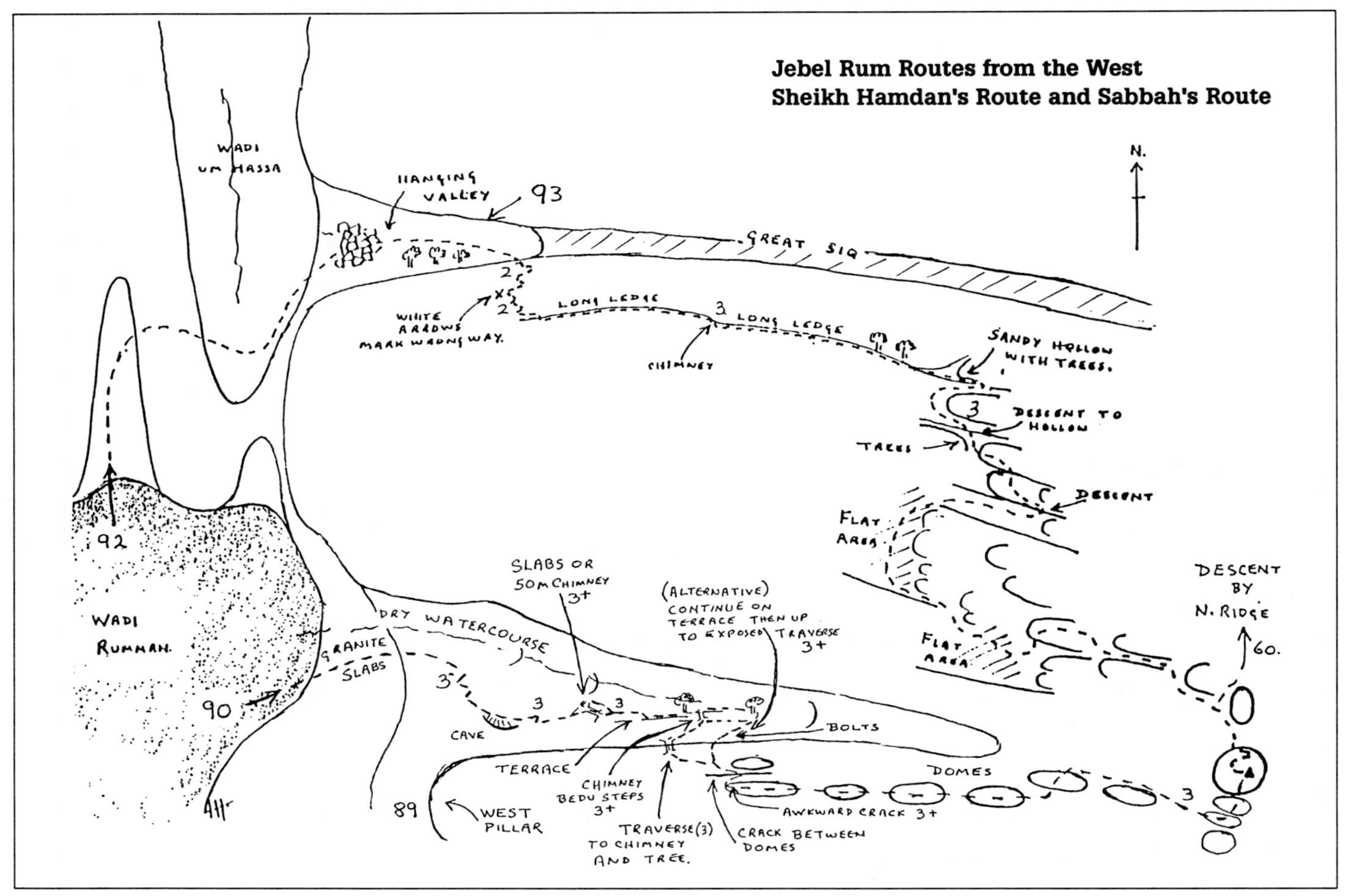

Jebel Rum Routes from the West
Sheikh Hamdan's Route and Sabbah's Route
N.
WADI UM HASSA
HANGING VALLEY
93
GREAT SIQ
WHITE ARROWS MARK WRONG WAY.
2
X
2
LONG LEDGE
3
LONG LEDGE
CHIMNEY
SANDY HOLLOW WITH TREES.
3
DESCENT TO HOLLOW
TREES
DESCENT
FLAT AREA
FLAT AREA
DESCENT BY N. RIDGE
60.
92
WADI RUMMAN.
90
GRANITE SLABS
DRY WATERCOURSE
SLABS OR 50M CHIMNEY 3+
3
3
3
(ALTERNATIVE) CONTINUE ON TERRACE THEN UP TO EXPOSED TRAVERSE 3+
BOLTS
CAVE
TERRACE
CHIMNEY BEDU STEPS 3+
TRAVERSE(3) TO CHIMNEY AND TREE.
CRACK BETWEEN DOMES
AWKWARD CRACK 3+
DOMES
3
89
WEST PILLAR

Once on the start of the domes do NOT head directly east towards the summit but go 50 metres south (right) and take a long easy angled crack (2) with some harder moves (3) eastwards towards the summit, then another in the opposite direction, on to the higher domes. Here, trend slightly north east, winding up slabs and cracks on and between domes until the summit can be identified and gained from this direction.
Descent: Via Hammad's Route. Topo page 74.

92. Sheikh Hamdan's Route *Sheikh Hamdan Amad, Sylvia Branford and Charmian Longstaff November 1952.*
The first recorded climb in Wadi Rum, the easiest way to the summit of Jebel Rum and a real classic. The following excerpt is taken from the Ladies Alpine Journal of 1953:

"We started off up broken scree to enter a wide gully leading into the heart of the mountain. Usually these gullies, so promising at first, end, as my husband put it, inhospitably, but we circumvented this by taking to cliff ledges on our right and traversed along always making height until we reached a narrow cleft which led us still further into the mountain along a level gravelly bed. I remember a few bushes beside which we had our first rest. To the right of us was vertical cliff and to the left, broken rock leading upwards to a red palisade a thousand feet high.

"Hamdan climbed with bare feet as surely as a mountain goat. We had gym shoes and were glad of them. I suppose really that it was very easy climbing but it was very exposed.

"Sometimes holding one or both of us by the hand, Hamdan led us along horizontal ledges in the cliff face. there always came a time when we had to climb from one ledge to the one above. Once we did this up a small gully that held two tall trees: we found afterwards that they were a kind of juniper. Then there were two vertical pitches, and suddenly, we were among the gleaming white of the summit domes. 'The top!' cried Hamdan.

"We looked round us and saw that although we were indeed on the summit plateau we were a long way from its highest point. 'We must go there', we said, pointing towards it. 'If you go there', replied Hamdan, 'You will be very tired'. But by now, the spirit of the intrepid woman explorers was in us and it must be the top and nothing but the top.

"'You English women', said Hamdan, 'are as strong as men. You should see our husbands', we replied.

"It had taken us about two hours up to the plateau and it took us another hour up and down the complication of white domes to reach the summit. Between the domes were beds of gravel and these must hold moisture after the rare rains, or perhaps dew, because to our surprise we found junipers growing in them up to two or three times the height of a man."

A fascinating way to the top of Jebel Rum, with few difficulties but nevertheless requiring a head for heights. The route takes the shaded N facing wall of the Great Siq, utilising a long ledge which rises all the way to the domes, from where, with some Bedouin cunning all major obstacles are passed by a circuitous but enjoyable bit of route finding which arrives at the col immediately N of the top.

For non-climbers this is a route well worth doing with a guide and perhaps spending the night up in the flat area in the domes just below the summit, before returning by the same route. About 2km. P.D. Allow 3 - 4 hours for the ascent from Wadi Rumman. Map p.87.

From the foot of the canyon taken by Sabbah's Route, scramble northwards up a dry stream bed to the saddle between Jebel Rum and Jebel Rumman. Here, go right (E) crossing the head of Wadi um Hassa, and scramble left along ledges to enter the mouth of the Great Siq. Continue up through large boulders and walk into the tree filled upper hanging valley.

The route ascends the right (S) wall of the Great Siq, from the inner end of the canyon. The occasional white arrow or cairn mark the line of the route. The only route finding problems in the lower half are at the very start where the way zig-zags up (never more than 2+) to reach the long and obvious ledge which rises gently up the S side of the siq, all the way to the domes, the exit being marked by giant old junipers. A short chimney (3) is the only obstacle along this ramp line.

Once in the little hollow at the start of the domes (possible water) care must again be taken with route finding. The way goes east, then back west above the hollow, then SE towards the summit, past an awkward descent (3), and up domes, before turning back right down slabs W, to a sandy plateau. The route then goes SE again to the col just below the top, on the N ridge.

PLEASE DO NOT CARVE YOUR NAME ON THE SUMMIT!

Approach: By Bedouin taxi (10km) to below Sabbah's Siq.
Descent: Either reverse the route (2 - 3 hours) or make a traverse of the mountain, descending by Hammad's Route. (Hammad is the son of Sheikh Hamdan.) See R.60. If you carry enough water, it is of course possible to spend the night near the summit, where there are good bivouac sites on the W side, to watch the sunset (or you can bivouac on Hammad's Route, on the way down). Like R.91 this is a popular and unforgettable trip for guided parties but well worth doing by anyone.

Amen Dome, South Face

93. Simsalabim. *A. Precht, S. Inhoger, W.Haupolter, 15th April 1990.*
Nice climbing up the obvious ramp and crack system in the middle of the big flat wall on very good rock, especially the two top pitches which are fascinating and really great! 300m. T.D. 3 hours. Maps page 56 and 87.
Approach: By Bedouin taxi and up R.92 to enter the

Amen Dome, South Face, Simsalabim

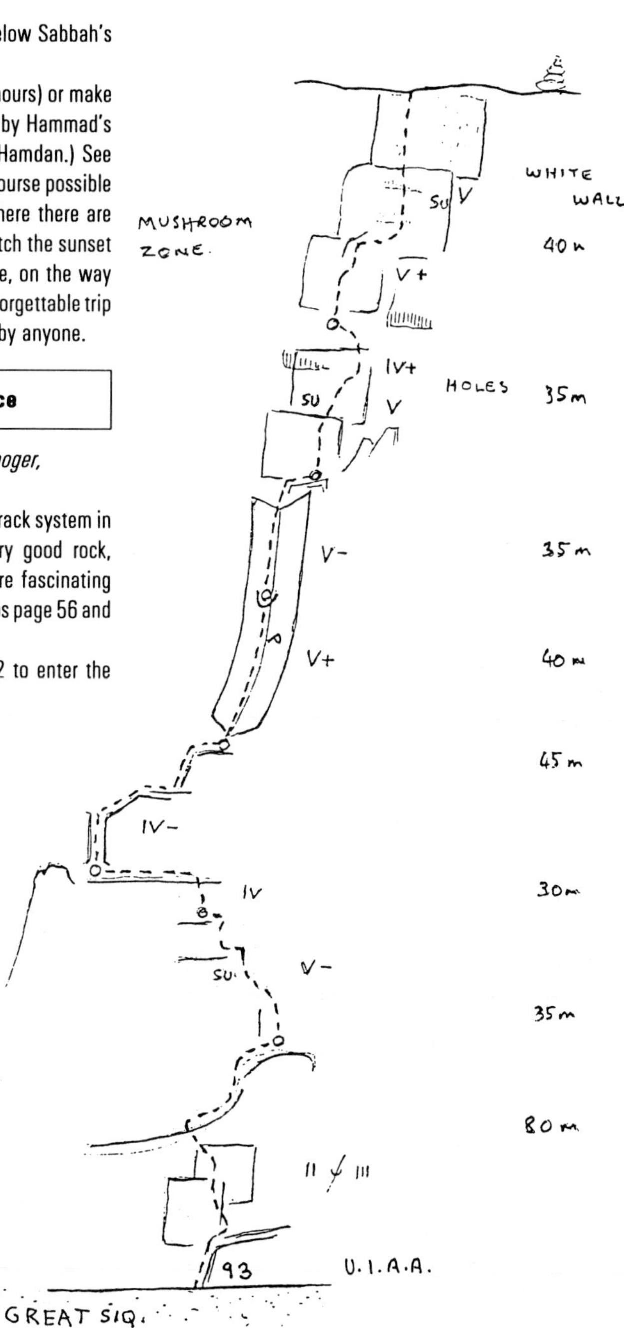

Great Siq. The wall is located left (north) of the siq (1 hour).

Descent: Walk towards the north and down climb into the northern canyon and walk back to the start along the terrace, above Wadi Hassa (45 mins).

94. Sabbah's North West Passage *First recorded ascent, Sabbah Atieeq, C. Jaccoux, B.Domenech and party April 1987.*

A typically long, technically easy but beautiful and spectacular Bedouin route with the usual peculiar route finding aided to some extent by Bedouin cairns.

The route covers about three kilometres to the North Plateau bivouac, from where it picks up the summit route of Al Thalamiyyah to the top, another kilometre away across the Great Siq (abseil).

A splendid outing. Allow 3 - 5 hours to gain the bivouac sites and another hour to the top. About 4km. Overall grade P.D. 4 - 6 hours.

Complete trip, up the NW Passage and down Hammad's Route. P.D. Sup. Allow 6 - 9 hours. Maps pages 41, 48, 56.

Follow Sheikh Hamdan's Route to below the Great Siq. Continue N, below its entrance, and along the obvious ledge below the W Face, passing a hanging siq and eventually arriving at a huge overhung cave used by Bedouin as a shelter for sheep and goats.

To gain the hanging valley above, ascend Bedouin steps left of the cave. Continue up, trending left, then go right to enter the right-hand siq with trees inside its 50m wide canyon. This is the highest point reached by the Bedouin shepherds and their animals.

Enter the siq and continue as it narrows, passing a little siq on the left and eventually reaching an impasse. Return about 100m to the small siq and ascend a stepped wall, 40m (2), to the top. Descend 10m and traverse right along a little ledge, 50m (3) to regain the main siq at a point beyond and above the impasse which is overcome by a short passage of 3/4, to arrive on a ledge, some 30m long.

The siq now presents a fissure after which there is a ridge in its centre, which is taken to its top (2, 3). After a 30m chimney (3) a ledge on the right is followed to the plateau NW of Wave Dome. The route joins Al Thalamiyyah just beyond this point, where it drops into the North Desert. Continue by that route to the abseil across the Great Siq, and thence the summit.

Approach: By Bedu taxi as for Sheikh Hamdan's Route.

Descent: By Hammad's Route (R.60)

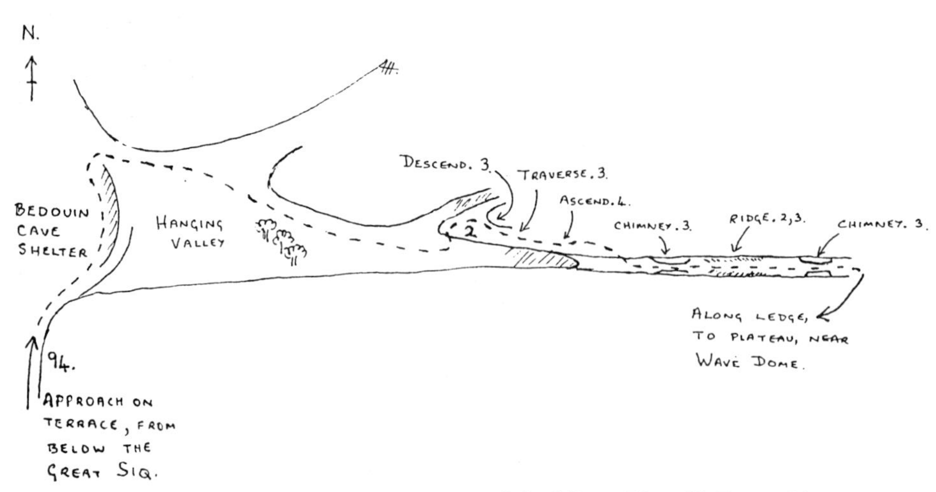

Jebel Rum Massif, Entry Siq, Sabbah's North West Passage

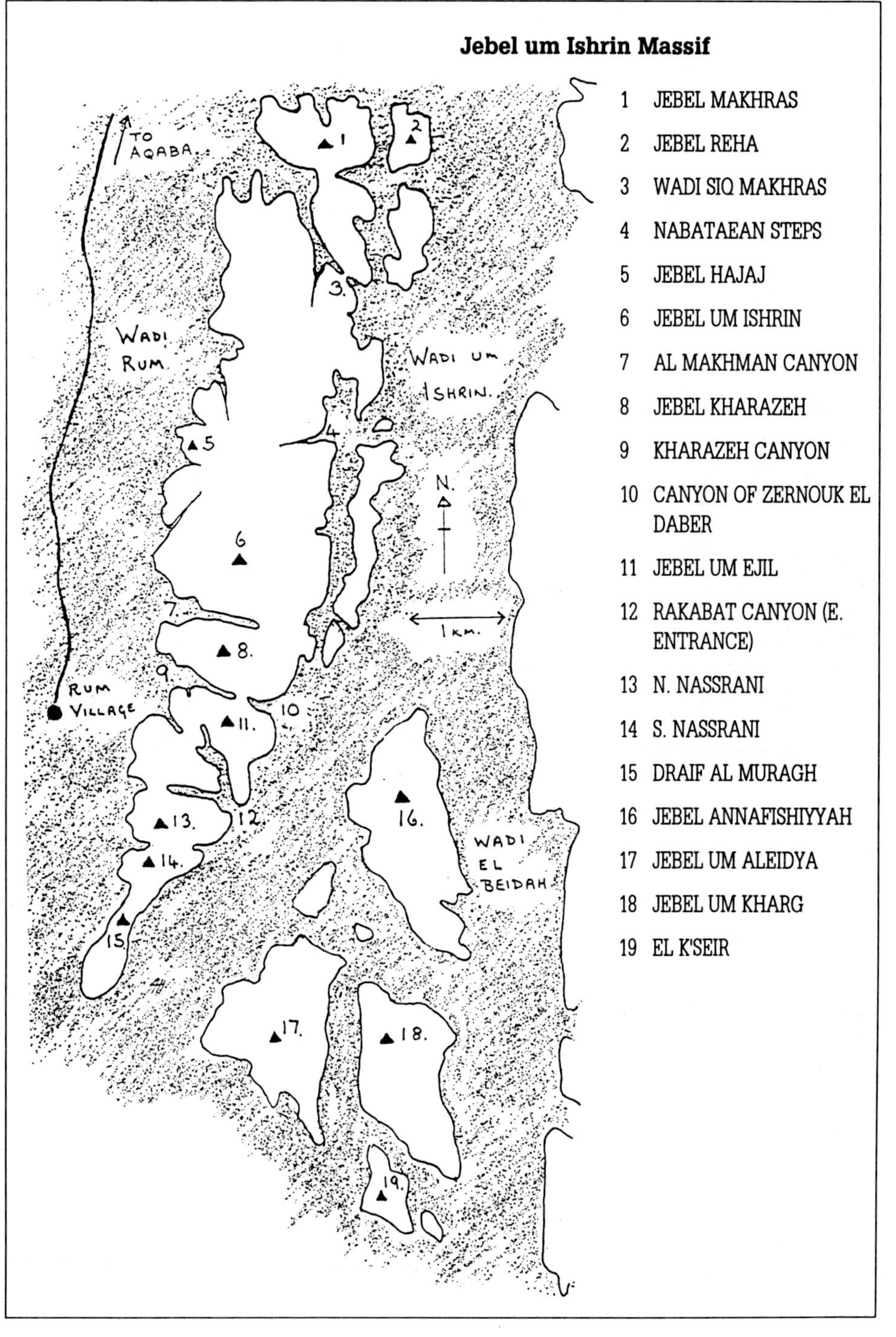
Jebel um Ishrin Massif
1 JEBEL MAKHRAS
2 JEBEL REHA
3 WADI SIQ MAKHRAS
4 NABATAEAN STEPS
5 JEBEL HAJAJ
6 JEBEL UM ISHRIN
7 AL MAKHMAN CANYON
8 JEBEL KHARAZEH
9 KHARAZEH CANYON
10 CANYON OF ZERNOUK EL DABER
11 JEBEL UM EJIL
12 RAKABAT CANYON (E. ENTRANCE)
13 N. NASSRANI
14 S. NASSRANI
15 DRAIF AL MURAGH
16 JEBEL ANNAFISHIYYAH
17 JEBEL UM ALEIDYA
18 JEBEL UM KHARG
19 EL K'SEIR
TO AQABA
WADI RUM
WADI UM ISHRIN.
N.
1 KM.
RUM VILLAGE
WADI EL BEIDAH

JEBEL UM ISHRIN MASSIF

Major features of Jebel um Ishrin (1753m)
The massif is divided by canyons into a number of obvious (and not so obvious) separate peaks. The actual summit of Jebel um Ishrin is 1,753 metres, one metre less than Jebel Rum, or so the map says. It is midway along the massif, with numerous minor summits further north. Immediately south is the canyon of Al Makhman, whilst the next huge canyon to the south is known to the Bedouin as Bahr al Kharazeh, at its western (Wadi Rum) end, and as Zernouk el Daber at its eastern (Wadi um Ishrin) end. Between Al Makhman Canyon and Kharazeh Canyon is the peak we named Jebel al Kharazeh (ref: 366748) with east and west summits at 1,580 metres.

Immediately south again is a rather complex area split diagonally from NW to SE by a labyrinth of canyons known as Rakabat Um Ejil, giving an easy but intricate passage through the massif. East of this passage and just south of Kharazeh Canyon is the prominent flat topped peak of Jebel Um Ejil (1,431 metres). Immediately below to the west and splitting the north end of the ravines of Rakabat Um Ejil are the north and south tops of Jebel Rakabat with a small col between (ref: 360740). South of here across more narrow ravines is Jebel Um Ejil South Summit (1,380 metres) with the slightly lower West Summit (1,320 metres) between it and Wadi Rum when viewed from the Rest House.

South again are the gloomy depths of North Nassrani Canyon, then the two great domes of North and South Nassrani. Beyond here, the range tails off to the minor summit of Draif Al Muragh.

East of here is the huge and beautiful desert valley of Wadi um Ishrin with a group of smaller peaks in its southern entrance. Only the northern one - Jebel Annafishiyyah - has any climbs on at the moment.

Jebel Makhras 1200m

This is the small summit at the extreme N end of the massif. Its W face is split by four major couloirs. The left-hand one is:

95. Finir En Beaute *Y.Astier, M.Kunkler 1988.*
The route follows the line of the chimney. Poor rock to start but improving above with a 5+/6A slab to enter the upper chimneys, the final rope lengths are best taken out to the left up overhanging rock (4 and 5). "Magical ambience". Easier variations possible, up the chimneys. 300m. D. Sup.

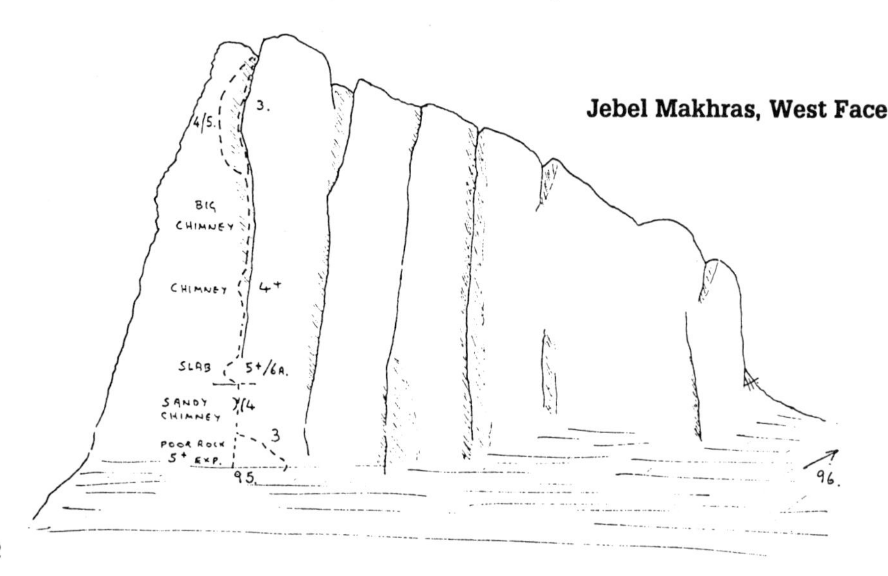

Approach: By Bedouin taxi up Wadi Rum to the foot of the climb (7km).
Descent: By abseil down the route.

96. Wadi Siq Makhras (Valley of Stones).

This pleasant little valley separates Jebel Makhras from the main bulk of Jebel um Ishrin and, apart from the maze of ravines that form Rakabat Canyon, this is the only easy way to cross through this mountain, from Wadi Rum to Wadi um Ishrin.

The entrance is 7km north of Rum village and immediately S of the first summit (Jebel Makhras). 2.5km. Allow 3/4 hour to walk through to Wadi um Ishrin. Map page 91.

From the mouth of the valley, it is an enjoyable walk following the wadi bed generally SE as it narrows to a small ravine, rising up to emerge suddenly just above the red sands of Wadi um Ishrin.

200m or so further on, and slightly right, a light coloured flat topped mushroom of rock can be easily gained. On it's top are inscriptions of feet, two separately and pointing in different directions and another set which appear to be a family group.

Once in Wadi um Ishrin, a number of possibilities present themselves for the walker: it is of course simple to return by the same route, total distance approx. 5km, or:

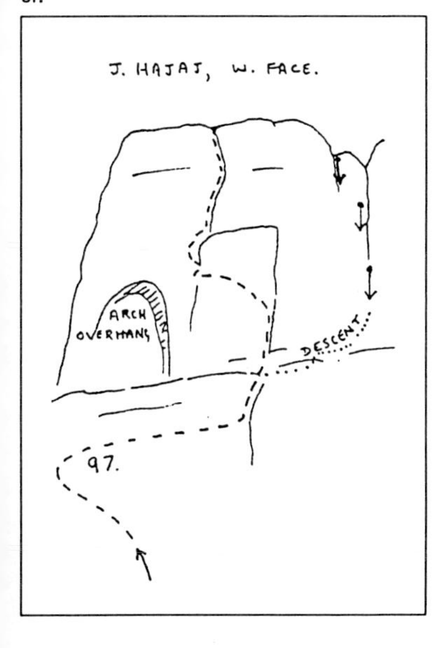

Jebel Hajaj, N. Summit, West Face

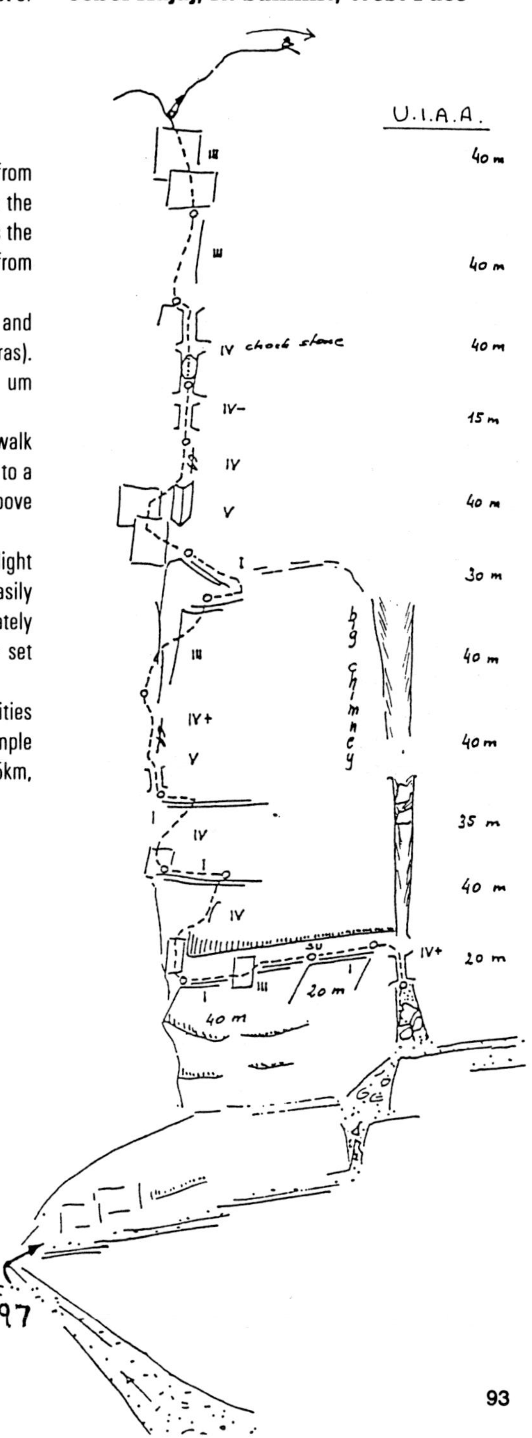

Jebel Hajaj, S. Summit, Mohammed Musa's Route

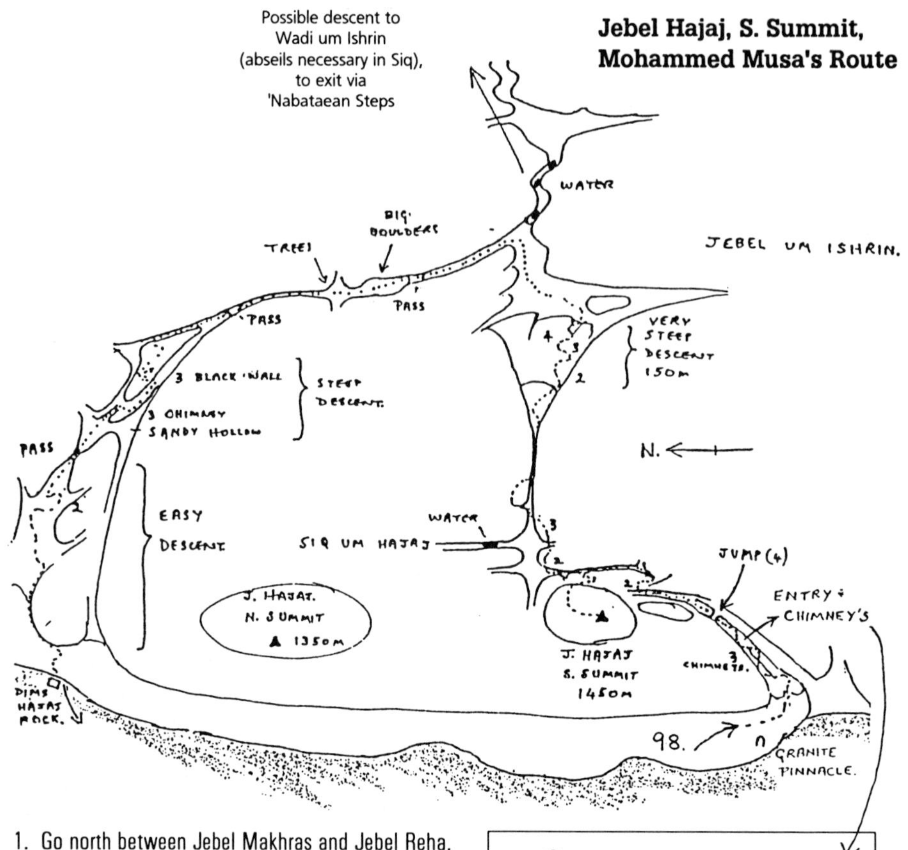

1. Go north between Jebel Makhras and Jebel Reha, then W round Makhras to return to the starting point in Wadi Rum. Total distance approximately 8km.
2. Go E across Wadi um Ishrin, and NE to Disi through Siq um Tawagi (R.186). Total distance approx. 10km.
3. Continue SE across Wadi um Ishrin passing N of Jebel Barrah, to reach the N entrance of Barrah Canyon. Total distance about 11km. From here, the walk can be continued through Barrah Canyon and back to Rum on a second day.
4. Go S keeping close to the E flank of Jebel um Ishrin to enter a desert canyon running down its E side after 2km. (At the entrance to this valley, is a side valley going into the mountain on the right. Here will be found Nabataean steps cut into the rock on the S side and leading up into a higher valley, to a narrow ravine with pools of water - see R.101.)

Continue down the desert canyon to the S for about 2.5km and 1km further on, pass the impressive

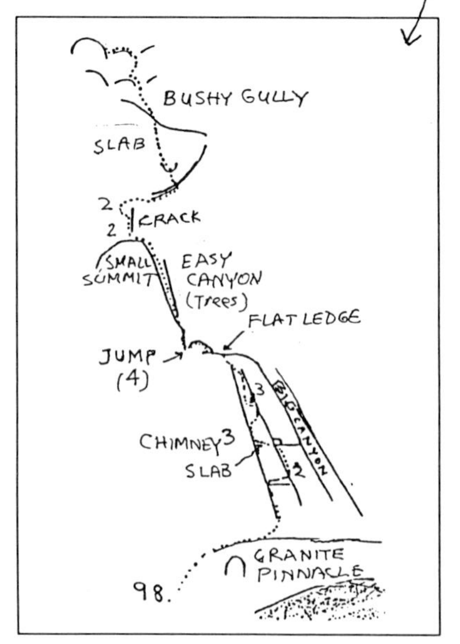

ravine of Zernouk el Daber which cleaves its way dramatically W to Wadi Rum but is not passable without ropes. Just over another kilometre further S, will be found the entrance to Rakabat Canyon with many bushes, just before the big red dune. This makes a fascinating way back through the mountain to the Rest House. (R.130). Total distance, approximately 14km.

Jebel Um Hajaj, N Summit 1350m

This summit is NW of the high point of Jebel um Ishrin. Its W face is identified by an arched overhang to the left and an obvious chimney-crack to the right. This is the line of:

97. West Face Route *W.Haupolter, A.Precht, H.Gufler 20th April, 1989.*

A nice climb with interesting route finding on good rock. 300m. D. Sup. 3½ hours. Top page 93.

Approach: Walk 3km NE across Wadi Rum (or take a Bedouin taxi). Reach the foot of the climb by ascending screes below the arch, then going right and up the big chimney until it is necessary to rope up, just before a leftward traverse.

Descent: Go. S, and abseil down the couloir S of the tower, to a long ledge which goes round N to the start of the climb 1½ hours.

The next summit immediately south, and separated from the main top of Jebel um Ishrin by a huge diagonal couloir, easily seen from the Rest House is:

Jebel Hajaj, South Summit 1450m

98. Mohammed Musa's Route *First recorded ascent: Sabbah Atieeq, D.Taylor, A.Howard 8th April 1992.*

Named in memory of one of our best friends in Wadi Rum whose tent used to be in the valley just below Jebel Hajaj, from where he showed us the line of the route many years ago. Mohammed was later tragically killed in a car accident.

The route is simple in concept, but confusingly complex in detail if the easiest way is to be followed, with only a couple of moves harder than grade 3. In fact, it is a masterpiece of Bedouin route-finding! The ascent route goes up left of the diagonal couloir below and left of the summit of Jebel um Ishrin, seen from the Rest House. The top is reached in 2 hours.

If you have done a Bedouin Route to the top of Jebel Rum, and been through the Rakabat Canyon system and want a really challenging adventure, this is the route to try. You need to be climbing grade 3 without ropes and above big canyons and crevasses, with confidence. 3km with 400m of ascent and descent. P.D. Sup. 5 hours. N.B. A Bedouin Guide (Sabbah Atieeq) is recommended! Map and topo page 94.

Approach across the desert (½ hour) and go up scree left of a granite pinnacle and walk behind it to reach the starting chimneys left of the main gully.

Descent through a maze of 'siqs' to the major canyon of Siq um Ishrin takes 1 hour approx., and a similar time is necessary for the return to Wadi Rum through more canyons. With an abseil (or 2) it should be easy to go down Siq um Ishrin to Wadi um Ishrin, the last section being down Nabataean Steps (see R.101). This would

Jebel um Ishrin Massif, West Face from Wadi Rum

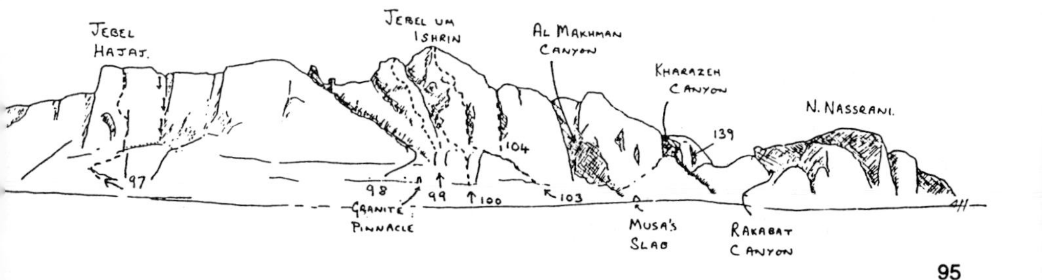

make an excellent 'through-route'. Driver required to pick up at the end!

Jebel um Ishrin, North Top 1560m

West Face

99. Hot Dog *W.Haupolter, A.Precht, S.Inhoger 9th April, 1989.*

In spite of big variations in pitch difficulty, the route offers excellent climbing with a magnificent roof at the end. 400m. E.D. Inf. 4 hours. Map page 95.

Approach: Cross the desert (30 mins) to the start of the climb in the left-hand of two chimneys right of Mohammed Musa's Route.

Descent: Abseil down to the terrace and cross south to 'Thunderstorm', which is then abseiled and down-climbed 1½ - 2 hours.

Jebel um Ishrin, West Top

West Face

100. Thunderstorm *A Precht, W.Haupolter, S.Inhoger 9th April, 1990.*

Enjoyable climbing in great scenery. It is possible to gain the summit of Jebel um Ishrin by crossing over to join The Left Crack. 400m. T.D. Sup. 3½ hours. Map page 95..

Jebel um Ishrin West Face Climbs

Jebel um Ishrin, West Face, Hot Dog and Thunderstorm

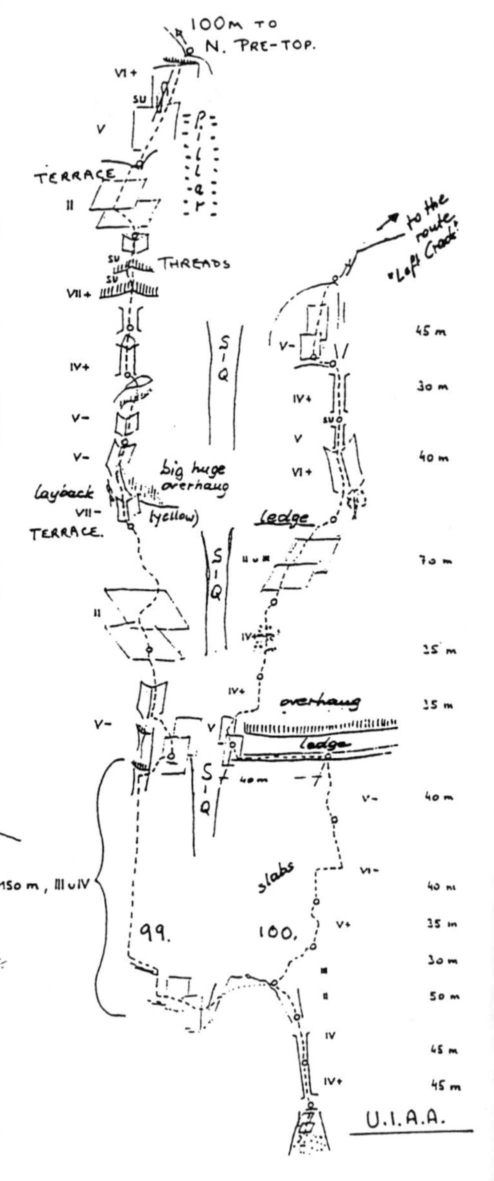

Wadi um Ishrin

Top right:
View south to Jebel Khazali
photo Howard

Centre:
View north west to Jebel um Ishrin
photo Howard

Climbs on Jebel um Ishrin Massif

Below:
Mohammed Musa's Route, Jebel Hajaj, with Sabbah Atieeq
photo Howard

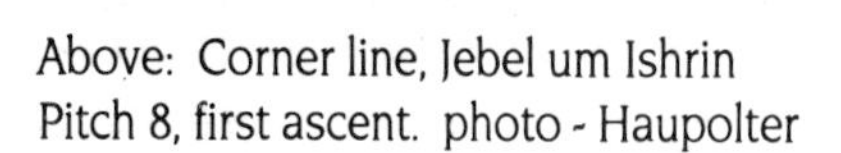

Above: Corner line, Jebel um Ishrin
Pitch 8, first ascent. photo - Haupolter

Below: Vanishing Pillar, Jebel Kharazeh,
first ascent - photo Taylor. Above right: Essence of Rum, Rakabat Canyon - photo Howard

Approach: Cross Wadi Rum ($^1/_2$ hour).
Descent: Abseil and down-climb the route ($1^1/_2$ hours).

Jebel um Ishrin (Mountain of the Mother of Twenty) 1,753 metres (ref: 367758)

Named after a flash flood which killed 20 Bedouin in it's canyons.

101. Jebel um Ishrin Subsidiary Wadi

This runs parallel to Wadi um Ishrin and just west of it hidden by a row of small peaks on the east side of Jebel um Ishrin. It is about $2^1/_2$ kilometres long from ref: 375750 to 380772. Halfway through the wadi is a siq dropping down vertically from um Ishrin with a deep pool at the bottom - The waters of um Ishrin, ref: 376761.

About 1 kilometre further north at ref: 378771 is the entrance to another siq system going west into the um Ishrin Massif where a well defined series of Nabataean steps will be found on its south wall leading to a hidden valley above a ravine filled with deep pools of water, (these being the reason for the steps). It may in fact be possible to reach the summit of Jebel um Ishrin by following this valley west and then south towards the top.

102. Eastern Route

A Bedouin route to this peak is reported from Wadi um Ishrin. Leave this for the above mentioned Subsidiary Wadi on its west at 375750. Take a gully system from this point just inside the entrance of the small wadi heading slightly west of north for about half a kilometre eventually rising round west onto the shoulder of Jebel um Ishrin. The summit is then due south about half a kilometre away

103. Jebel um Ishrin, West Face: The Left Crack *A.Precht, W.Haupolter, H.Gufler 23rd April 1989.*

A long and intimidating route which is less difficult than its appearance suggests. Great scenery, and excellent black and water polished rock in chimneys, cracks and slabs, finishing 100m below the main summit, on a pre-top-500m T.D. Inf. 5 hours. Mapspages 95 and 96.
Approach: Cross the desert from the Rest House for 2km

Jebel um Ishrin West Face, Left Cracks

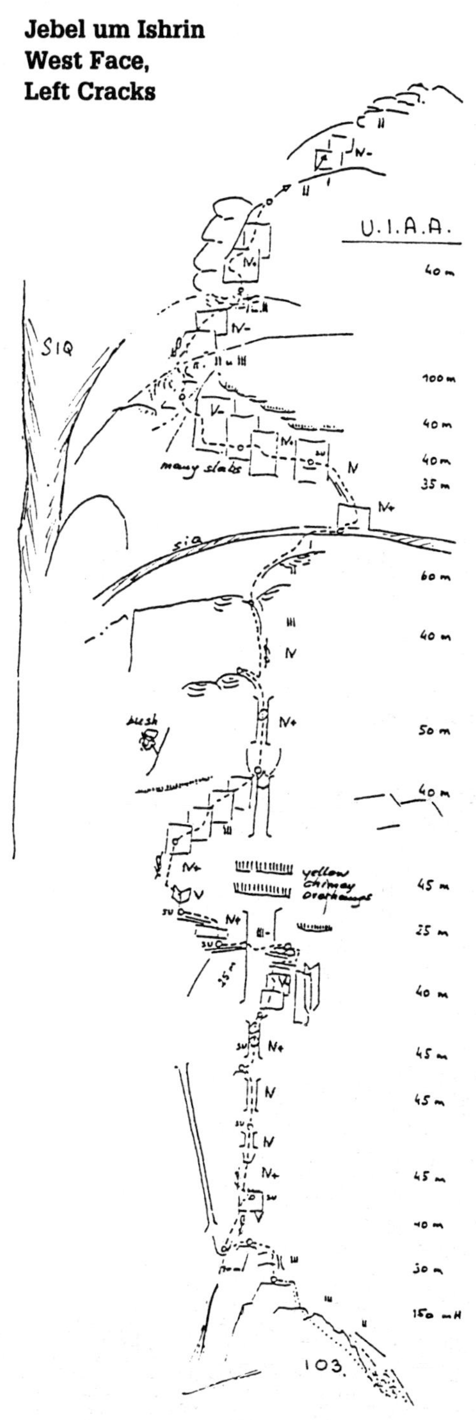

Jebel um Ishrin
West Face, Gluntz and variations

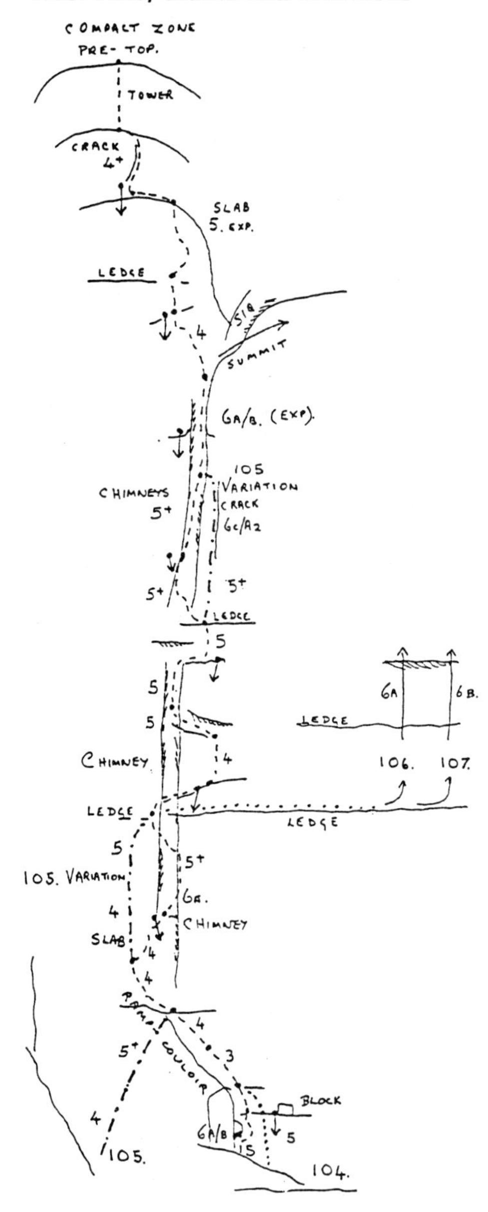

NE to below the left-hand of the two great crack lines. Go left up a little siq behind a tower to the foot of the chimney.

Descent: Down-climb and abseil the route. 2 hours.

104. Gluntz *C.&Y. Remy 23rd April, 1986.*

A long and interesting route with some difficult and exposed passages, following the system of cracks and chimneys, on the right of the West Face. The route finishes at a tower below a compact zone of rock; from there, it should be possible to gain the summit by making two rappels, to the right of this compact zone to reach route R.117. 500 metres T.D. (not sustained), 6 hours ascent. Maps pages 95, 96 and 103.

Alternatively to reach the summit: from belay 13, at the level of the Siq go to the right through an area of domes to reach Le jour le plus long (R.117).

Approach: From the Rest House, to the north east, 20 minutes (or by 4-wheel drive) and five minutes up scree to the climb.

Descent: It is preferable to descend by route 117. 2 hours.

105. Gluntz Ameliore Variation *Yves Astier & Party 1987.*

A parallel and (its first ascentionists claim) better climb but with a section of A2. Both routes seem to share a common crux shown on the topo as 6A/B but reported by Astier as 7A. The first 300m like Gluntz includes some sandy rock, T.D. or 500m T.D. Sup if the route is taken to the top.

Immediately right of Gluntz but sharing the same start are two more Astier routes:

106. Voie Astier-Beauvais (1987)

Completed Astier and party 1990.

No precise details are available but the route traverses right out of Gluntz along the prominent ledge for about 200m, and ascends the wall above. 500m. T.D. Sup.

107. Guerre Et Paix *M.Kunkler Y.Astier. 1988.*

"A very recommended route, one of the most beautiful on the mountain" starting up Gluntz then right along the ledge to an obvious direct line of cracks and chimneys just right of the previous route with pitches of 6B. 500m. T.D. Sup. Precise details not available.

108. Canyon of Al Makhman (The Ambush, or Hiding Place) (ref: 360753)

Also referred to as "Mukman el Jaheleen", the Jaheleen

being a tribe of this area.

A walk of $1\frac{1}{2}$ kilometres approximately North East from the Rest House brings one to the entrance of the canyon. The highest summit of Jebel um Ishrin is above to the left (north). The summit to the right is Jebel Al Kharazeh.

The canyon bed is followed fairly easily, first up through a bed of polished water worn granite, and then up through various levels of sandstone, the huge walls closing in above. At the point where the granite finishes two little side canyons enter from left and right. Just left of the left canyon and immediately below the light coloured sandstone cliff will be found a Bedouin store place - a pile of stones with a cavity below and a trap door entrance. Nearby here and also below the next tower to the north are some Thamudic rock drawings.

Just left of the right canyon will be seen another pile of stones, these being Bedouin steps to a terrace along which goats are led into the upper main ravine. After this, a little scrambling along the line of the stream bed passing bowls cut into the floor by the action of the water, eventually leads to the head of the canyon where the walls meet. The length of the ravine is about one kilometre. Allow $1\frac{1}{2}$ - 2 hours for the return journey from the Rest House. Maps pages 95 and 103.

The next giant cleft is little more than half a kilometre to the south, and immediately east of the Rest House. This is the canyon of Bahr Al Kharazeh, with the nearby Rakabat Canyon.

Both Al Makhman and Kharazeh Canyons can be easily visited in a morning and give an interesting half day excursion, mostly in the shade, the foot of the cliffs of Jebel Kharazeh which divides the two canyons being the site of numerous 'enclosures' of single course stones, probably pre-Thamudic.

This area is also the location of:

Musa's Slab

A beautiful granite slab 20m high on the S side of the entrance to Al Makhman Canyon, 20 minutes walk from the Rest House. Named in memory of Mohammed Musa (see R.98). Maps pages 95 and 103.

The slab is in the shade until midday and is also a great place in the evenings. All the routes were originally climbed with top-rope protection but bolts have now been placed on some climbs which look very unsightly. In fact, some were removed by the Bedouin, but were later replaced. Left to right, the routes are:

109. The Nose *6B W.Colonna 14 April 1989.*

110. The Joker *6A A.Howard, D.Taylor 14 April 1989.*

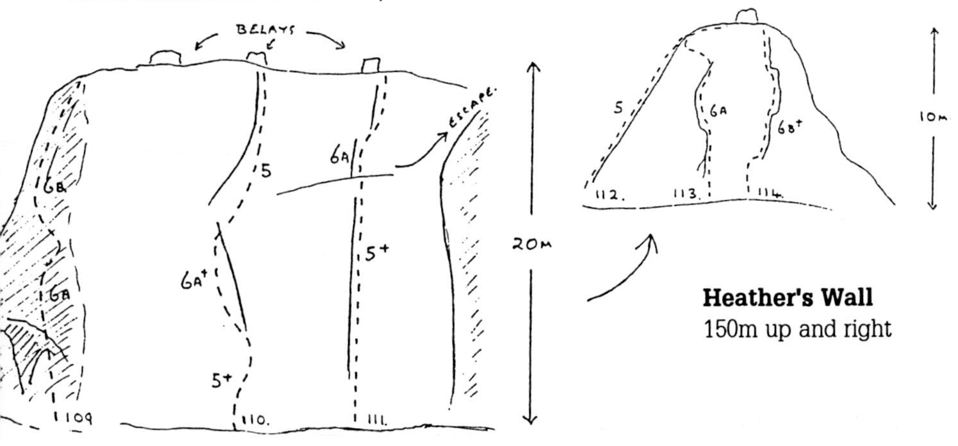

Heather's Wall
150m up and right

Musa's Granite Slab

Jebel um Ishrin
S.W.Pillar
De Grès ou de Force

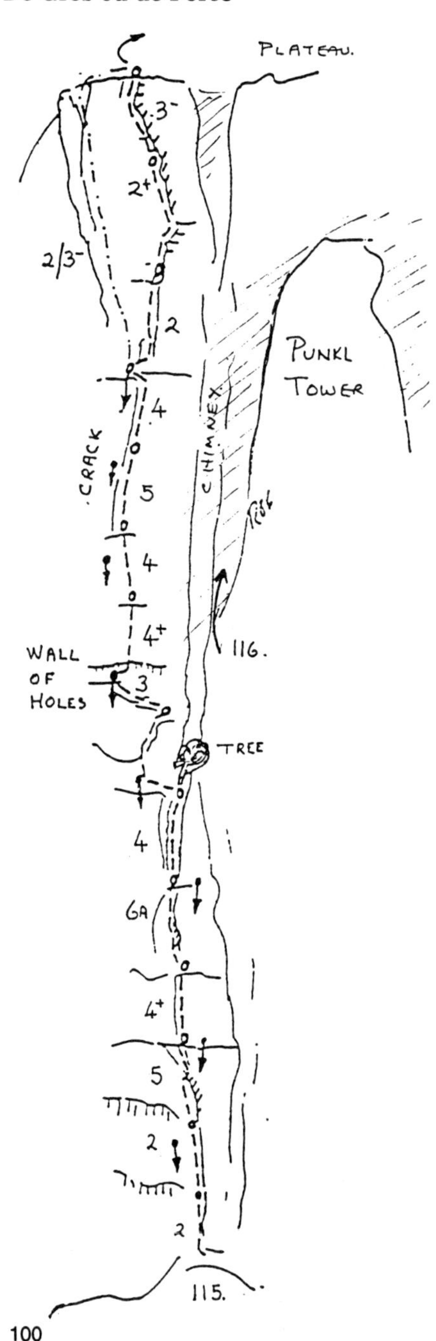

111. The Scorpion *6A A.Howard, D.Taylor 14 April 1989*

Just before going to press, some belated notes were received from M. Pearce and P. Laver indicating that they climbed these three routes on 5th October 1988. "Like you, we also used top ropes as we did not wish to place bolts in this unspoilt area." The bolts should be removed again!

150m to the right of here and higher up are three more top-rope problems of 10m length, also on granite. First ascentionists not known. Topos page 99.

112. Left Arête *5*

113. The Wall *6A*

114. Heather's Route *6B+.*

Jebel um Ishrin

SW Pillar

115. De Grès Ou De Force *C.&Y.Remy 23 October 1986.*

Situated inside the entrance of Makhman Canyon, the route ascends an obvious line of chimneys 50m left of an immense diedre, passing a tree and moving left to ascend the ridge, evident from the Rest House. Once above the big diedre it is possible to join Le jour le plus long to gain the summit: like it says, a long day! 400m. T.D. Inf. Maps pages 101 and 103.

Approach: As for R.108, and up left ¾ hour.

Descent: Down-climb and rappel the route. 1¼ hours.

Just right of the previous route is a prominent tower on the left side of the left wall of the big corner.

Punkl Tower

116. Corner Line *A.Precht, W.Haupolter 18th April 1990.*

The obvious corner up the left edge of the dark tower can only be reached through the chimney system of De gres ou de force. The upper part offers excellent and difficult climbing mostly in cracks. There are two short passages of poor rock (good protection). Impressive and steep! 350m. E.D. Sup. 6 hours. Maps and topos 101 and 103.

Approach: As R.108.

Jebel um Ishrin
Punkl Tower, Corner Line

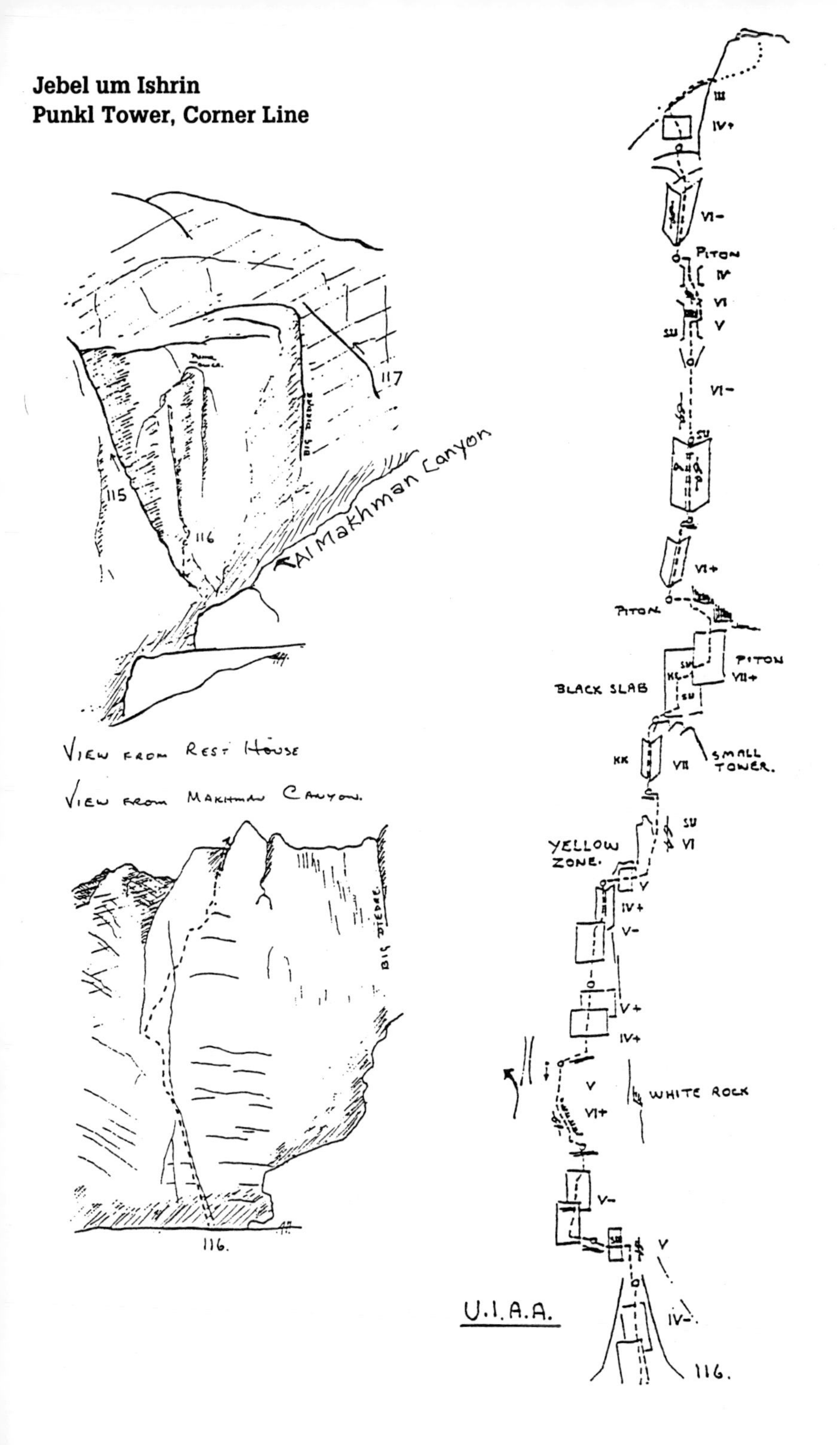

Jebel um Ishrin, South West Face, Le Jour Le Plus Long

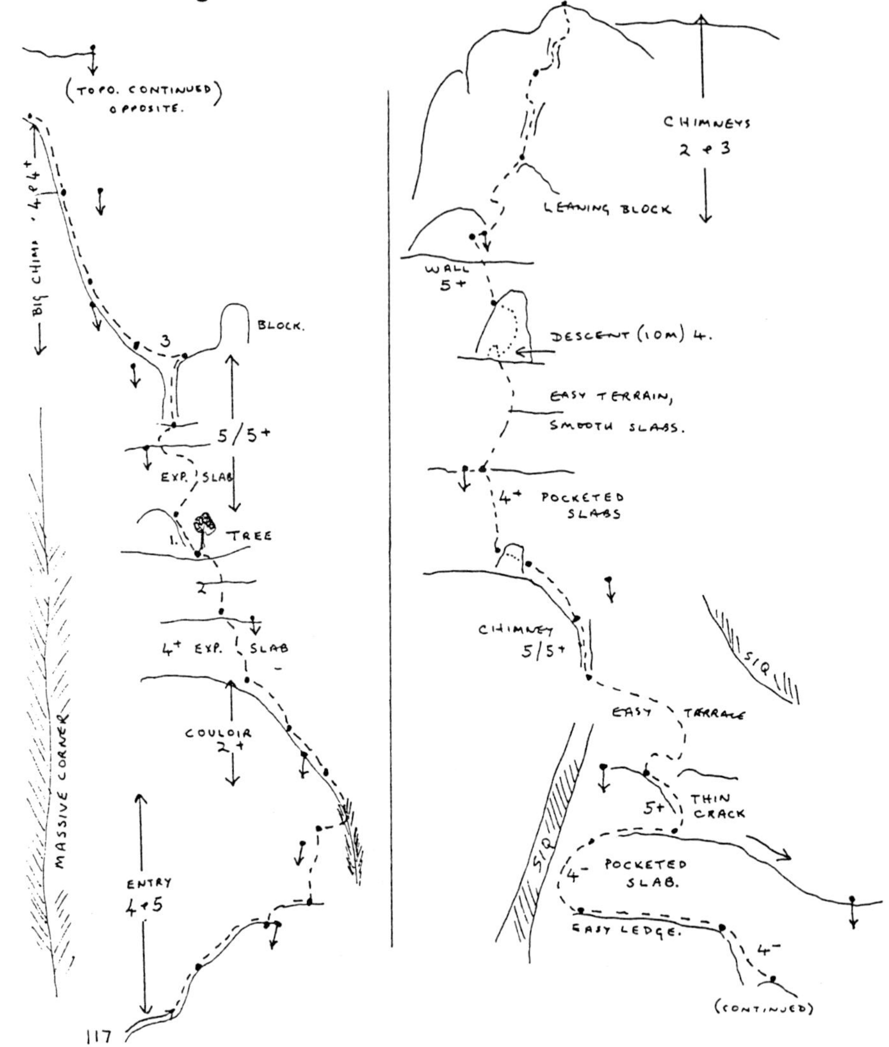

Descent: Abseil and down-climb a small siq to the west to reach R.115. Down this $1\frac{1}{2}$ hours.

117. SW Face, le Jour le Plus Long

C.&Y.Remy 1st May 1986.

Beautiful and long climb, not very sustained. Protection obvious (exposed passages in 8th and 11th pitches). Good belays. The climb ascends large flakes and passes the big tree in the middle of the wall, easily seen from the Rest House. From belay 16, the way to the summit through the domes is long and not obvious but not sustained. T.D. Inf. 600 metres (400 metres on the wall). Ascent 6 hours. Maps pages 101 and 103.

Approach: From the Rest House, towards the north east 20 minutes, (or by 4-wheel drive) to Al Makhman Canyon (route 108), and then to the left through a

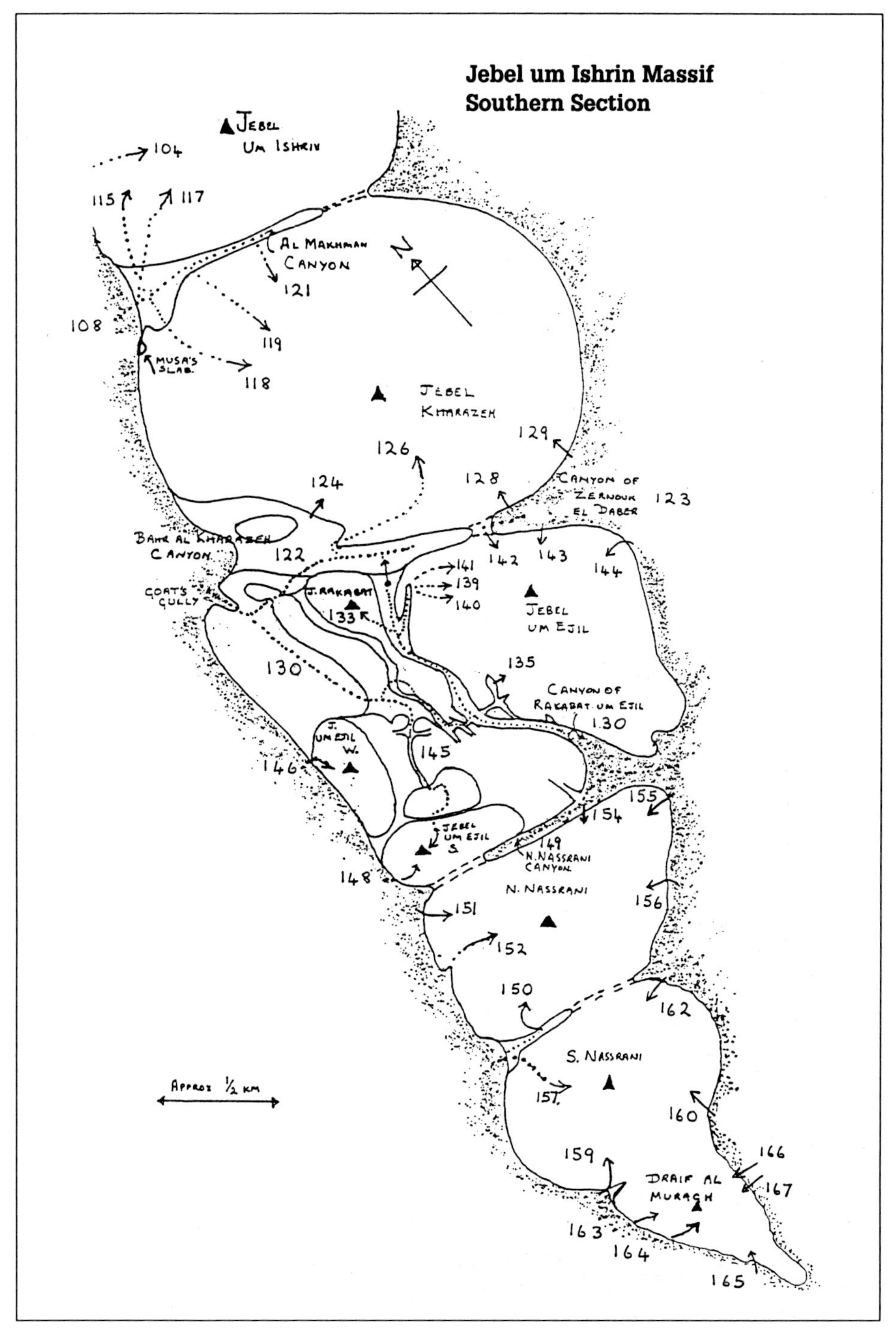

Jebel um Ishrin Massif
Southern Section
Jebel
Um Ishrin
104
115
117
Al Makhman
Canyon
121
108
119
Musa's
Slab
118
Jebel
Kharazeh
129
126
124
128
Canyon of
Zernouk
el Daber
123
Bahr al Kharazeh
Canyon
122
142
143
144
141
139
140
Goat's
Gully
J. Rakabat
133
Jebel
um Ejil
130
135
Canyon of
Rakabat um Ejil
130
J.
um Ejil
W.
145
146
155
154
Jebel
um Ejil
S
149
N. Nassrani
Canyon
148
N. Nassrani
151
156
152
150
162
S. Nassrani
Approx ½ km
157
160
159
166
Draif al
Muragh
167
163
164
165

couloir with some sections of 2 to the foot of the red flakes, right of the immense diedre (10 minutes).
Descent: Long and not so obvious between the domes but rapid and direct down the face. 3 hours.

Jebel Al Kharazeh. (Mountain of the Sea-Stone Canyon) 1,580m (ref: 367748)

The first routes on this peak start from Al Makhman Canyon.

118. North West Pillar, Le Jardin Secret

C.&Y.Remy 2nd May 1986.
Good varied climbing, not too sustained and with good protection except in the last exposed pitch. 200 metres. D. Sup. Ascent 3 hours. Map page 103.
Approach: From the Rest House, 20 minutes to the north east into the canyon of Al Makhman (Route 108), then enter the little siq on the right, and follow it until directly below a big diedre. Continue on a ledge on the left until directly below a big chimney and ascend 20 metres by climbing a crack (3) in a slab and then follow a good ledge on the left (many cairns). Arrow scratched on the start of the route (20 minutes).
Descent: Abseil down the route (7 abseils) from below the summit domes. 1 hour.

Jebel Kharazeh, North Face

119. Barraud *C.&Y.Remy 30th April 1986.*

Nice route, varied and not very sustained; the rock is a little broken at the base but becomes good higher up. Good belays and protection (except for the 4th rope length). 350 metres. T.D. Inf. Ascent 5 hours. Maps and topos pages 103 and 105.
Approach: From the Rest House, 20 mins to the north east to enter Al Makhman Canyon (Route 108). Continue up it for 150 metres (10 minutes).

The route ascends the obvious lines of cracks on the left, right of a huge couloir. The start is defined by three parallel cracks. Take the centre one.
Descent: Abseils are not always easy to find. Descend to the left of the route, down a couloir chimney. 1½ hours.

120. Nos Amis *Astier and Beauvais 27th September 1987.*

300m left of Barraud, the route ascends cracks and slabs for eight pitches of 4 and 5+ finishing in a 6C/7A corner (4 pegs in place). 300m. T.D. Sup 4½ hours.
Approach & Descent: The route is at the inner end of Makhman Canyon but precise details are not known.

121. Rock Fascination. *A.Precht, W.Haupolter, W.Leitenecker 12th April, 1990.*

The route offers excellent climbing on very good rock

Jebel Kharazeh, N.W. Pillar

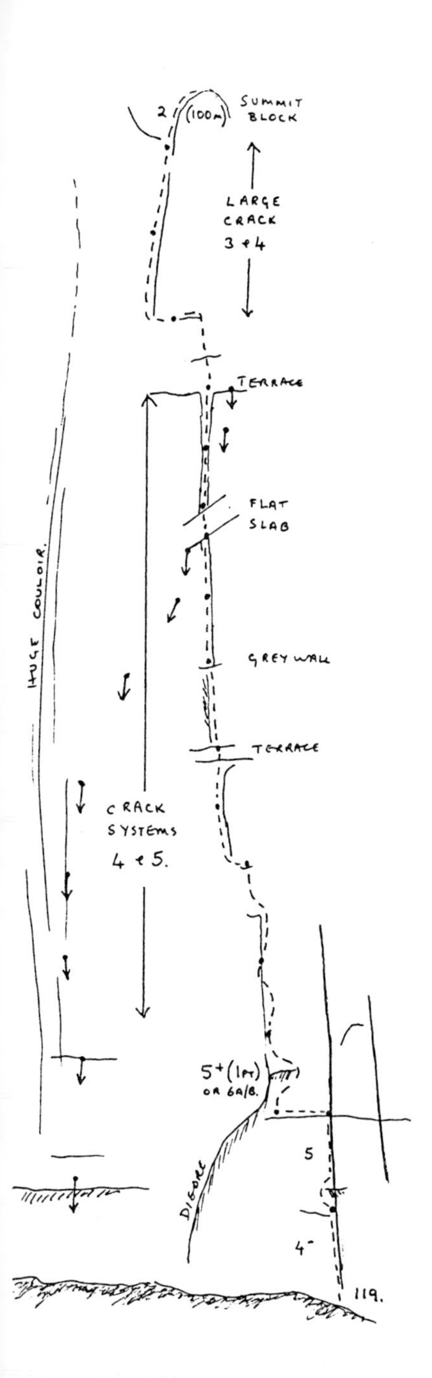

Jebel Kharazeh,
N. Face, Barraud

Jebel Kharazeh, North Face
Rock Fascination

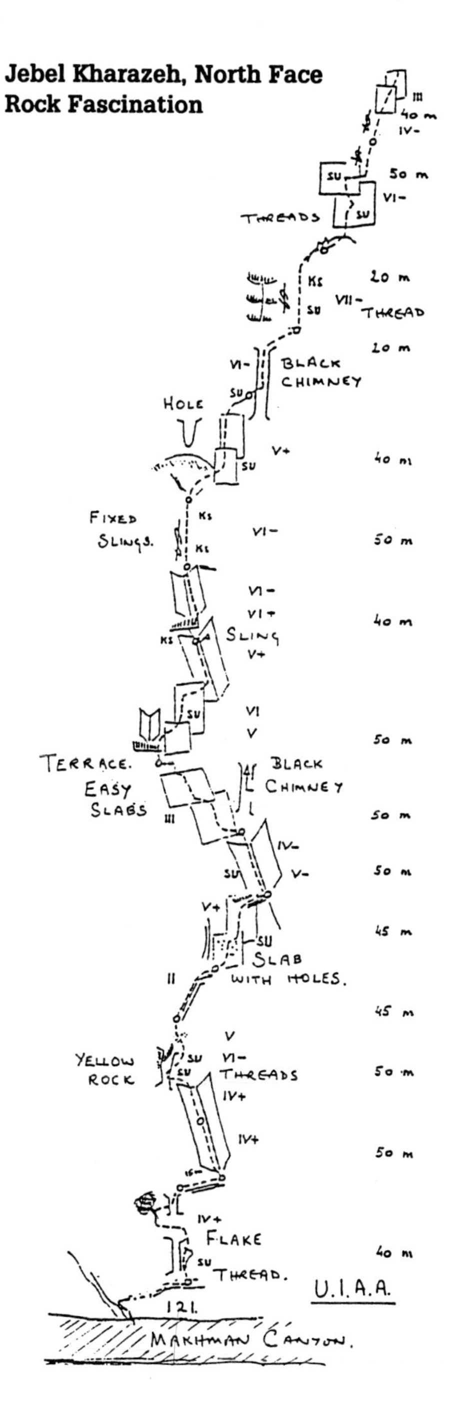

mostly in beautiful cracks (handcracks and corners). Some very interesting and surprising passages but with good protection. Many slings mark the route. A really great climb for a hot day! 500m. E.D. 6½ hours. Map and topo pages 103 and 105.

Approach: From the Rest House cross the desert and enter Makhman Canyon (R.108). The beginning is marked by a crack and chimney system in the inner part of the canyon (sling in the first pitch).

Descent: From the end of the climb, continue to the south to a slab traverse (3). Abseil 15m to a lower terrace and walk towards the north in the direction of the South West Pillar of Jebel um Ishrin till you reach some trees. Down-climb easily then abseil now along the route The Secret Garden. First abseil point a little bit north of the crack system. 1½ hours.

122. The Canyon of Bahr Al Kharazeh (Canyon of Sea Stones)

A walk of just over 1km from the Rest House leads to the entrance of the canyon visible as a huge gash in the skyline to the East. Just before this point three ways in exist. The left way involves a little scrambling and leads up to a plateau and round the left side of a tower before walking back into the main ravine. It is the most complex and least pleasant. The central way follows the most obvious water course and has a short steep section of climbing (4) to gain the first plateau and then goes more easily above, round the right side of the tower.

Most easily take R.130 up Goat's Gully to the plateau, across which a bushy gully will be seen going diagonally left up to a saddle.

Ascend this, then descend into the Canyon, above the lower cliff barrier, and walk easily up into the inner recesses with bizarre cliffs above. (It is possible to continue up and over the col (4) to reach the climbing routes in Zernouk el Daber, the eastern end of this canyon.) Allow 1½ - 2 hours for the return journey from the Rest House. Maps pages 95, 103 and 110.

The eastern continuation of Kharazeh Canyon can either be approached as above, or from Wadi um Ishrin:

123. Zernouk el Daber (Canyon of the Hyena)

When approached up Wadi um Ishrin this huge cleft is obvious, just over 3km from the S end of the massif.

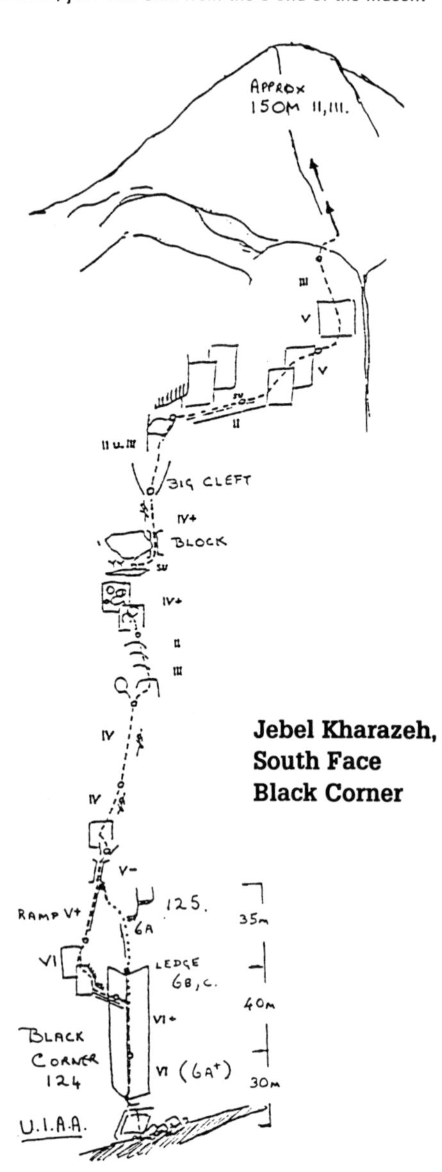

Jebel Kharazeh, South Face Black Corner

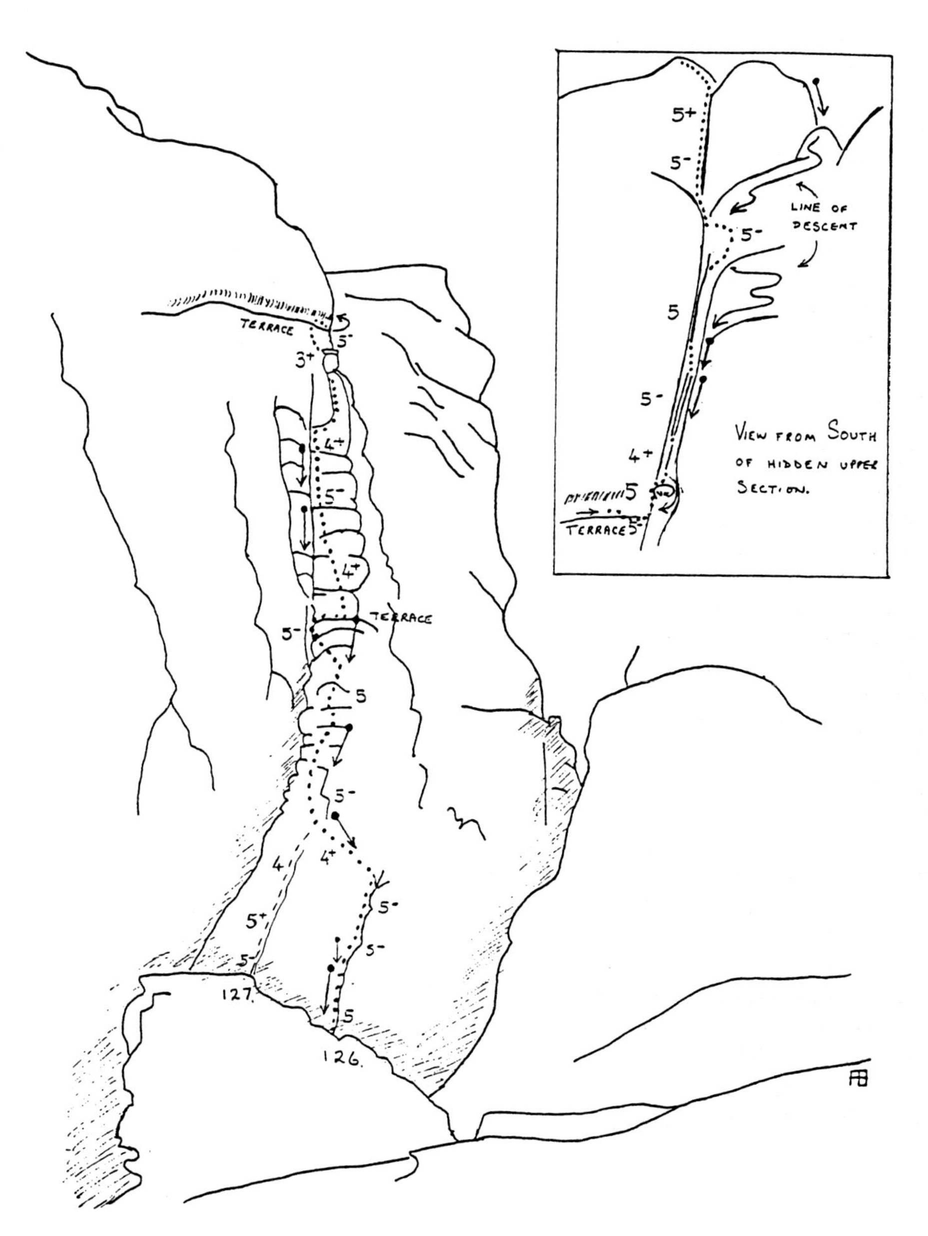

Jebel Kharazeh, South West Pillar
The Vanishing Pillar

From Wadi um Ishrin, walk into the secluded basin and scramble right up a boulder filled gully to a tree with many branches. From behind the large boulder on its left, make a long stride out (2) on to slabs. Go up these, and 10m higher move on to the top of another big boulder (1) then up a ramp into a chimney and bushy gully. Leave this for the easy ridge on its left, which is crossed leftwards on slabs to the next easy gully. After passing a boulder (1), carry on up, under a boulder and out on to the col. 0.5km. F. Allow 1/2 hour. Maps pages 103, 110.

Descent: Either by the same route, or usually by abseil into Kharazeh Canyon, and so to Wadi Rum (see R.132).

Jebel Kharazeh

South Face

124. Black Corner *W.Haupolter, A.Precht March 1988.*

Superb and varied climbing on very good black rock taking the obvious steep corner and crack line left of The Vanishing Pillar. 350m. E.D. Inf. 6 hours. Maps and topos pages 103 and 106.

Approach: Follow R.122 into Kharazeh Canyon and go N to gain the small canyon on the N side of The Vanishing Pillar. 3/4 hour.

Descent: Best down the NW face. From a small terrace with an obvious tree, a canyon and corner lead down the face via 4 abseils. 1 1/2 hours.

Starting from the same place as Black Corner, is an excellent three pitch climb:

125. Cat Fish Corner *W.Colonna and party November 1992.*

Ascend the Black Corner and continue for three pitches up pure finger cracks. 6A+/6B-6C/6A. Belays and abseil chains in situ. Topo page 106.

126. South West Pillar (Vanishing Pillar)

First ascent M.Shaw, A.Baker, A.Howard, D.Taylor 19th October 1984. (The first non-Bedouin route in Rum, and first ascent of this summit.)

The route follows the vanishing pillar of rock that rises above the north west edge of the entrance of Bahr al Kharazeh. From the end of the pillar, hidden chimneys,

Jebel Kharazeh, South Face South Corner

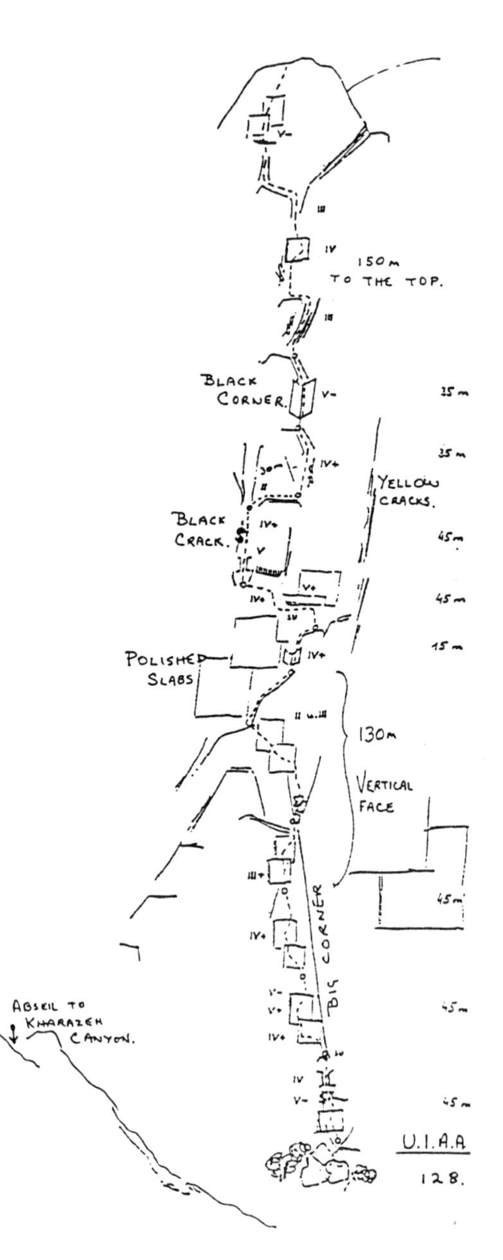

cracks and slabs lead up to the summit. The route gives good climbing on good rock with plenty of variety. 400m. Overall grade T.D. Inf. Allow 6 hours Maps and topos, pages 103 and 107.

Approach: From the Rest House cross the desert and enter the canyon of Al Kharazeh (R.122). The climb starts at the entrance of the upper narrow canyon, 70 metres left of the large fallen block in the sandy gully floor.

Descent: Just east of the summit a short descent of easy slabs (20 metres) leads to a lower terrace of easy angled rock above a 20 metre high wall. About 50 metres along this terrace to the right (south) is an in-situ peg for an abseil down the wall. A spare 5 or 6 metre length of tape or rope will be needed to form the abseil loop as the peg is well back from the edge. Descend easy slabs to regain the route. Abseils in situ where necessary (see topo). All abseil pegs and slings are in place though some will probably need replacing. A few metres of spare tape should be carried for this purpose and half a dozen pegs would be advisable, mostly long angles. Allow 3 hours. (Or it should be possible to use the quicker Secret Garden descent, 2 hours.)

127. The Disappearing Act Direct Start

G.Hornby, S.Sammut 9th November 1992.

This follows the left hand and more integral of the two grooves in the lower half of the pillar for three pitches (5-,5+,4), rejoining R.126 at the low angled area before the ridge steepens again. Topo page 107.

Jebel Kharazeh, South East Face
Eulenverschneidung

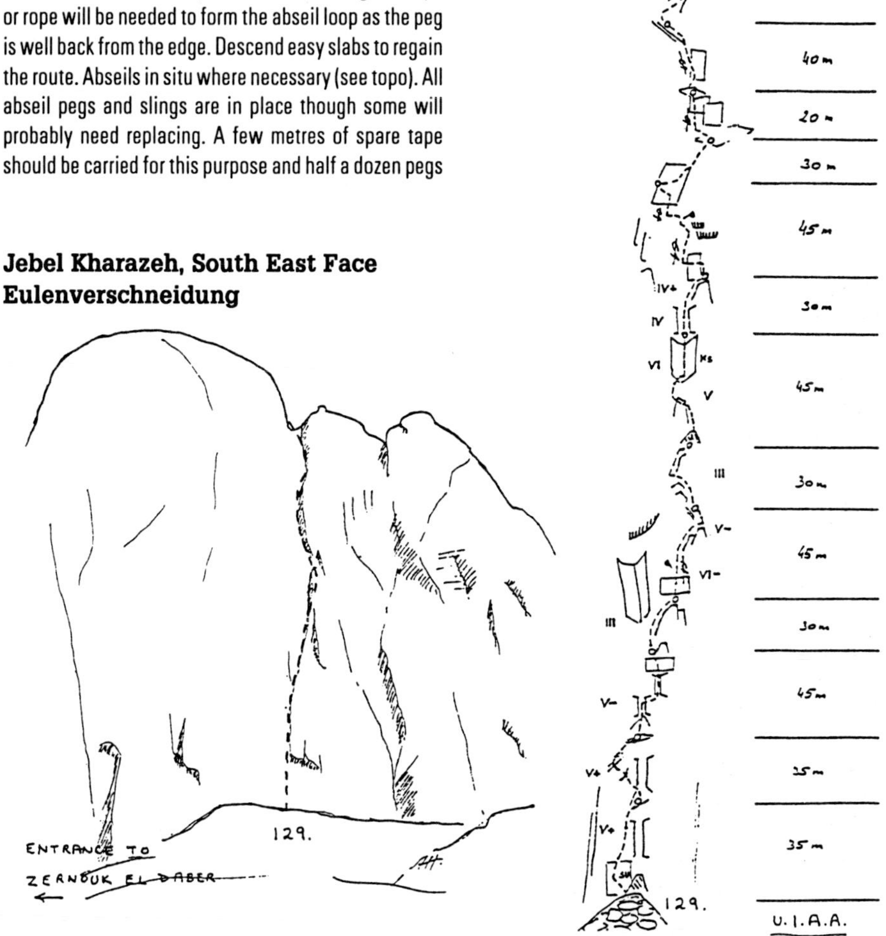

128. South Corner *A.Precht, W.Haupolter, H.Gufter 18th April 1989.*

A recommended climb on slabs and cracks with good protection up the big corner system at the inner end of Zernouk el Daber. 400m. T.D. Inf. 4 hours. Maps and topos pages 103 and 108.

Approach: Follow R.122 into Kharazeh Canyon and climb up to the col at its head (60m, 3+/4, some poor rock), then descend into Zernouk el Daber to below the huge SE facing corner (1 hour). Alternatively, take a Bedouin taxi round to the canyon entrance in Wadi um Ishrin.

Descent: From the summit, down-climb slabs to the W (3), to terraces and go N to reach the top of The Secret Garden. Abseil this (2 hours).

SE Face

129. Eulenverschneidung *A.Precht, W.Haupolter March 1988.*

The SE Face, N of the entrance of Zernouk el Daber has a series of flakey corners, of which the left-hand one gives the route. 300m. T.D. Sup. 6 hours. Maps and topos pages 103 and 109.

Approach: Either via R.122 through Kharazeh Canyon and Zernouk el Daber ($1^1/_2$ hours), or by Bedu taxi.

Descent: From the end of the climb, go up some terraces and keep right (W), before down-climbing and rappeling the S Face to the col between Zernouk el Daber and Kharazeh Canyon (2 hours), then down R.132 for another $^3/_4$ hour back to the Rest House.

The intricate key to the cluster of peaks between Kharazeh Canyon and N Nassrani is the superb through-route of:

130. The Canyon of Rakabat um Ejil (The Neck, or Narrows of the Mother of the Calf)

Known simply as Rakabat Canyon, this maze of ravines

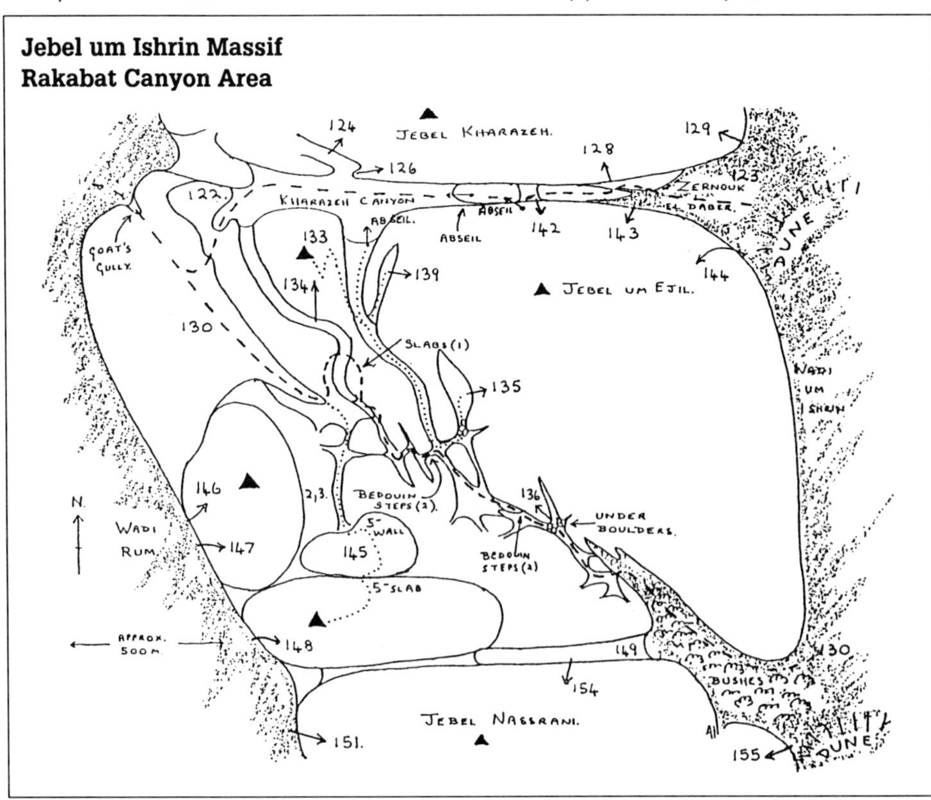

Jebel um Ishrin Massif
Short climbs in Rakabat Canyon

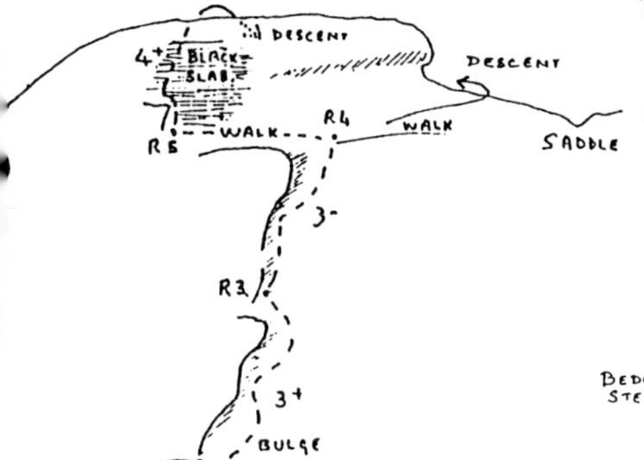

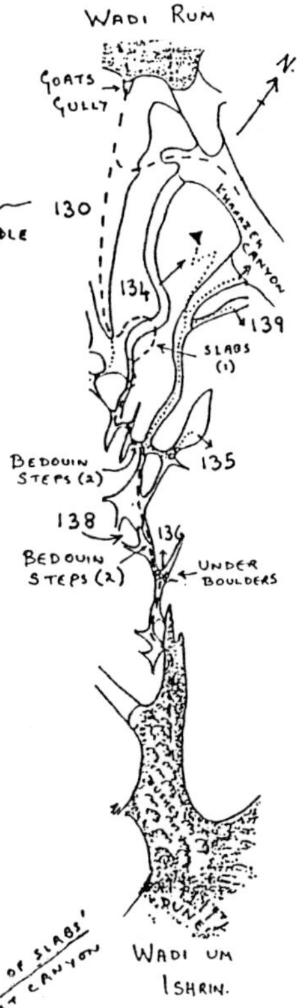

gives access to the climbs on the West Face of Jebel um Ejil as well as the North and East faces of Nassrani and the peak of Annafishiyyah in Wadi um Ishrin. In addition, they also provide a beautiful walk and rock scramble in its own right giving a wonderful half-day in some amazing mountain and desert scenery.

For the walker, it is possible to return to Wadi Rum either the same way, or south down the big red dunes of um Ishrin, round the end of the mountain and back up the valley of Rum. Either way takes about the same time.

Alternatively, for those with ropes and climbing experience an entertaining round trip can be made, by going north up Wadi um Ishrin from the end of Rakabat Canyon to enter the huge cleft of Zernouk el Daber. Go through this with two 40m abseils, and so down Kharazeh canyon and back to the Rest House. The round trip takes about 5 hours (see R.132).

Also, of course, these canyons can be used as part of a longer trek out to the stupendous Barrah Canyon, or as part of a circuit of Jebel um Ishrin (R.96). Either of these journeys takes a full day. You can also arrange to be met in Wadi um Ishrin with camels, and so combine a canyon walk with a camel trek (R.131). The Rakabat Canyon from the Rest House to Wadi um Ishrin is approx. 3km. F. Allow $1^1/_2$ - $2^1/_2$ hours. Maps pages 95, 103, 110 and 111.

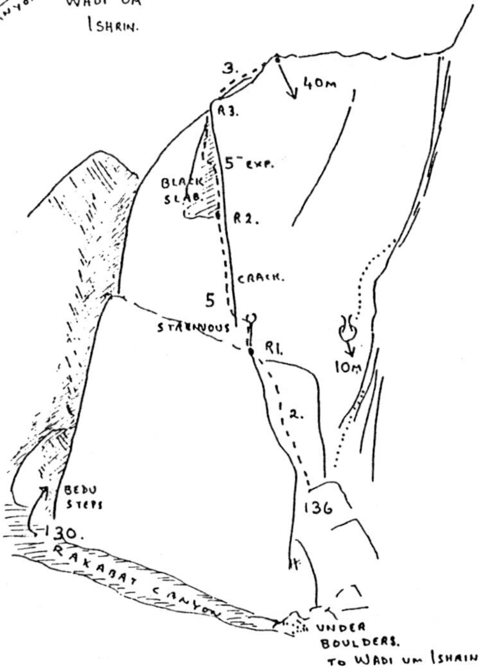

From the Rest House, cross the desert towards the giant ravine of Kharazeh Canyon. 100m right of the bushy wadi basin below its mouth, a small gully will be seen (not too obvious at first) with a large overhang on its right. This is Goat's Gully and provides the way in through a barrier of cliffs, to a plateau, $^1/_2$ hour from Rest House.

Walk almost south, along the plateau (bearing 160°) towards the smaller (left hand) of two gullies. Scramble up this, still in the direction of a thumb shaped tower on the distant skyline to arrive in a bay. On the left is a saddle above a ravine which marks the entrance to the Rakabat Canyons. However, it cannot be entered directly. Instead, go left, and down to cross the little stream bed at an S-bend and climb up some smooth pink slabs on the opposite side. Walk rightwards along their top (exposed) and descend into the ravine above the first barrier.

50m further on is another small steep barrier. Either ascend it directly (1), or pass it on the left. Continue, until 10m before the end, Bedouin steps lead up left to enter a side canyon.

At the next junction, turn right, then almost immediately left and up a narrow ravine (more Bedouin steps) to reach the pass. Descend, down an awkward 5m wall (Bedouin steps), (2), to emerge in the upper Rakabat Canyons at a 'cross-roads'. Here, there are three ways. To the left (N) is the way to the climbs on the W Face of Jebel um Ejil. If this is followed to its end, a 20m abseil goes down a corner and gully into Kharazeh Canyon.

Straight on, a narrow cleft goes into a concealed canyon known as the Hanging Garden with some rock climbs, whilst to the right is the way out into Wadi um Ishrin (this point is approx. 1 hour from Rest House).

Go right, keeping to the left side and descending to a lower wadi (which goes back up another ravine into the concealed canyon). Continue down it, again keeping to its very left edge. Rise up over a rock bulge, (do not go down the canyon), then through a defile and down steep slabs (Bedouin steps and 'ladder'), (2), into the lower ravine.

50m down this, pass under a big boulder and carry on down keeping to the right side through a little defile for the first magnificent view of um Ishrin's red dunes. Descend the gully from here, squeezing past a jammed boulder on to slabs. Keep right, still close to the mountain, finally descending to the valley floor 10m below, through the lowest little wadi, down smooth rock (1).

(To find this point from the opposite direction, it is opposite a tongue of rock which descends into the valley from Jebel um Ejil, and about 50m before the inner end of the valley.)

From here, walk out through bushes into Wadi um Ishrin, at the foot of the big dunes. Ascend to their top for superb views.

131. Camel Trek to Rakabat Canyon.

This is an excellent short camel trek which is ideally combined with a walk back to the Rest House through the canyon of Rakabat um Ejil:-

Go south with the camels, down Rum, rounding the south end of the um Ishrin Massif (Jebel Draif al Muragh) to head back into Wadi um Ishrin. Either go directly up um Ishrin to the mouth of Rakabat um Ejil (365730). (Distance 7km $1^1/_2$ - 2 hours), or detour through the interesting narrow wadis south of Jebel Annafishiyyah (shown as Jebel er Raka on map, ref: 381733), passing east and then north of this mountain, before working south west again to Rakabat. (About 14km 3 - 4 hours).

The entrance to Rakabat is a nice area for lunch before walking back through the shaded canyons and across the Wadi Rum to the Rest House. Walking distance about 3km. Allow $1^1/_2$ - 2 hours. See Route 130.

132. Round Jebil um Ejil

A very enjoyable day amongst varied and continually changing rock and desert scenery, passing by many rock climbs. A great introduction to walking and climbing in Rum. The return journey from the Rest House is about 7km. F. Allow 5 hours. Map page 110.

Take R.130 through the Rakabat Canyons, to Wadi um Ishrin. Walk North up this in inspiring desert scenery for less than half an hour, along the foot of the E Face of Jebel um Ejil, passing some new route possibilities, to enter the Canyon of Zernouk el Daber. Up this (R.123) to the col above Kharazeh Canyon.

An abseil chain will be found 10m down on the left. Abseil 40m into a chimney (mostly free hanging) and descend this to the canyon floor by some awkward bridging (3) in chimneys, or by a second abseil.

Walk out of the canyon reversing R.122 between impressive mushrooming walls to where it suddenly opens out. (The abseil descent from the Rakabat Canyon,

Climbs on Jebel Rum's East Face

Left:
Flight of Fancy, pitch 4, first ascent - photo Colonna

Right:
Pillar of Wisdom - photo Verin

Bedouin Climbs on Jebel Rum Above left: Hammad's Route. Abseil into the Great Siq
Above right: Sabbah's Route. The exposed traverse
Below: Sheikh Hamdan's Route, view west down the Great Siq - all photos Howard

below the W face climbs of um Ejil comes down the gully on the left.)

Continue down R.122 until the wadi drops down a cliff. Here, rise left up a bushy gully to a saddle. Cross it and descend in the same direction, starting from the right, down another bushy gully which leads down to a plateau. Goats Gully (R.130) will be found across the plateau and slightly right. Descend it and cross Wadi Rum back to the Rest House.

Jebel Rakabat (Mountain of the Neck) 1,229m (ref: 360740)

133. From the East *First recorded ascent October 4th, 1985 W.Colonna, M.Shaw, A.Howard.*
The narrow summit ridge of this mountain which lies between Wadi Rum and Jebel um Ejil, and splits the north end of the Rakabat ravines is reached easily by climbing its east side, from the ravine that divides it from the West Face of Jebel um Ejil. There are numerous ways between grades 2 and 3 winding up the face which is only about 50 metres high. The highest summit is to the north. Obviously climbed by the Bedouin. Time from the Rest House about 1½ hours, via Rakabat canyon (R.130), to below West Face of Jebel um Ejil. Grade F. Maps pages 103 and 110.

The easiest way starts at a very easy angled ramp opposite the ramp leading from the canyon bed to the 'Beauty' climbs. Follow this rising rightwards with an awkward step (2) eventually zig zagging a long way back left almost to a col, then right again to the summit.

If you're looking for a pleasant walk and a good introduction to climbing in Wadi Rum or a rest from cranking up the big walls, then here's a few nice little routes to choose from:

Jebel Rakabat, West Face

134. L'Aperitif *D.Taylor, A.Howard 2nd November 1991.*
Entertaining climbing up a variety of features on an otherwise mushroom festooned wall. The route starts at an obvious finger-thin crack line 200m left (N) of the "smooth pink slabs" on the walk through Rakabat Canyon (R.130). 150m. 5-/5-/3+/3. 1½ - 2 hours. Maps and topos 110 and 111.
Approach: Via R.130, approx. 30 - 45 minutes from Rest House.
Descent: The climb ends on a large terrace below the summit. Walk right (S) and cross the ridge as soon as possible to the col at the top of a chimney-crack on the E face. Now reverse R.133, via a long descending zig-zag (some steps of 2), first to the left (N), then to the right. (10 mins). If the Black Slab variation finish is taken to the summit, simply traverse the E face to pick up the same descent. From here, follow R.130 back to the Rest House (1 hour), or abseil into Kharazeh Canyon and return via R.122.

The other little climbs are further along Rakabat Canyon:

Jebel um Ejil 1431m

SW Face, Lower Wall

135. Little Gem *J. Smith, A.Howard April 1992.*
Brilliant technical climbing up a smooth dihedral in a flat black wall. 35m 6B (abseil descent). Maps pages 103, 110 and 111.
Approach: Up Rakabat Canyon to the 'cross-roads', then straight on E through a narrow steep walled ravine and left up boulders into the Hanging Garden. 1 hour. (Other possibilities for routes exist here.)

SW Facet

More games in Rakabat Canyon!

136. Essence of Rum *D.Taylor, A.Howard 31st March 1992.*
A nice canyon walk, superb views of the red dunes of um Ishrin, a good strenuous crack and a delicate sparsely protected black slab leading to a small top via a sunny south face make this little climb 'the essence of Rum'. 80m. 2/5/5-/3.1 hr. Maps and topos 110 and 111.
Approach: 1 hour through Rakabat Canyon, turning right at the 'cross-roads' towards um Ishrin, on and down the Bedouin steps to the entrance of the little tunnel under big boulders. The climb is immediately above, on the N side.
Descent: Abseil 40m from the summit belay down slabs to the E, into the gully. Scramble down its right side (1) to a big thread and abseil 10m to arrive in the gully close to the start of the climb. 15 mins.

Just 10m left of the previous route is:

Jebel um Ejil, West Face

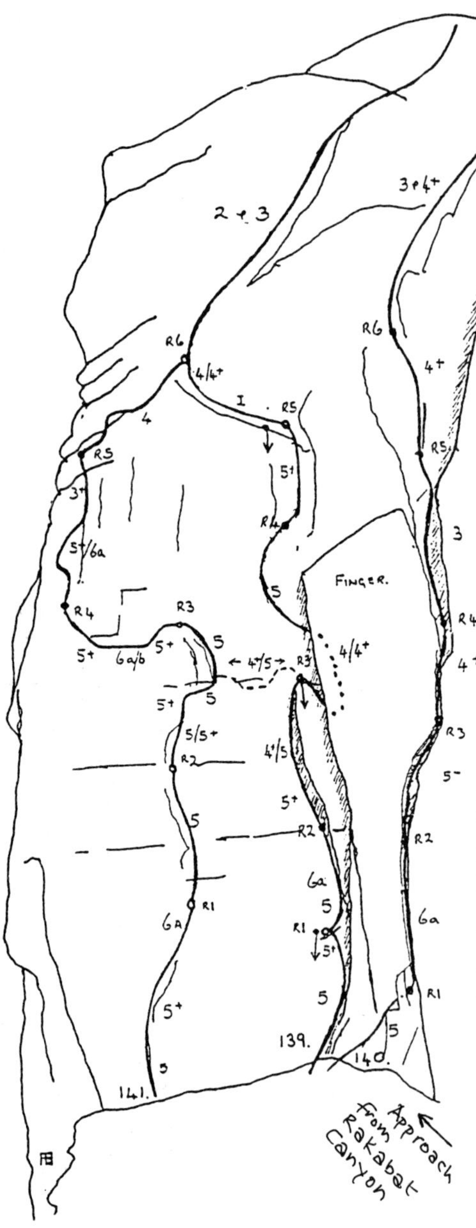

137. Slingsby's Wall *P. Talling, P. Williams 24th May 1992.*
Climb the wall, starting at a thin crack. 4+. *Descent* via R136 abseil.

138. Point Alexandre *G. Hornby, S. Sammut 11th November 1992.*
Pleasant climbing with some exposed steps of 3. 100m. Map page 111.
Approach: From the inner valley of Rakabat, instead of rising up left to reach the top of the descent of Bedouin steps, continue in the valley bottom and descend cut steps, then go S into a siq and behind the tower which is diagonally opposite R.136.

Jebel um Ejil

The West Face of this mountain, easily seen from the Rest House, just south of Kharazeh Canyon has an obvious NW Diedre split by a giant finger of rock. The foot of the face is reached easily through the canyons of Rakabat um Ejil (1 hour) from where a scramble up scree slopes leads to the bottom of the two big corners (see route 130).

139. The Beauty *W.Colonna, A.Baker 10th October 1985.*
A classic! This route follows a superb line of sustained layback flakes up the left hand side of the finger, the last one being poorly protected (no. 4 Friends high up). 200m. T.D. Allow 4 hours. Maps pages 95, 103 & 110.
Descent: A fast and easy descent is given by the line of The Beauty the top of which is in a corner below some slabs about 50m right (facing out) of The Beast. Descend the top pitches easily to the easy traverse ledge where abseil rings mark the first abseil of 45m to the top of the pedestal above pitch 3. The next two abseils of 45m and 30m go directly to the ground. Allow 1 - $1^{1}/_{2}$ hours.

To return to the Rest House, either walk back through Rakabat um Ejil or, perhaps more logically, take the alternative abseil descent into Kharazeh Canyon. Either way about $^{3}/_{4}$ hour.

140. The Beast *M.Shaw, D.Taylor, A.Howard 10th October 1985.*
A thuggish route up the righthand side of the finger, with only one hard pitch and loose rock above. 200m. T.D., 3 hours. Maps and topos, pages 103 and 114.
Descent via The Beauty.

141. Alan and his Perverse Frog
W.Colonna, A.Baker The first three pitches were climbed on 24th October 1985 and the last three on 28th October 1985, entering by a traverse from the top of pitch 3 of The Beauty.
A superb and sustained route, taking a line up the centre of the square black wall left of The Beauty, and finishing where it meets the easy upper slabs of that route, 150m. T.D. Sup. Allow 4 hours. Maps and topos, pages 103 and 114.
Descent: Simply traverse a few metres right to reach the start of the first of three abseils down The Beauty.

N Face
There are two routes on this wall, starting from the Canyon of Zernouk el Daber.
Approach: As R.122, up Kharazeh Canyon to the col (1 hour).
Descent: Down to the west, and abseil The Beauty. The first route starts from the col:

142. Edge of Zernouk el Daber *W.Haupolter, W.Bogensberger, A.Precht March 1988.*
Nice climbing on good rock from the notch and up the NE Pillar. 350m. D. Sup. 3 hours. Maps and topos 110.

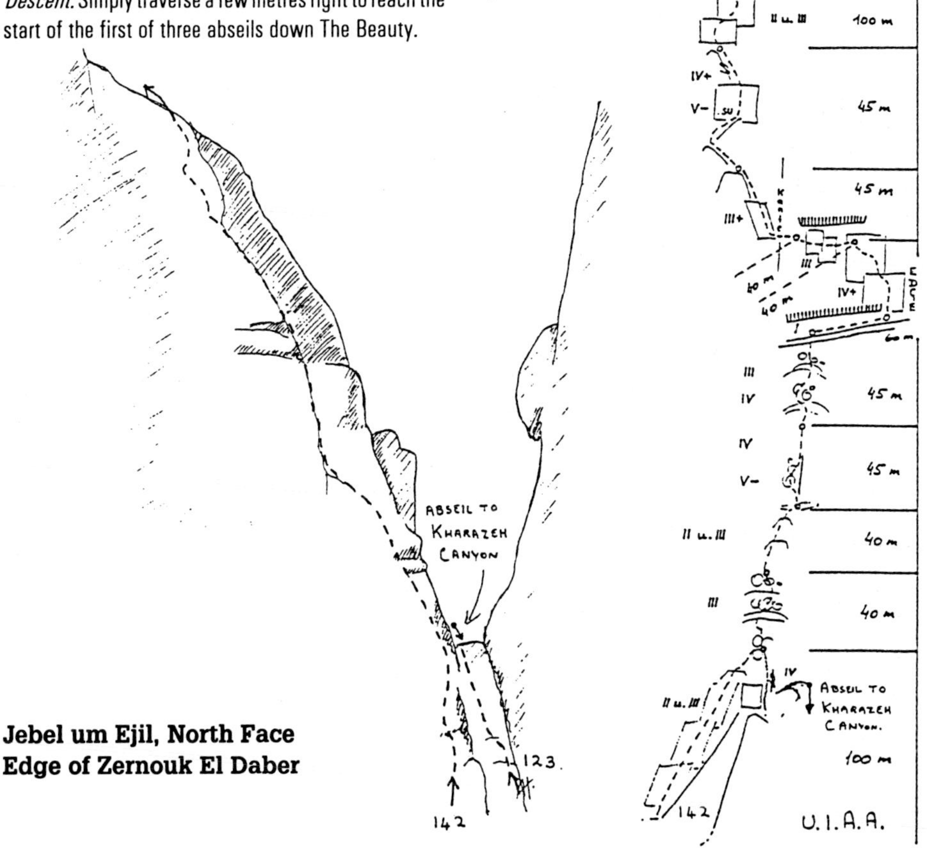

Jebel um Ejil, North Face
Edge of Zernouk El Daber

143. Straight Up *A.Precht, W.Haupolter 3rd April 1989.*

An interesting and varied route on good rock up a poorly visible crack-corner which splits into two, in the middle of the face. Take the left one directly up the black wall finishing by low angled but poorly protected slabs 300m E.D. Inf. 4 hours. Maps pages 103 and 110.

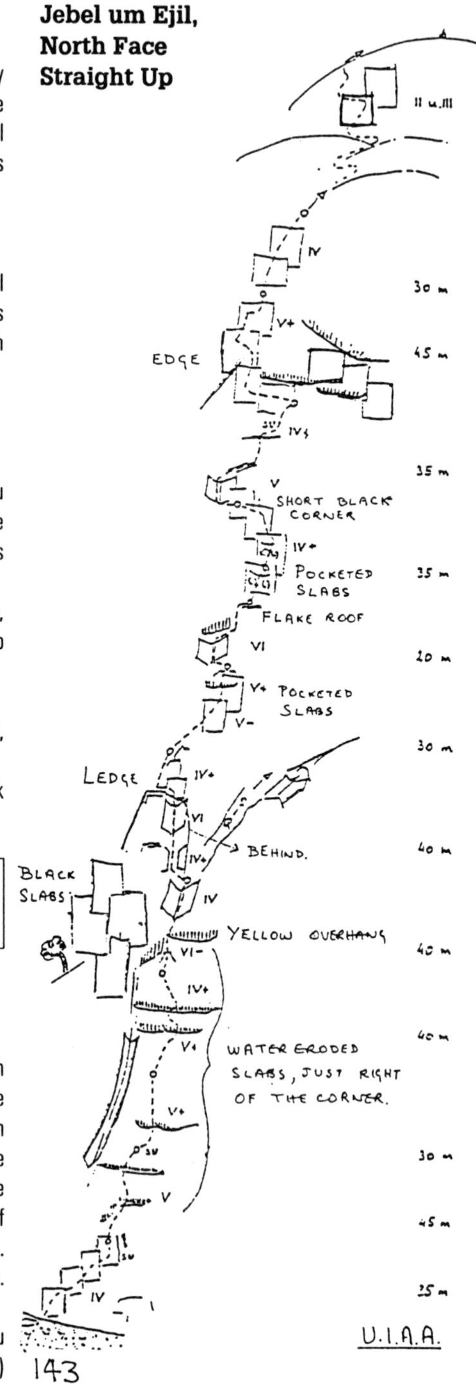

North East Face

Above the far left side of the entrance to Zernouk el Daber is an expanse of smooth water washed slabs rumoured to have been climbed by Bedouin, though neither Hammad nor Sabbah could verify it:

144. Local Knowledge *Geoff Hornby, Susie Sammut 2nd November 1992.*

Ascends the S-shaped slabs. A strange route in that you can climb almost anywhere but on three occasions, are forced to make harder moves due to bands of continuous overlaps or steepening of the walls (4+).

Above the slabs, climb either of the obvious cracks, then go left on to the big traverse, then a long way up easy slabs to the top. 400m. A.D. Sup. (2 - 3 hours). Map & topos pages 110 and 117.

Approach: Either through Rakabat Canyon, (1½ hours), or by Bedu taxi.

Descent: Down the route, 3 abseils necessary and back via Zernouk el Daber (3 hours), or via The Beauty.

Jebel Um Ejil, South Summit. 1,380 metres (ref: 356735)

145. Via the North Ravine *A.Howard, D.Taylor, M.Shaw, A.Baker October 8th, 1984. (The first tentative exploration in Rum.)*

An enjoyable day out in interesting rock scenery (though the rock itself is sometimes suspect). There are some route finding problems but the summit domes are an excellent place with good views over Wadi Rum village and south to the looming walls of Nassrani. Distance covered, approximately 1km with maybe 200 metres of climbing at grade 2 or 3 and a couple of pitches of 5-. Overall grade A.D. Allow 3 - 4 hours from Rest House. Maps pages 110.

Approach: Via the Goat's Gully, then across the plateau at a bearing of 160° as for Rakabat Canyon (R.130)

Jebel um Ejil,
from N. Barrah Summit
N.E. Face
Local Knowledge

until a hidden gully is entered, above the lip of Rakabat Canyon. This gully gives the line of the route.
Descent: 2 - 3 hours. Reverse the route. No abseil points in place, but the crux pitches can be avoided (see R.148).

Jebel um Ejil, West Summit

NW Face

146. Alia *C.&Y.Remy 4th May 1986.*
Nice, varied climbing, except for a passage of poor rock at the start. The 3rd pitch is an athletic crack (6A/B) but it can be done on nuts at 5 A1. Good belays and runners. 200 metres. D. Sup. Ascent 3 hours. Maps and topos, pages 103, 110 and 118.
Approach: 15 minutes, directly east from the Rest House, and 10 minutes up the scree.
Descent: Obvious rappels to the top of pitch 5 then down easily, following the ridge (cairns) and finishing with two abseils to the north. 1 hour.

SW Face

147. Aqua Marina *C.&Y.Remy 11th November 1986.*
Interesting climbing with several nice pitches taking the line seen easily from the Rest House up the right side of the face. Some slings and a peg in place, but carry an extra blade peg. 200m. T.D. 3 hours. Maps and topos pages 110 and 118.
Approach: Cross the desert and go up screes to the foot of the chimney-crack (1/2 hour).
Descent: Either rappel and downclimb R.146, or go via the South Summit, (numerous cairns). Some downclimbing (2) joins a large terrace 50m below the South top at a col on its E side. Continue to a tree, and descend into the siq: a tortuous but interesting hour to reach the desert!

Jebel um Ejil, South Summit

West Face

148. Via Salim Musa *N.Christie, Salim Musa, C.&Y.Remy 31st October 1986.*
Interesting climbing up the obvious line easily seen from the Rest House, (some slings in place). 200m. D. 3 hours. Maps and topos pages 103, 110 and 118.
Approach: Cross the valley and ascend the scree to the crack between the two towers 1/2 hour.
Descent: Go back down to the big platform on the W Face and contour N and E to a big tree. Descend the siq passing numerous cairns (2+) 1 hour to the desert, via Goat's Gully (R.130).

149. Nassrani North Canyon
The entrance to the giant cleft which divides Jebel Nassrani North Summit from Jebel um Ejil South Summit is in the green wadi basin of Rakabat um Ejil (ref: 365739).

Enter the wadi basin from Wadi um Ishrin and take the left fork into the narrow high walled ravine which can be followed to its end, below Nassrani North Face

Jebel um Ejil, West and South Summits, West Face Routes and Descents

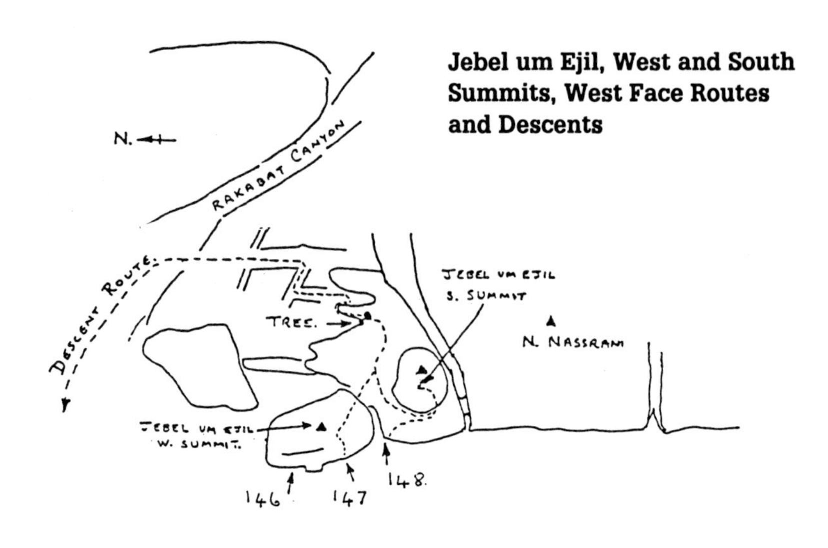

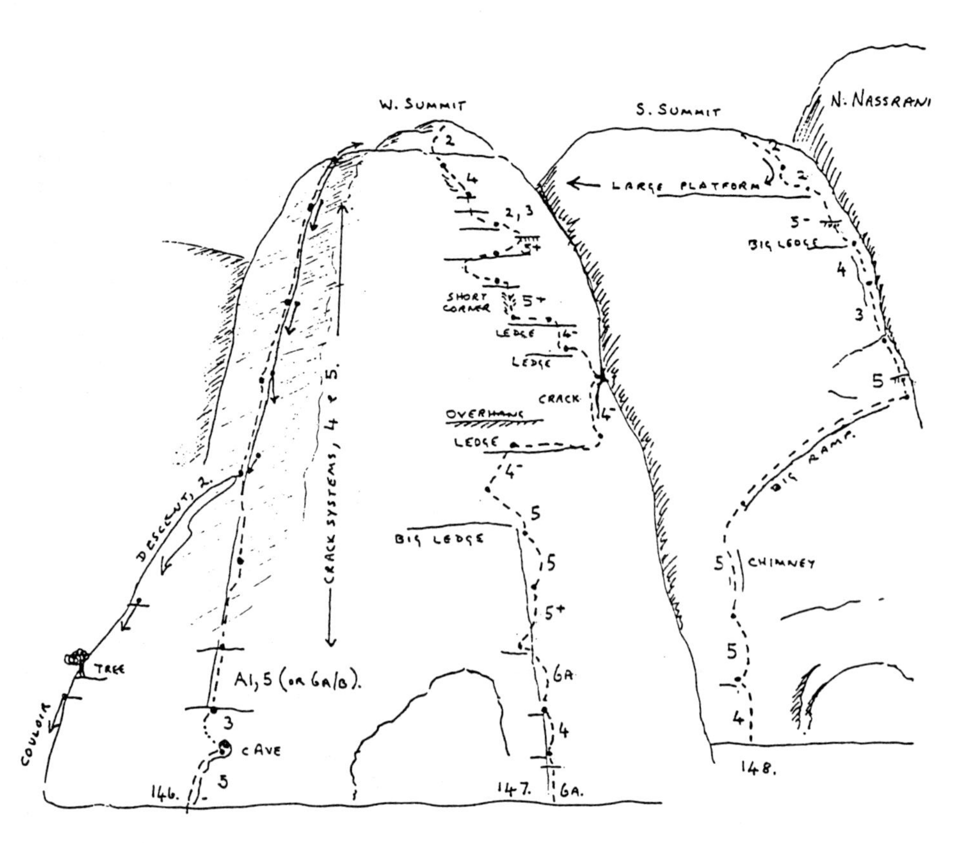

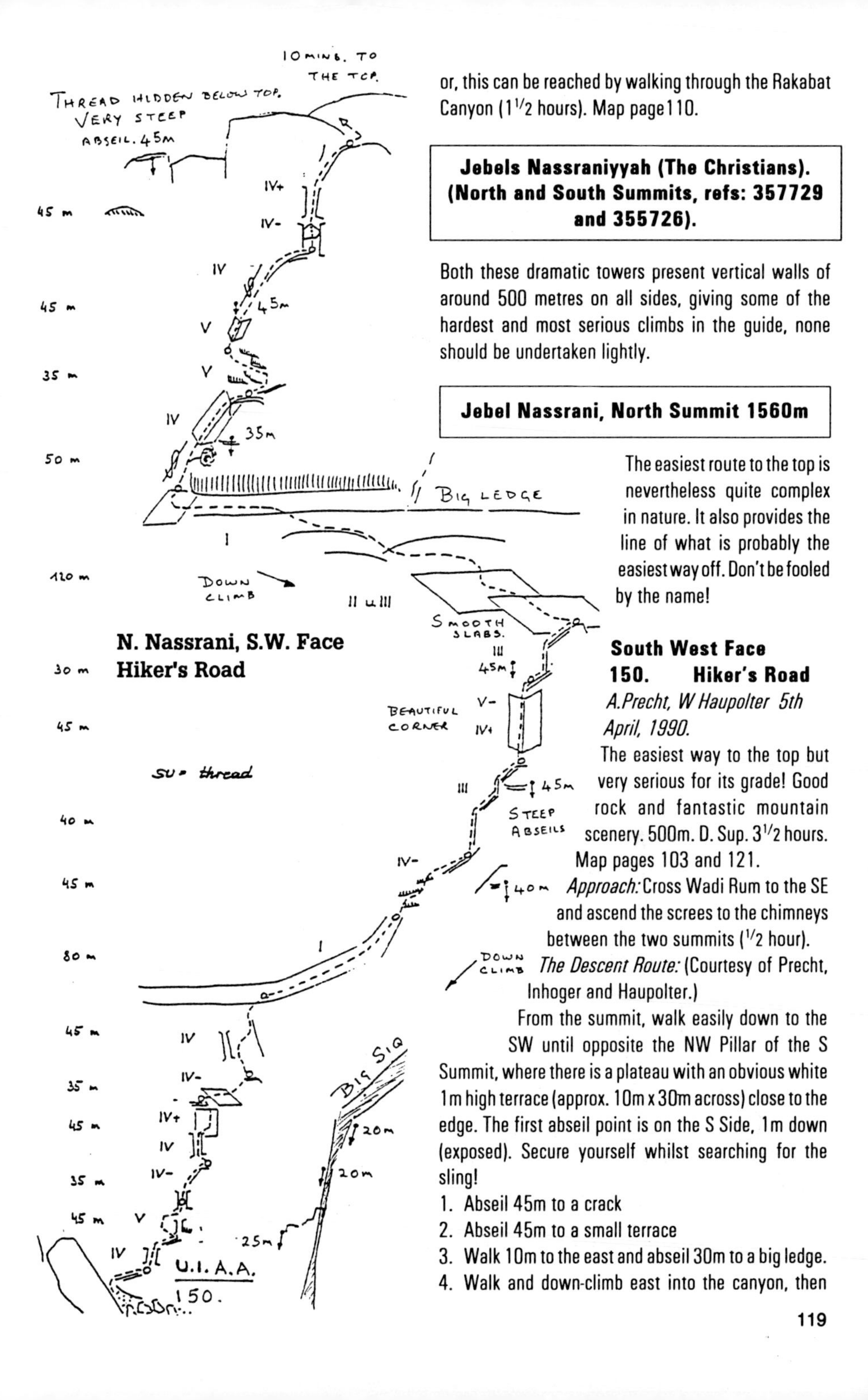

N. Nassrani, S.W. Face
Hiker's Road

or, this can be reached by walking through the Rakabat Canyon ($1^{1}/2$ hours). Map page110.

Jebels Nassraniyyah (The Christians). (North and South Summits, refs: 357729 and 355726).

Both these dramatic towers present vertical walls of around 500 metres on all sides, giving some of the hardest and most serious climbs in the guide, none should be undertaken lightly.

Jebel Nassrani, North Summit 1560m

The easiest route to the top is nevertheless quite complex in nature. It also provides the line of what is probably the easiest way off. Don't be fooled by the name!

South West Face

150. Hiker's Road

A.Precht, W Haupolter 5th April, 1990.

The easiest way to the top but very serious for its grade! Good rock and fantastic mountain scenery. 500m. D. Sup. $3^{1}/2$ hours. Map pages 103 and 121.

Approach: Cross Wadi Rum to the SE and ascend the screes to the chimneys between the two summits ($^{1}/2$ hour).

The Descent Route: (Courtesy of Precht, Inhoger and Haupolter.)

From the summit, walk easily down to the SW until opposite the NW Pillar of the S Summit, where there is a plateau with an obvious white 1m high terrace (approx. 10m x 30m across) close to the edge. The first abseil point is on the S Side, 1m down (exposed). Secure yourself whilst searching for the sling!

1. Abseil 45m to a crack
2. Abseil 45m to a small terrace
3. Walk 10m to the east and abseil 30m to a big ledge.
4. Walk and down-climb east into the canyon, then

follow a ramp back west (cairns)

5. Down-climb 20m (2+) and abseil 45m in a big corner.
6. Go 10m east to a 45m abseil, then a 35m abseil to the bottom of the canyon.
7. Now climb down easily and walk out towards the mouth of the canyon.
8. A 10m steep step is passed by climbing down (2+) on the right wall
9. Continue out and traverse the left wall (10m) to a 25m abseil, then a 20m abseil
10. Down-climb a ramp system to the N and abseil 20m to the bottom.

Some cairns and abseil slings with carabiners (the slings will need renewing) mark the route and the lower abseils can be down-climbed. Allow $1^1/2$ - $2^1/2$ hours - the latter is more realistic!

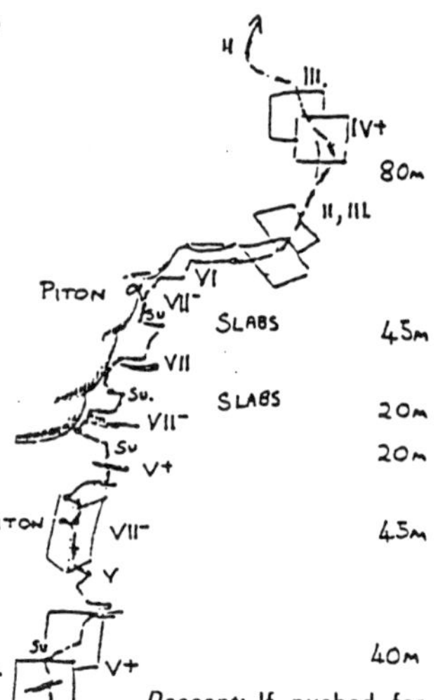

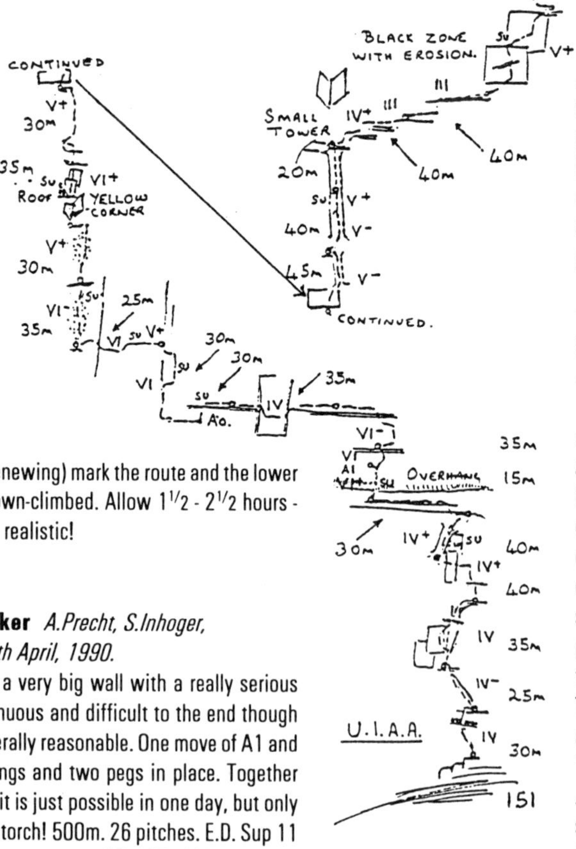

West Face

151. Jolly Joker *A.Precht, S.Inhoger, W.Haupolter 16th April, 1990.*

A great climb on a very big wall with a really serious atmosphere: strenuous and difficult to the end though protection is generally reasonable. One move of A1 and one Ao; many slings and two pegs in place. Together with the descent it is just possible in one day, but only just! Take a head torch! 500m. 26 pitches. E.D. Sup 11 hours. Maps and topos pages 95, 103, 110 and 121..

Approach: Walk SE from the village and up screes to below a 70m high tower ($^1/2$ hour).

N. Nassrani, W. Face Jolly Joker

Descent: If pushed for time you don't need to gain the summit but instead, can traverse round the top to reach the SW Pillar and the abseil point (R.150).

152. West Face. L'autre Dimension

C.&Y. Remy 21st April 1986. The first ascent of this summit.

A route of great character in crack-chimneys up the only really obvious line on this face. The diedre of the 3rd pitch is splendid. Belays and protection are good throughout. 500 metres. T.D. Ascent 6 hours. Map and topo pages 103 and 121.

Approach: Cross the wadi, south east from the village (30 minutes, or by 4-wheel drive), and up scree. (10 minutes).

Descent: Obvious abseils

N. Nassrani, W. Face

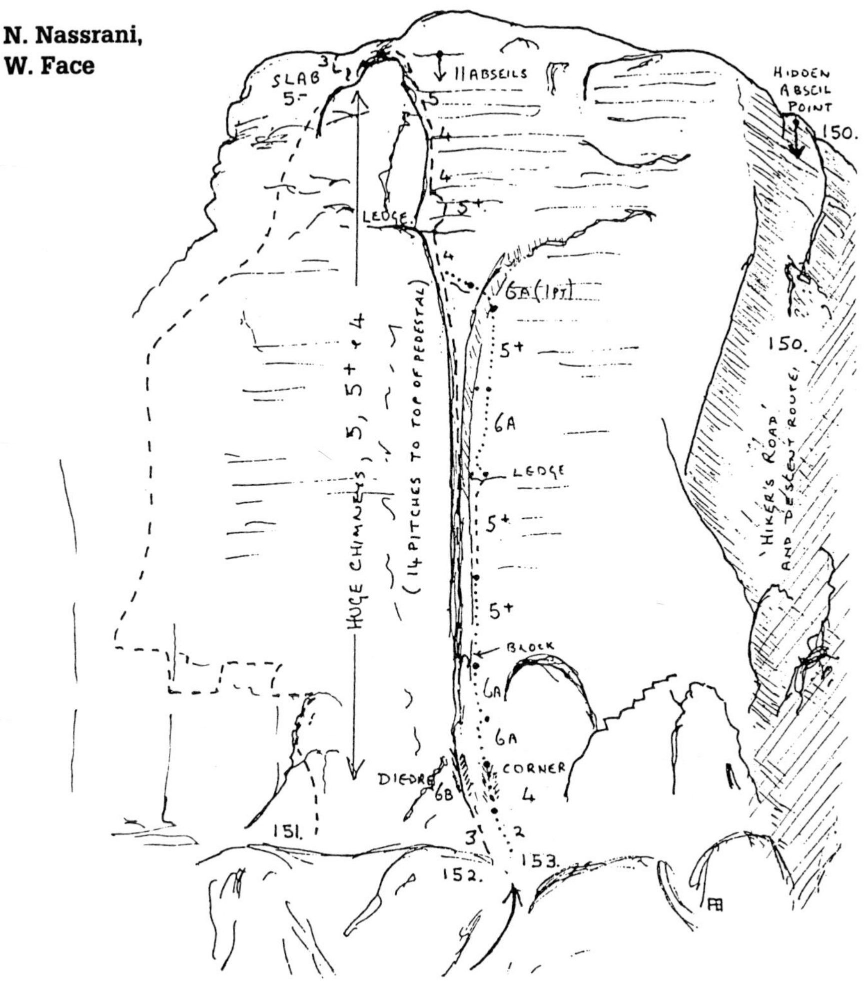

down the route. 2 hours, (or by Hiker's Road).

153. Le Mot De La Fin *C.&Y.Remy 13th November 1986.*
A great line on good rock with impressive surroundings. Numerous slings in place, also 2 pegs and a bolt. 250m to the junction with R.152, (500m to the top). T.D. Sup. 4 hours.
Approach: Cross Wadi Rum and ascend the screes as R.152.
Descent: By R.152, 2 hours (or down R.150, also by abseil).

North Face

154. King's Wall *A.Precht, S.Inhoger, W.Haupolter 6th April, 1990.*
Another 'big feel' route offering good climbing on superb rock. Highly recommended, with interesting pitches especially in the upper part on the white slabs where protection is minimal! Carry a full rack and many slings. 450m. E.D. 6 hours. Maps and topos pages 110 and 122.
Approach: Either through Rakabat um Ejil though this takes 1$^1/_2$ hours, or by Bedouin taxi up Wadi um Ishrin to the E entrance of the Rakabat Canyon. Go into the bush-filled valley, and N Nassrani canyon is on the left

N. Nassrani, North Face
King's Wall

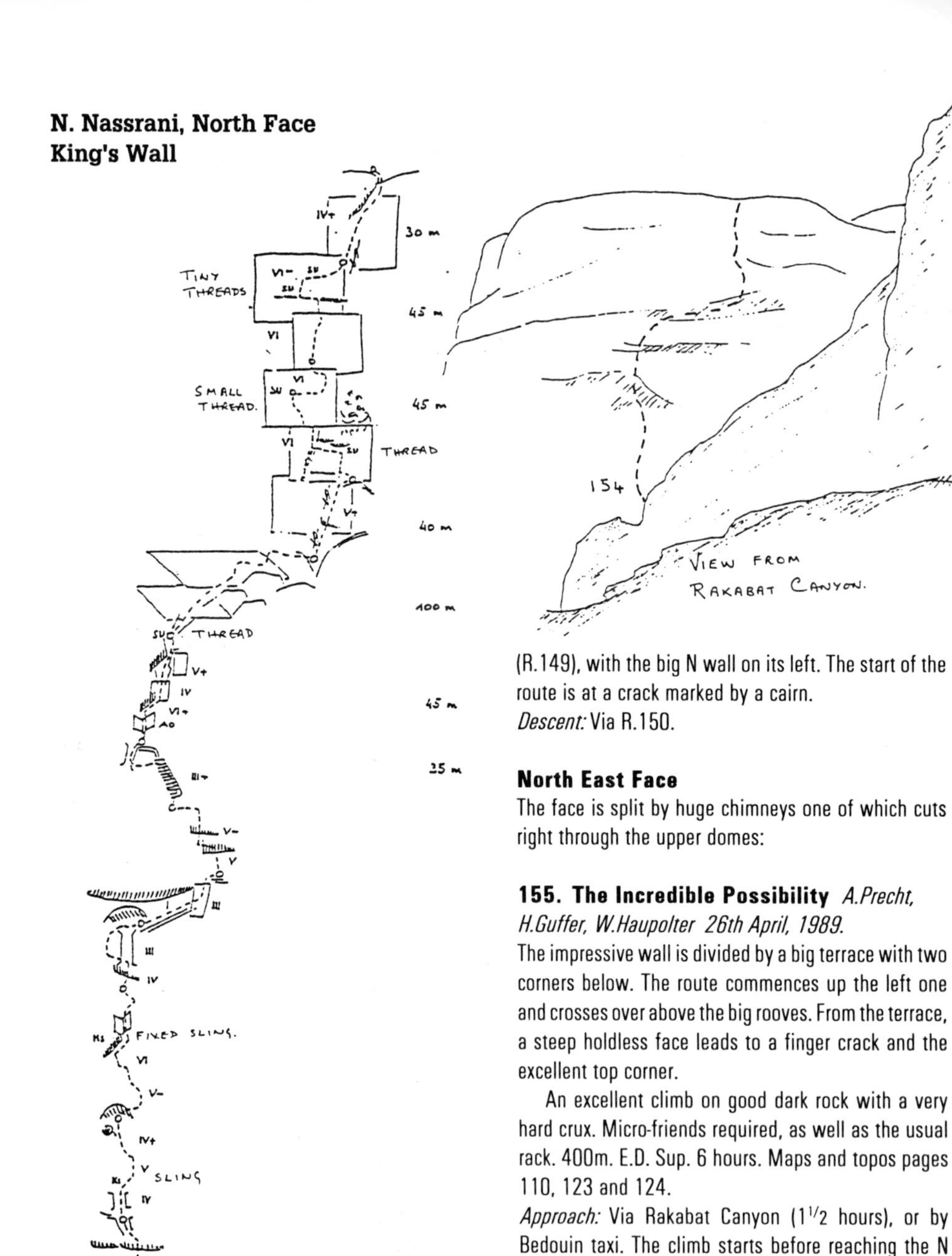

(R.149), with the big N wall on its left. The start of the route is at a crack marked by a cairn.
Descent: Via R.150.

North East Face
The face is split by huge chimneys one of which cuts right through the upper domes:

155. The Incredible Possibility *A.Precht, H.Guffer, W.Haupolter 26th April, 1989.*
The impressive wall is divided by a big terrace with two corners below. The route commences up the left one and crosses over above the big rooves. From the terrace, a steep holdless face leads to a finger crack and the excellent top corner.

An excellent climb on good dark rock with a very hard crux. Micro-friends required, as well as the usual rack. 400m. E.D. Sup. 6 hours. Maps and topos pages 110, 123 and 124.
Approach: Via Rakabat Canyon (1½ hours), or by Bedouin taxi. The climb starts before reaching the N Nassrani Canyon (R.149).
Descent: Down R.150, 1½ - 2½ hours.

N. Nassrani, N.E. Face
The Incredible Possibility

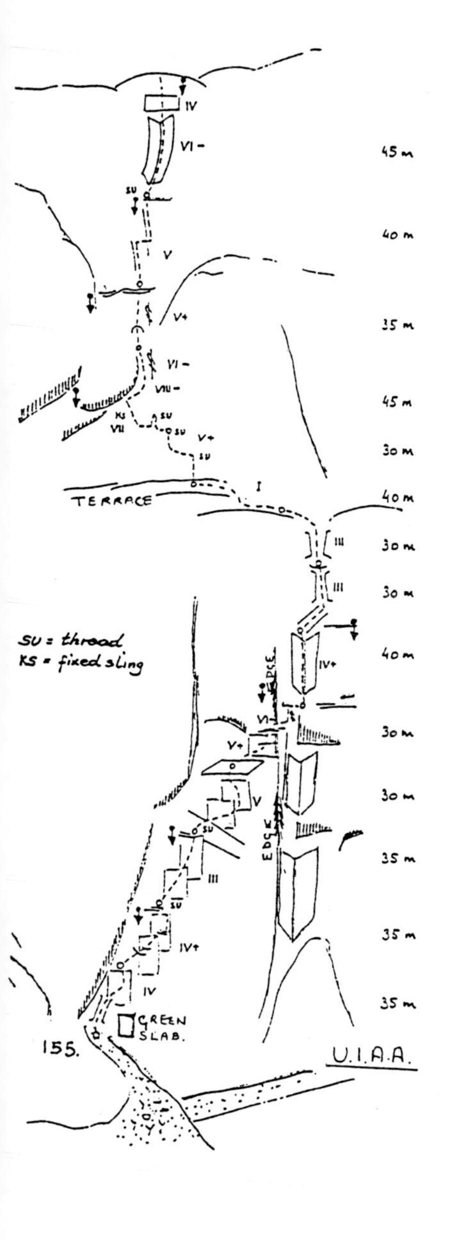

N. Nassrani,
East Face
Muezzin

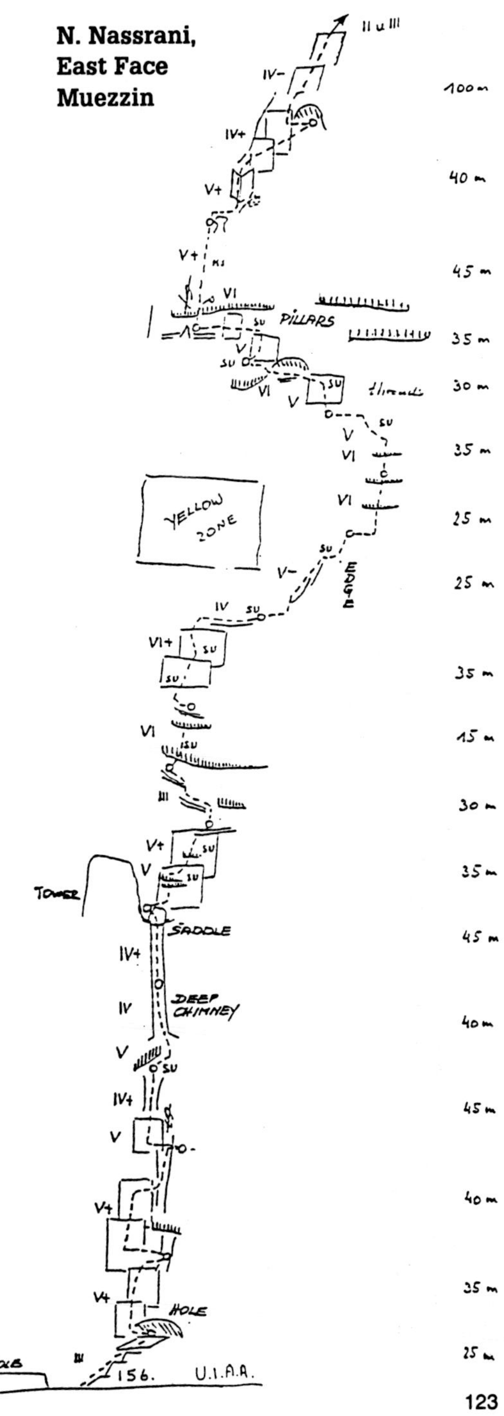

N. Nassrani, East and N.E. Face

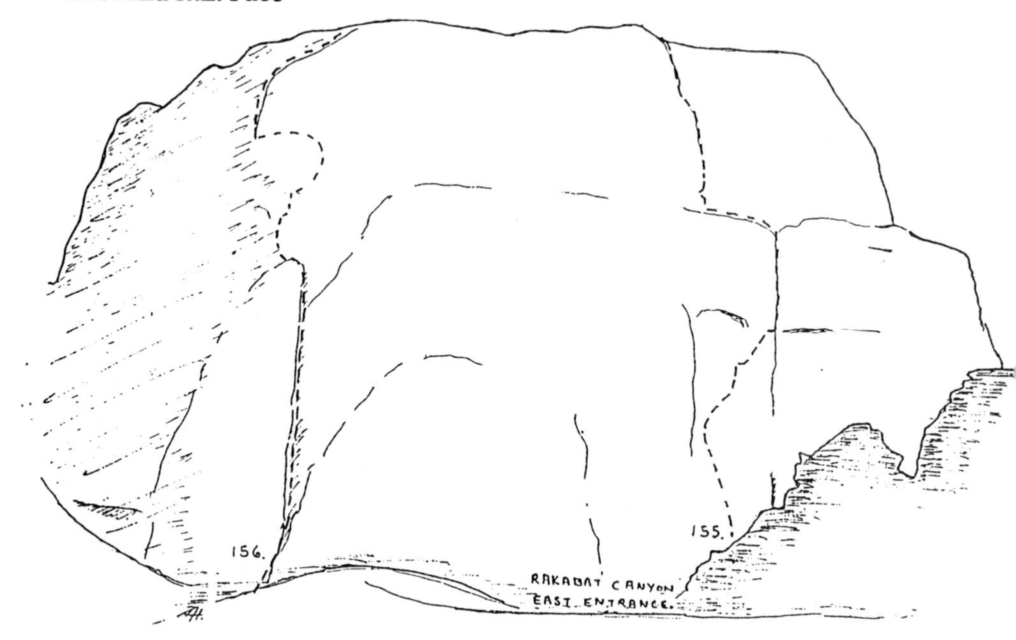

East Face

This presents a massive front to Wadi um Ishrin, and bends round to the huge smooth sweep of the SE face. The next climb swaggers up and around the arête between the two, finishing up bottomless cracks in the SE wall:

156. Muezzin *A.Precht, W.Haupolter, S.Inhoger 11th April, 1990.*

A superb climb up an impossible looking pillar. Really fascinating and very exposed with committing climbing on usually good but sometimes doubtful rock. One of the 'big' climbs of Wadi Rum which should be on the list of any competent party. A comment from the second ascent team: "It is possibly not a coincidence that the Muezzin makes the call for prayer - get on it and discover just how great Allah can be!" 400m. E.D. 6 hours. (Second ascent by good climbers took 7 - 8 hours). Maps and topos pages 103, 123 and 130.

Approach: Take a Bedouin taxi directly to the start, or walk there through Rakabat Canyon (1½ hours). The first pitch is marked by a big cairn and a rusty petrol can, about 10m up.

Descent: Walk up to the main top (½ hour) and down SW to the abseils (R.150).

Jebel Nassrani, South Summit 1560m

157. North West Pillar, Merci Allah

C.&Y.Remy 7th May 1986. The first ascent of this summit.

A route of great atmosphere but mixed character. This climb is fairly straightforward and obvious in its lower two thirds but becomes devious in its upper part winding through the overhanging zones. Belays and protection are good except for some aid moves.

In-situ: slings and two bolts. Take a selection of at least eight pegs including long pointed blades. 500 metres. T.D. Sup. 6½ hours. Map and topo pages 103 and 125.

Approach: From the village, cross the desert to the south east (30 minutes) and then up the scree to the foot of route (10 minutes).

Descent: Obvious abseils, but delicate! 2 hours.

S. Nassrani, West Face
Merci Allah

SW Face

158. Aqaba *A.Precht, W.Haupolter March 1988.*
A long route going through some impressive walls, generally on good rock, by crack systems. One peg and some slings in place. 500m. E.D. Inf. 6 hours. Top page 126.

Approach: Walk down Wadi Rum and scramble up below the far end of the SW face. Continue on a ledge to reach a small canyon at the foot of the route and start by a chimney system on the right of a small tower (1 hour).

Descent: Down-climb and rappel the route 2½ hours.

S. Nassrani, S.W. Face

S. Nassrani, S.W. Face
Aqaba and Stairway to Heaven

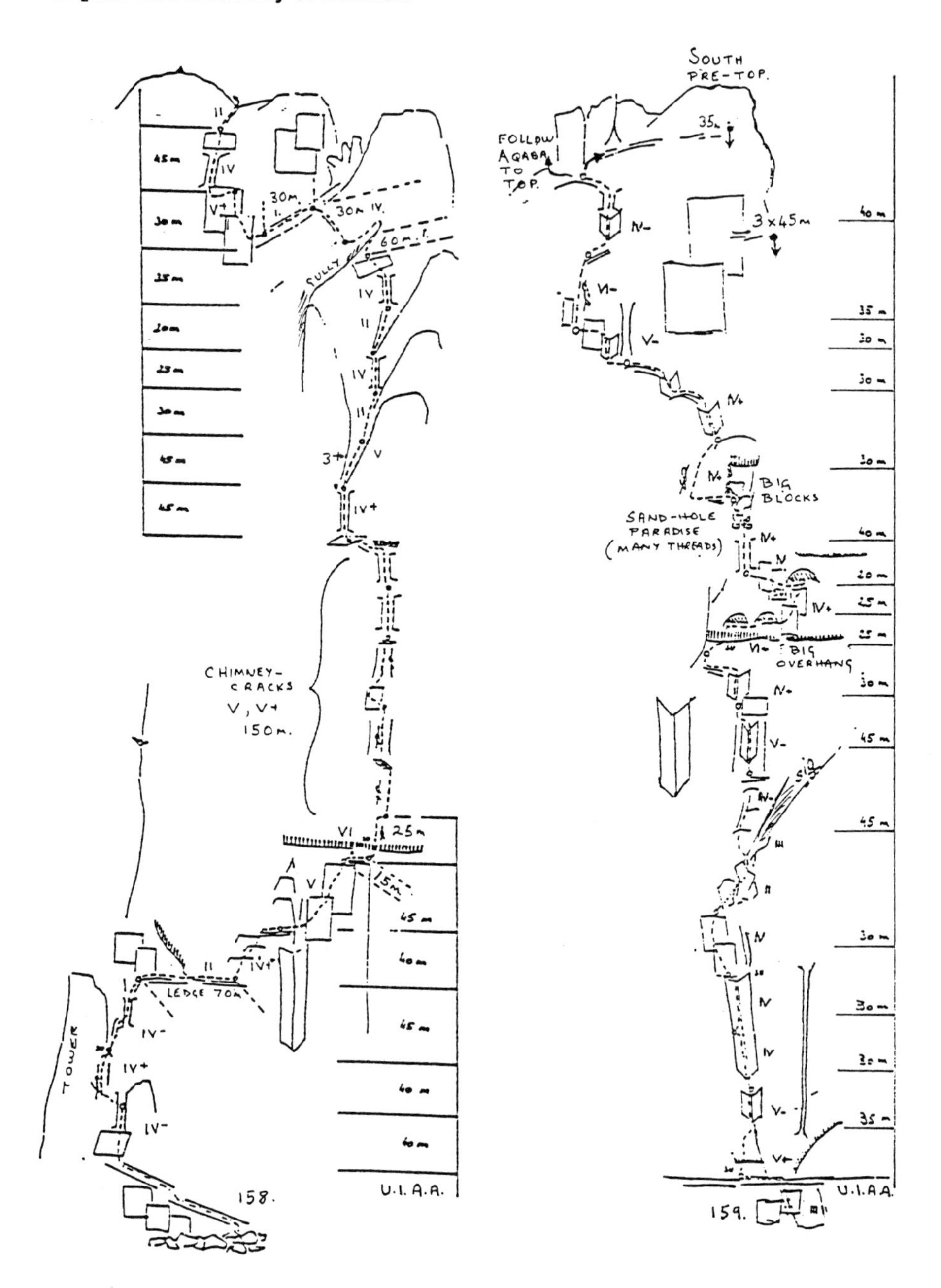

159. Stairway to Heaven *W.Haupolter, A.Precht 28th April 1989.*
Situated at the right end of the SW Face, just left of the corner and chimney systems which separate it from Draif al Muragh. Extolled by its first ascentionists as "one of the most beautiful climbs in Wadi Rum".

The route takes the left-hand chimney, crosses a big siq to reach the overhanging zone, then ascends crack systems left of the steep top slabs. The summit can be reached via 'Aqaba'. 400m. E.D. Inf. 4½ hours. Maps and topos 103, 125 and 126.
Approach: Walk down the valley and ascend screes (1 hour).
Descent: Go along a ledge to below the S pre-top, make 3 abseils then abseil the lower part of the route (2 hours).

160. SE Diedre: Warriors of the Wasteland *R.&M.Edwards 22nd March 1987.*
A superb line - the most striking as you look up Wadi um Ishrin from the South: a massive corner rising straight up from huge multi-coloured dunes. 450m. E.D. Inf. 6 hours. Maps pages 103 and 130.
Approach: By Bedouin taxi to the foot of the dunes.
Descent: Abseil down the route (1½ hours) then - unless you have arranged to be met - another hour to walk back to the Rest House!

161. The Warrior *6A/5+/5+* The first three pitches of the above route. A splendid climb in its own right.

162. North East Pillar: Zamarama Dama *A.Precht, W.Haupolter, H.Gufler 24th April, 1989.*
Excellent climbing on good steep rock mostly in chimney systems, finishing by slabs. 400m. E.D. Inf. 5 hours. Maps and topos pages 103, 128 and 130.
Approach: By Bedouin taxi into Wadi um Ishrin. The start of the route is behind an obvious small round tower. Go up an easy face to the foot of the cracks.
Descent: Abseil first down the route, then down the pillar on its right. Pre-arrange a Bedouin taxi, or walk back!

S. Nassrani, East Face Warriors of the Wasteland

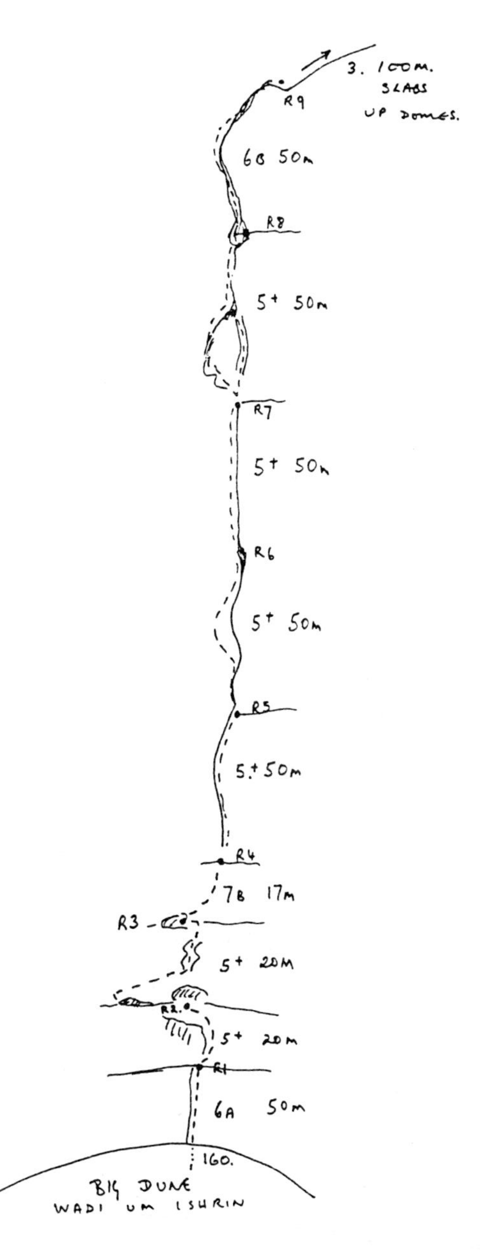

S. Nassrani, East Pillar Zamarama Dama

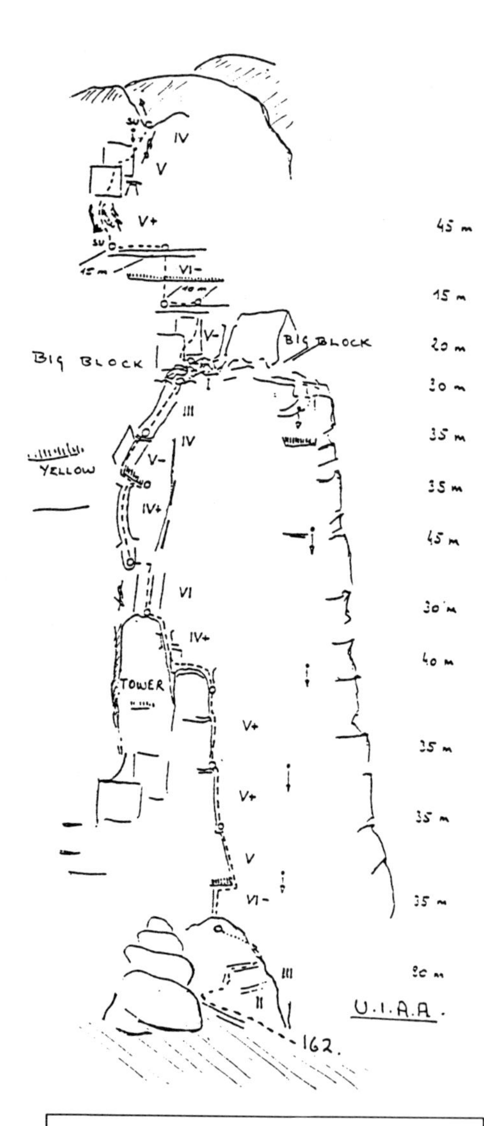

Draif Al Muragh 1360m

West Face

163. Never Say Never *A.Precht, W.Haupolter, S.Inhoger 8th April, 1990.*

A very sustained climb on good rock, ascending the face right of the big arch. Many slings and 2 pegs in-situ (1 move Ao) 300m. E.D. Sup. 5 hours. Map and topo pages 103 and 129.

Approach: Walk 20 minutes to the S and ascend screes to just right of the arch, where a small tower leans against the wall.

Descent: Down-climb easily to the col below S Nassrani tower and descend by the abseil of Stairway to Heaven (R.159).

164. Red Balcony *W.Haupolter, A.Precht, H.Gufler 30th April, 1989.*

Interesting climbing up a steep face with many overhangs and ledges. The climbing is surprising and it's a skill to find the way through the overlaps. 300m. T.D. Sup. 4 hours Map and topo 103 and 129.

Approach & Descent: As R.163. The route begins in the right hand corner system.

165. From the South West "Help"

C.&Y.Remy 11th May, 1986. (First ascent of this summit.)

The route takes a line of crack-chimneys. (On its right is a vast couloir, and right again is the south ridge.) There are, unfortunately, areas of poor sandy rock, but with good belays and protection.

Draif al Muragh, W. Face

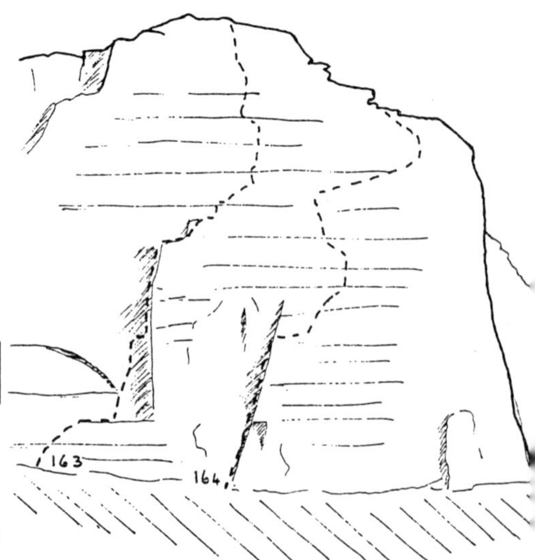

Draif al Muragh, W. Face Never Say Never and Red Balcony

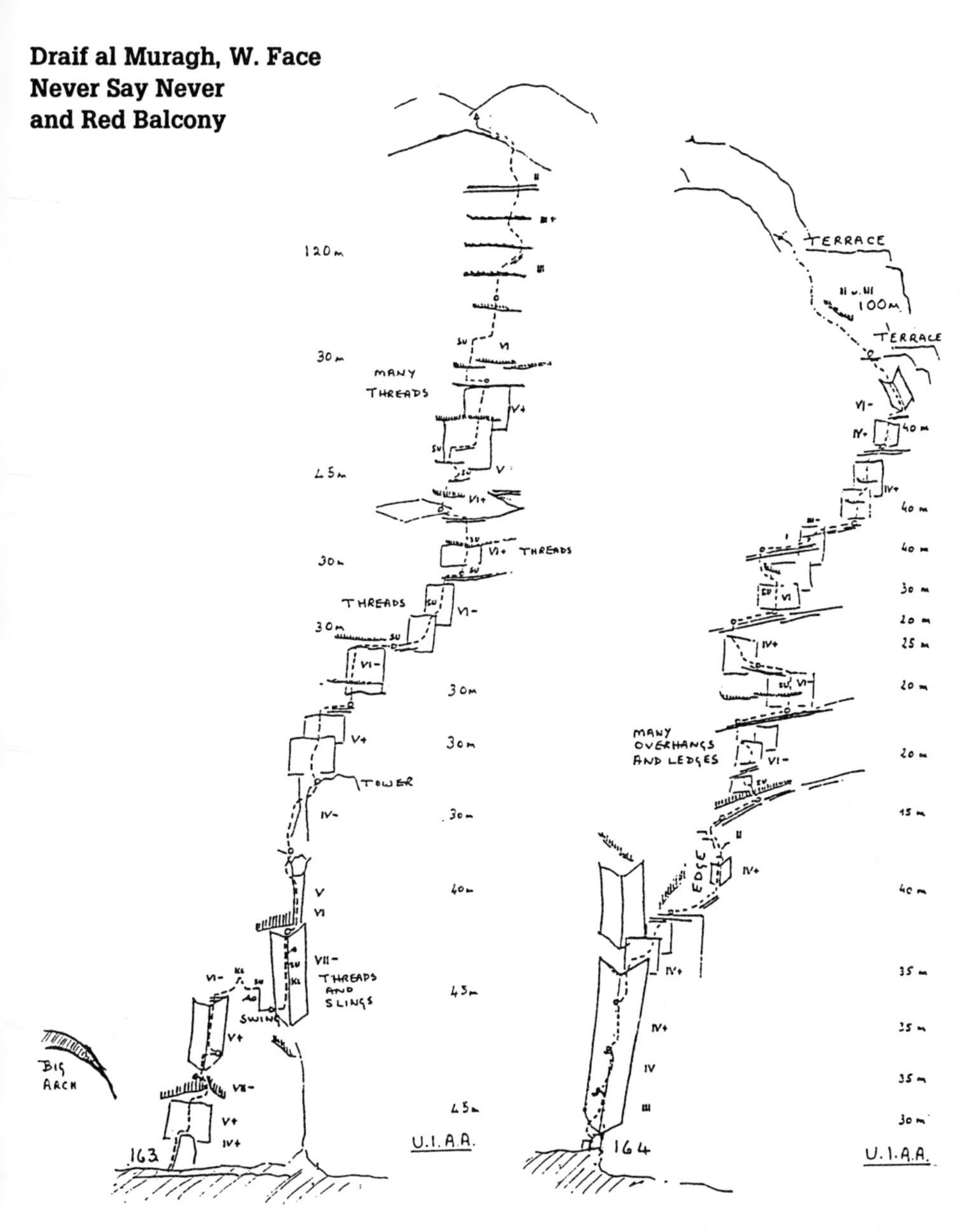

In-situ: Slings and one peg. Carry 2 pegs (1 blade 1 angle). 300 metres. T.D. 4 hours. Map and topo pages 103 and 130.

Approach: From the village, south east down Wadi Rum for about half an hour (or by 4-wheel drive) and up the scree to the foot of the climb (10 minutes).

Descent: Obvious abseils down the route. 1 hour.

166. East Face. The Beautiful Last Day

A.Precht, W.Haupolter March 1988.

The long vertical wall is broken by two parallel corners. The climb commences in the right one for a rope-length, then takes the left one to the top. "A high quality climb on the best sandstone". 300m. T.D. Sup. 3½ hours. Map and topo pages 103 and 130.

Draif al Muragh,

S.W. Face, Help | **East Face, Sandstorm** | **East Face The Beautiful Last Day**

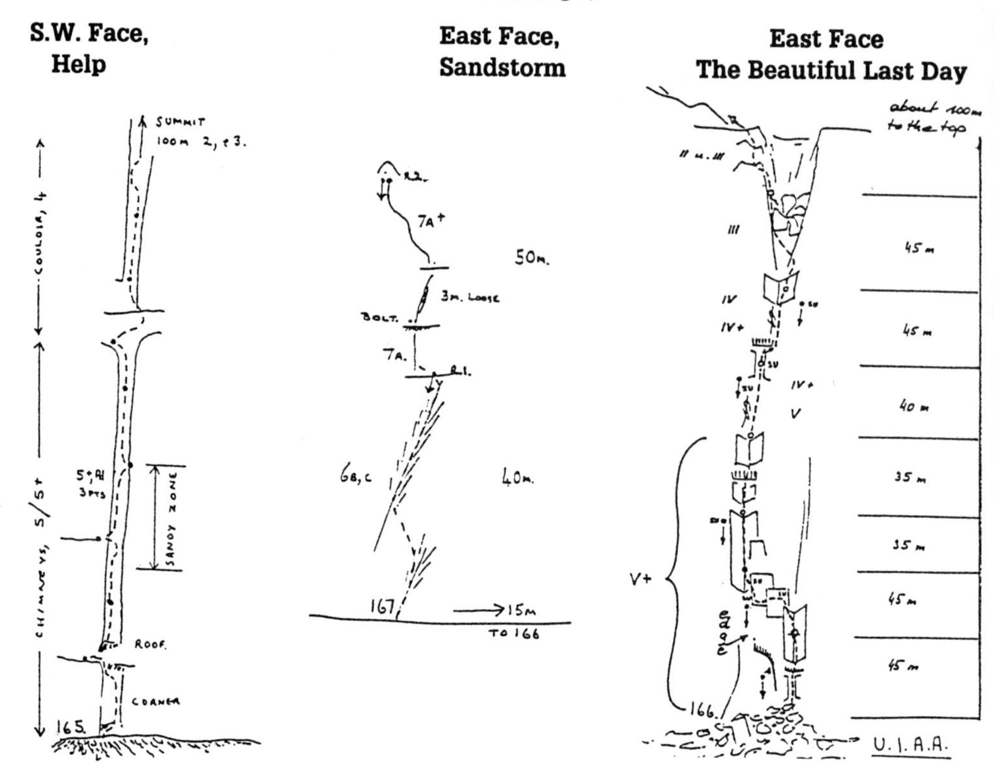

Approach: By Bedu taxi.
Descent: Abseil down the route.

Just left of the above route is a very hard two-pitch climb:

167. Sandstorm *M.&R.Edwards 15th March 1987*

"A star route". Small cams necessary for the second pitch.

The route ascends a superb little groove and crack-line left of a larger groove, capped by a large roof. 6B,C/7A+ (E5 6B, English).

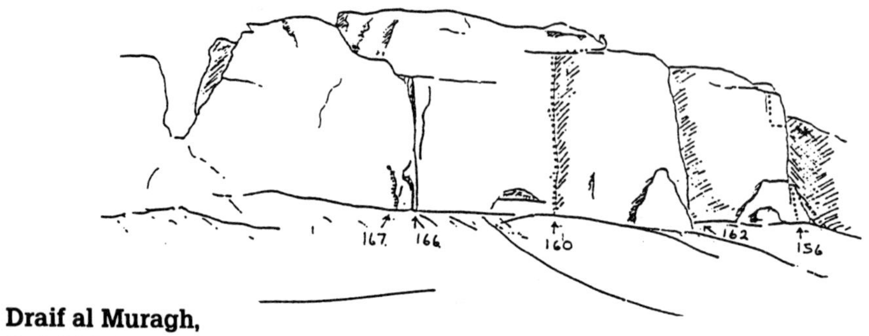

Draif al Muragh,
S. & N. Nassrani, East Faces

Jebel Annafishiyyah 1,424m (ref: 381733)

Named Jebel er Raka on the map, this peak is apparently wrongly named and should be Jebel Annafishiyyah. It is the largest and most northerly of the cluster of peaks in the southern end of Wadi um Ishrin.

West North West Face
168. Where Angels Fear to Tread

W.Colonna, A.Howard 14th April, 1987.

Interesting and varied climbing, first up an excellent grey slab by fine finger laybacks, then up a water washed ribbon of mostly good rock with little protection, winding between pockets and hollows with 'mushroom walls' on either side, to reach a large juniper at the mid-way terrace. The sandy overhanging crack above is unclimbed and looks horrendous! 150m. T.D. Inf. 2 1/2 - 3 hours. Map page 91.

Approach: By 4-wheel drive up Wadi um Ishrin until opposite the canyon of Zernouk El Daber (the East exit

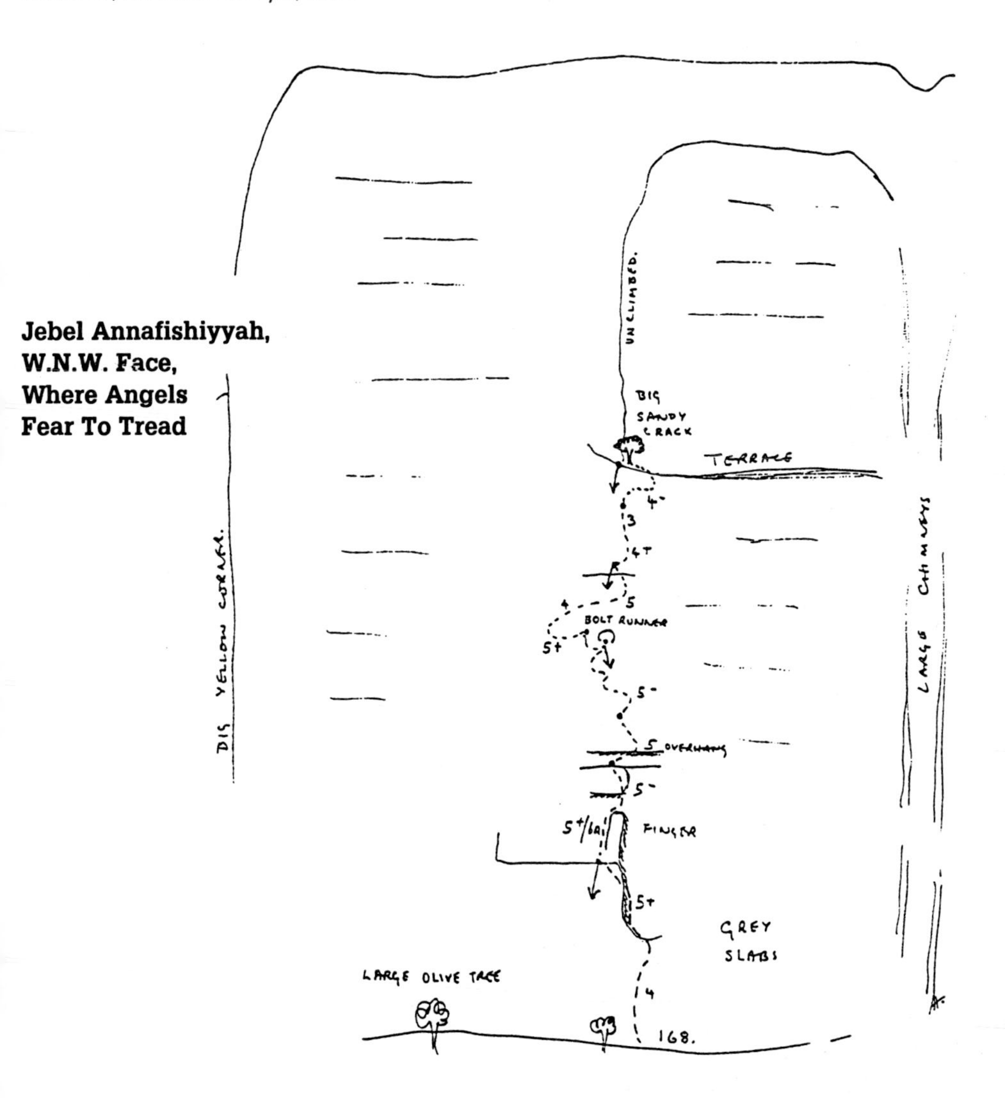

Jebel Annafishiyyah, W.N.W. Face, Where Angels Fear To Tread

of Kharazeh Canyon). On close inspection the route is obvious, and is identified by the grey slab at its base, with a prominent finger of rock pointing up the route. The start is below this, 50 metres right of a large old olive tree which itself is right of a big corner with a blank white wall to its left.

Descent: Four abseils straight down the route. Bolts etc., in place $\frac{3}{4}$ hour. (It is possible to return to Rum via Zernouk El Daber, 2 hours).

West Face

169. Slab & Canyon Route *First recorded ascent: A.D.Erskine, R. M.Austin 11th April 1988.*

A long and circuitous route with an equally long and complicated description supplied by the first ascentionists! No map or topo were made and the notes are difficult to follow. Here is a simplified version: ascends extensive red slabs to a terrace (3) then goes left and up a corner (3+) to ridges leading to a red terrace below white walls.

Go S then E above a deep canyon with some airy steps to the next ledge above. (Large Bedouin wall cairn just further on.) Gain a ramp via Bedouin steps and follow it to a short corner. Up this (4) and go right (5) to enter a chimney. Follow this (4 and 3) to roofs. Avoid them to the left or right (4/4+) and continue along easy angled ridges going N (some 3). $1\frac{1}{2}$km. A.D. Sup.

Descent: By the same route (a few small cairns).

There is also another route on this West Face which again is not described too precisely:-

170. Jordan Express *G.Villa, G.&P.Crimella, P.Chiocchetti 26th April 1989*

Very good rock ascending the big spur of the right wall

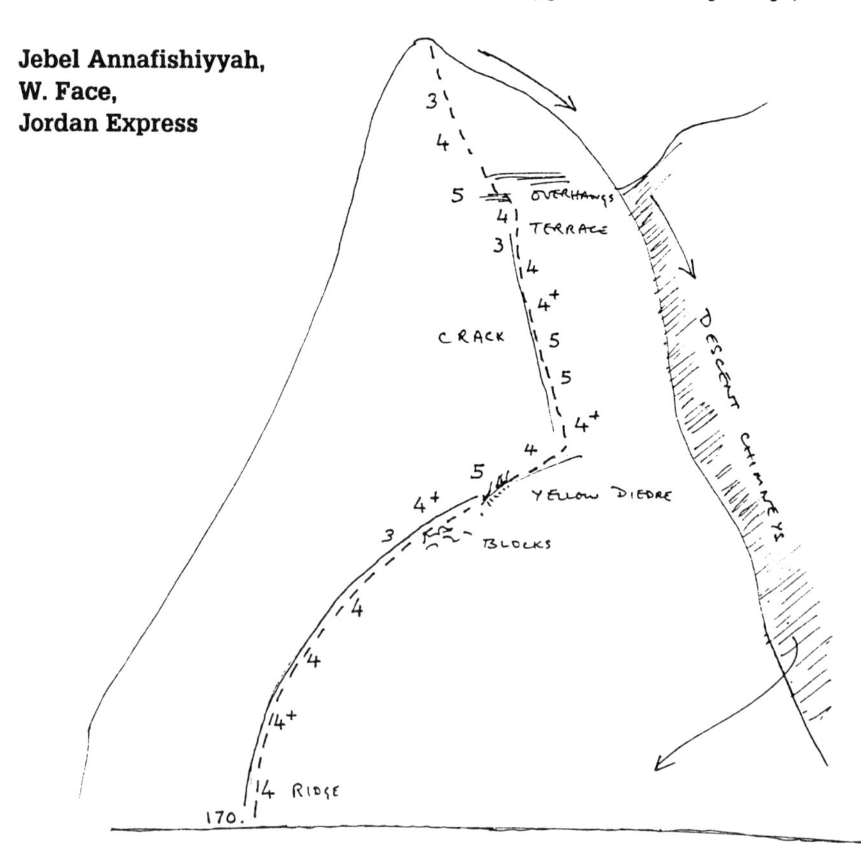

Jebel Annafishiyyah, W. Face, Jordan Express

in which are two big channels that come all the way down to the foot of the face. The start is close to a big niche. Carry a few Friends and chocks, and a few pegs. 320m. T.D. Inf. 3 hours. Topo page 132.
Approach as R.168
Descent to the right (S) down chimneys.

Jebel Annafishiyya. SW Summit 1,160m, ref: 377723

Presents a typical 'pocketed' red south west face, below and in front of the higher white wall of the main massif from which it is separated by the north-south couloir taken by the descent route.

171. West South West Face. April Fools

W.Nairz, D.Taylor, A.Howard 1st April, 1987.

A fairly intimidating crack and ramp goes diagonally up the left side of the face, from left to right, separating the rough red rock from a small white wall. Surprisingly easier than it looks! 1½ hours. 200 metres. D.
Approach: ½ hour by 4-wheel drive up Wadi um Ishrin. The face is opposite the entrance of Rakabat um Ejil. The route may also be reached on foot via Rakabat. 2 hours.

Descent: From the summit, go a few metres NE and down an easy diagonal ramp in the east face for 10 metres with an awkward step at the bottom (3) to a terrace. Down another 2-metre step (2) to the next terrace then right (S) for about 50 metres, and down easily to another terrace. Back left for 50 metres to large blocks beyond which a 45 metre abseil from a big thread goes exactly to the couloir. Easily down this (S) to the desert. 1 hour.

Immediately south of Annafishiyya is:

Jebel um Kharg (Mountain of Holes) 1,386m (ref: 377702)

172. A small peak climbed by the Bedouin.
The narrow wadi of um Kharg is to its west whilst Wadi Beidah, which is the south-east entrance to Wadi um Ishrin is to its east where a Nabataean building and dam are located, known as Um el Qeseir.

No modern climbs have been done on any of the peaks in this area. The locations of Bedouin routes are not known.

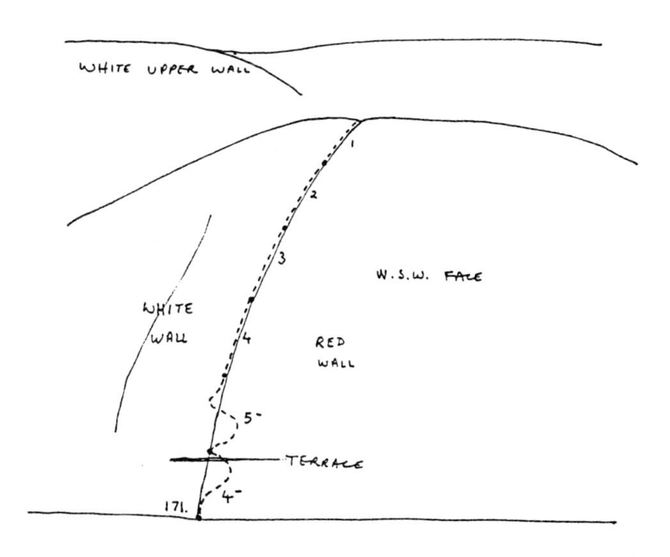

Jebel Annafishiyyah, S.W.Summit West South West Face, April Fools

BARRAH CANYON AREA

Major Features

For the purpose of this guide I have included under this heading the numerous peaks immediately east of Wadi um Ishrin, with the Disi oasis road forming its far north eastern limits and the Wadi of Khor el Ajram its south boundary.

The most striking peaks of this group are the three pyramidal peaks to the north east of Wadi um Ishrin. As far as we can ascertain none of these have specific names, the name Barrah seemingly being applied to the whole group. However, the most prominent of these peaks from most directions is the one directly above the north east end of Wadi um Ishrin. this one in particular became known to us as Jebel Barrah and is referred to as such in this guide.

From this peak, the range continues directly south with an almost unbroken West Wall for five kilometres, passing the undercut vertical wall of Al Riddah El Baidah at half way. South again across some wadis is the flat topped peak of Al Raqa.

Immediately east of the above group of peaks is Abu Judaidah only easily approachable on its western side by camel (or on foot!) by a long narrow desert canyon, which also gives access to the south east side of the Barrahs. With a competent Bedouin driver, the canyon can be entered by four-wheel drive.

There are as yet only a few recorded ascents of these peaks though the Bedouin have been up many of them. The canyon of El Barrah is, however, a climber's wonderland with a number of superb routes of around 100m to 250m. It is a 'must' on anyone's agenda and worth taking food and water in for a couple of days. Bivouac sites are, of course, numerous.

173. The Camel Trek to Barrah Canyon.

For aficionados of desert travel, camels can be used to ride into the concealed narrow canyon of El Barrah which is without doubt the best known area for this type of trek (ref: 410730).

Day 1: The shortest way of approaching this canyon which has many good sheltered camping areas is to leave Rum and head south, turning up Wadi um Ishrin and crossing east as soon as possible through dunes between red and purple towers (370719) to enter the little desert at the south end of the canyon at a narrow rock col (398707) known as El Mezeileqeh (Little Slippery Place), thence north east into the actual canyon, to the campsite (at 410724) which is on the left just before reaching a 'neck' in the canyon with an old fence. Distance about 12 kilometres, about 2½-3 hours riding time.

A variation on this journey is to continue south east from the end of Wadi Rum, rather than turning north east. At ref 380580, (after 4 or 5 kilometres down the Khor), go north up Wadi el Beidah along the east side of small rocky mountains, to Jebel um Kharg where there is a small building (383693) and an ancient dam (382699). The ruins are probably those of Nabataean building known as Um El Qeseir. From here, trend north east to the rock col at 398707 where the other route is joined to El Barrah Canyon. Distance about 15 kilometres. Riding time about 3 - 3½ hours.

If camels are only hired for one day, it makes a good trek to use the camels by any of these routes, to the campsite in El Barrah Canyon, from where they return to Wadi Rum with their owners. Next day it is a very enjoyable 4 kilometre walk through the Barrah Canyon to its north east entrance where a four-wheel drive vehicle can be met, to go back out to Disi via the flats. Near the fence inside the southern canyon entrance, on its east side is the site of the Nabataean dam known as Um Sidd.

Alternative: A longer way, with a slightly difficult entrance to the little desert south of the canyon is to go south down the Rum Valley, then south east down Khor el Ajram passing Jebel Khush Khashah and Jebel Qabr Amra, to Wadi Qabr Amra (375670). Go south down this, eventually turning east then back up north with the white jebels of Abu Khsheiba to the right. Cross Khor el Ajram again (390670) and rise up through an area of dunes north north east to a rocky escarpment between small towers (405693). Descend this with care (probably

Barrah Canyon Area
(see key opposite)

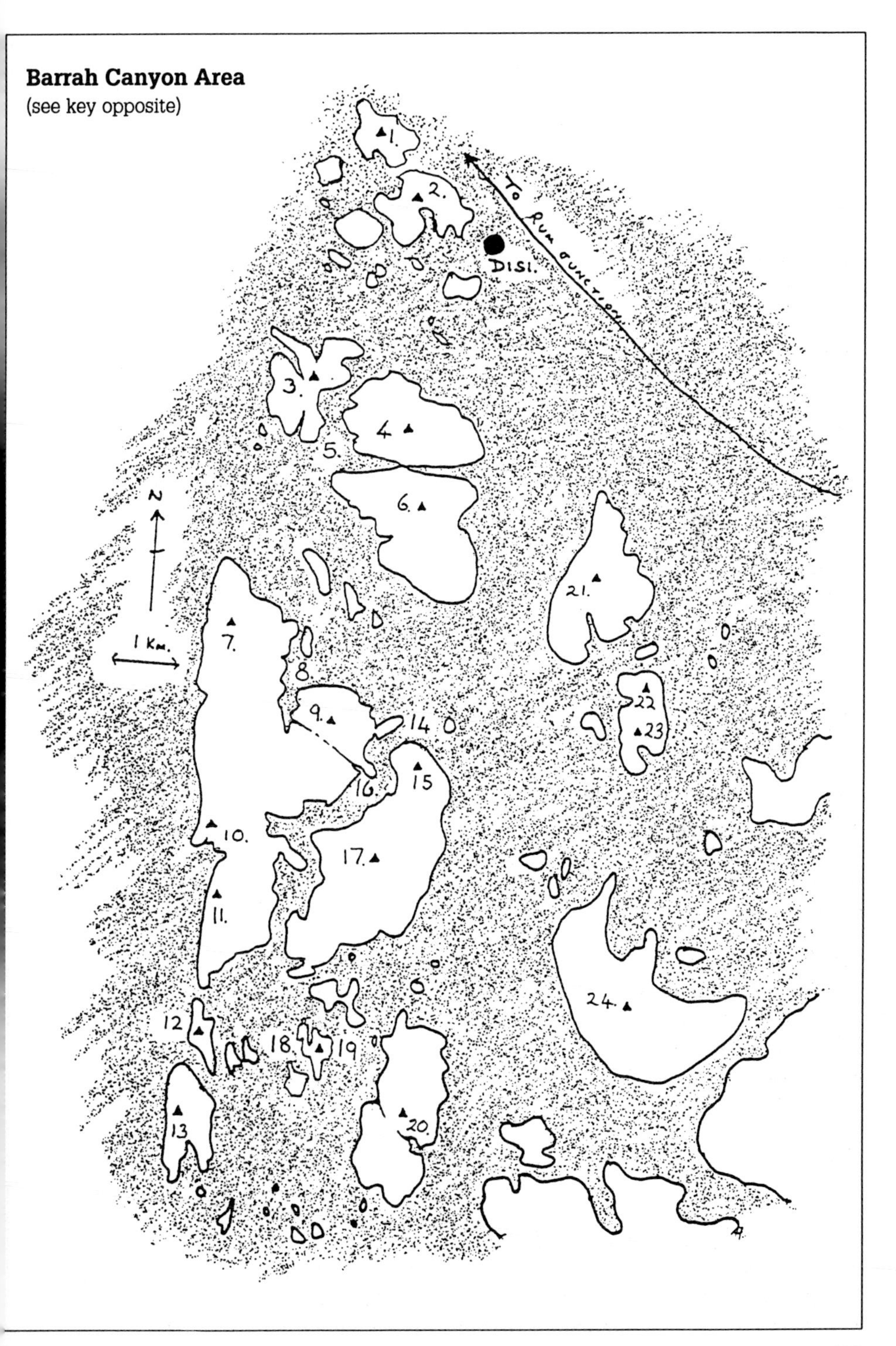

KEY TO MAP OPPOSITE

1 TOWER LAWRENCE
2 JEBEL UM ZERNOUK
3 JEBEL AL HASANI
4 JEBEL UM ANFUS
5 UM TAWAGI
6 JEBEL ABU ARASHRASHA
7 N. BARRAH
8 THE CANYON OF RAD AL BEIDAH
9 E. BARRAH
10 AL RIDDAH EL BEIDAH
11 S. BARRAH
12 JEBEL AL M'ZAYGEH
13 JEBEL AL RAQA
14 ARCH TOWER
15 N. SUMMIT OF ABU JUDAIDAH
16 BARRAH CANYON
17 JEBEL ABU JUDAIDAH
18 SOUTH BARRAH CANYON (UM HASHAD)
19 JEBEL UM SAURA
20 JEBEL UM HARAG
21 SEIFAN KEBIR
22 SEIFAN S'RIR
23 JEBEL UM'S DAIAT OF SEIFAN
24 JEBEL NASB

necessary to dismount) to the desert area immediately south of the canyon and follow the canyon as previous for 1$^1/_2$ kilometres to the campsite area. Distance about 20 kilometres. About 4$^1/_2$ - 5 hours riding time - an excellent full day with stops for 'chai' (tea) and lunch!

Day 2: From the campsite of El Barrah Canyon, follow the winding spectacular ravine north east to its exit above the salt flats of Disi which can be seen in the distance and then turn north west along the first possible valley for about 3 kilometres, until north east of the pyramidal summit of the N Barrah. From this point (409769), go between rocky towers to the north and then trend slightly west of north for another 1$^1/_2$ kilometres to a small rocky mountain with a smaller rocky tor on its left. On a flat face of rock on the south west corner of this mountain are some Thamudic inscriptions (403793). (A good place for chai or lunch, 10 kilometres.)

From here, cross the upper end of Wadi um Ishrin bearing north west to a concealed canyon (38500). Take this to the north, over dunes, then bear west round the north end of the um Ishrin Massif (Jebel Al Makhras) eventually rounding the end of the mountain (more rocks with inscriptions, though poor quality), into the north end of wadi Rum. Follow this south for 7 - 8 kilometres to the village. Total distance about 23 kilometres. Riding time about 5 hours. Another excellent day.

Alternatives: If it can be arranged to finish at Disi, it is possible either:
(a) To follow the above journey to the inscriptions (10 kilometres) and then go back east, then north, through a canyon (413790) before heading north east to Disi. Distance from inscriptions 5 kilometres, (15km from campsite). Time about 3 - 3$^1/_2$ hours.
(b) From the campsite, go down the canyon and desert beyond to the north east then directly north to Disi across the mud flats. Approximately 11 kilometres. About 2$^1/_2$ hours.

Jebel Barrah (The Outside Mountain) N Summit, 1,584m (ref: 400758)

This pyramid shaped summit stands at the east side of the north end of Wadi um Ishrin about 15 kilometres drive from the Rest House, up the road for 7 kilometres, then across the desert to the east past the north end of Jebel um Ishrin Massif.

174. Via the N Face - The Hunter's Slabs *First recorded ascent. M.Shaw, D.Taylor, A.Howard 2nd November, 1985, after being shown the route by Sheikh Kraim.*
The route starts near the north west tip of the mountain on a detached tower about 100 metres right of the end of the mountain and 50 metres left of a bushy hollow. After a devious start where care must be taken with route finding, pleasant slabs go all the way up to the East Ridge, where there is a choice of line. The route covers about 1$^1/_2$ kilometres.

Jebel Barrah, Hunter's Slabs

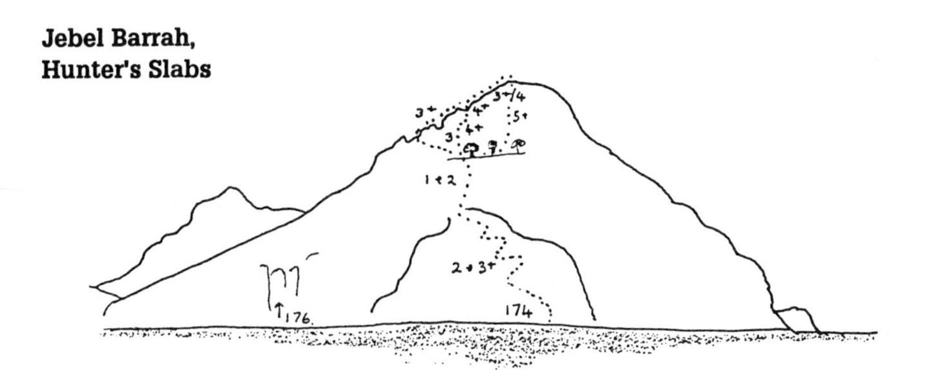

300m. Grade A.D. Inf. Direct finish, A.D. 2 hours.
Approach: By 4-wheel drive (1/2 - 3/4 hour - some soft sand!)

Descent: Take the easy line back down, taking care with route finding in the lower section. 1 3/4 hours. No abseils necessary.

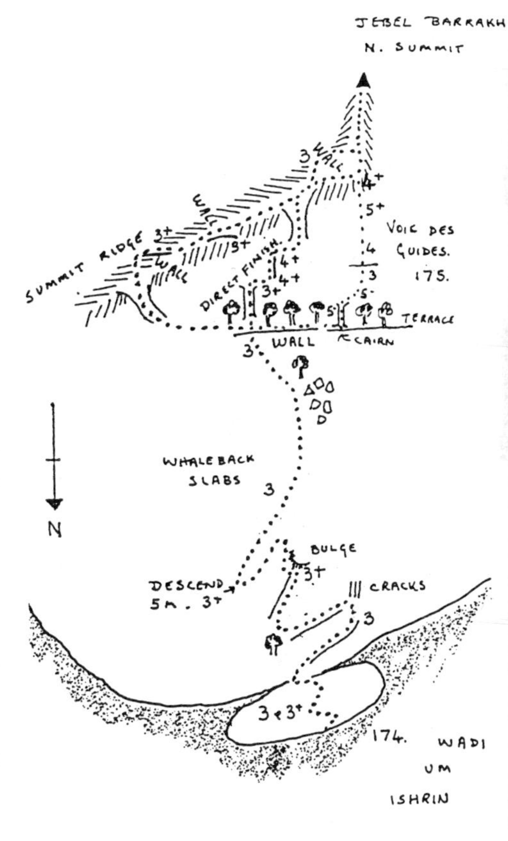

175. Voie Des Guides *Alberto Re, W.Nairz, B.Domenech October 1986.*

A more difficult but equally enjoyable variant of Hunter's Slabs. 300m D. 2 hours.

176. NNE Face. La Rose du Desert

Y.Duverney and J.P. "Dolby" Monnet. October 1986.
An excellent climb on very good black rock with a hard and technical start. Situated on the steep lower walls of the NNE side of the N Barrah, easily identified from the topo. Good protection on the first part (crack system), and after more exposed in some places. 200 metres. T.D. Sup. Allow 3 hours. Topo page 138.
Approach: About 1/2 hour in four-wheel drive from the Rest House, as for the Hunters Slabs.
Descent: 1 hour, 5 rappels in place, starting from the top of the main crack corner.

To the south of the steep wall below the west face slabs of N Barrah is a small cove with a huge hidden flake chimney in its back wall, giving access to a hanging valley above, frequented by Bedouin hunters. The way on from here up the S ridge of the mountain is barred by a huge siq and steep wall but a W - E traverse of this part of the mountain has been done:.

Jebel Barrah, N.N.E. Face, La Rose du Desert

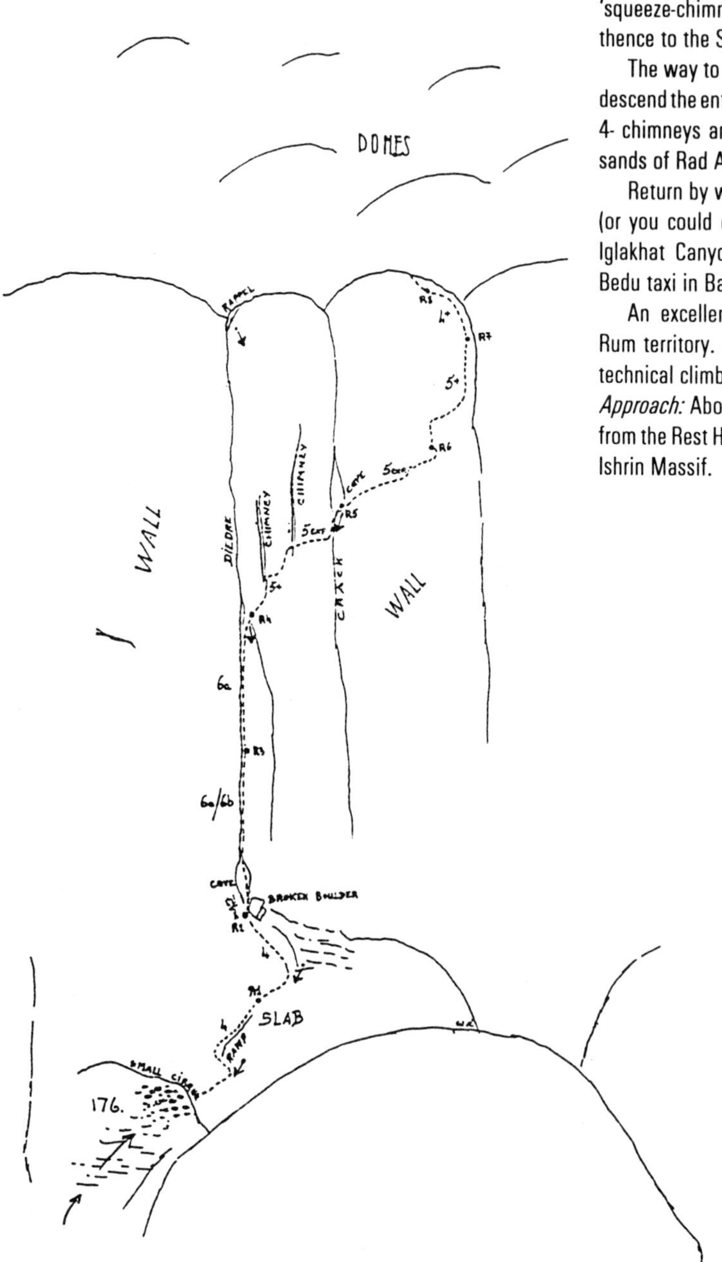

177. The Black Iris. (The flower of Jordan) *G.Hornby, S.Sammut 11th November, 1992.*

From the cove, the route ascends the 'squeeze-chimney' to the hanging valley, thence to the S Ridge of the mountain.

The way to the summit is prevented, so descend the entertaining 'skinny-siq' by 3+/4- chimneys and two abseils to reach the sands of Rad Al Beidah.

Return by walking round the mountain, (or you could even continue through Abu Iglakhat Canyon (R.190) and be met by Bedu taxi in Barrah Canyon!).

An excellent day out through classic Rum territory. Just over 1k with 200m of technical climbing. D. Topo page 139.

Approach: About 1/2 - 3/4 hour by 4 W.D. from the Rest House, round the N end of the Ishrin Massif.

N. Barrah, South Col Traverse, The Black Iris

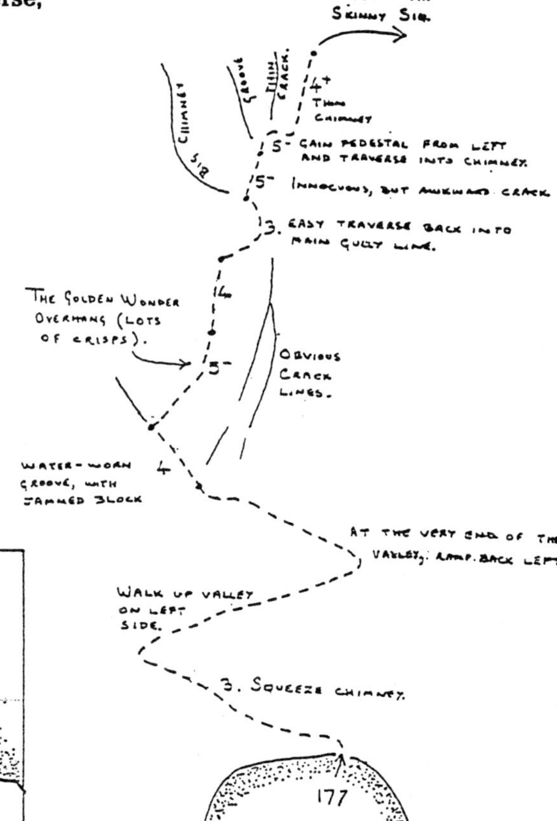

1. N. Barrah
2. Rad al Beidah
3. Skinny Siq.
4. Abu Iglakhat
5. Barrah Canyon.

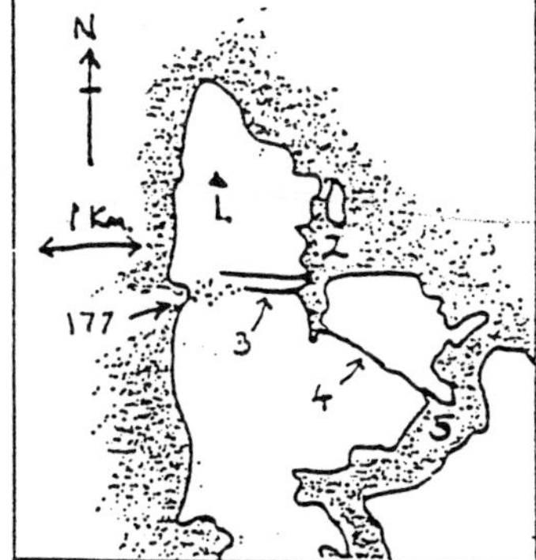

Al Riddah el Baidah (Mountain of the White Cape) 1,360m (ref: 398734)

Presents a large vertical south wall with a huge incut dome shaped overhang at the base. This peak is 1½ kilometres due south of Jebel Barrah, North Summit. No record of any ascents.

Jebel Barrah (South Summit) 1,653m (ref: 401720)

178. Via the south west ridge. This route is reputed to have been climbed by the Bedouin.

179. Via the West Face. As yet unclimbed, but presents a very prominent vertical crack line leading directly to the summit.

Jebel Al m'Zaygeh. 1,200m ref: 397703

South Summit

Situated just south of S Barrah and divided from it by the desert pass of El Mezeileqeh (Little Slippery Place). These two little summits bisected by a siq present a smooth black wall to the west, with prominent corners up each side.

Jebel al m'Zaygeh, West Face

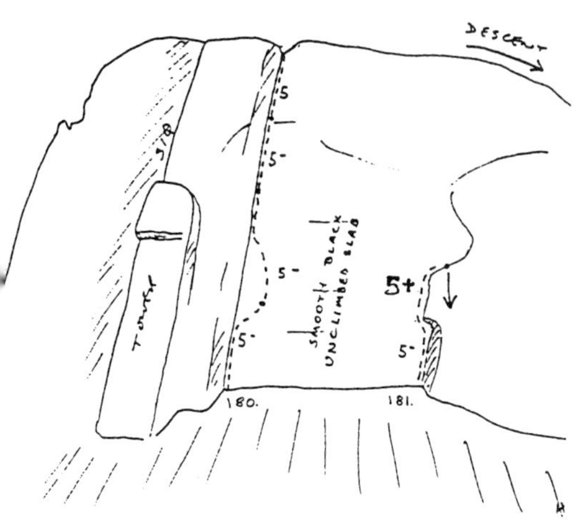

Approach: By Bedu taxi (on the way to Barrah Canyon).

180. Runner-Up *First ascent unknown (slings found in-situ by Colonna and Howard, 5th April 1987)*

The big left hand corner 5-/5-/5-/5-.

Descent: Take the ridge south from the summit, descending domes and couloirs, to the south and south south west. Some moves of 3, 15 minutes.

181. A Pale Moon Rising *W.Colonna, A.Howard 5th April, 1987.*

The lower half of the question mark shaped right hand corner. A little gem! Perfect rock, nice climbing, good protection 5+. 40 metres.

Descent: One abseil from a huge thread. (It should be possible to add a nice top pitch up the slab.)

Jebel Al Raqa (The Ragged Mountain) 1,375m (ref: 394687)

This peak is situated directly E of the SE entrance to Wadi um Ishrin, known as Wadi el Beidah. It is identifiable when approaching down Khor al Ajram by its long flat summit and west face, on which there is one major feature, towards its right side:

182. West Face Route *M.Kunkler, Y.Astier 1988 (variations by Astier and M.Simon, 24th April, 1990).*

Steep climbing with a choice of difficulty up the line of cracks and chimneys exiting on the S ridge. Peg belays in place. 300m T.D. (with harder variations). Map page 141.

Approach: 20 mins by 4-wheel drive.

Descent: Abseil down the route, or via the S ridge (not so obvious with 3 abseils). 1 hour.

183. East Face. La Terre du Soleil *C.&Y.Remy 28th April, 1986.*

A magnificent line and good climbing. 250 metres T.D. Ascent $3^{1}/_{2}$ hours. Map and topo page 141.

Approach: 20 minutes by four-wheel drive, and then go behind a huge dune and up to the end of the cirque, 10 minutes, where the line of cracks will be seen at the last moment. Just right of the starting point is a source of water with a pipe.

Descent: Along the south ridge, not so obvious, eventually finding three abseils, 1 hour.

Jebel Raqa, West Face

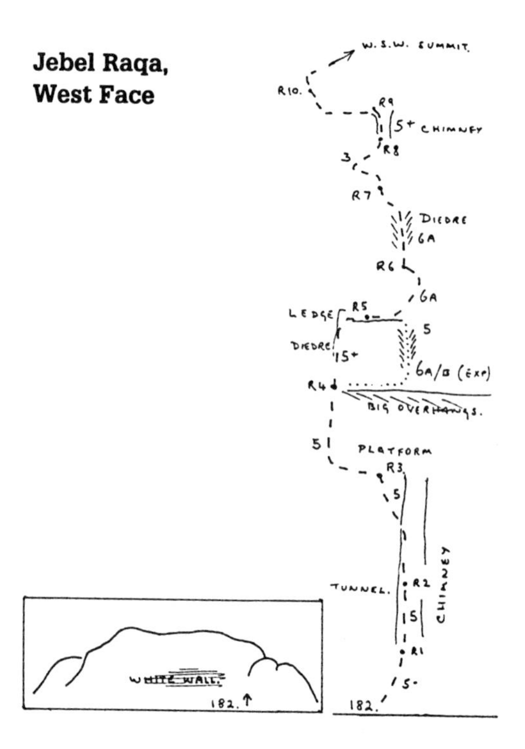

Jebel Raqa, East Face

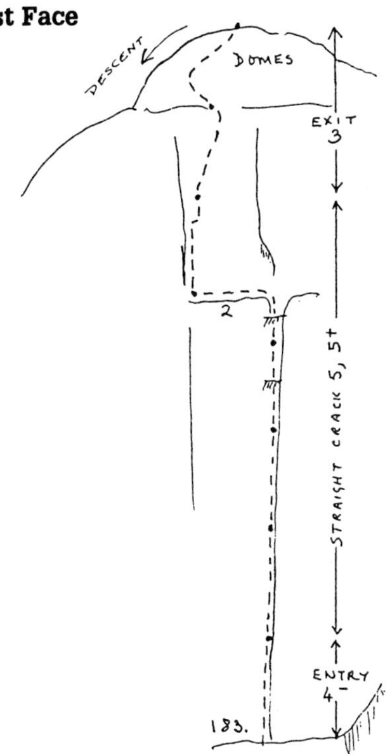

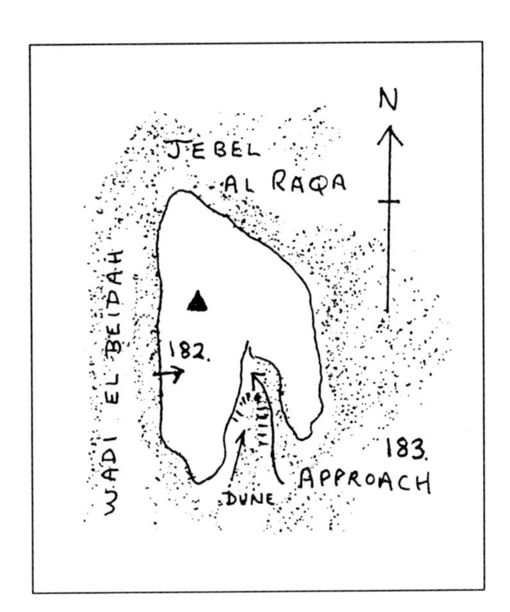

Tower Lawrence, West Face, My Friend Khalid

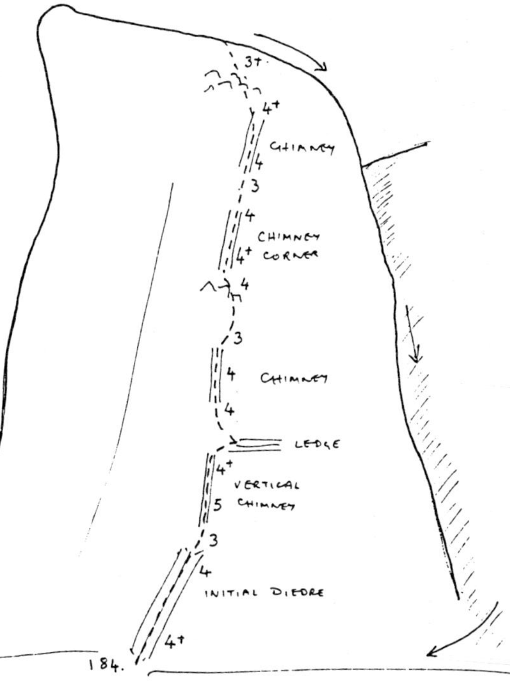

At the far northern extremity of the Barrah Canyon Area are a group of peaks just to the NW of Disi. They may be approached from Rum across the desert N of the um Ishrin Massif (about 12km. allow 1/2 hour) or by driving round the Rum-Disi road. The northern peak is:

Tower Lawrence 1016 m

184. West Face. My Friend Khalid *G.Villa, G.&P.Crimella, P.Chiocchetti 25th April, 1989.*
Good rock except in places where the sun has caused exfoliation. 250m D. 4 hours.
Approach: Cross the desert, to the start in a dihedral chimney.
Descent: To the right (S).

Immediately S of Tower Lawrence and W of Disi is:

Jebel Um Zernouk 990 m

185. SW Wall. Bello Camellino *G.Villa, G.&P.Crimella, P.Chiocchetti 29th April 1989.*
The route ascends the left of two big corner cracks on rock of variable quality. 250m D. 3 hours.
Approach as R.184.
Descent to the NW.

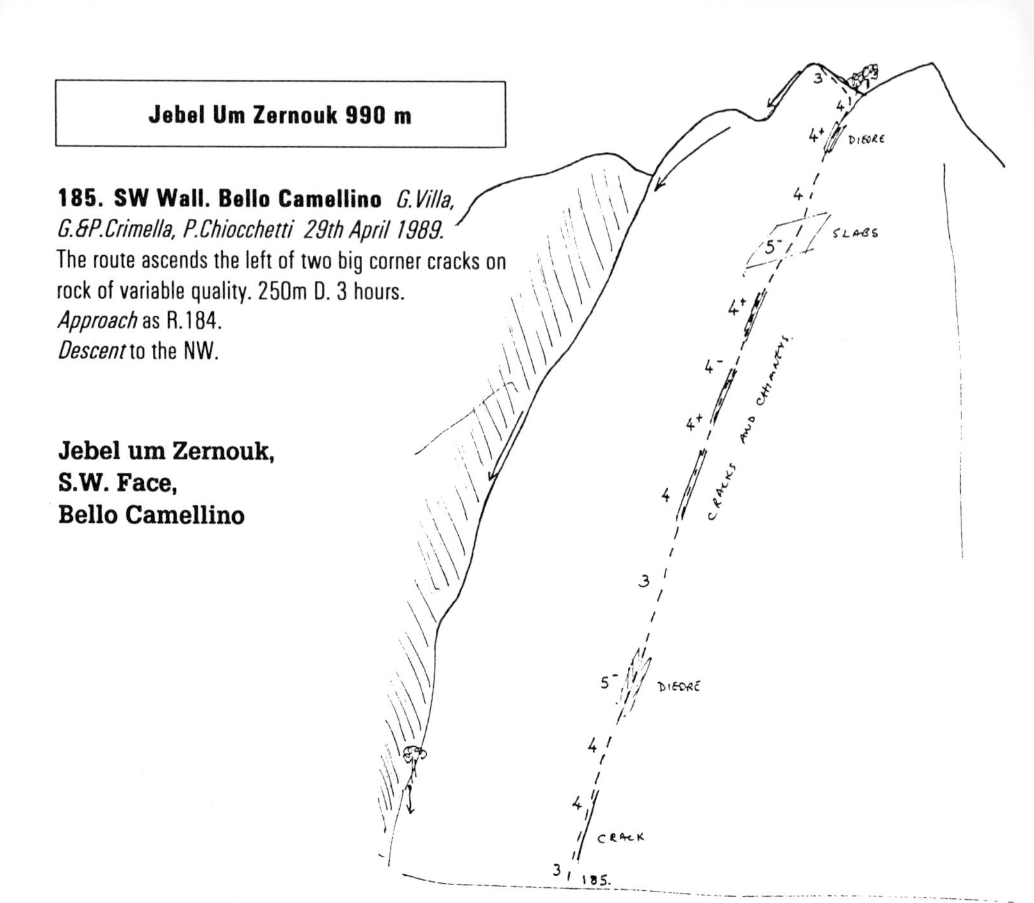

Jebel um Zernouk, S.W. Face, Bello Camellino

Jebels Al Hasani, Um Anfus and Abu Arashrasha

This cluster of peaks with its impressive canyons and inscriptions is 3km N of the Barrah group and 3km SSW of Disi. Seldom visited it has some spectacular mountain scenery. It is split into three summits by the siq and wadi of:

Um Tawagi. A secluded valley hidden away in the SW side of these peaks and approached by 4-W.D. from Wadi Rum, crossing an area of dunes N of Jebel um Ishrin (15km). There is scope for climbing here, and there are also rock inscriptions nearby, and a pleasant walk:

186. Round Jebel um Anfus.
An enjoyable canyon walk with a surprising variety of scenery. 7km. Allow 2 hours. Map page 135.

From the S entrance of Siq um Tawagi, walk E along the obvious valley, coming to a surprising drop above its lower continuation and an excellent view out across the mud flats to the green oasis of Disi.

Descend into the lower valley and walk N then W, round Jebel um Anfus to enter the N end of Siq um Tawagi. Walk up through dramatic rock scenery and back to the starting point.

Just W of the Siq entrance on a black slab above a boulder slope will be seen a variety of rock drawings depicting hunting scenes. Half a kilometre WSW on an isolated rock tower are more inscriptions again on a black slab, on its SW side (Ref: 403793).

Jebel Al Hasani, (Mountain of the Stallion) 1,142m (Ref: 413798)

This is the NW summit of the group. One climb has been recorded to the summit of Hasani, up its N side, starting right of an obvious dry waterfall above a fertile area:

187. North Siq, to North Summit - Siq and ye shall find *B.N.H.Scott, C.D.Wagstaff 15th September 1989.*

The rock is mostly solid, with good protection if required. The route is about 1km long rising 350m A.D. Inf. 2½ hours.

Approach: By 4 wheel drive, either from Rum or Disi. Look out for the dry waterfall which descends from a hanging valley and siq to soft white sand and a tree.

Descent: Down the route. 2 hours.

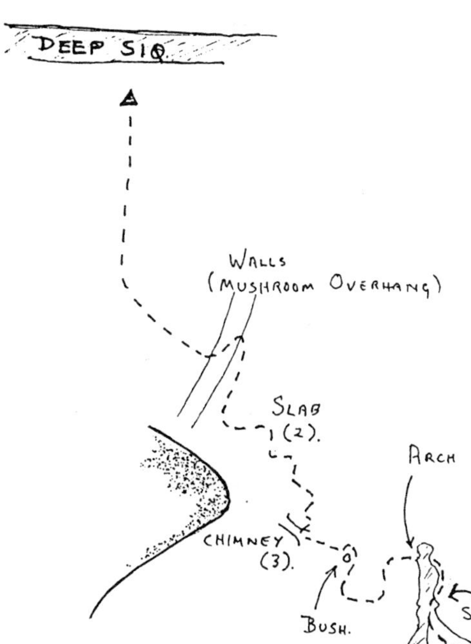

Jebel um Anfus (1,218 m) and Arashrasha (1,466 m).

As yet no climbs recorded on them though there is a Bedu route:

188. Ascends to semi permanent water supply in a canyon on the NE side of Um Anfus.

South of these peaks and just over 1km west of the N end of Barrah Canyon is a hidden box canyon cutting into the Barrah Massif. This is:

Rad Al Beidah (Canyon of White Sands)

To reach this canyon, take 4-W.D. from Wadi Rum (approx. ¾ hour turning S behind the E side of N Barrah, through soft sands. Concealed within are a number of side ravines including the curiously named Um Khera Said (the toilet of Said!). Poor Said who ate too many of the figs which grow here was 'taken short', and the name lives on much to the mirth of the Bedouin!

In the western side of Rad Al Baidah, in the concealed cleft of Abu Lasafa is a very recent discovery:

189. The New Super Crack *Partially climbed by W.Colonna, May 1992* no details yet, but look out for details in the new routes book at the Rest House.

Opposite on the E side of Rad Al Baidah will be found a fascinating ravine forming a through-route to Barrah Canyon:

190. Abu Iglakhat Canyon *Traversed by Sabbah Atieeq, W.Colonna, B.Domenech, D.Taylor, A.Howard spring 1990.*

An excellent through route with some climbing (3) and an abseil necessary, regardless of direction taken. On an overhung terrace near the western end and concealed from the outside world are some old stone shelters or food and equipment caches once used by Bedouin.

Barrah Canyon Area,

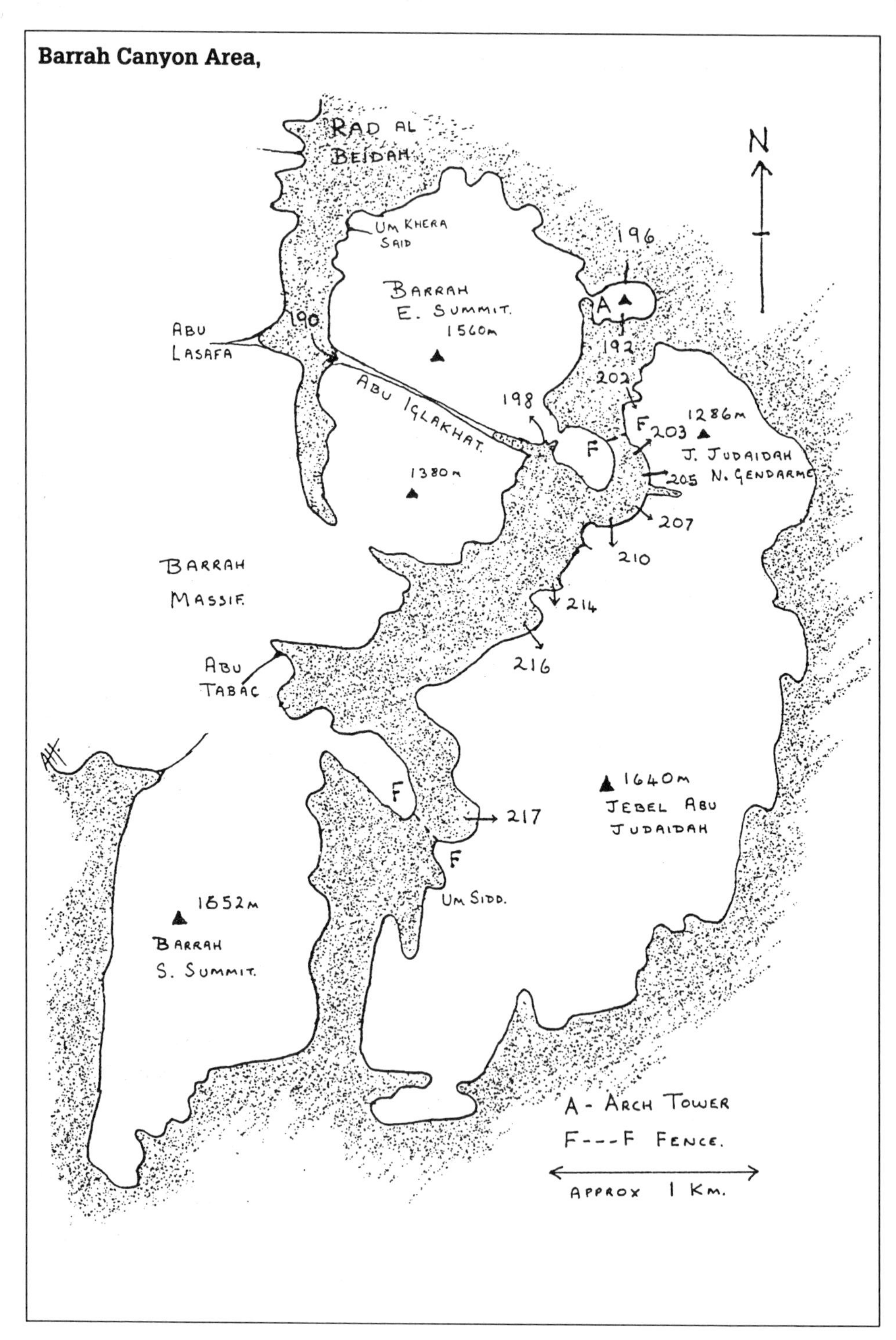

Muezzin, N.Nassrani. Pitch 14.
first ascent - photo Haupolter

Aqaba, S.Nassrani
Pitch 5, first ascent, - photo Haupolter

Climbs on the Nassrani Towers

Climbs on Jebel um Ishrin Massif

Sandstorm, Draif al Muragh, first ascent - photo Edwards

Climbs on Jebel um Ishrin Massif

Above: Jolly Joker, N.Nassrani. The big traverse, first ascent - photo Haupolter

Climbs in Barrah Canyon

Above: Merlin's Wand (note small figure at two-thirds height) first ascent - photo Taylor

Left: Sheikh Yerbouti first ascent - photo Howar

1km. F. Allow 1 hour. Map page 144.

From the West: Approach by 4-W.D. through soft sand to enter the recesses of Rad Al Beidah. Abu Iglakhat Canyon is at the back and is approached from the right. Pass the hidden shelters and climb chimneys to the col (30m, 3). Continue on the left side and abseil down the left wall to a ledge leading down into the E end of the canyon. Follow this out into Barrah Canyon.

From the East: (Barrah Canyon). Just past the fence at the N end of Barrah, go E alongside big dunes to enter the siq. Go almost to the end, before going up the right (N side) by a ramp and wall (30m, 3). Continue to the col and descend by abseil. Follow the canyon out, past the stone shelters and descending left at the end.

There are a number of rock climbing possibilities at the E (Barrah Canyon) end of this canyon, where three single pitch parallel cracks mark the entrance. (Routes 199 - 201).

Barrah Canyon

The climber's playground of Barrah Canyon winds between steep cliffs for five kilometres. There are huge sand dunes below some of the rock faces which makes driving difficult, particularly if travelling up the valley from N to S - far better to go through on foot, or with camels, the easiest way being from the S end. However, most of the climbs are near the N end and if climbing here, the driver will probably drop you off just inside the entrance.

The approach from Wadi Rum by any route goes through spectacular scenery: allow 1 hour by 4.W.D. or a half day with camels.

191. Through Barrah Canyon.

Simply follow the track down (or up) the canyon, making exploratory excursions as the fancy takes. (There are fences near both ends. Please leave the 'gates' either open or shut, as you found them - they are there to allow or prevent camels from passing through.) 5km. Allow 1½ - 2 hours.

Near the E end of the S fence an old Nabataean dam named Um Sidd will be found in a side canyon, whilst the area inside the N fence is where most of the rock climbs are. There are also some huge dunes here, close to the cliffs on the W side and not immediately apparent. Some of the 'siqs' on the W side hold pools of water for much of the year.

The major 'sports-climbing' area is at the N end and the first feature is the Arch Tower, which almost closes the mouth of the canyon.

Arch Tower

There are three routes on this tower which is situated in the North Entrance of Barrah Canyon, on a peninsula of rock projecting East from the East Barrah. Map page 144.

South Side

192. Le Bal des Chameaux *Y.Remy 26th April 1986.*

An enjoyable climb, which ascends the obvious diedres which come down 100 metres left of the summit. 4+/4/5-. 100 metres. 1 hour. Map and topo pages 144 and 147.

Variations: Y. Astier and B.Beauvais have climbed two alternatives to the upper pitches of this route:

193. The vertical wall on the right (6B)

Arch Tower, South Face

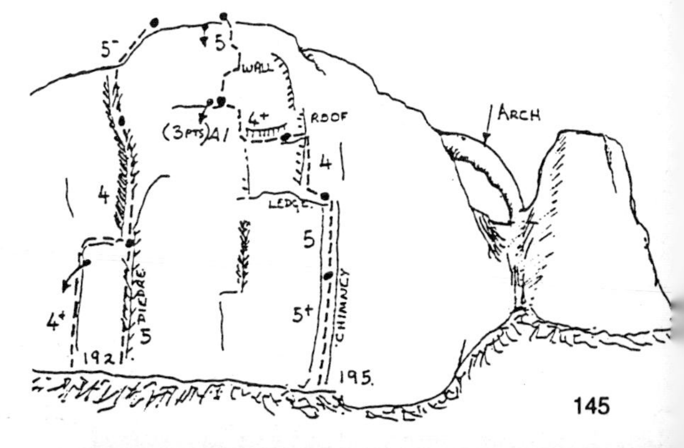

E. Barrah,
East Face
Ocean Slabs

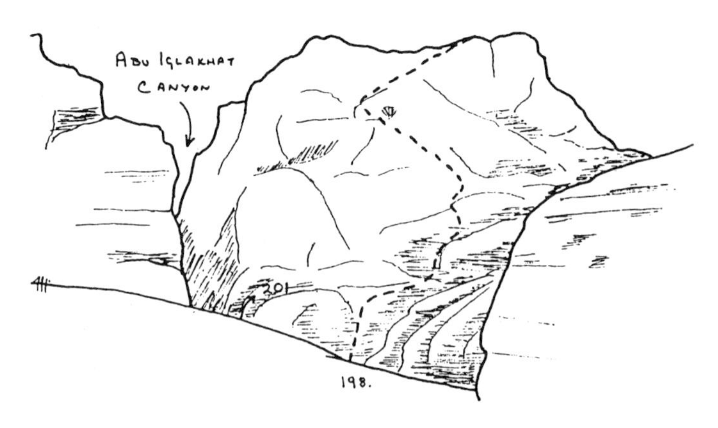

194. Further right, the diedre (6C)
Descent: 3 rappels near R.192, with some down climbing (3) $\frac{1}{2}$ hour.

195. Avant la Nuit *C.&Y.Remy 12th May 1986.*
Interesting climbing up the chimney and the corner directly below the right end of the summit, finishing by a slab. Carry 3 pegs (2 blades and an angle). Belays and protection obvious. 100 metres. 5+/5/4/4+A1/5. $1\frac{1}{2}$ hours. Maps and topo pages 144, 145 and 147.
Descent: 30 mins. (R.192).

North Side

196. Jogging *Y.Remy 26th April 1986*
Nice climbing up the chimney on the right of the ridge which leads to the summit with a pitch of 4+ at the start, followed by pitches of 3/4 and 5-. 100 metres. Ascent 1 hour. Maps pages 144 and 147.
Descent: (Route 192) $\frac{1}{2}$ hour.

Barrah Canyon, Central Dome
On the W side of the fence, when approaching from the N entrance is a small dome with a little climb on its N Side.

197. Tamer. *Jamal Ashab, N.Christie, C.Remy 5th November 1986.*
A nice little climb up the obvious line, with some pleasant climbing in the upper corner. 2+/3/3+/2. 1 hour. Map page 147.
Descent: By the same route.

Barrah Canyon, West Side
Only one major route has been recorded to date on the West Side of the canyon:

Jebel Barrah, E Summit (1,560m)
(Ref. 414745)

The prominent pyramidal peak NW of Barrah Canyon

198. East Face, Ocean Slabs *Chris Forrest, Louise Thomas November 1989.*
Exposed, with impressive situations. The easiest line up the vast sea of slabs opposite Merlin's Wand. 500m A.D. 3 - 4 hours. Maps pages 144 and 147.

Start at an easy chimney (cairn) and go up to the centre of the slabs. Follow them to a cave which is exited to the right (3). Continue to the barrier wall which is taken by the easiest line, starting with a leftward traverse (4), and so to the broken rocks of the summit ridge. Go right to the summit.
Descent: By the same route.

Immediately left (W) of the start of Ocean Slabs is the concealed Eastern entrance of Abu Iglakhat Canyon (R.190). Three parallel cracks mark the entrance, all 45m high and climbed by a French guide in November 1992. Map page 147.

From left to right, they are:-

199. Le Truand 6B+. Medium quality rock.

200. La Brute 6B. Sandy and slippery.

201. Le Bon 6A+. Superb.

Barrah Canyon, East Side
North Gendarme of Abu Judaidah 1,286m.

North Facet

202. Antibut *C.&Y.Remy 13th May 1986.*
Good climbing, not sustained, taking the parallel cracks just to the right of a couloir. These cracks are situated at the end of a small siq which is itself near the north entrance of the Barrah Canyon. The passage of 6A can be climbed in artificial with nuts. 200 metres. T.D. Inf. Ascent 3 hours. Map page 144.
Descent: Follow the cairns and go to the south, crossing the domes, to reach the top of Enervit, marked by a crack and a tree. The first abseil is situated a little below on the left (horizontal crack). 1 hour.

Once inside the N fence, one enters a huge gladitorial amphitheatre of desert climbing! The first route on the left is on a S facing wall:

203. Fauteuil D'Orchestre *C.&Y.Remy 5th November 1986.*
The obvious crack left of Enervit. 250m T.D. Sup. 3½ hours. Maps and topo pages 144 and 148.
Descent by Enervit. 1 hour.

204. Enervit *C.&Y.Remy 24th April, 1986.*
A superb line in the middle of a large yellow wall in magnificent scenery (1 peg and 1 bolt in place. Carry a couple of angles). 250 metres T.D. Ascent 4 hours. Topos pages 148 and 149.
Descent: Follows the line of the climb but the second rappel is delicate to attain, because it is situated some metres under the ledge of belay 5. 1 hour.

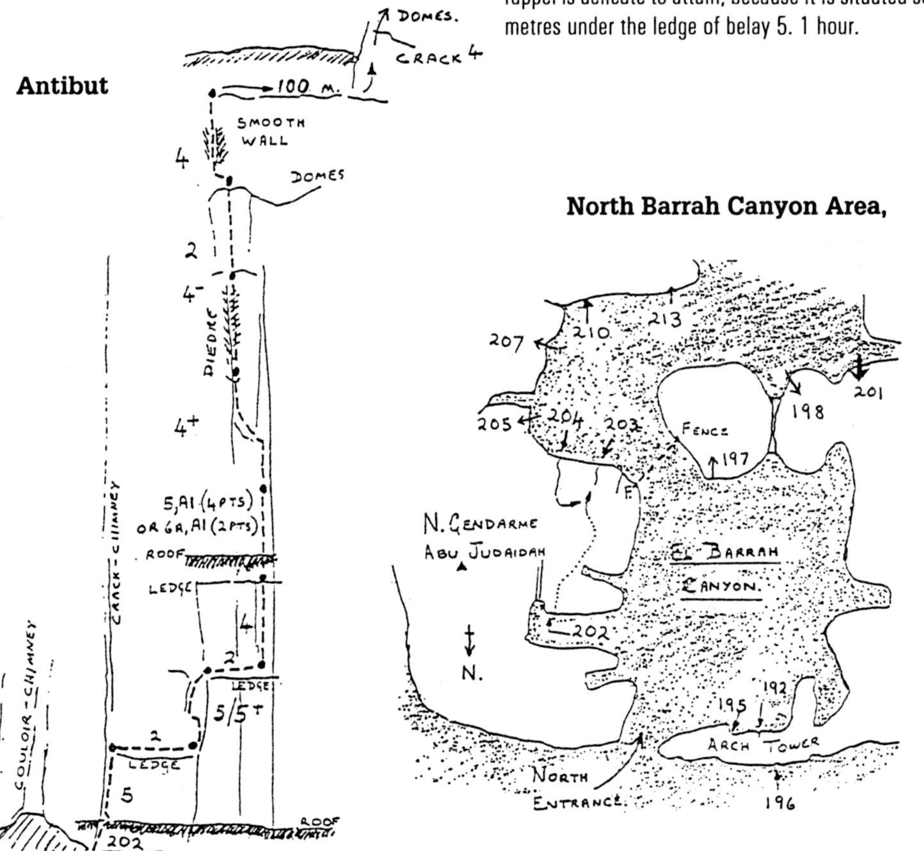

Antibut

North Barrah Canyon Area,

Barrah Canyon, Fauteuil d'Orchestre

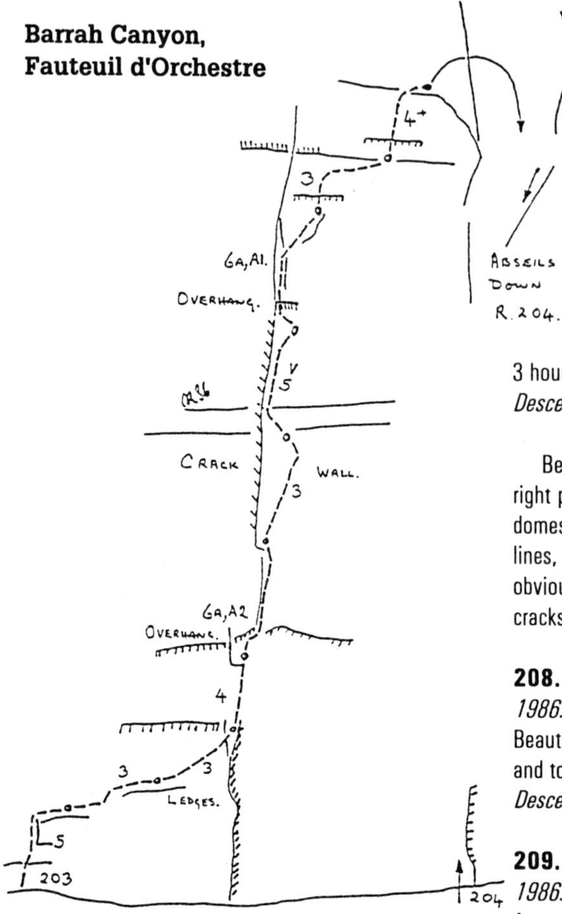

205. Neige dans le Desert *C.&Y.Remy 12th May, 1986.*
Very beautiful and aesthetic climbing (diedres, crack, slabs), situated just to the right of R.204. Good belays and protection but the seventh pitch of grade 6A/B up the slab is exposed. In place: slings, 1 bolt and 4 pegs. 250 metres. T.D. Sup. Ascent 4 hours. Maps and topos pages 144, 147 and 149.
Descent: Down Enervit, which is marked at the top by cairns and a tree. 1 hour.

206. A Siege of Jericho *Alex Renshaw, Dave Green September 1988.*
A really superb climb up the magnificent flake line immediately right of Neige dans le Desert. All pitches are sustained and on perfect rock. "Unfortunately lack of time and a drill made a lead of the last pitch impossible. Once protection is in place, the route will be a real classic." 120m, 7A/6A+/7A/6C/7A. Topo page 149.
Descent by R.204. 1 hour.

Over to the right, past a side ravine is a massive 'open-book' corner.

207. Les Rumeurs De La Pluie *C.&Y.Remy 27th October 1986.*
Good climbing up a powerful line. 250m T.D. 3 hours. Maps and topos pages 144, 147 and 149.
Descent: Down-climb and rappel the route.

Beyond here, the canyon wall sweeps round to the right presenting a north facing steep lower wall, with domes above. It is split by a number of superb crack lines, the most stunning being Merlin's Wand, very obvious when approaching up the canyon. Two other cracks parallel it to left and right, respectively:

208. Honte A Vous *C.&Y.Remy 1st November 1986.*
Beautiful climbing up a finger crack. T.D. 200m. Maps and topos pages 149 and 150.
Descent by abseil down Merlin's Wand.

209. Fesse Tival *C.&Y.Remy 27th October 1986.*
A good sustained and exposed line in a compact wall though aid is necessary (8 pegs in situ). 200m T.D. 4 hours. Maps and topos pages 149 and 150.
Descent: Delicate abseils down the route (1 hour).

210. Merlin's Wand. (Super Crack of Rum) *W.Colonna, A.Howard 7th October 1986.*
An incredibly straight crack-line slicing through the steep north facing wall.

Sustained, superb and surprising situations, with excellent protection requiring a good selection of nuts and many Friends. Magic climbing. 150 metres. 5+/6A/6A+/5+/5. 3 - 4 hours. Maps and topos 144, 147, 149 and 150.
Descent: The first abseil bolts are on the slab west of the tree in the basin at the top of the route. Descend the crack line with 4 abseils (pegs and bolts are in place), the last being right of the crack, on the pedestal. 1 hour.

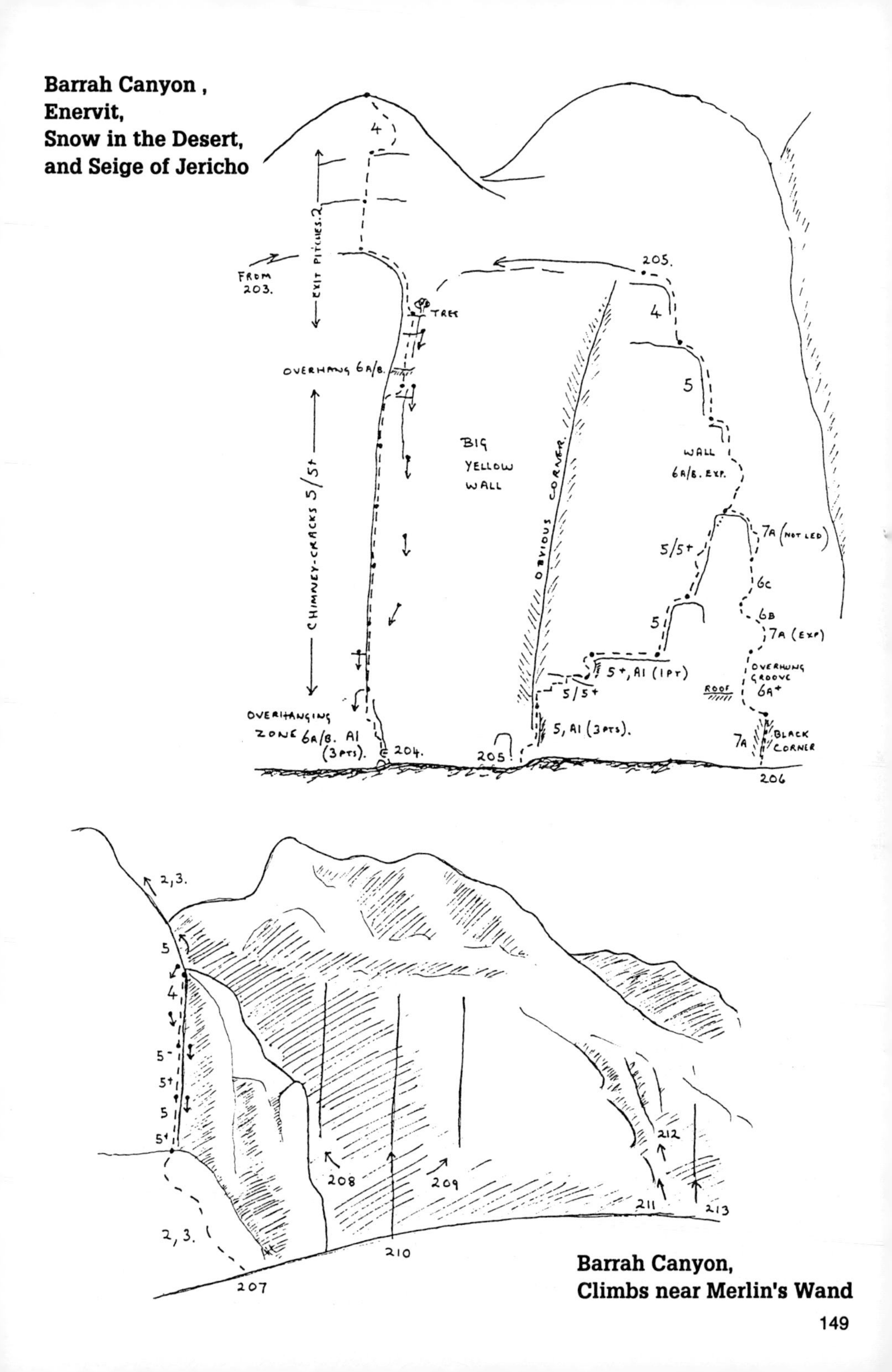

Barrah Canyon, Enervit, Snow in the Desert, and Seige of Jericho

Barrah Canyon, Climbs near Merlin's Wand

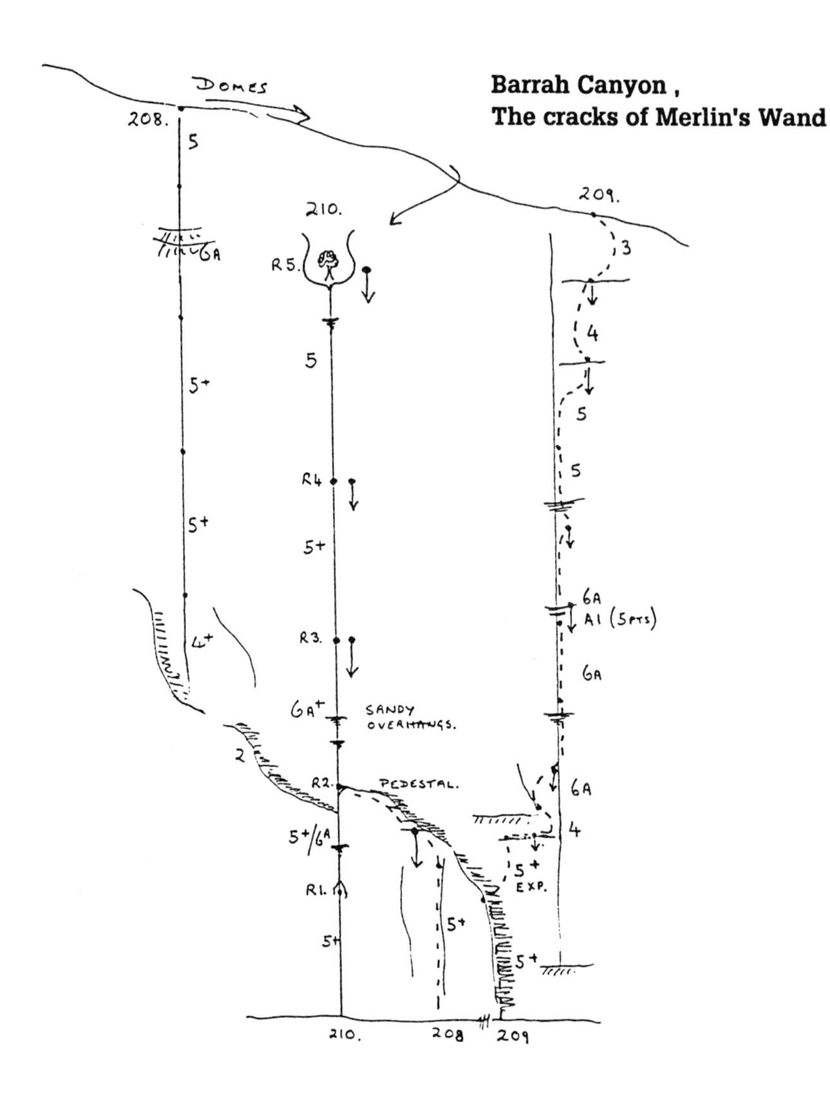

The next three crack-lines will be found at the right (W) end of the wall of Merlin's Wand:

211. Rain in the Desert *Y.Duverney and J.P.Monnet 27th October 1986.*

Athletic climbing, mostly in a corner-crack and a chimney. Good rock. Good belays and protection. 120 metres 5+/5/6A/4. 1½ hours. Maps and topos pages 147, 149 and 151.

Descent: ½ hour with a short 5/6 metre abseil to the top of Sundown and another of 45 metres, beyond here (SW) to the canyon.

212. Storm *Gilles Claye and Francois Lenfant 27th October 1986.*

Very nice crack climbing on excellent rock. Good belays and protection. 120 metres. 5+/5+6A/4/6A/4. 1½ - 2 hours. Maps and topos pages 147, 149 and 151.

Descent: As for Rain - ½ hour.

213. Sundown *Y.Duverney and J.P.Monnet 27th October 1986.*

A nice straight and vertical crack. Very good rock. Excellent climbing. Good belays but large Friends required and the final pitch up the wide crack is committing. 100 metres 5+/6A/5. 2 hours. Maps and topos pages 147,

149 and 151.

Descent: To the south west with one abseil, as Rain. 20 minutes. (The abseil point is not obvious. There is an alternative abseil point above the canyon to the SW but this involves some awkward down-climbing to reach the desert.)

After the wall of Merlin's Wand, the canyon bends to the south and is broken by chimneys. After nearly 200m there is a big black wall split by a crack:

214. Degage Cancer!

C.&Y.Remy 1st November 1986.

Interesting and sustained climbing. 1 peg and 4 slings in place. 200m T.D. 4 hours. Map and topo pages 144 and 152.

Descent: Cross the domes northwards for about 200m (cairns) and descend by abseil into the ravine, opposite the descent route of the Sundown climbs.

Still on the E side of Barrah Canyon, and continuing south west round the next bend in the NW Face, one comes to the next two routes, located by obvious crack-chimneys and pillars.

Barrah Canyon , Rain, Storm and Sundown

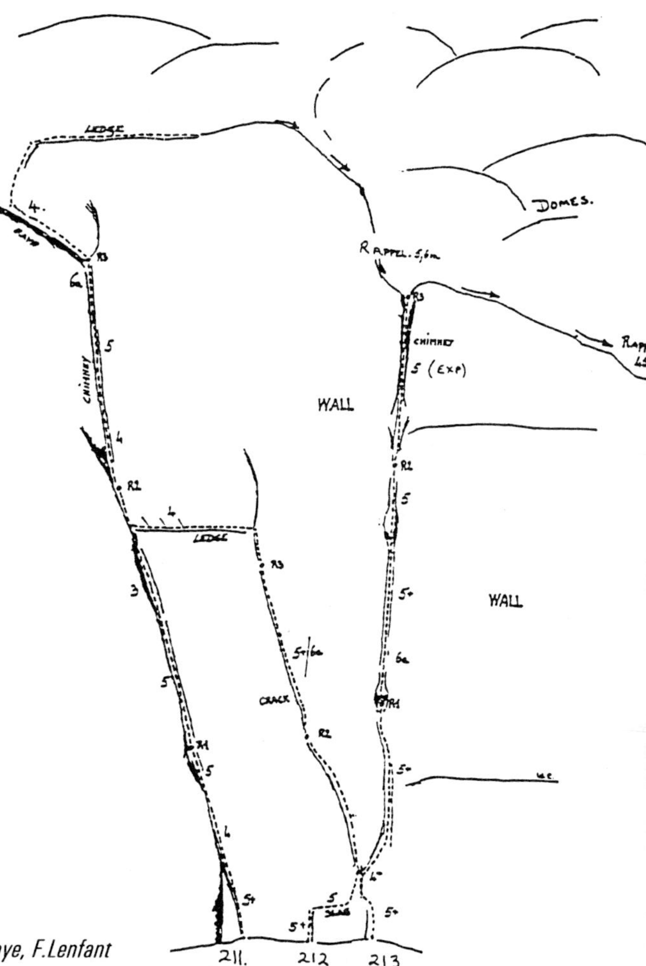

215. Voyage in the Aura *G.Claye, F.Lenfant 29th October, 1986.*

A brilliant climb - should become a classic! 75 metres 5+/6B. Map and topo pages 144 and 153.

Approach: From the wall of Merlin's Wand, continue into the Canyon for a further 300 metres (south), finally arriving at a large pillar, beyond which will be seen the characteristic beautiful walls and large chimneys.

Descent by 2 abseils.

216. The Star of Abu Judaidah *Y.Duverney and J.P.Monnet October 1986.*

The best Duverney/Monnet climb in the Wadi Rum Massif. All the pitches are sustained but on an excellent dark rock, with fine finger crack climbing, following a very pure line. Protection and belays are good. One angle peg is needed for the 6A move in the second pitch. 220 metres. E.D. Inf. Allow $4^1/2$ hours. Map and topo pages 144 and 153.

Descent: $1^1/2$ hours to gain the rappels of R.213, or 214. It would be better to rappel down the route. No abseil points in place.

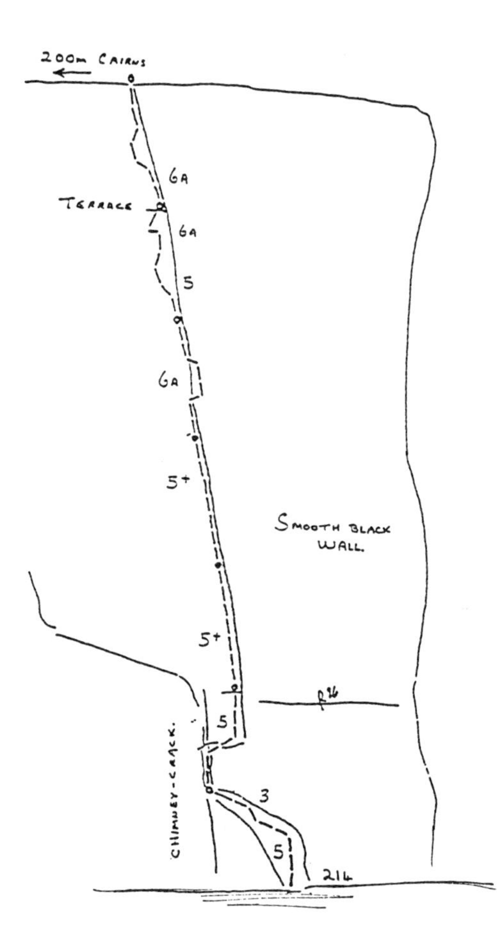

Continuing S down the canyon, one eventually arrives below the huge W face of:

Jebel Abu Judaidah, 1,640m

217. South West Corner: No way for Ibex
W.Haupolter, A.Precht 2nd May 1989.
A long, fantastic and bold climb on good rock. Recommended. This remote 'big wall' is situated towards the S end of Barrah, in a bay to the NE of the southern fence. The west face offers a hidden corner which points a little to the south. This has to be reached by difficult slabs which are hard to protect. The route then takes a line up the right side of the face with a detour right just above the top of the big flake. Some slings and

Barrah Canyon Area, Degage Cancer!

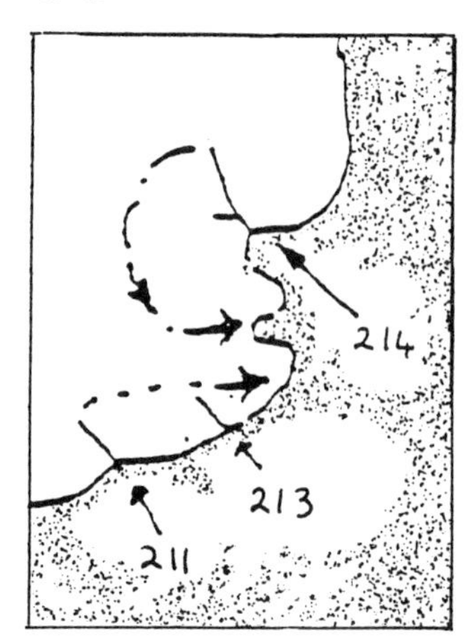

a peg in place. 400m E.D. 6 hours. Map and topo pages 144 and 154.

Approach: By 4-wheel drive to just beyond the S fence then a 10 minute walk up to the foot of the climb. *Descent:* From the summit, walk to the saddle in the E then down-climb and abseil moderate slopes and slabs to the N and W into the Canyon. (1½ hours).

El Barrah, South Canyon (ref: 412693) Um Hashad (Place of small stones)

This canyon is located approximately 2km south of the south entrance of the main Barrah Canyon and 1km west of Jebel um Harag. It runs in a south south east direction and has excellent faces on both sides offering great potential for 2 - 4 pitch crack and wall climbs. Only one route has been climbed to date.

218. Sheikh Yerbouti *A.Perkins, W.Colonna April, 1990.*
A powerful layback pitch up the big corner. Superb Friend protection 45m 6B (American 5.10c, English E3 5C).
Approach: Entering the canyon from its SE end (difficult driving through dunes), there is a large west facing slab on the right. This has a prominent left facing corner on its right. The route is 200m to the left, up the big square cut dihedral with a steep 100m high wall on its left. Map page 135..

Barrah Canyon, Voyage in The Aura & The Star of Abu Judaidah

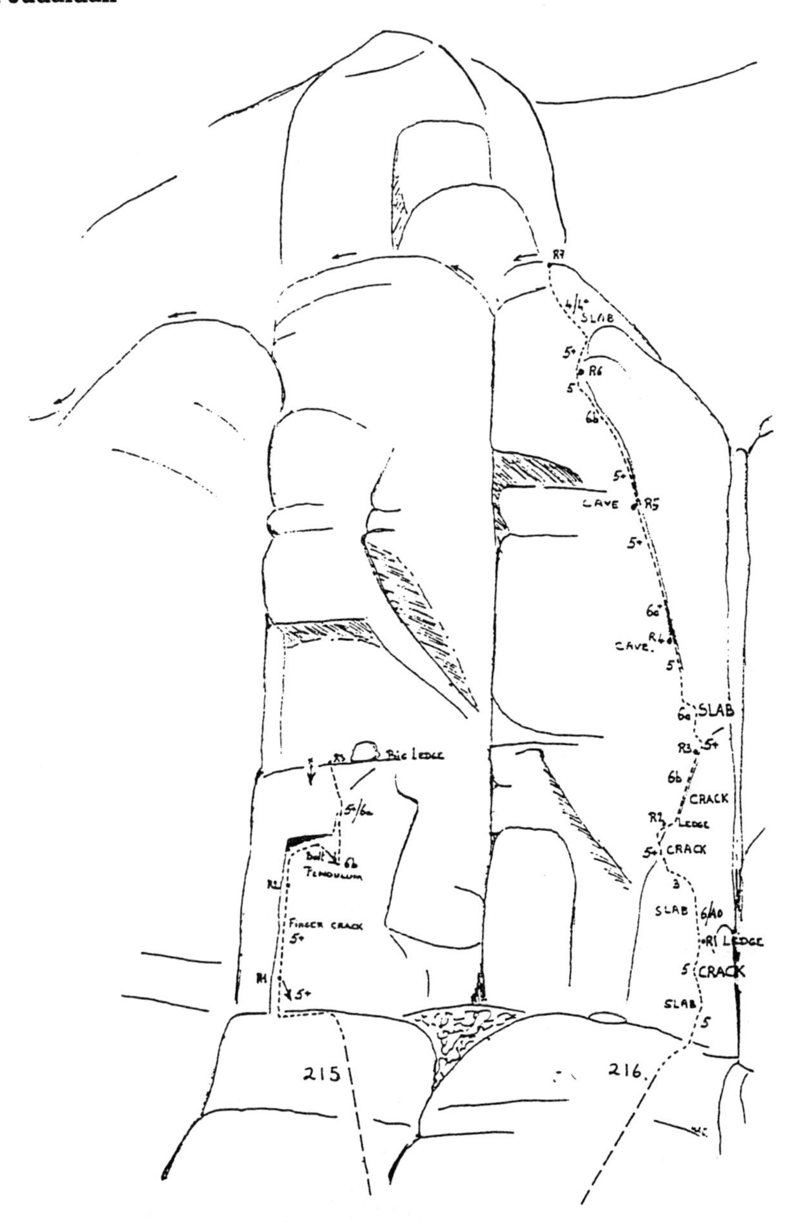

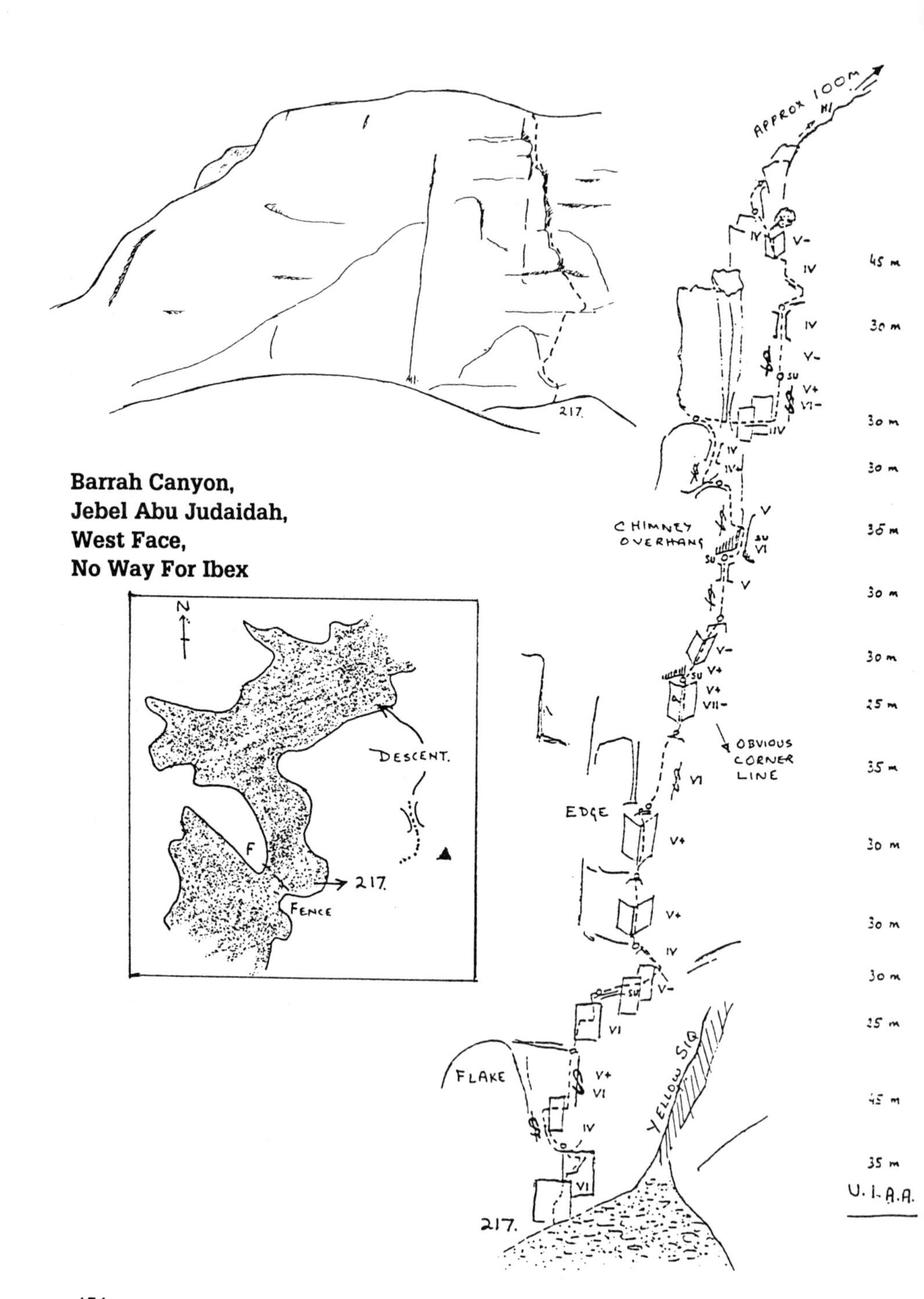

Barrah Canyon,
Jebel Abu Judaidah,
West Face,
No Way For Ibex

Jebel Seifan Group

This is actually a group of three peaks situated 2km E of Abu Arashrasha and 5km SSE of Disi. From N to S they are Seifan Kebir, Seifan S'rir and Umm's daiat. All are striated with crack lines, particularly the latter.

Four routes have been recorded on these peaks though the locations given are not precise.

Seifan Kebir 1256m (Ref: 452773)

219. West Face. Pensees pour Laurianne *Y.Astier and party 1987.*
The line starts left of a black wall and trends left to the summit. Mostly 4 and 5, 350m T.D. inf. 3½ hours.

220. S Ridge. A l'heure des scorpions *Y.Astier and party 1987.*
Pitches of 4+ and 3. 350m P.D. Sup.

Jebel Umm's daiat of Seifan 1104m (Ref: 460748) N Summit. (Seifan S'rir)

221. Pour quelques dinars de plus *Y.Astier and party 1987.*
Ascends the left side of W Ridge and the N face of the canyon, for 100m, to join the W ridge. 4+ with a section of 6B. 300m T.D.

222. Pour une poignee de dinars *Y.Astier and party 1987.*
Ascends the W ridge with pitches of 4 and 5+ and a passage of 6A. 300m T.D. Inf. 1½ hours.
Descent of both routes, by abseil and down climbing.

MASSIF OF KHUSH KHASHAH AND KHAZALI

Major Features
This is the block of peaks south of the main valley of Wadi Rum forming a giant flat topped mass on the horizon, split into two sections - Khazali to the west and Khush Khashah to the east - by the North Canyon of Khazali. East of Khush Khashah is the wadi of the same name, bounded on its east by a myriad of cumulus shaped white domes amongst which is Jebel Qabr Amra. That again is bounded to the east by the wadi of Qabr Amra (Amra's Grave).

Jebel Khazali (Gazelle Mountain) 1,420m (Ref: 345676)

The peak was referred to as Qasr Ali (or Ali's Castle) by Charmian Longstaff and spelt Khazail by Lawrence:

"My mind used to turn me from the direct road, to clear my senses by a night in Rumm and by the ride down its dawn-lit valley towards the shining plains, or up its valley in the sunset towards that glowing square which my timid anticipation never let me reach. I would say, 'Shall I ride on this time, beyond the Khazail, and know it all?' But in truth I liked Rumm too much."

North Face: This face can be seen from Wadi Rum village, with its overhanging NW arête, and in the centre of the wall, the big gash of Khazali Canyon.

223. Khazali Canyon
The northern ramparts of Jebel Khazali are split by a gigantic canyon or 'siq' in which are numerous inscriptions dating back to Thamudic times.

To reach the canyon, either go by 4-W.D. (about 8km), or of course, it is possible to walk or hire camels. The canyon is entered by a ledge on its right and the first hieroglyphics will soon be seen above on the left wall. Others will be found on both sides of the ravine at various levels.

As one goes up the canyon, it gets progressively narrower, often with pools. The rock walls are worn

Khazali, Burdah and the Domes of Abu Khsheibah

1 JEBEL KHAZALI
2 KHAZALI CANYON
3 JEBEL KHUSH KHASHAH
4 WADI KHUSH KHASHAH
5 JEBEL QABR AMRA
6 WADI QABR AMRA
7 JEBEL ABU EISALAN
8 JEBEL IKHNAYSSER
9 JEBEL UM FRUTH
10 JEBEL ABU KHSHEIBAH
11 JEBEL UM GOOR
12 AERAYQ ASSEJA (ROCK OF GAMES)
13 JEBEL ABU KHASHABA
14 JEBEL UM SAISIBAN
15 JEBEL UM HAMATA
16 JEBEL FARATA SHAIB
17 JEBEL UM S'DAIAT
18 THE ROCK BRIDGE
19 BURDAH

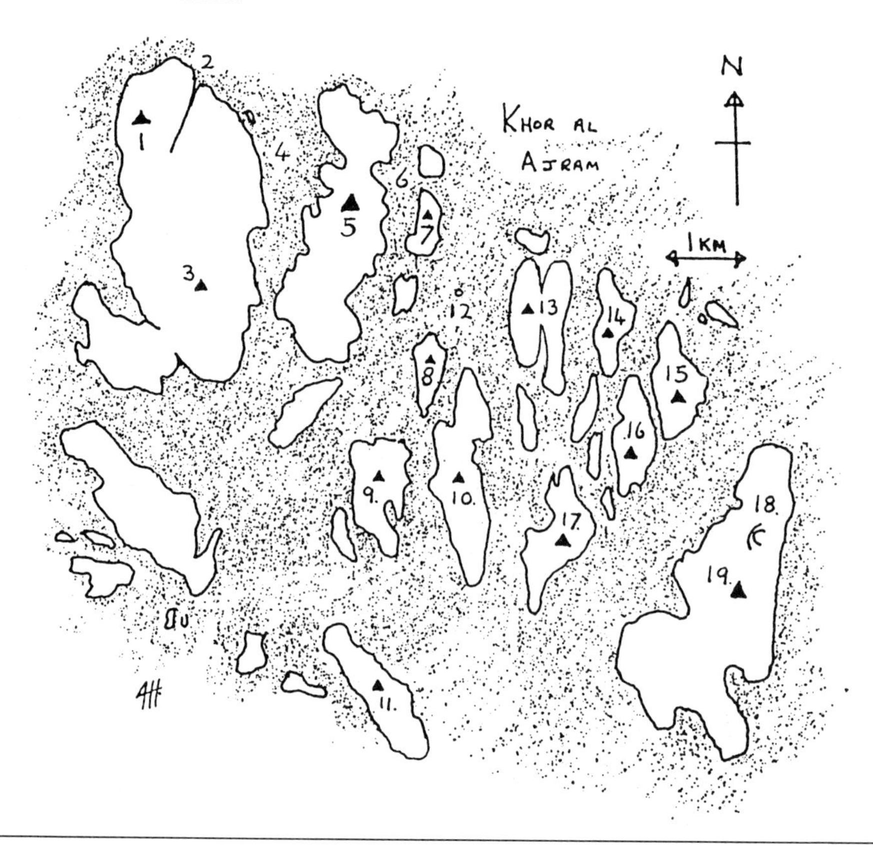

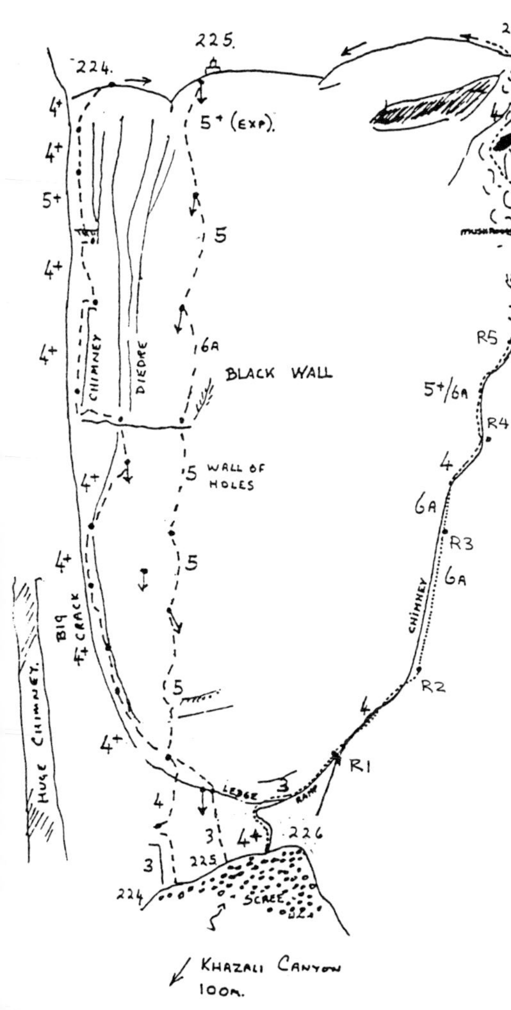

Jebel Khazali, N. Face

smooth by water. It is possible to continue for 200 metres or so, with some climbing (2) to reach the final box canyon, where there is a bull carved on the rock.

Near the end of the canyon, there is a route up its left side (going in), up the west face of the N summit of Jebel Khush Khashah (see R.239).

There are three climbs 100m right (W) of the canyon entrance, the first two are on the left side of a black wall, above the screes. Approach and descent for all three is the same:

Approach: By 4-W.D., 20 mins from Rum, then 10 mins scramble up the scree. Map page 158.

Descent: By rappel down Mazyed (R.225). 1 hour.

224. Rebelote *C.&Y.Remy 22nd October 1986*
Interesting climbing up big cracks and chimneys. 220m D. Sup. 2 1/2 hours.

225. Mazyed *C.&Y.Remy 22nd October 1986.*
Interesting climbing up cracks on the left side of the black wall. 220m T.D. 2 1/2 hours.

The third route goes up the right side of the black wall:

226. Les Petits Ramoneurs *Y.Duverney, J.P.Monnet, October 1986.*
Mostly chimneying in excellent black and red rock, finishing through a mushroom section (50m). Good belays and protection (no.4 Friends useful!). One good peg in place on the third pitch. 200m T.D. 3 hours.

NW Diedre

227. Le Commencement du Sabbah
C.&Y.Remy, 19th April, 1986.
This way ascends the big corner in the north west ridge, defined on its right by the smooth, yellow, overhanging wall. Interesting climbing, except for a short passage of bad rock in the 7th pitch (A1) but great character in the upper pitches. Protection is not always good, with some pitches rather exposed.

In place, one bolt and some slings. A selection of at least 5 pegs should be taken. 300 metres. T.D. Sup. Ascent 6 hours. Map and topo page 158.

Approach: 1 1/2 hour walk south, down Wadi Rum (or by four-wheel drive to the foot of the climbs).

Descent: By abseil along the line of the route. 1 hour.

Khazali, N.W. Diedre, Le Commencement du Sabbah and Selma Tower

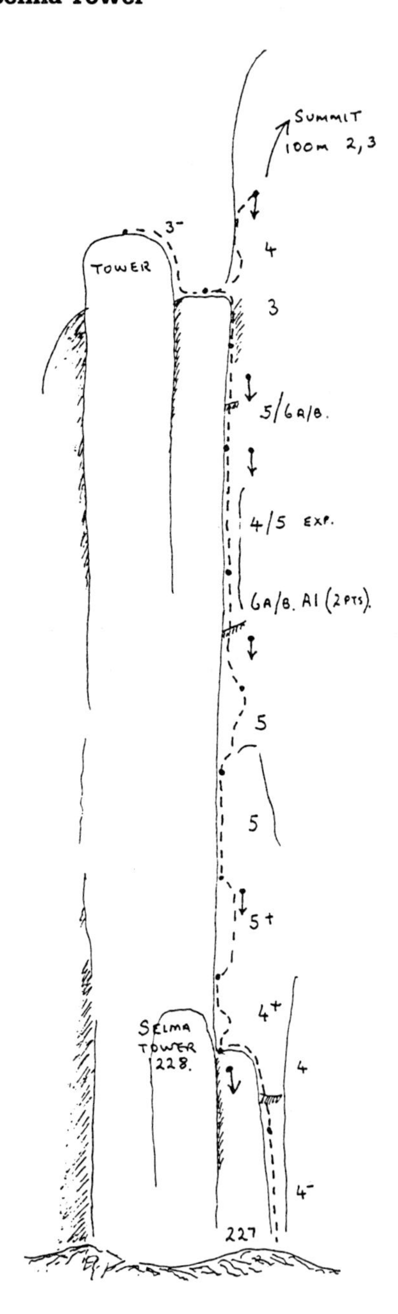

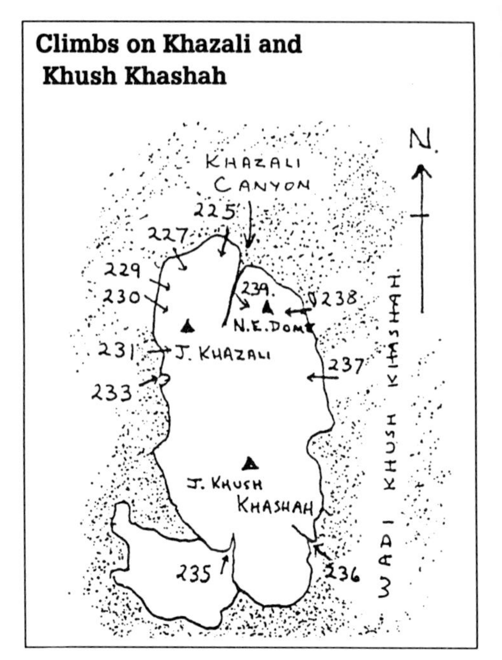

The tower at the foot of this route has a small climb on its S Face:

228. Selma Tower, Ugla Route. *Y.Astier and party 1987.* 100m Grade and line of route not known.

West Face

Past the prominently overhanging NW arête is the 300m high, 2km long vertical west face with some dramatic crack lines (not all climbed). The first route, just right of the hanging wall is:

229. Le Couchant *C.&Y.Remy 20th April, 1986.* Beautiful varied climbing up the obvious line of cracks on the left of the West Face. There is also an alternative start, from the right, which is much easier than the original. Good and obvious protection and belays.
In place. Slings and one bolt (for abseil). Carry two blade pegs for the second pitch. 300 metres. T.D. Ascent 5 hours. Topo pages 159 and 160.
Approach: By 4-W.D., 20 mins
Descent: Via abseil points alongside the route. 1 hour.

230. Jamal *C.&Y.Remy 3rd May, 1986.*
Nice climbing, with magnificent character, up the obvious

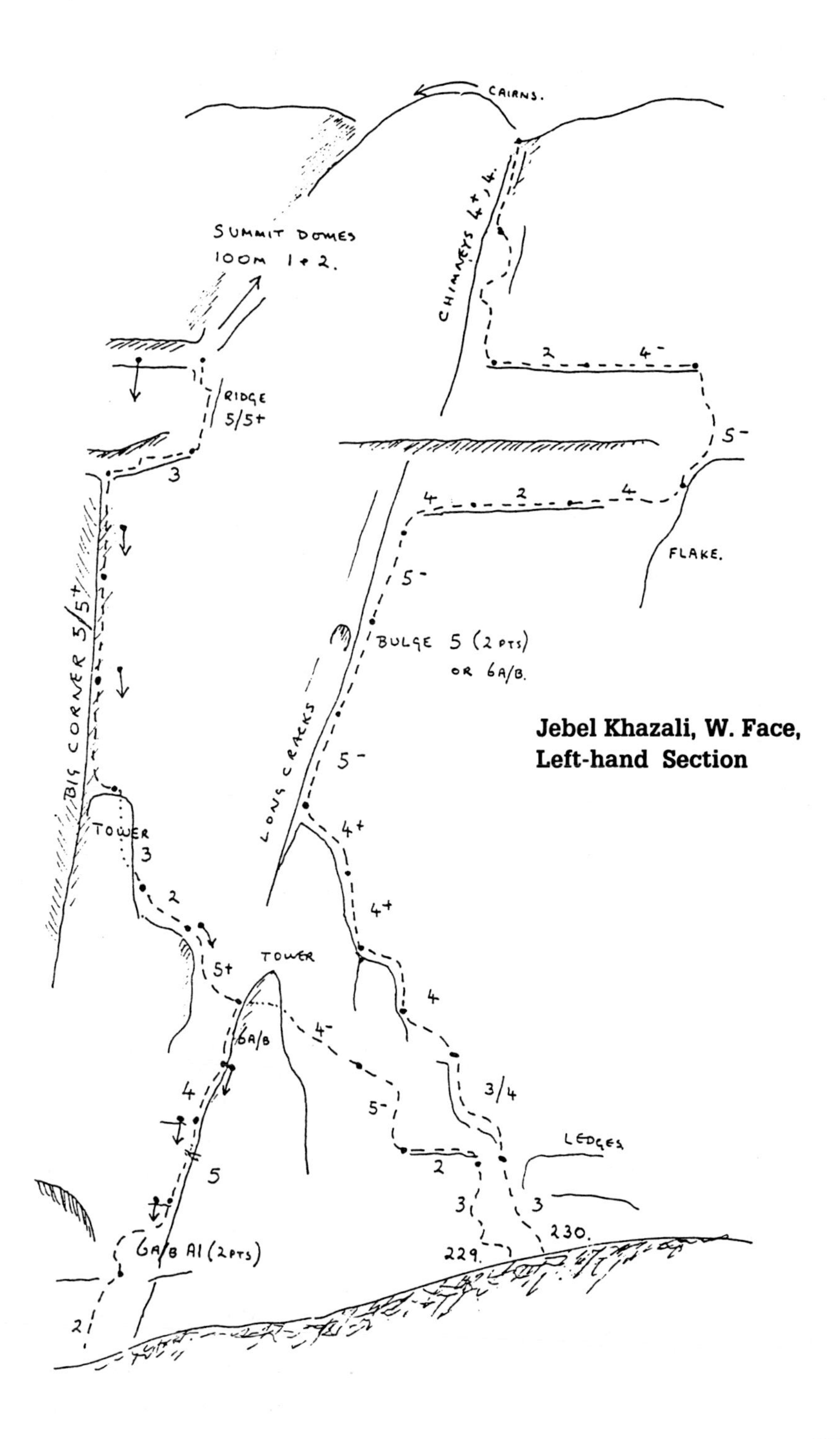

Jebel Khazali, W. Face, Left-hand Section

Jebel Khazali, W. Face, Crack of Cracks and Martha's Steps

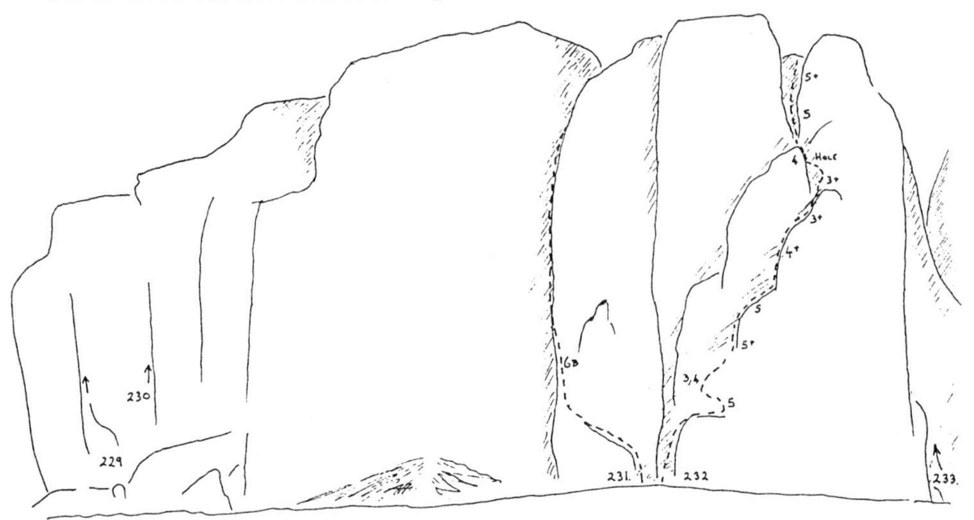

line of cracks in the centre of this west wall. Belays and protection good. Slings in place. 300 metres T.D. Ascent 4 hours. Map and topo pages 158 and 159.
Approach and Descent, as R.229.

Continuing S, the next route that has been climbed is at a big prominent corner:

231. Crack of cracks *D.Scott, S.Prabhu. 16th April 1987.*
A strenuous climb on good rock. Few pitch details available! The climb starts as for Martha's Steps, traversing left after 40m below a white wall to gain the corner crack. The first overhang is passed on its right with difficulty (6b) before the main line is regained and followed to below a col set well back. (The last 30m to the col was not climbed and a forced bivouac was taken!) 300m T.D. Sup - 6 hours.
Approach: By Bedu taxi to the foot of the climb - 1/2 hour.
Descent: Abseil and down-climb the route. (2 - 3 hours)

232. Martha's Steps *B.Domenech, M.Scott, S.Prabhu, D.Scott 13th April 1987.*
Follows the lower line of 'steps' rightwards to the top step. Then left to a hidden chimney and a diedre and up the open slabs to a summit dome. A variety of enjoyable climbing on good rock. 300m D. Sup. 3 hours.
Approach: As the previous route
Descent: 6 abseils down the route, and some down climbing. 2 - 2 1/2 hours.

233. Al Uzza *First 3 pitches - W.Colonna & A.Howard 21st April, 1989. Route completed - W.Colonna, B.Domenech, D.Conderaux, 22/23 April, 1989.*
One of the hidden gems of Wadi Rum, being concealed in a little side canyon at the end of the main west face of Khazali. An exceptional and intimidating line up a smooth walled diedre. Steep starting cracks finish with a bold layback or a better protected but harder finger crack and lead to the diedre.

The diedre is escaped by a bolted traverse to the right arête, then continue up more diedres to the top. All belays in place. Carry 4 or 5 blade pegs as well as a full rack from R.P.'s, to Friend 4. Technically difficult, but not unduly serious for the grade. 300m E.D. Sup. Allow a full day for ascent and descent. Map and topo pages 158 and 161.
Approach: By Bedu taxi 1/2 hour, and 10 mins up the screes in the little valley.
Descent: By abseil down the route. Pegs, bolts and karabiners in place. 1 1/2 - 2 hours.

Two views of Jebel Khazali

Above: View from the summit of Jebel Rum, to Khazali and the south - photo Verin

Below: Le Couchant, first ascent, Khazali West Face - photo Remy

Outlying areas of Rum

Desert Rats, Al Maghrar, pitch 4, first ascent - photo Howard

The Rock Arch of Jebel Kharaz - photo Howard

Jebel Khazali, W. Face
Al Uzza

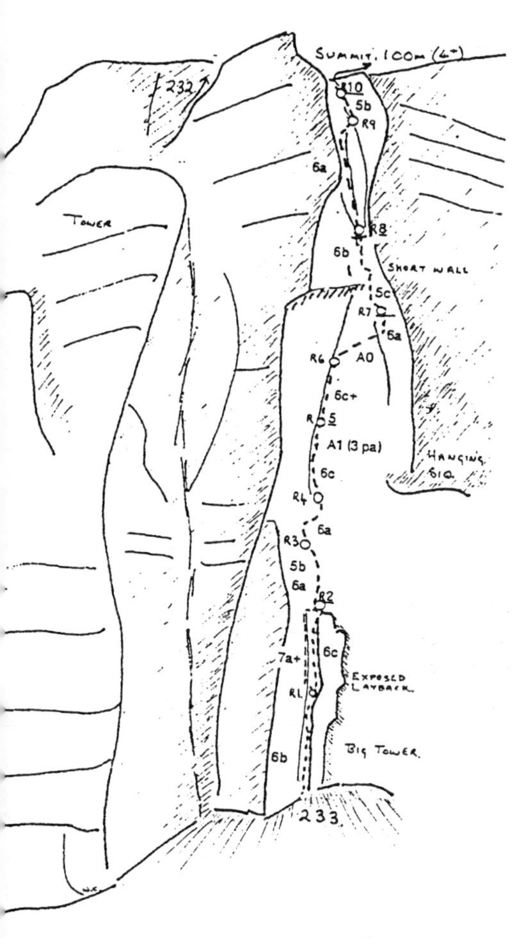

234. South of here, are many broken buttresses, up which there is at least one Bedouin route but no recorded climbs.

Jebel Khush Khashah 1,514m
(Ref: 350663)

235. Far South Summit via South Siq. The Ribbon of Moebius *First recorded ascent, D.Taylor, A.Howard 22nd April, 1989.*
Another of Sabbah's routes! Pleasant scrambling with good views to the south. (Better to omit the west siq and chimney and start from the tree-filled little valley to the S. 1.5km (500m of ascent). F. 2 hours. Map and topo pages 158 and 162.
Approach: By Bedouin taxi to the S end of Khazali. 3/4 hour.
Descent: By the same route (1 1/2 hours).

East Face

This 4km long wall has a number of interesting features, the lower section tends to be split into small buttresses and ravines. Near the S end is a particularly large canyon with a big black smooth wall on its left with obvious rock-climbing potential. On the right of the canyon is:

South Summit

236. Sabbah's Route *First recorded ascent, Sabbah Atieeq, S.Prabhu, M.&D.Scott, B.Domenech April 1987.*
A pleasant rock scramble up slabs and grooves on the right of the canyon, always interesting and in great desert scenery. Popular as a guided route for less experienced climbers. One of Sabbah's specialities! He will tell you the story of the old lady who, a long time ago, was coming down near this route with her goat skin full of water in a time of drought when a rock broke and she fell into the canyon below: there are some wooden branches sticking from the rock, placed there as handholds which are still visible.

Half-way up, a shoulder is reached and above, a corridor leads up through sometimes steeper rocks (sections of 2) to the upper slabs. Cross these trending right (some exposed moves) to the summit plateau. The final dome is larger and trickier than it looks! 1km. P.D. Allow 1 1/2 - 2 1/2 hours. Map and topo pages 158 and 163.
Approach: Down Wadi Rum and up Wadi Khush Khashah with 4-W.D. to the canyon near the S end, marked by a huge black smooth wall on its left. 1/2 hour.
Descent: By the same route, 1 - 2 hours.

237. Falcon Corner *Y.Duverney and J.P.Monnet October 1986.*
This very obvious large open corner is situated in the upper white walls, well left of Purple Haze and above the lower red rock walls. It gives superb climbing on very

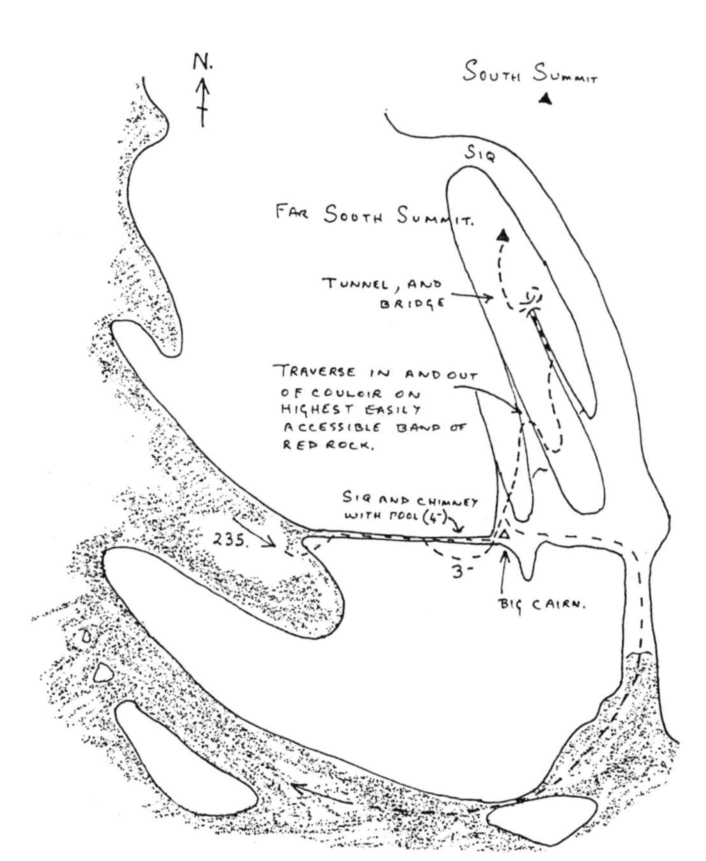

Jebel Khush Khashah, Far South Summit, The Ribbon of Moebius

good yellow and black rock. The only problem is the approach through the bottom wall. Despite that, a recommended climb! 350 metres. T.D. Allow 1 hour for the approach up the lower red rocks and $1^1/_2$ hours for the corner itself. Map pages 158 and 163.

Approach: Enter Wadi Khush Khashah (as for Purple Haze) and continue south down the wide wadi until the big corner is seen high on the East Face. (30 minutes by 4-W.D). To reach the corner, climb the left-hand siq through ledge systems in the red rock (3 and 4 not always obvious). The bottom of the Falcon Corner is at the obvious big ledge and change of rock colour.

Descent: 3 abseils down the corner followed by down climbing and some abseils on the lower walls.

NE Dome 1,420m (ref: 353673)

N E Face

238. Purple Haze

A.Baker, A.Howard, W.Colonna, D.Taylor 14th October 1985.

An enjoyable climb up cracks and slabs. Mostly at a medium standard, with the occasional harder section. 300 metres 3 - 4 hours. D. Map and topo pages 158 and 164.

Approach: The route lies just inside the N Entrance of Wadi Khush Khashah up a band of cracked slabs left of and above a long arched overlap. Driving in from the north, on desert tracks, two small tors are passed below the wall. Beyond these is another tor, closer to the face. Behind this, a long diagonal crack line will be seen starting just left of and above a long overhang 40 metres above the saddle between the tor and the East Face.

Descent: Just south of the sandy bay at the top of the actual climb, a gully will be found descending diagonally down the East Face in similar line to the ascent route. Descend this with scrambling behind chockstones and through caves, and three abseils (in situ) $1^1/_2$ hours.

West Face

239. Nostalgia Di Cima *Gianbattista Villa, Chiocchetti Paolo, Crimella Paolo, Crimella Gianbattista. 28th April 1989*

Mostly good but sometimes poor rock ascending from the depths of Khazali Canyon. Carry the usual rack, and a few pegs and slings. 400m 4 hours. T.D. Inf. Map and topo pages 158 and 165.

Approach: Via R.223. The route starts about 200m inside Khazali Canyon, at a dihedral-chimney, on the left going in.

Descent is down a chimney line to the N, down-climbing with some abseils. About $1^1/_2$ hours.

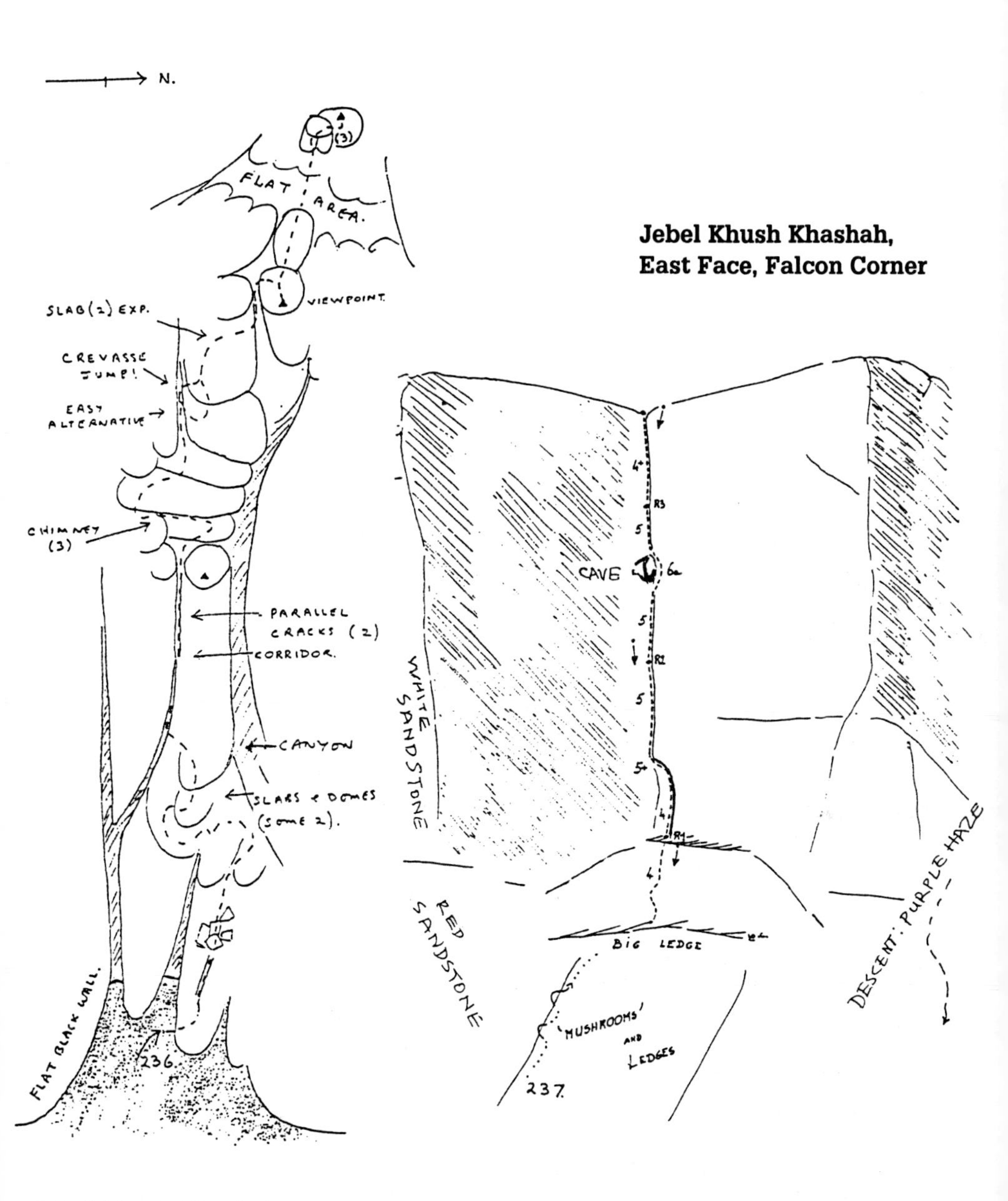

Jebel Khush Khashah, East Face, Falcon Corner

Jebel Khush Khashah, South Summit, Sabbah's Route

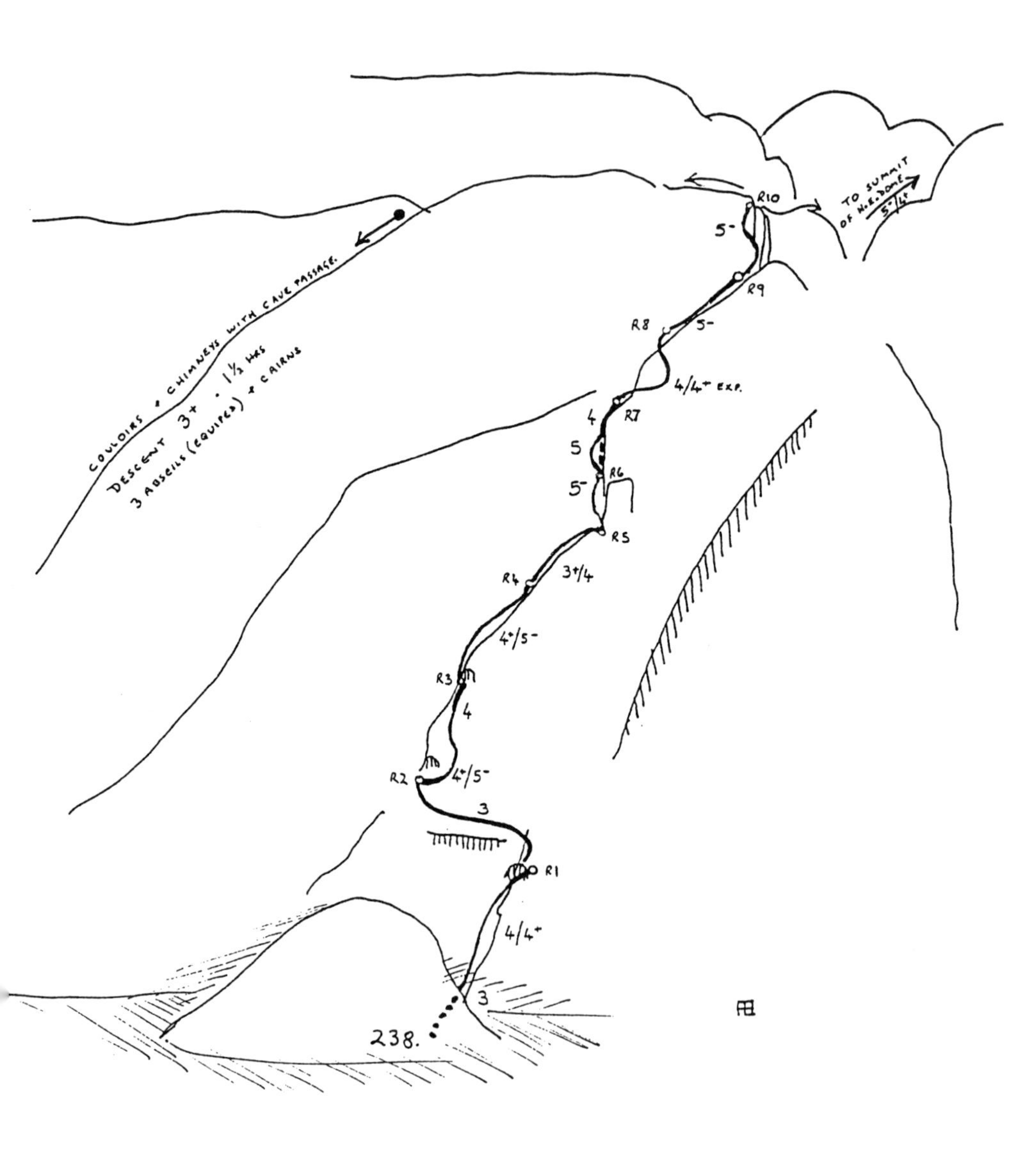

Jebel Khush Khashah, N.E. Dome, Purple Haze

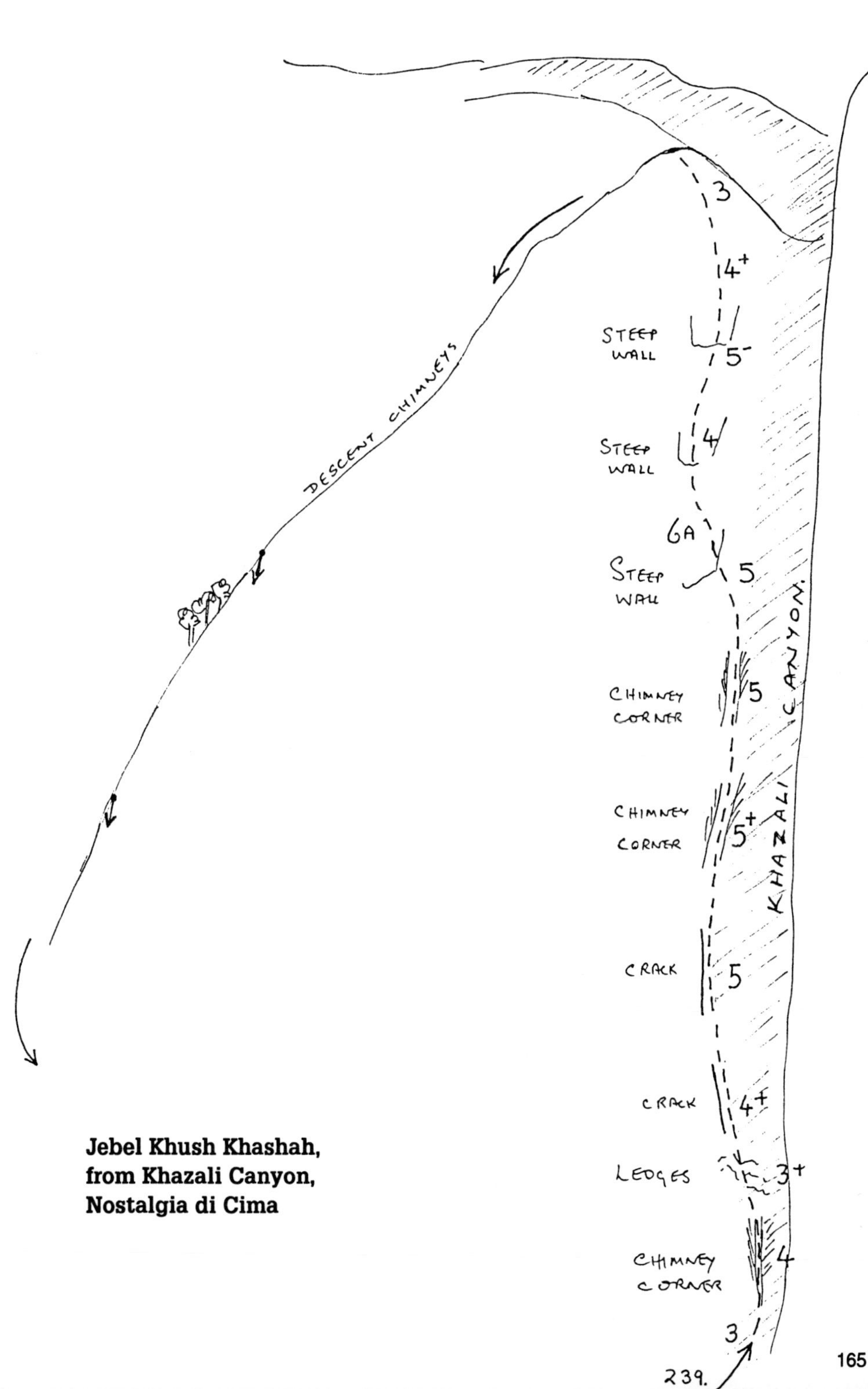

Jebel Khush Khashah,
from Khazali Canyon,
Nostalgia di Cima

BURDAH AND THE DOMES OF ABU KHSHEIBAH

Major Features

This is the area of domes we originally referred to as the "Pleasure Domes". About 12 - 15km SW of Rum village. They are a playground of rock, varying in height from 10 metres or so up to 200 metres and offering all kinds of problems. To their north they are defined by Khor el Ajram, and to the east and west by Burdah and Qabr Amra, respectively. The 'Rock Bridge' of Burdah is now a famous landmark.

Jebel Qabr Amra (Mountain of Amra's Grave) 1,329m (ref: 372663)

No details are available concerning this ridge of 'cumulus' peaks east of Wadi Khush Khashah. They should give some entertaining climbs. The Lion Rock is 2km in, along its W Face (see Pre-historical Sites).

Aereyq Asseja

This is the small rock pedestal in the centre of the wide desert valley E of Jebel Qabr Amra and N of Jebel Ikhnaisser, known as the Rock of Games (see Pre-historical Sites).

Jebel al Ikhnaisser (Small Finger) 1,250m (ref: 379645, map 3049-11)

A small fairly remote summit and the first of the many domes of Abu Khsheibah to be climbed by anyone other than the Bedouin. Situated south east of Rum in a pleasant part of the massif well worth visiting.

Approach: From Rum village, drive south and then south east down Wadi Rum and Khor al Ajram for about 9km

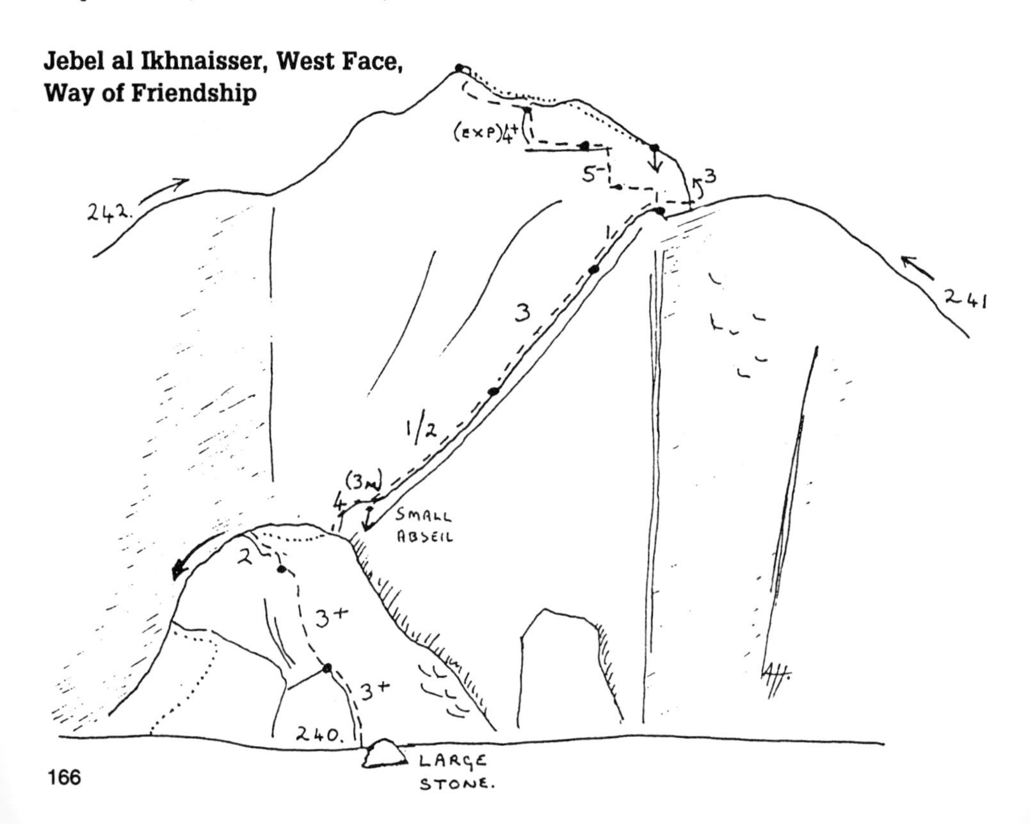

and then south for 1km down an open wadi, to the Rock of Games in the centre of the wadi. Jebel Ikhnaisser is another kilometre south south west.

240. West Face. Way of Friendship *Alberto Re, Wolfgang Nairz, Bernard Domenech 26th October 1986.*
Enjoyable climbing on good rock; the route is easily identified by the obvious ramp. 250 metres D. 2 hours. Map and topo pages 156 and 166.
Approach: As above, $^{3}/_{4}$ hour by 4-W.D.
Descent: $^{3}/_{4}$ hour down the South Ridge, with one abseil to reach the ramp top and a short abseil on the lower block.

241. The SW ridge has been climbed by Bedouin. No details.

242. The NW ridge has also been climbed by Bedouin. No details.

243. NE Face. Dayfallah's Lunch *Charles Read and Simon Beaufoy 14th September 1988.*
A pleasant way to the top up the left side of the smooth NE face, identified by a rightward curving crack-line. Three pitches of climbing to reach domes and ridges. 200m D. Inf. $2^{1}/_{2}$ hours.
Approach: as R.240, $^{3}/_{4}$ hour.
Descent: Down-climb then 2 abseils to finish. $1^{1}/_{2}$ hours.

**Jebel al Ikhnaisser,
N.E. Face,
Dayfallah's Lunch**

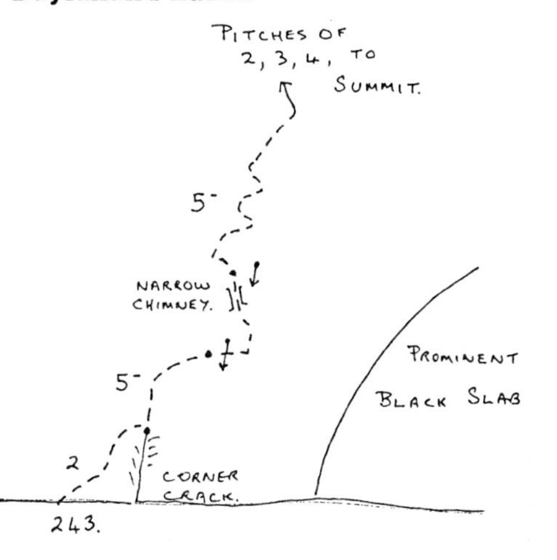

Jebel Abu Khsheibah 1,399m (ref: 383629)

This summit is SE of Jebel Ikhnaysser in a quiet and remote area reached by 4-W.D. in $^{3}/_{4}$ hour from Wadi Rum.

244. East Face. Juniper Siq *D. Green and Alex Renshaw 13th September 1988.*
A good route taking a line up the S Wall of the largest siq (with several trees) in the east face. Mainly good rock. 200m T.D. 4 hours. Map page 156.
Approach: Drive down the desert to below the E Face which has many siqs. The route is in the most prominent one. Climb up to the back of the siq, passing three large juniper trees to a well defined steep chimney, just before the siq becomes impassable. (1 hour from Wadi Rum.)
Descent: Follow the top of the cliff N, until it is possible to climb down to the valley floor (1 hour).

**East Face of Abu Khsheibah,
Juniper Siq**

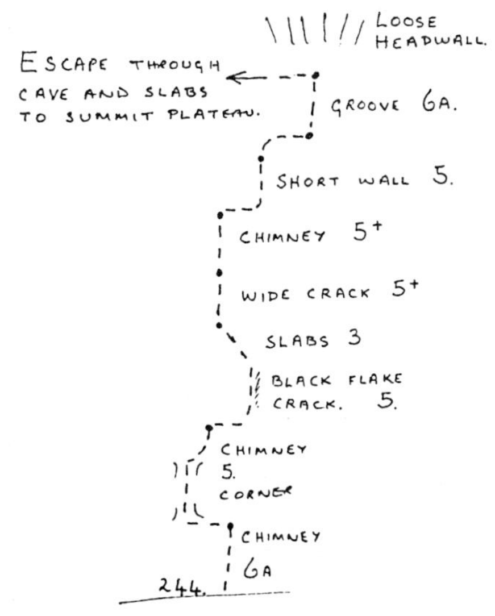

West Face: Immediately E of the S end of Jebel Ikhnaisser, the face is split by a number of vertical fissures.

245. The left-hand crack starts above fallen rocks, looks powerful and is unclimbed, though a quick foray up the pedestal at its foot revealed good rock!

The parallel crack to the right looks equally impressive:

246. Guelta Grooves *D.Scott, S.Prabhu 14th April 1989.*
A bold and strenuous route on good water-worn black rock, directly up the obvious groove. The first pitch is the crux and very strenuous. 150m. T.D. Sup. 3 hours. Map page 156.
Approach: By 4.W.D, 3/4 hour.
Descent: Abseil down the route. 1 hour.

Jebel um Fruth 1,214m (ref: 373634)

This is the small mountain opposite the W face of Abu Khsheibah. Just inside a little canyon at its SE end is:

247. The Rock Bridge of um Fruth
A rock arch similar to the famous one on Burdah, but only 20m above the desert floor and easily attained by slabs (2 to 4 dependent on route).

The only recorded climb is on the west face:

West Summit
248. Rats *C.D.Wagstaff, B.N.H.Scott 20th September 1989.*
A pleasant and easy way to the summit. The route starts in the western siq with many bushes below a barrel or urn-shaped rock, about 10m in height and 30m above the desert. Mostly scrambling, with two pitches (4+ and 5). 120m P.D. Sup. 1 hour. Map and topo pages 156 and 169.
Approach: By bedu taxi 3/4 hour, to the siq. Walk S through bushes past a concreted step in red rock. Ascend a nose on the left to white rock and a terrace which is followed leftwards for almost 100m below the 'barrel'. Pass through a gap, to the first pitch.
Descent: Abseil from a cave to the upper siq (peg in-situ) and follow the rest of the route down, or make a second abseil from the top of the crack (3/4 hour).

Jebel Abu Khashaba 1,262m (ref: 394653)

249. The Canyon This peak marks the east side of the entrance of the big open valley going S to Jebel Ikhnaisser. There are no recorded climbs but it is split by a huge N - S canyon which reputedly gives a good scramble in impressive surroundings.

To its south and east are a maze of small summits and tortuous little desert valleys between cliffs and dunes. Only two of these peaks have climbs on them and there is lots of scope for exploration. The most southerly peak of the group is approached via:

250. Um S'Daiat Canyon
The canyon takes its name from the very aptly named mountain at its west entrance:
Approach: About 1km south east of Aerayq Asseja, then left to eventually enter a canyon with the diagonally

Jebel Abu Khsheibah, West Face, Guelta Grooves

Jebel um Fruth, West Summit, Rats

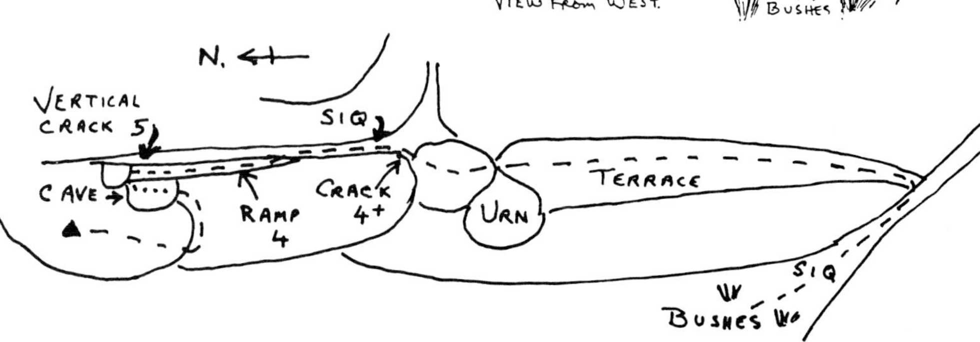

hatched West Face of Jebel Um S'Daiat to the right. The hatchings continue on the East Face which is quickly identified by two rock arches.

The little canyon has many obvious short 1 - 3 pitch lines on both sides, on good rock and is in a beautiful area about ¾ hour by 4-wheel drive from Rum. Map page 156.

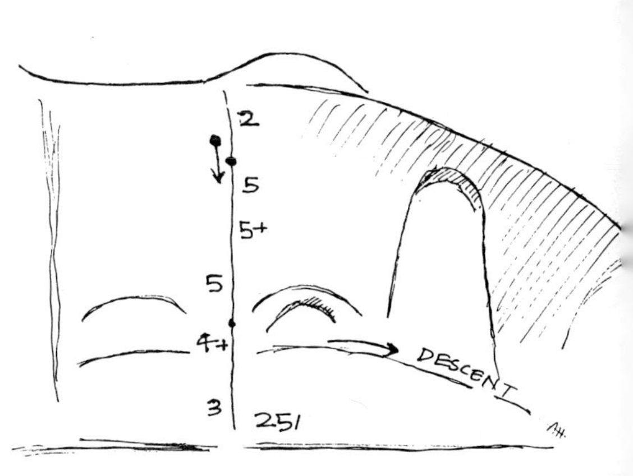

Jebel um S'Daiat (Mother of Little Cracks) 1,327m (ref: 397627)

East Face

251. Whilst Shepherds Watch *A.Howard, D.Taylor, M.Carr, C.Evans 16th April 1987.*

An enjoyable little crack climb, 4+/5+.

Descent: 1 abseil then easy to the north down a ramp.

252. North - South Traverse. A Short Walk with Dang *C.Read, S.Beaufoy 13th September 1988.*

An enjoyable outing up an attractive and easy line with excellent summit views. 1.5km. (200m of ascent). A.D. Inf.

Descent: Down the ridge with one abseil and down easy domes to the desert.

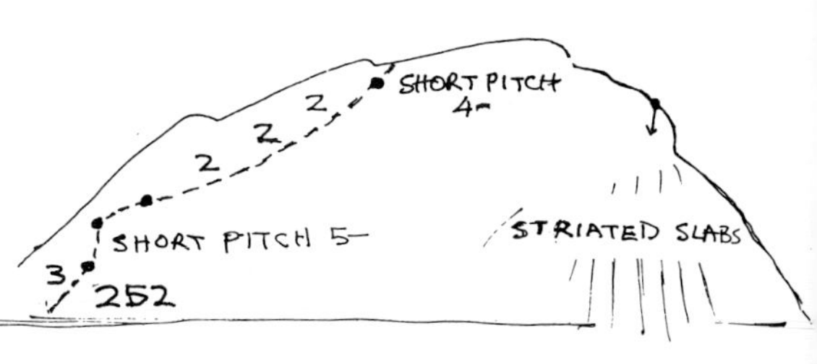

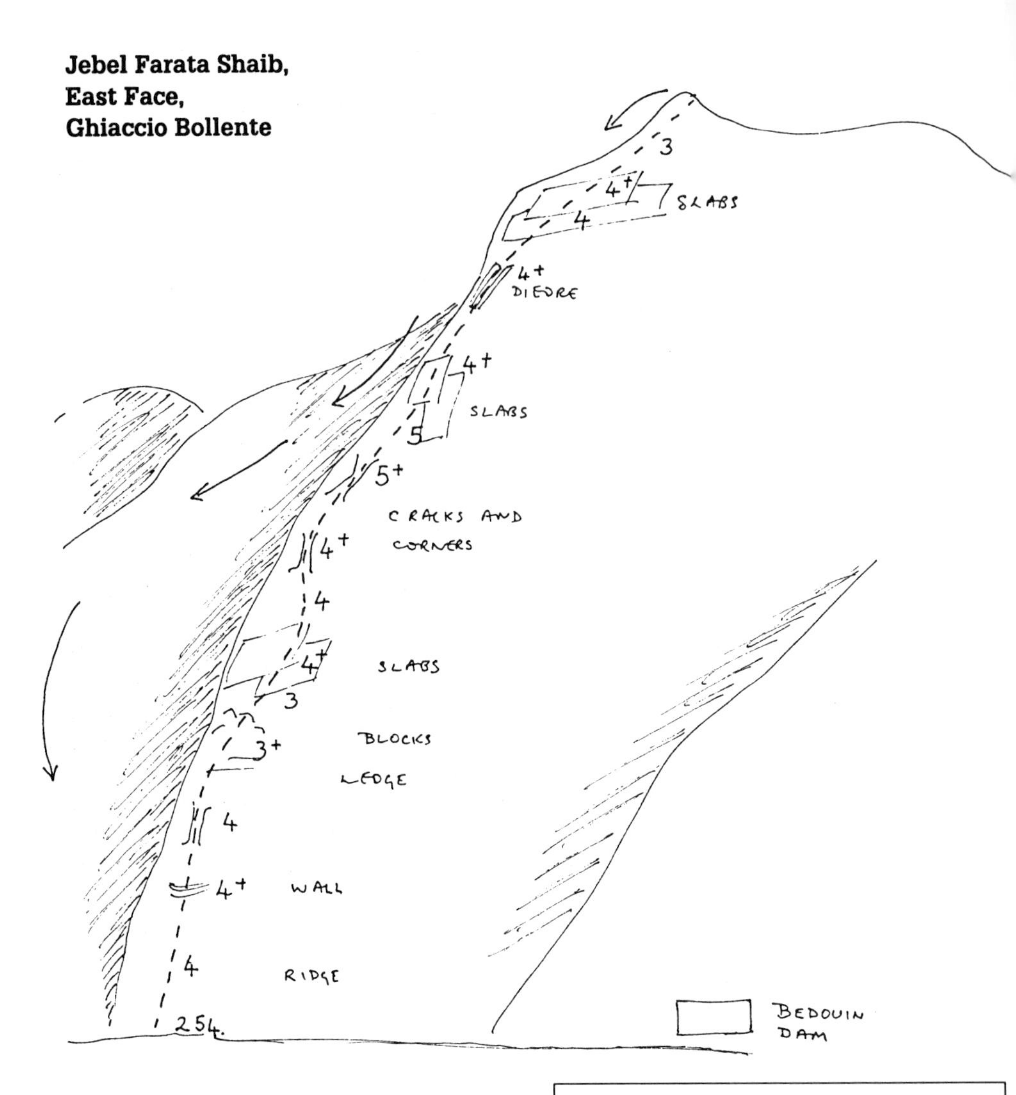

Jebel Farata Shaib, East Face, Ghiaccio Bollente

253. There is also a Bedouin route to this summit, location unknown.

North of here, and facing the W side of Burdah is:

Jebel Farata Shaib 1280m (Mountain of the little open valley, of the old man)

One route has been recorded to this summit:

254. East Face, Ghiaccio Bollente *G.Villa, G.&P.Crimella, P.Chiocchetti 28th April 1989.*
Very good friction climbing up slabs. 400m D. Sup. $2^1/_2$ hours. Map page 156.
Approach: Down Khor al Ajram to enter the valley W of Burdah. The route starts at the obvious spur near a water dam in a rocky chasm.
Descent is to the S.

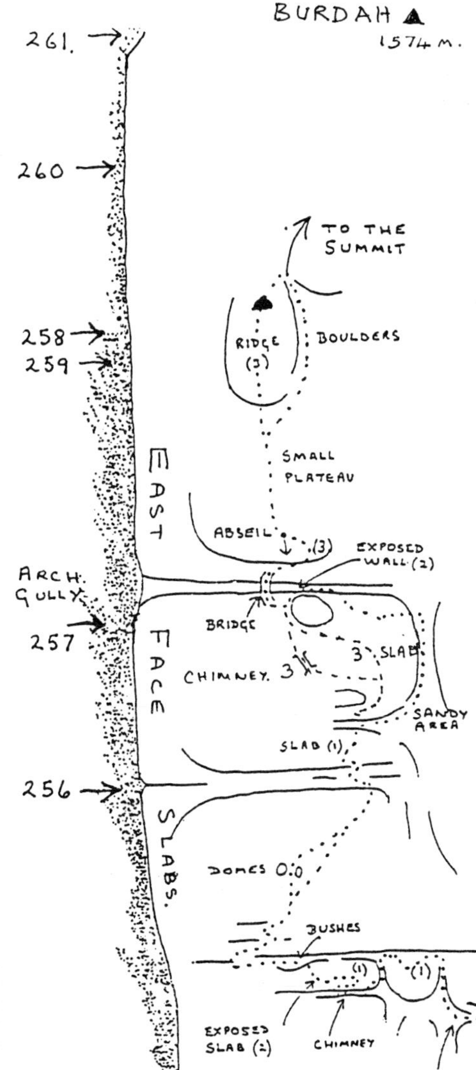

Burdah (Mountain of Cool Breezes). 1,574m (ref: 422626, Map No. 3048-1)

This peak is in the south east corner of the Wadi Rum area and has unsurpassable views of the whole region from its summit. There is also a very spectacular and famous rock archway on its north ridge with an easy and enjoyable route to it:

255. Burdah N Ridge *First recorded ascent D.Taylor. A.Howard 16th October 1986.*

A delightful scramble on good rock, well marked with cairns but sometimes a little exposed and with some moves of 2. Safety rope advised, and a Guide for anyone unfamiliar with rock.

The bridge is now a famous land mark in Wadi Rum and a 'must' for any fit visitor. The views around the Rum area are superb and even better from the actual summit, though to reach this, 20m of grade 3 rock have to be climbed just after the bridge. Most people stop at the bridge. Distance to the bridge about 1 kilometre. P.D. $^3/_4$ - 1 hour. $1^1/_2$ hours to the summit. Allow a similar time for the descent. Map page 156.

The route goes E along a pale ridge of rock, on the left side of a little valley, with a broken white rock 'mushroom' marking the start, to the saddle above the end of the valley. Here, trend right up slabs and over a dome. Carry on in the same direction and descend E for 10m to enter a gully. Go S up this, then down left at a rock barrier to a hollow.

Go up again, in the same direction, then left and right (1) on a slab to pass a steep chimney, after which walk easily E again, still below the rock barrier, to two big chimneys. Avoid them by going left and across a slab to enter the next parallel ravine.

Follow this up a short way, to 10m before its end. DO NOT go up the square walled chimney ahead but step right and walk back W on a ledge (exposed) passing under a yellow/white overhang and up a black chimney (1) to ledges.

Now, step onto the left side of the slab above (exposed) and climb rightwards across it (2) to enter the original gully above the two chimneys. Follow it, through bushes and continue E, then go right and zig zag S up slabs and domes above the barrier wall (some 1) to slabs which lead easily up past a rock tower on to a plateau (1/2 - 3/4 hour from start).

Go diagonally right to the far right corner and pass the next barrier of cliffs easily up slabs and domes (1) to the next plateau. Here there are three alternatives:

For the climber:

1. Cross the little gully and traverse right under an overhang (1) then go left and up three obvious corners (3) to reach the bridge.
2. Cross the little gully and traverse right under the overhang (1) then go diagonally right up a ramp in the slabs (3) to the bridge.

For the walker:

3. Descend to a flat sandy area, walk S along it then left, and up on to easy slabs. Up these towards the left side of a notch in the skyline, trending right below a barrier wall to enter the gully, when the bridge will suddenly be seen ahead. Follow the gully up, then just before the bridge climb its left wall steeply (exposed 2) to the big ledge.

To reach the summit:

Cross the bridge to the barrier wall ahead which is climbed by traversing right (3) then up and left to easier ground. From here the ridge may be followed directly (3) or go up the little valley on its W side to regain the ridge above the steep section. The final slopes go up to a superb viewpoint on the summit.

Approach: Take a 4-W.D. for the 15km drive down Rum and the long valley of Khor el Ajram, to the start of the route in a little valley 200m right of the N end of Burdah's W Face. (This journey is itself well worthwhile.) The driver will wait for you whilst you do the climb to the bridge and will also visit the Canyon of Khazali and its rock inscriptions on the way back, if you ask, as well as other sites of antiquity.)

Descent: Follow the easiest route down, taking particular care at the steep sections. (Abseil to reach the bridge.)

N.B. In 1984, there were no graffiti near the bridge, whilst now the rocks are full of carved names. Please do not add to this eyesore. It is a beautiful place - try to keep it that way.

Burdah East Face

Easily identified as the massive expanse of slabs with the 'Rock Bridge' half way along the N Ridge.

Approach: Down Wadi Rum and Khor al Ajram with four-wheel drive (about 3/4 hour), passing between small domes North of the North Ridge of Burdah to enter the wide valley below the East Face. (Soft, deep dunes at the foot of the face.) Maps pages 156 and 171.

256. Original Route *A.Baker, M.Shaw, D.Taylor, A.Howard 2nd November 1984*

A pleasant route with two variations, climbing initially up the clean slabs of the East Face on good rock starting about 100 metres right of Arch Gully, and then following the North Ridge over the Arch. 1 kilometre (about 250 metres of climbing). Overall grade A.D. 3/4 - 1 1/2 hours to the bridge. 1 1/4 - 2 1/2 hours to the summit. Maps and topos pages 171 and 173.

Descent: Follow the same route back to the bridge, taking the easiest way left (west) of the ridge to the top of the gully which is entered easiest by its north side opposite the corner/flake crack. Descend the gully line with a difficult section at the bottom down which it may be better to abseil. Angle pegs required. 1-2 hours (1/2-3/4 hour from the bridge). Alternatively descend by the N Ridge (R.255).

257. Bedouin Bridge Route *First recorded ascent W.Colonna, G.Claye, P.J.Lange, P.Longuet 1987.*

The route which is well cairned starts just right of the

Arch Gully and follows ledges and corridors (some 3) to arrive on the ridge just north of the Rock Bridge. 200 metres. P.D. Sup. 3/4 - 1 hour. Map page 171.

258. Orange Sunshine *M.Shaw, A.Howard, D.Taylor, W.Colonna, A.Baker. 27th October 1985.*
About 150 - 200 metres left of the Arch Gully is another gully slanting right towards the arch. Left of this is a broad expanse of slabs which form the skyline when viewed from below Arch Gully, going up to a subsidiary summit on the N Ridge.

The climb goes directly up the centre of the above mentioned slabs following a shallow depression and starting at a 30 metre high leftward leaning corner. Very enjoyable throughout. 300 metres. D. Inf. About 2 1/2 hours to the shoulder and a further 1/2 hour to the summit. Map page 171.

259. Orange Sunshine Variants. It is of course possible to go almost anywhere on the slabs, and a number of alternative pitches were climbed on this route, including a parallel line about 50m to the right, at a similar grade (22nd October 1986 Edwards and Arkless).

Descent: Follow the N Ridge back down and descend as for the Original Route or down the N Ridge 1 - 2 hours.

260. The Animated Slab *R.&M.Edwards 17th March 1987.*
"The neckiest of Burdah's Slab Routes. Belays are sometimes an illusion".

Some fine climbing on the steep lower wall and the final head wall. 250m. T.D. 3 hours. Map page 171.
Approach: Walk left along the dune for 60m from Orange Sunshine to a vertical finger crack with a cave depression above to the right.
Descent: Down the N Ridge.

Going left again from Animated Slab to a point almost directly below the main summit, one reaches:

261. Tangerine Dream *G.Hornby, S.Sammut 4th November 1992.*
"The intention was to climb a direct line to the summit." The initial black groove is obvious and pleasant, then come the mandatory Burdah slabs. Fortunately a slight rib avoids the rubble.

The real meat starts at the big terrace where a cute 5+/6A curving crack followed by a bulge leaves you stuck below a blank wall. To the right is a pure crack

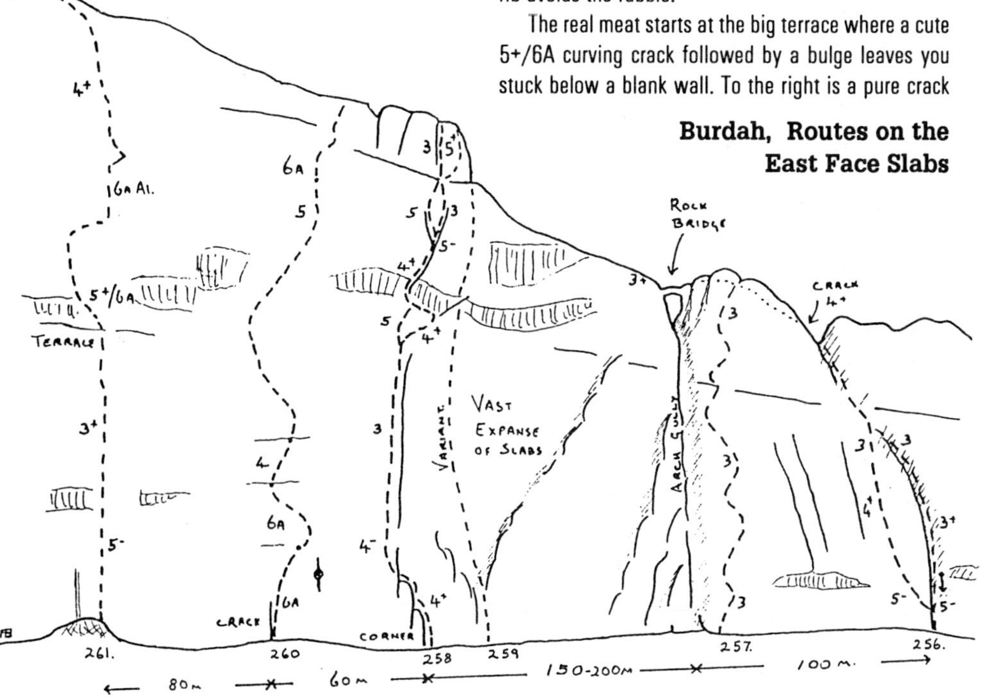

Burdah, Routes on the East Face Slabs

overhanging at the top which should go free at 6C (English E4.6A) but where aid was used on the first ascent. Above, a pleasant rake leads to the summit. "Really enjoyable." 350m. T.D. Inf. 5 hours. Maps pages 171 and 173.
Approach: As R.260 but continue another 80m or so to the S, to boulders below a big cleft, almost in line with the summit. The route starts in a cracked groove line to the right of the cleft, at the top right of the boulder slope.
Descent: As R.255.

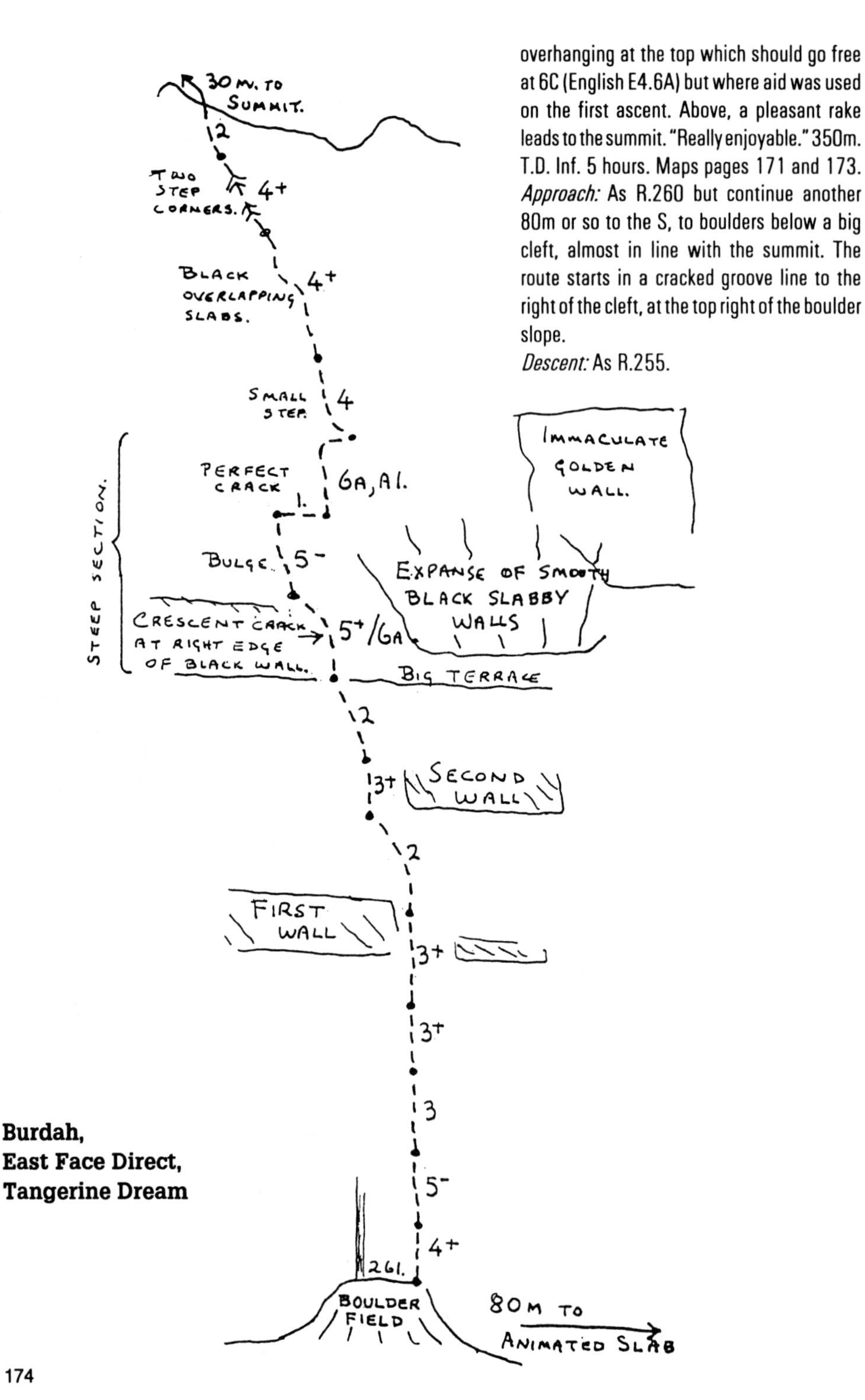

Burdah, East Face Direct, Tangerine Dream

OUTLYING AREAS: NORTH OF RUM

Quweirah - Disi

This desert area, despite having a couple of major roads through it, is seldom visited. It has some wild and beautiful scenery and some interesting sites of antiquity as well as remote camps of the usual hospitable Bedouin.

262. Jebel Humeima, Nabataean village

These twin peaks of dark rock are some 20km N of Quweirah as the crow flies and 12km W of the point where the road starts to climb up to the plateau of Ras en Naqb.

Situated at their foot are the ruins of a Nabataean village, with the ancient quarry workings along the valley side to the west.

Access is by 4-W.D. from the Desert Highway.

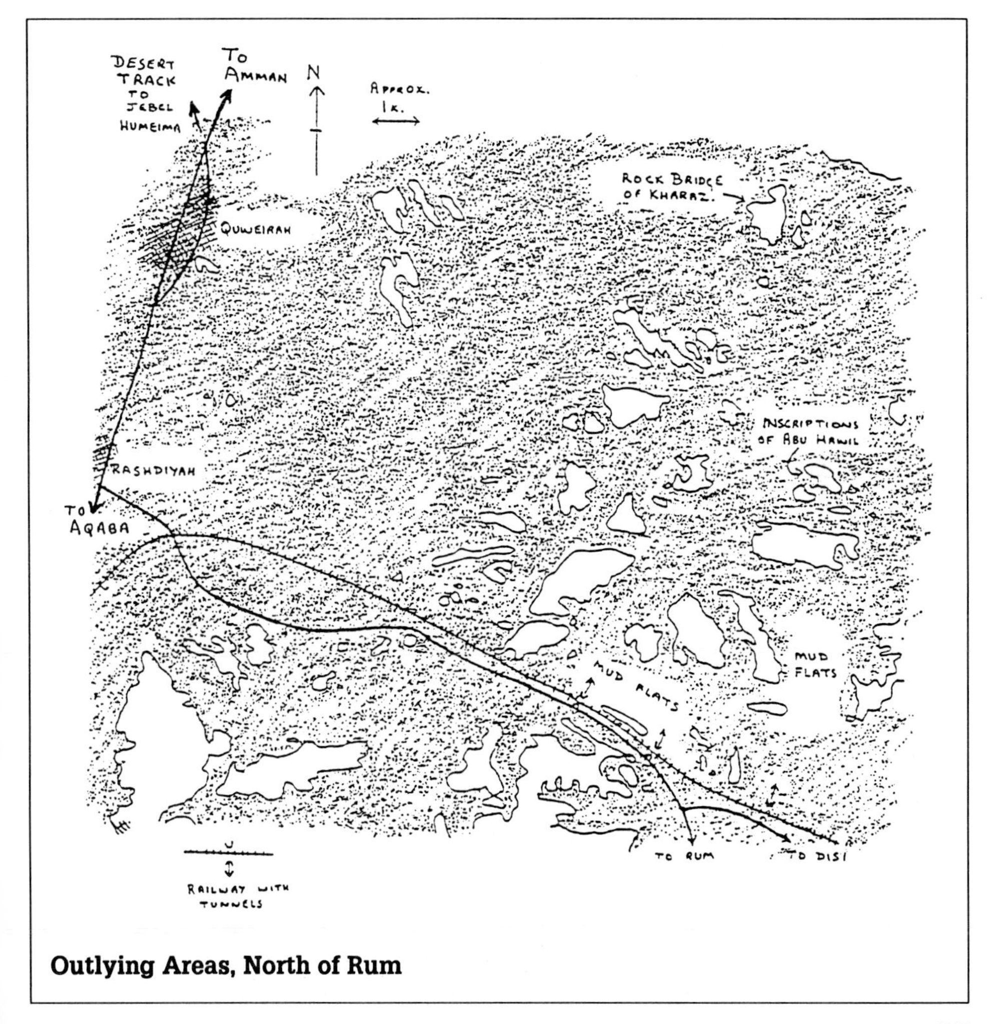

Outlying Areas, North of Rum

263. The Rock Arch of Jebel Kharaz
This is 15km directly E of Quweirah and a 27km drive N of Rum village, in a remote and beautiful setting with vast desert panoramas. A visit from Rum to this huge natural rock arch, combined with a small detour to the inscriptions at Abu El Hawil makes a wonderful journey through a variety of desert scenery. The high desert N of Disi is also a good place to view the sunset.

264. The Inscriptions of Abu el Hawil
There are a number of inscriptions on the walls of this mountain which is part of the Jebel um Rathah massif 7km N of the Disi - Rum road junction. They include some long-horned cattle but the most amazing are two 5,000-year-old anthropomorphic figures over a metre high, which are well worth seeing.

To reach here from Wadi Rum, leave the road 12km N of the village (1km past Disi Junction), go under the railway and N and NW past Jebel Abu Rashrasha for 10km to Abu el Hawil inscriptions, on the SW side of a small mountain, with excavations below.

The return journey to the road is about 12km, first E then S down mud flats to pass under another railway bridge on to the Rum - Disi road.

265. Horse, camel & 4-W.D. Safaris. The whole of this quiet area can be visited by any of these methods. There are also some nicely situated camping areas for a 2-day journey.

266. A 3 - 6 day safari by horse or camel, from Wadi Rum through this area and all the way to Petra can even be arranged! Ask Sabbah or Dayfallah Atieeq at Wadi Rum. (For horse-treks, contact W.Colonna - see 'Guided Holidays.')

Rock-climbing. Though there is obviously plenty of rock, no really good lines have been found, and no routes recorded.

OUTLYING AREAS: SOUTH OF RUM

267. The Domes of Al Maghrar and the Sunset Site
This beautiful area of desert and small white rock domes is 20km. S of Rum Village and just a couple of kilometres S of the Rum to Aqaba desert track. It is very green in spring, with many flowers and a maze of small valleys between the rock domes. There are various old dams here, in the mouths of the little 'siqs', some from Nabataean times and some more modern. There are also old burial mounds and inscriptions, and numerous cave shelters, again some of them quite new with walls and even doors! It is a pleasant place to spend a day and night, and a good area for watching the sunset and sunrise. Maps pages 177 and 178.

Arrange transport out from Rum village and a time and place to be picked up for the return journey.

Al Maghrar (Place of Caves)
Approach: With four-wheel drive. Follow the Aqaba desert track for 14 kilometres to the south, turning west between small white sandstone domes on the left and black volcanic scree to the right. Just after this point, turn south west down a wide wadi towards two dark flat topped domes (Al Maghrar). After about 5 kilometres up this wadi, broken rocks are reached about 1 kilometre north north east of the two domes marked as 1,232 metres and 1,260 metres on map 3048-1, Ein El Hashim, the map ref. of 1232 Dome is 545596.

An easy walk of 20 minutes now leads to the East Face of 1232 Dome, through a narrow defile (stone cabin hidden to the left). The route of Desert Rats is obvious, up the big diedre left of the huge smooth East Wall.

This region is also a pleasant walking area, with narrow passages and superb desert scenery. There also seems to be plenty of possibilities for new routes on the small domes just to the east.

Outlying Areas, South of Rum

1 JEBEL KHUSH KHASHAH, S. SUMMIT
2 JEBEL ABU KHSHEIBAH
3 BURDAH
4 UM SAMMEN
5 AL MAGHRAR, 1232 DOME
6 JEBEL SUWEIBIT
7 JEBEL ABU HAMATA
8 WADI SAABIT
9 JEBEL UM ADAAMI

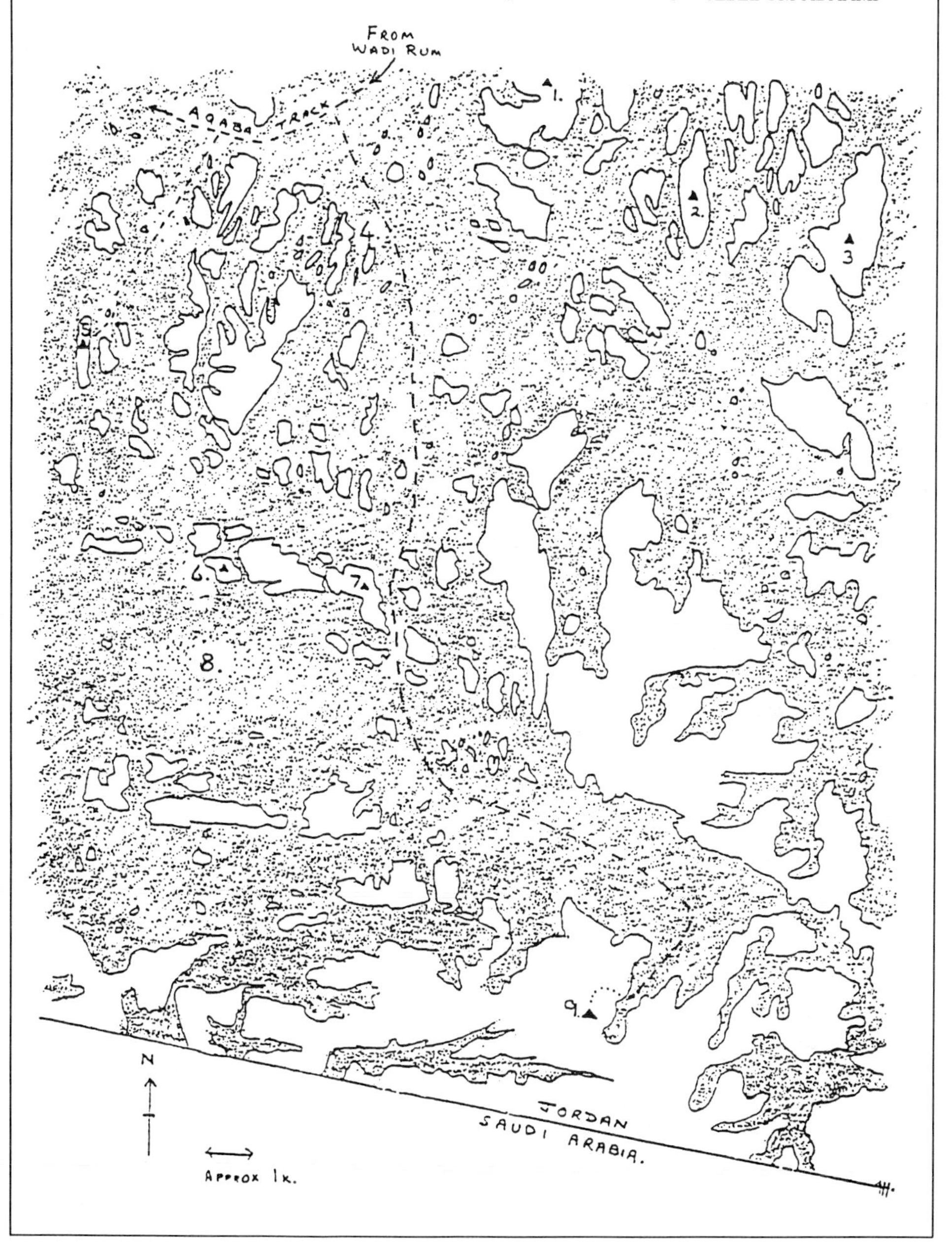

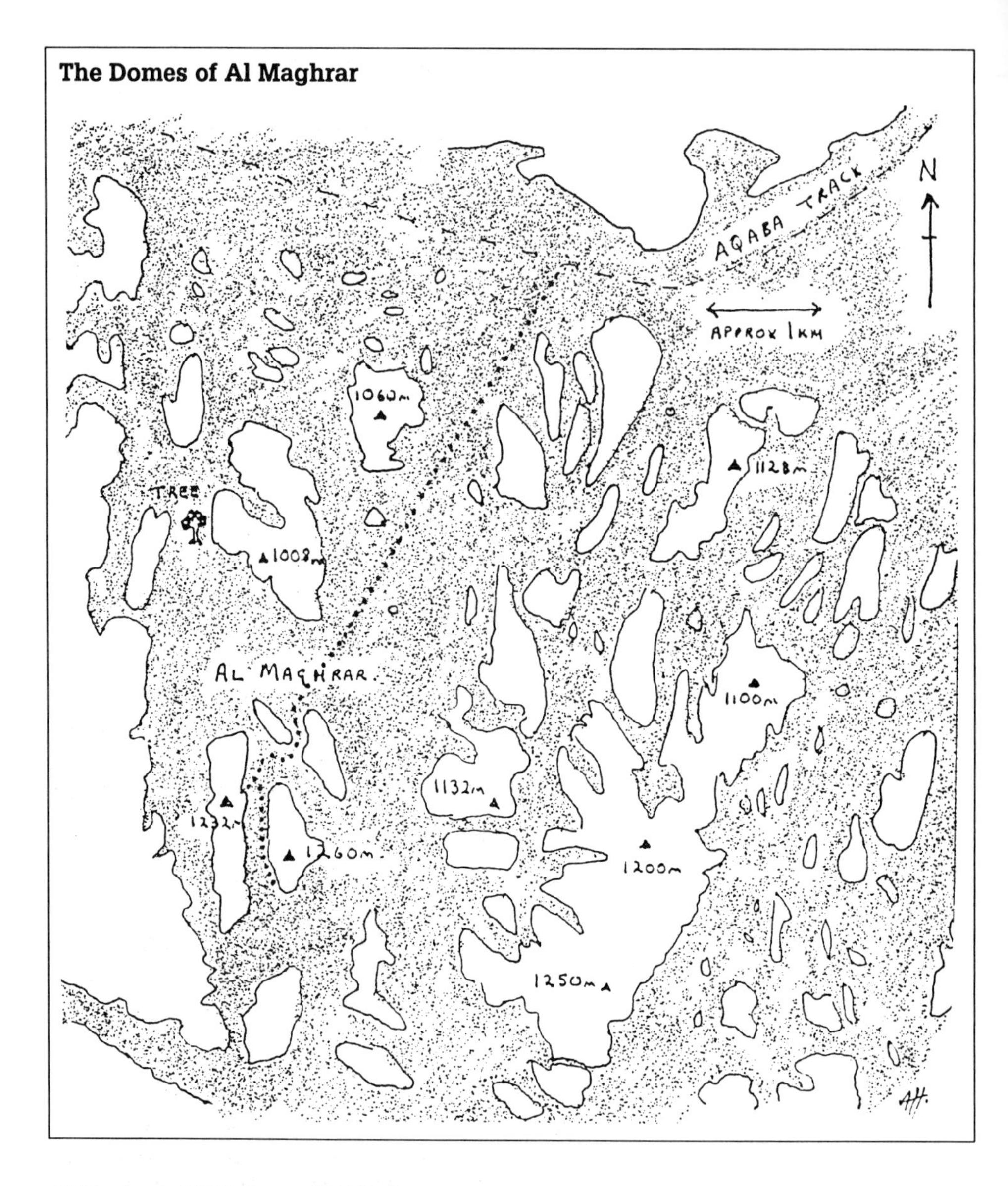

Al Maghrar, 1232 Dome, NE Diedre

268. Desert Rats in the Shade *W.Colonna, D.Taylor, A.Howard 15th October 1986.*

Good climbing in a remote and beautiful setting, first up a very sustained and steep corner with varied crack climbing, Arizona style, then easily up slabs to the summit. 200 metres T.D. 3½ - 4 hours. Maps and topo pages 177 and 179.

Descent is by abseil down the route. 1 hour.

269. N Ridge. Angel's Steps *Pierre Jean Lange 15th October 1986. First ascent of this summit.*

The route takes the easiest line (3 and 4) up to the breche north of the summit from the north west side and the easiest line up the ridge (three steps of 5-) taking care with sandy rock. 250 metres. A.D. 2 - 3 hours.

Approach: As for Desert Rats in the Shade and contour round the foot of the North Ridge until below the North

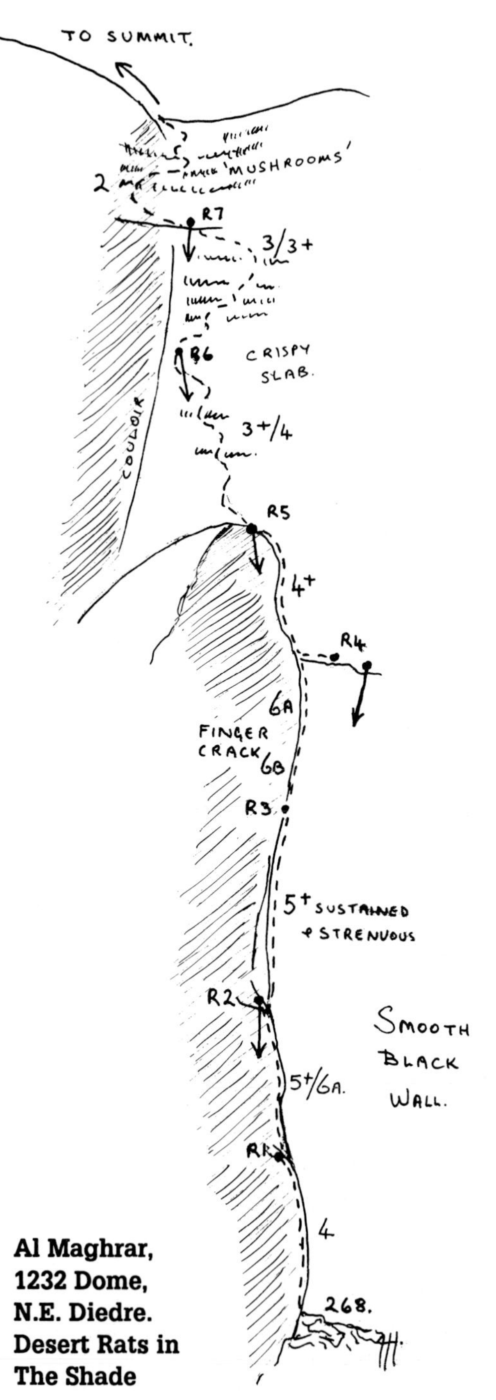

Al Maghrar, 1232 Dome, N.E. Diedre. Desert Rats in The Shade

West Face (1/2 hour from the desert).
Descent by Desert Rats (5 abseils), starting about 50 metres down the East Face, through a basin directly east of the summit. 1 hour.

Al Maghrar 1,260 Dome

270. West Face. Tranquille Emile *First ascent to this summit Yves Duverney and 'Dolby' Monnet 15th October 1986.*

Not sustained climbing but with harder steps through 'mushrooms'. 150 metres A.D. 1 hour. Map page 178.

Climb up a system of terraces in the area of the crack which gives the general line with some short moves of 5. The summit is gained by an obvious scramble.
Approach: As for Desert Rats and when in the valley between the two domes (1232 and 1260) go up to the South col (1/2 hour from the desert). An obvious crack line will be seen on the West Face.

Descent by:

271. Relax Max *Y.Duverney and J.P.Monnet 15th October, 1986.*

This route is situated on the south east side on a nicely sculptured slab. It has only been climbed in descent, but would also make a pleasant ascent. 120 metres. A.D. Sup. Map page 178.
Descent: From the top of the crack of Tranquille Emile go down by easy scrambling in a wide basin, then on the right side, down a vegetated corridor followed by a chimney at the bottom of which is a scree. Gain the nice slab to the right which goes to the bottom (4, 4+) or better, abseil down, and then contour round to the south col. 1 hour.

272. Jebel Um Adaami 1830m *First recorded ascent D. and S.Atieeq and party. 1992.*

Jordan's highest summit, situated in an extremely remote part of the desert, 40km from Rum, and only a couple of kilometres from the border with Saudi Arabia.

Assuming the driver has managed to get the vehicle up the narrow and tortuous sandy wadi, to a point just E of the summit, it is then simply a pleasant scramble up the boulder covered hillside to a little saddle 1/2km NE of the top, where amazing views open out over the Rum mountains to the N. From there, continue up the rounded ridge to the rocky summit, and the splendid panorama, S into Saudi Arabia, and N across the whole area of Rum. 1km. Allow 2 hours for ascent and descent. Map page 177.

Approach: The 4-W.D. journey out there is itself well worth while, passing through ever changing rock and desert terrain and past isolated Bedouin camps. The last 3 or 4km. is particularly difficult driving and requires considerable skill. At the time of writing, only Dayfallah and Sabbah Atieeq know the precise location of this summit, (in fact it was Dayfallah who brought the peak to our attention in 1992!). Allow 2 hours each way for the drive, more if you visit the rock inscriptions on the S side of Wadi Saabit, (ask your guide).

273. The Desert Track to Aqaba

A great way to get from Rum to Aqaba 'in the footsteps of Lawrence', involving about 50 - 70km. (dependent on route) of desert driving. The route goes S down Rum, then W through valleys (not always obvious) to meet the Desert Highway in Wadi Itm about 12km N of Aqaba, or alternatively, to emerge on the Red Sea coast, just N of the border with Saudi Arabia. Take a competent driver who knows the area!

PETRA

In the first edition of this guide, some treks were described in the areas of Petra and Dana Nature Reserve.

A separate guide is now under preparation to these areas and the routes are not therefore included here. However, it is worth stating that the guide to these areas will be a trekking guide and not a climbing guide.

Rock-climbing in the immediate environs of Petra was described as 'sacrilegious' in the earlier edition of this guide. Furthermore, it should be obvious to anyone that you DO NOT rock climb on ancient national heritage sites or where there are hundreds of tourists who could be injured by falling rock. Even so, I have been sent details of climbs in Petra! They will not be published, and no further rock climbing should be done in or close to the ancient city of Petra, or in areas adjacent to it frequented by tourists.

Outside Petra, in the lesser known canyons, there is potential for climbing but the area, like Dana to the north is first and foremost one of remote and unspoilt beauty ideal for wilderness treks. Hire a guide, and a camel or horse, or just go on foot and take a look!

1996 UPDATE

Visas

Visas now last only 14 days. They can be renewed within that period, free of charge at Aqaba Police Station, opposite the bus station.

Medical Advice

It is possible to catch Cutaneous Leishmaniasis from the bite of sand-flies particularly at dawn and dusk when sleeping out near vegetation or spring water in semi-desert areas, or near gerbil colonies. Sleeping high up (on a roof top for example) virtually eliminates the problem since they cannot jump more than 60cms above the sand. Mosquito nets are of little use since the smaller sand-flies are only 2 or 3mms long, and can pass through them!

The disease is transferred from desert rodents and foxes etc. to humans via the sand-fly. It is frequently incorrectly diagnosed since you are unlikely to be aware of the bite at the time it happens and it does not manifest itself until about three months after the incident, when an unsightly sore appears, colloquially known as "the Baghdad boil"! The sore continues for up to nine months, finally disappearing a year after the initial bite and leaving a small permanent scar of the type often seen on faces in the Middle East.

If all this sounds awful, don't be over concerned - I know of only one incident happening to a climber in the last twelve years and the really good news is that once you've had it, you're immune forever after!

Travel to Jordan

With the advent of peace in the Middle East and the opening of borders between Israel and Jordan, it is now possible to reach Wadi Rum easily via Eilat. There are flights and holidays there for less £200. From Eilat it is a short taxi journey to the Aqaba customs point then 3 J.D. by taxi to Aqaba and so to Wadi Rum. The border is usually closed for religious reasons on both Fridays and Saturdays!

Transport to and in Rum

The 1 J.D. fee to enter the valley has already been put to good use enabling the Wadi Rum Community to buy a bus. This operates daily, except Fridays, leaving the village around 7 am to Aqaba bus station from where it returns about midday. You should let the driver know if you intend returning with the bus from Aqaba.The ticket is 1 J.D. each way. There is also a bus which runs most days to Petra for 2 J.D. - again, advise the driver when you wish to return with it.The Petra entrance fee is now 20 J.D. and may be increasing to 30!

In Rum itself, prices have also risen somewhat over the past two to three years and the list of prices on page 18 has been updated overleaf:-

Stop Press: In late summer 1996, telephone reached Wadi Rum! Some useful contacts are:

Tourist Police	03 315 661	Rum Rest House	03 318 867
Rum Rest House (fax)	03 314 240		

Fees for Travel and Accommodation in Wadi Rum

	JD
1. Entry to Wadi Rum Desert (40% is paid to the Rest House where you will be given a drink and 60% to the local community projects)	1
2. Use of Tourist Campsites (Rest House and Abu Aina Bedouin Camp). Tents and water are available at both sites. The Rest House site also has self-catering facilities, showers and toilets.	2

3. Hire of camels or 4 wheel-drive vehicle and driver.

Destination	CAMEL	4 W.D.
Abu Aina Campsite	5	6
Khazali Canyon (rock inscriptions)	13	15
Sunset-site	15	18
W Side of Jebel Rum (for Sheikh Hamdan's Route)	-	18
Burdah (rock bridge) - includes waiting whilst climbing	31	28
Barrah Canyon includes waiting whilst climbing	-	45
Jebel um Adaami - (highest mountain) includes waiting whilst climbing	-	45
Any area for full day	31	45

Eating out in Rum

I have already mentioned the excellent meals provided at the Rest House by Ata, the chef, who has made himself a great favourite amongst climbers. You should also ask Ata or Ali Hillawi for permission if you want to use the 'climber's kitchen' at the back of the Rest House. If you do cook here there are now a couple more shops in the village to get food from. Please keep the kitchen clean. If you fancy a snack elsewhere, there are now also a couple of 'Bedouin Cafes' in the village where you can get 'chai', felafels and soft drinks etc. and thereby support and experience something of the local community rather than the sometimes crowded touristic atmosphere of the Rest House.

Guides in Wadi Rum

In addition to Sabbah Atieeq, Sabbah Eid and Atieeq Auda have been doing a lot of guiding recently. Both are excellent climbers and becoming very knowledgeable in modern rope techniques and the needs of clients. Ask for them at the Rest House.

Environmental Concerns

Further to my notes on pages 26 and 27 I would like to add some comments received from other climbers visiting Rum, with which I wholeheartedly concur. For example, I was sent a copy of the climbing guide to the Lofoten Islands of Norway with a suggestion that the advice on bolts and natural protection should apply to Wadi Rum: "Climbers are strongly encouraged to learn to place nuts and natural protection and to leave their electric drills at home...don't bother coming here to go sport climbing. Natural and all-nut protection is the rule, not the exception." Also, a quote from the American magazine

Climbing May 1994 debating 'Climbing and Fixed Anchors in the Wilderness' which states "Fixed anchors, where appropriate, must be substantially unnoticeable and must not have a significant adverse impact on the primeval character and influence of the wilderness area."

Other climbers have expressed similar concerns about the use of chalk: in recent years, trails of chalk have started to leave their tell-tale dotted lines up some of the more popular routes regardless of difficulty, despite the fact that some of the routes of 6b and below were put up chalk free. This has two unfortunate repercussions: from the non-climber's point of view it is unsightly and detracts from the "wilderness experience". For the concerned climber it not only looks unsightly but, worse still, it detracts from the spirit of adventure as the way is marked by previous ascentionists. D. Compton, writing in *On The Edge* is obviously in agreement "A climb whose beauty depends at least partly on subtle route finding is debased to an exercise in following the white dotted line". It is this very aspect of climbing which is one of the main joys of Wadi Rum and could so easily be lost.

These negative results of chalk are exacerbated by the fact that it never rains in Rum in the summer, so chalk remains through the year and the build-up is unlikely to be removed unless there are unusually heavy mid-winter rains. It's a problem that could and probably will go worse: do your bit for the environment and for the pleasure of those coming after - use a chalk ball or make it a chalk-free ascent!

The rock, route times and grades

Not everyone finds Wadi Rum rock suites their taste ; some have written to say it's frightening, with remarks like "If you don't enjoy Gogarth, don't go". Well, most people would consider Gogarth to be one of the best adventure climbing cliffs in Britain - Rum is every bit as good and lots bigger! Unlike Gogarth, it also has climbs of all standards.

With regard to route times, though they are all based on reality, there are many who find the times in this guide unforgiving. It may be wise to allow more on your early ascents (and descents), though I think the party that took two and a half days on Al Thalamiyyah without even reaching the summit was overdoing it a bit!

Grades, so far, have had few criticisms and whilst I am not happy about having to use both U.I.A.A. and French grades in this book there is not, as yet, sufficient feedback to convert all the grades to French. Consequently, some of the new routes in the following section retain the U.I.A.A. grades given them by their first ascentionists. If so, their topos are marked U.I.A.A.

Rescue

There have now been two accidents in Rum involving helicopter rescue and the expert services of The Royal Jordanian Airforce. However, it would be well to remember there is no official rescue service and to pick your routes and climb them accordingly!

Prehistoric sites

It seems the Bedouin have a long and notorious history of benefiting from those who pass their way: a report in *The Geographical Magazine*, May 1993, informs us that "Protection rackets were not invented by Chicago gangsters. Bedouin nomads were extracting protection money from hapless farmers living in what is today southern Jordan thousands of years ago. Evidence for the existence of these Bedouin gangsters comes from an interpretation of the world's oldest stone map, or petroglyph, carved some 5,000 years ago.

Discovered in 1978 by the Italian palaeontologist Dr Edoardo Borzatti von Lowenstein in a cave in the Jebel Amud [to the north west of Rum]. It was not until recently that the features depicted on the petroglyph were identified. It is approximately circular, with a diameter of about five metres, and looks rather like a giant shortbread. The markings on the stone are a few centimetres wide, connected up by small channels. The area covered by the map is some 2,500 square kilometres, on a scale of 1:16,000.

To decipher the petroglyph, Borzatti copied the markings on to paper. Gradually, he realised he was looking at a topographical record, a map of the Bronze Age villages in the region.

Twenty of these had already been excavated in Borzatti's earlier searches of the area. To prove his case, Borzatti succeeded in using the stone map itself to locate another 100 villages in the area."

Professor Borzatti's book on Wadi Rum is shortly to be published and should make fascinating reading.

The Earthquake!

In November 1995 an earthquake measuring 5.6 on the Richter Scale with its epicentre in the Red Sea south of Aqaba (part of the Rift Valley), shook Wadi Rum. There were rock falls into the approach gully of Hammad's Route (which is now ankle-deep in dust) and from the top of 'Jack Daniels'. Otherwise, the area seems remarkably undamaged despite a few subsequent minor tremors.

New Routes (since March 1993)

Since our 'discovery' of Wadi Rum in 1984, the area has become (to quote from *On The Edge*), "one of the world's leading desert climbing areas". As a result, visiting Rum every spring is no longer sufficient to keep pace with events. Within the limitations of time imposed in preparing this third edition, I have consequently had to rely more than ever on the first ascent notes in the New Routes Book with little opportunity to check any of the details. However I have included the name, location and first ascent information of all of the new routes climbed between spring 1993 and 1995 (approximately one hundred). I have also included all the new climbs in the graded lists which follow with, as previously, stars for the better climbs. As a consequence,visitors to Rum can see at a glance beforehand not only where all the routes are, but also where the best routes are, and where the spaces are for new routes!

Any more recent new routes climbed since spring 1995 and not included here will be found at the Rest House in the New Routes Book provided by Troll Safety Equipment. It is hoped a fourth edition of this guide will follow incorporating full details of all climbs, but at the continuing rate of development each edition is out of date within months of it's publication. However, with almost four hundred routes in this guide, half of which have 'star-status', including fifty with three stars, there should be enough in these pages to keep everyone happy!

Keep on rocking, and "Keep Wadi Rum Clean".

JEBEL RUM MASSIF

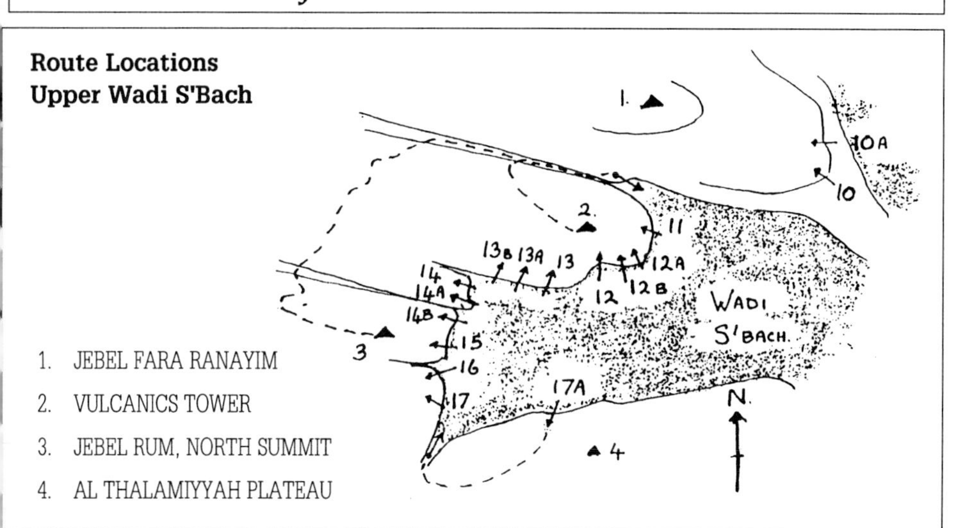

3A. A Bedouin route exists from Wadi es Sid to Wadi Rumman, descending just N of R.94. It also connects with other Bedouin routes which traverse Jebel Rum from N to S: a potentially excellent expedition!

Jebel Fara Ranayim

10A. East Crack *G. Stari, F. Kroll 10th March 1994.* To the right of the East Ridge (R.10) a fairly obvious crack and chimney line leads up the tower. 200 metres of climbing (1 kilometre to the summit, as R.10) A.D. 2 hours.

Descent: From the summit, follow small domes west for about 500m, then left (S) to the saddle below Vulcanics Tower. Descend to Wadi S'bach (some 3).

Vulcanics Tower

12A. South Pillar. *A. Precht, S.Brochmayer 17th April 1994.*

Varied climbing, taking a fairly direct line to gain the pillar which it then follows. Many slings and a peg in place. 300m. E.D. inf. 4 hours. Topos pages 186 and 189.

Vulcanics Tower
South Pillar

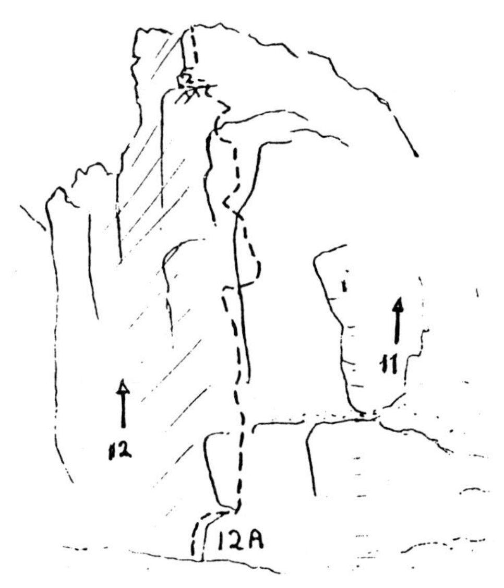

South Face

12B. Und Jetzt Gehts Los *A. Precht, S. Brochmayer 13th April 1994.*

Good climbing up a logical line up the wall right of South Cracks. 300m. E.D. 3-4 hours. Topo page 186.

Vulcanics Tower
South Pillar

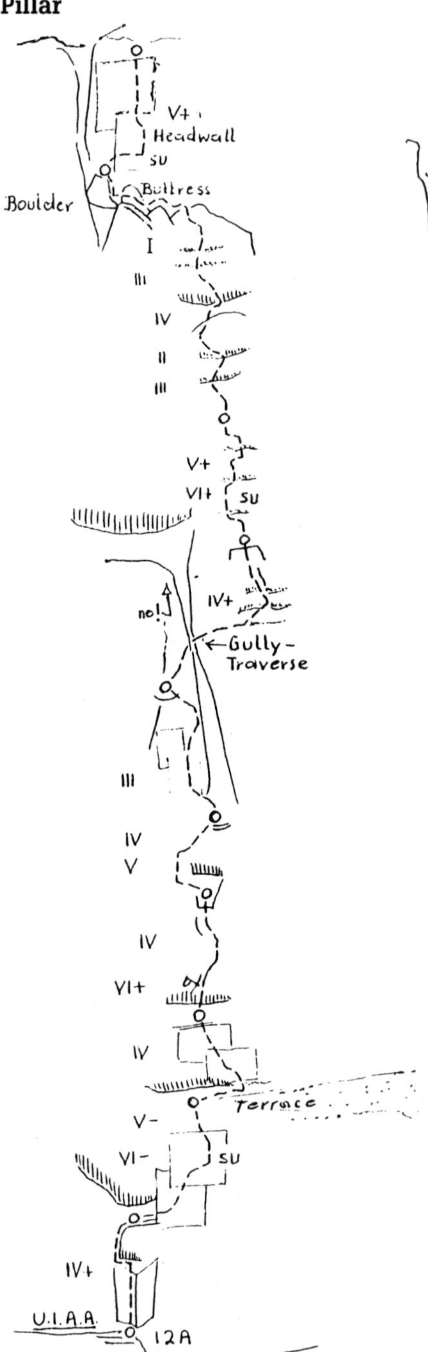

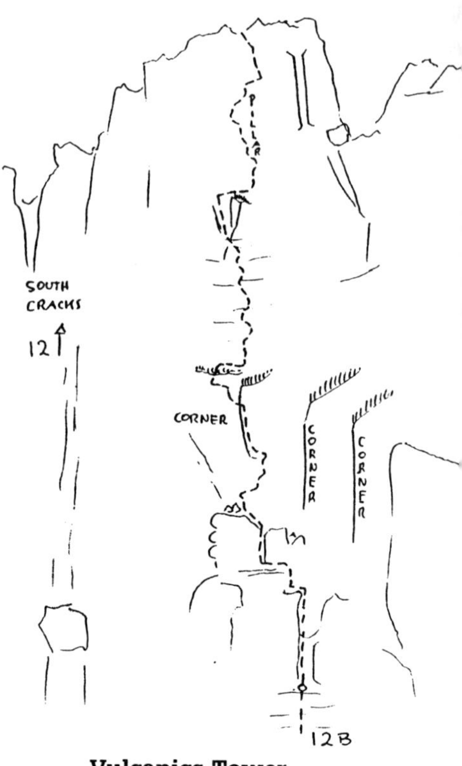

Vulcanics Tower
South Face
Und Jetzt Gehts Los

13A. Ata *A. Precht, S. Brochmayer 20th April 1994.*

Good climbing up the steep south east pillar left of First Road. Slings and pegs in place. 280m. E.D. 3 hours. Map & topo pages 185 and 187.

Vulcanics Tower
Ata

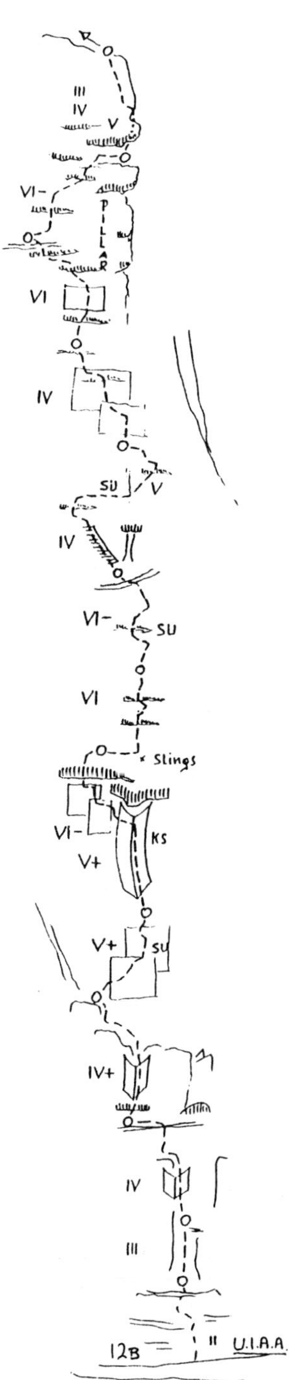

Vulcanics Tower
Wonderland

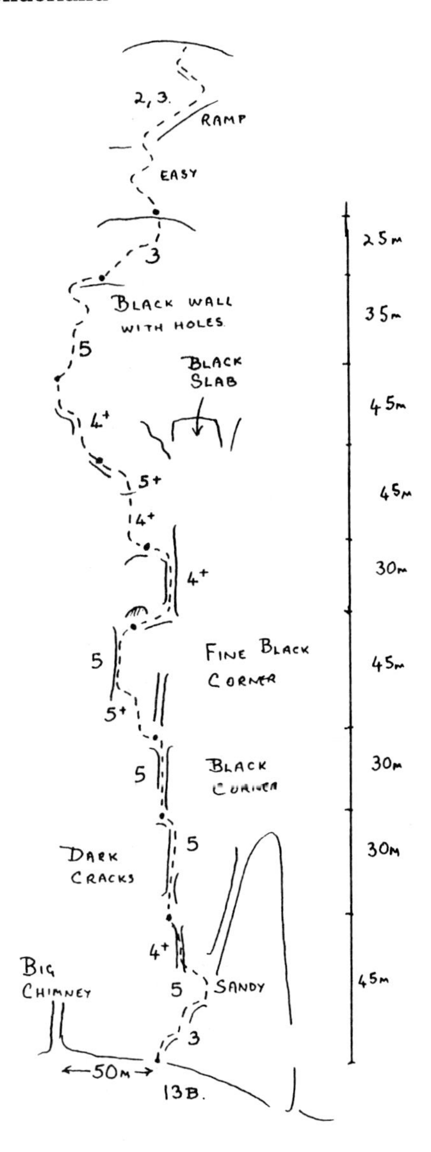

13B. Wonderland

Alfred Reidl, Thomas Behm 9th April 1995.

Climbs the left, dark part of the wall. Beautiful climbing on very good rock, with good belays and protection, starting 50m right of a big chimney. 280m. T.D. 3 hours. Map page 185.

East Face

To the left of R.14 is the outstanding but previously ignored:

14A. Forgotten Pillar *A. Reidl, T. Behm 14th April 1995*.

Good climbing up cracks on very good rock with excellent protection (many slings in place). A classic line. 300m. T.D.Sup. 3-4 hours. Map page 185.

Descent: Cross the domes to the Vulcanics Tower descent, (or abseil the route - not easy. 4 abseils on in-situ gear).

Jebel Rum, North Summit East Face Forgotten Pillar

Between here and the Rainbow Edge is yet another pillar.

14B. The Austrian Pillar *A. Precht, S. Brochmayer April 1994.*

Powerful and challenging; a fantastic tour on good rock. 300m. E.D. 4 hours. Mpas pages 185 and 189.

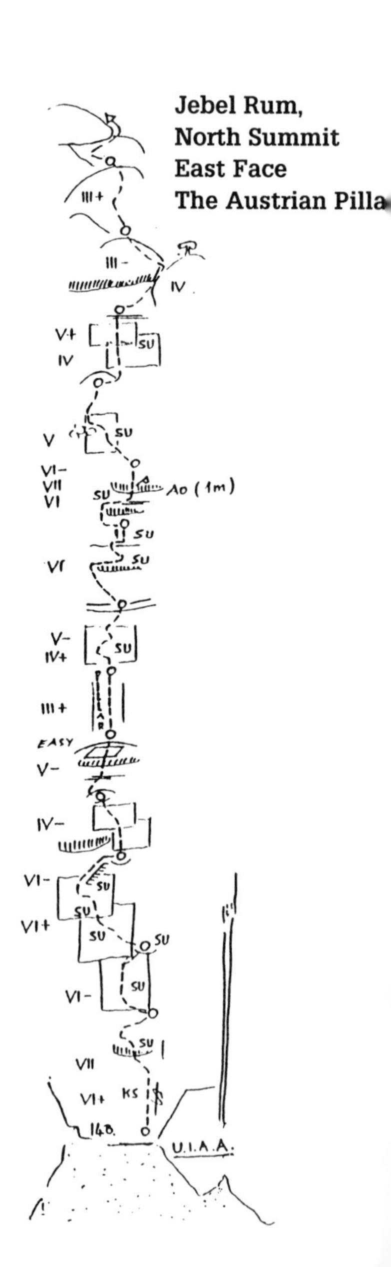

Jebel Rum, North Summit East Face The Austrian Pillar

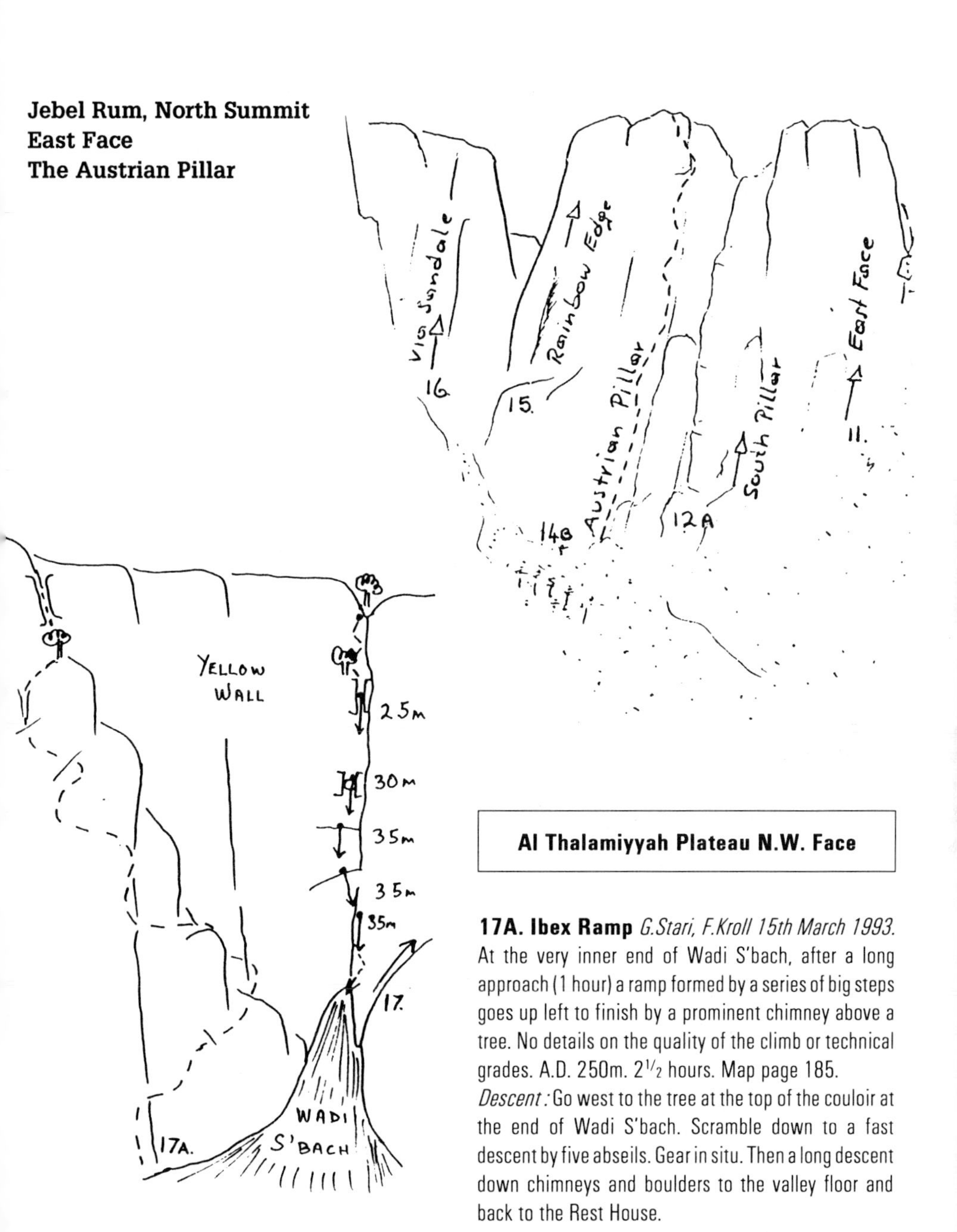

Al Thalamiyyah Plateau N.W. Face

17A. Ibex Ramp *G.Stari, F.Kroll 15th March 1993.* At the very inner end of Wadi S'bach, after a long approach (1 hour) a ramp formed by a series of big steps goes up left to finish by a prominent chimney above a tree. No details on the quality of the climb or technical grades. A.D. 250m. 2½ hours. Map page 185.

Descent: Go west to the tree at the top of the couloir at the end of Wadi S'bach. Scramble down to a fast descent by five abseils. Gear in situ. Then a long descent down chimneys and boulders to the valley floor and back to the Rest House.

The Dark Tower

25A. Spiel Fur Heisse Tage *S. Brochmayer, A. Precht 14th April 1994.*

A pleasant way up the shady wall right of the tower on the right of the upper half of Black Magic. 200m E.D. 3 hours.

North East Domes

31A. Khadra *Cristophe Moulin, Pomme Depras 10th April 1995.*

An excellent and obvious line just right of King Hussein, though the rock quality is not always good. The route starts up the first 3 pitches of King Hussein and involves quite a lot of aid. Take a full rack of nuts and cams, 5 knife blades, 5 Lost Arrows and 5 angles. 300m. E.D.sup. 10 hours.

Descent: By abseil down King Hussein.

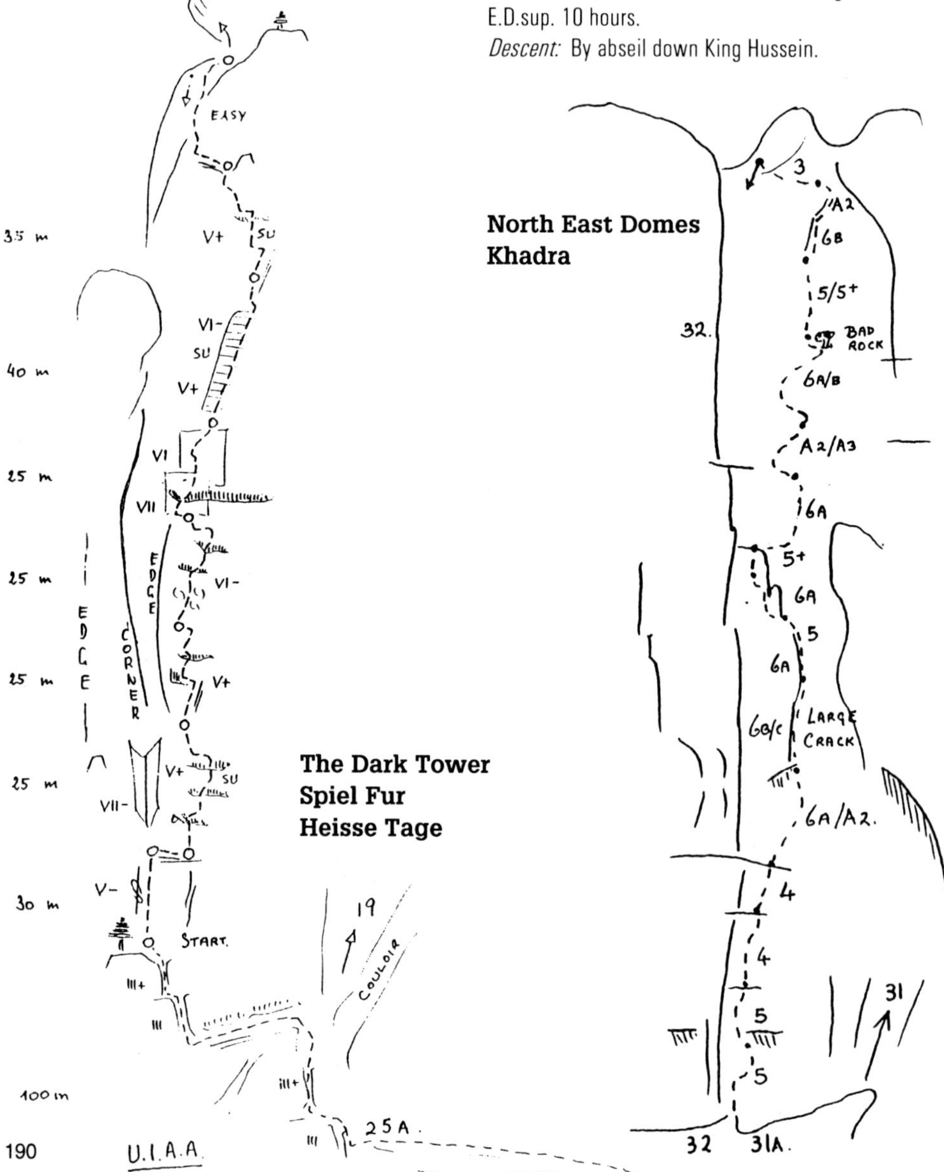

North East Domes
Khadra

The Dark Tower
Spiel Fur
Heisse Tage

32. King Hussein The upper chimney (6A/B) is notoriously unpleasant. The route also provides the abseil piste for all the climbs in this area and has a bad reputation for jammed ropes!

East Dome, East Face

36A. Raid Mit the Camel *Claus Obrist, Hainz Cristoph 14-20th February 1995.*

An excellent line and one of the major new routes of the year. Reputedly good and sustained mixed free and aid climbing up the centre-right of the wall. Bolts were placed sparingly and are in situ. A full set of nuts and cams should be taken, also 7mm cords for threads and 5 pegs. 450 metres. E.D.Sup. The second ascent took 7½ hours.

Descent: By abseil down the route (beware of bubbly rock - it may be better to abseil down Eye of Allah).

East Face Towers

41. Great Siq Route. Pitch 4 6A. *M.Shaw, D.Taylor, A.Howard April 10th 1994.*

An additional pitch up this unusual climb: after pitch 3, scramble into the depths of the siq to the edge of a black watery abyss. Climb the crack in the left wall to a hollow. Abseil, or the speleologically minded may like to try to re-enter and climb the apparently endless chasm of the Great Siq above, to join R.57!

Three new single-pitch climbs have been added between Ziggurat and Aquarius by the Tyrolean climbers who made the first ascent of Raid mit the Camel, and their friends. Unfortunately the line of these routes is marked only too obviously by bright, shiny bolts, which is a pity and should **not** set a precedent. From left to right, the routes are:

54A. Henngrint 6C+
54B. Petting 7B
and between Mano Negra and Aquarius:
55A. Chicken Heat 7A+

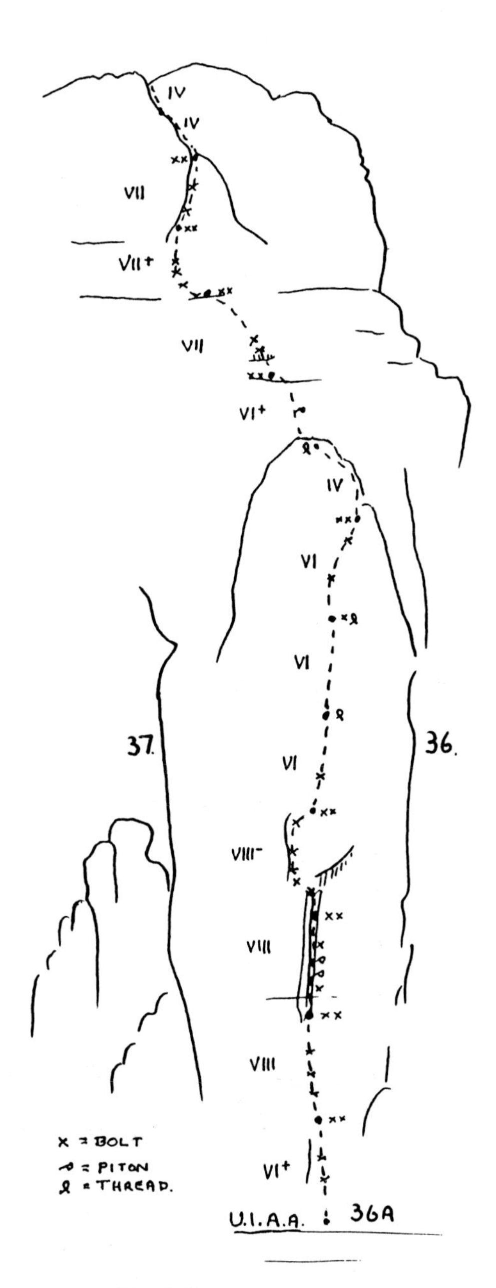

East Dome
East Face
Raid Mit the Camel

Jebel Rum Summit from the East

60. Hammad's Route. Variation start. *J.McIntosh, J. Shand November 1994*
Start 15m left of the ramp. Up easy corner 2m, cross ledge to left, up a step then obvious traverse right to join Hammad's Ridge about 5m north of cairn. Easier than original, and avoids loose blocks.

73. Rum Doodle Variation start *M.Shaw, A. Howard. April 21st 1994.*
After the grade 3 approach chimney, go down left for 10m. Climb the crack and chimney (30m 4+) then straight up the crack in the pillar, missing the traverse right to R.2 (see topo), to arrive directly at R.3 (45m 5)

Vanity Dome. N. Face

On the right side of the N. Face, rising above the inner siq of Wadi Shelaali is the hidden:

74A. Franny's Corner *G.Stari, F.Kroll 2nd March 1993.*
250m. A.D. $2^{1/2}$ hours.

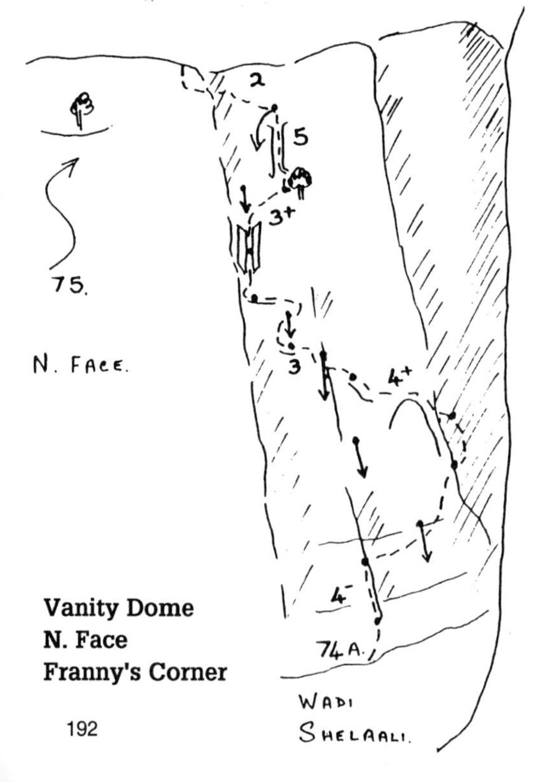

Following a very similar line is:

74B. North Corner *A. Precht. S. Brochmayer 23rd April 1995.*
Vegetated, but pleasant and in impressive surroundings. 300m. D. 2-3 hours.

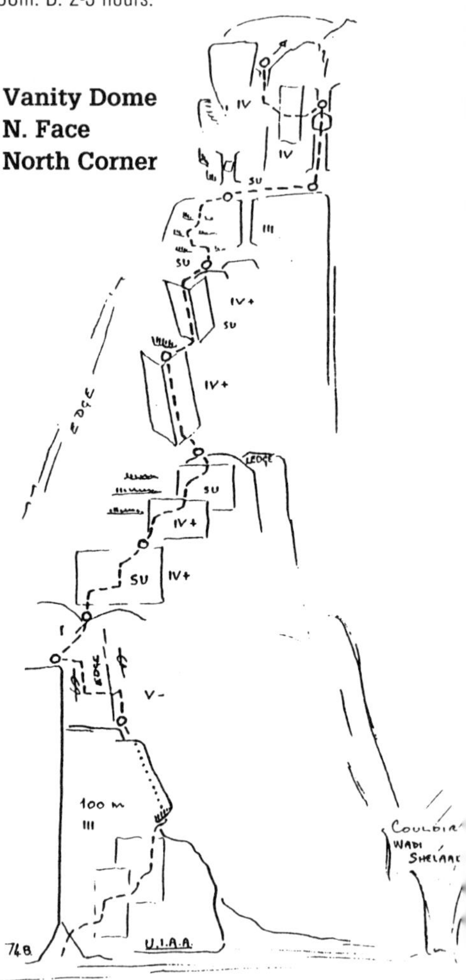

On the east side of the N. Face is an obvious pass, which is:

75A. Rakabat Abu Aina
A traditional and well used passage through the E side of Jebel Rum giving 1 kilometre of rock scrambling. P.D. Allow $2^{1/2}$-3 hours from the Rest House to Abu Aina Bedouin camp.

Take the path up to Lawrence's Well and into the valley above. R.76 goes up the black chimney in the S side of the valley. Head towards this but before entering go about 50m to the right, make an awkward step up (3) and continue the traverse right, to the bottom of an overhanging chimney. Go up this on its left (sandy, strenuous, 3) for a few moves, and continue up to the col with the occasional step of 3.

From the col, keep close to the cliffs of Jebel Rum on the right side and descend into the narrow canyon which leads to the valley of Abu Aina. Go down the canyon until it steepens and avoid the difficulty by taking the right side, then crossing to the left side and after a short traverse, descend a steep 10m wall (3) to the valley floor.

Continue S. down the valley past a 'cross-roads' where R.83 comes in from the left, and an unrecorded Bedouin route goes up the valley to the right into the S plateau of Jebel Rum. The tents of Abu Aina can be seen in the desert to the S. Either approach them directly, or via the springs and palm trees on the right side of the valley.

75B. From just beyond the col of the above route, 'Bedouin steps' lead up towards the summit of Vanity Dome - not yet checked, but Atieeq Auda knows the way.

Jebel Ahmar Al Shelaali, E. Face

A small but pleasant summit wall reached easily up R.78 provides two climbs and good views.
Approach from "the prominent gap between the mountain and tower" on R.78, then either walk along a ledge to belay on the edge of the wall, or descend past the pinnacle to belay at the foot of the wall. 3/4 hour from Rest House.
Descent: via R.78. 1/2 hour.

78A. Arabian Rock *D.Taylor, A. Howard 12th April 1993.*
The name describes the climb and the unusually loud and lively Arabic music playing in the village during the first ascent!

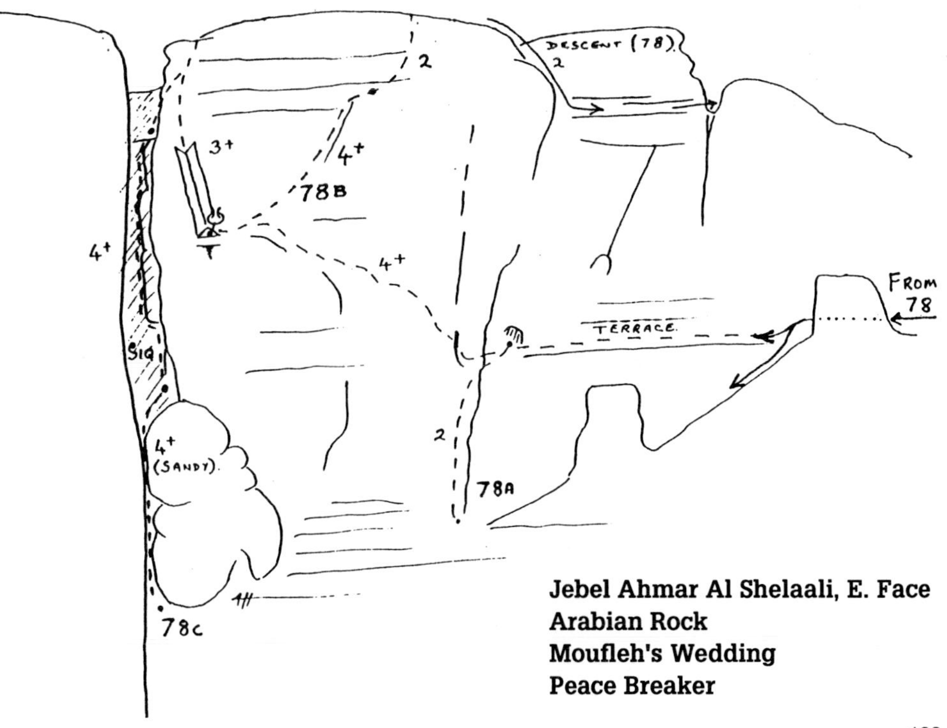

Jebel Ahmar Al Shelaali, E. Face
Arabian Rock
Moufleh's Wedding
Peace Breaker

The main pitch is interesting and delicate climbing on crisps, quite committing, with no obvious line - head for the groove line on the top left. 4+/3+ 1 hour.

78B. Moufleh's Wedding *M. Shaw, A. Howard 30th March 1994.*
A nice variation finish to 78A. 4+/2. Topo page 193.

78C. Peace Breaker *D.Taylor, A. Howard 17th April 1993*
This day, the peace was broken by the army on a military exercise! The climb ascends the chimney system on the left edge of the wall. Some sandy moves on the first pitch are more than compensated for by the fine ramp and crack system in the left wall of the huge upper chimney. 100m. 4+/4+. 1 hour. Topo page 193.

Jebel Um Rera

79A. Les Freres Mousson "Serendipity" variation *S. and M. Bissell 8th April 1994*.
After the Grade 2 pitch to reach the Big Flake chimney, move left above an undercut overhang onto a smooth black wall. Continue left and up the arete to an "imaginative" belay. Carry on up the arete to a tree near the top of the Flake then easier to the top. The pitches up the flake are all very exposed with just enough protection from medium wires. 6A/5/4/2.

Jebel um Rera, S. Summit

This is the next top S of Jebel um Rera. It can be reached via R.83 from Rum village or, in reverse, 15 minutes from Abu Aina. Two routes have been climbed on the N. wall:

81A. Strongfinish *A Reidl, T. Behm 8th April 1995.*
Soft rock leads to good climbing and a "strong finish". 5/6A/6A+ $2^{1}/_{2}$ hours.

81B. Ein Bischen Rax *A. Reidl, T.Behm 8th April 1995.*
A beautiful route on good rock 5+/5+/4/3.
Descent : Go left through a very short canyon to a 50m abseil then scramble down left through mushrooms (2/3).

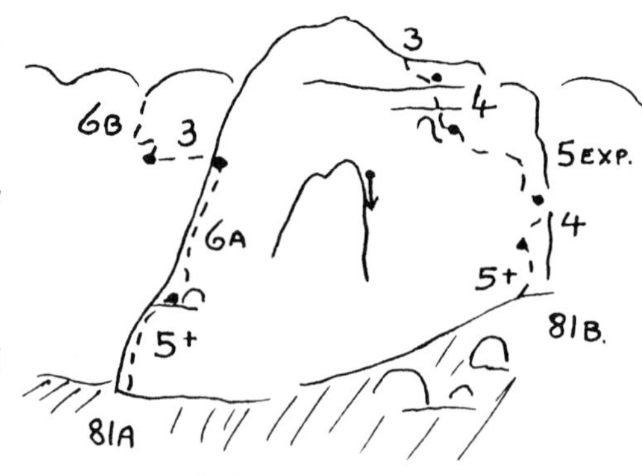

Jebel Um Rera
Strongfinish
Ein Bischen Rax

Abu Aina Towers

There are three towers to the left of Lionheart and directly above the water tank of Abu Aina camp.

86A. Quid Pro Co *Thierry Renault, Atieeq Auda October 1994.*

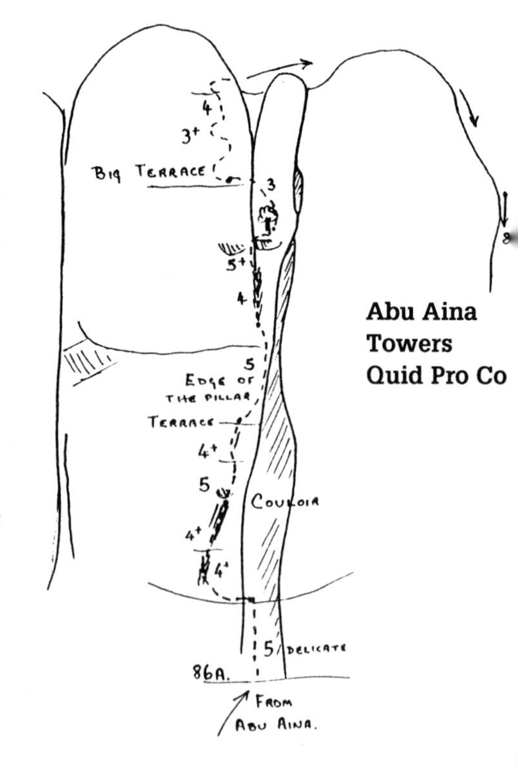

Abu Aina
Towers
Quid Pro Co

This enjoyable route climbs the central tower commencing up a delicate black wall below it's right-hand couloir. T.D.inf. No details of length or time. Topo page 194.
Descent: By Lionheart.

Abu N'Khala Towers

86A. Ecce Homo *Angel and Ana 18th October 1994.* A route has been recorded up "the obvious diedre "to the left of the palm trees. 170m. 5/5+/5+/4/4.

Jebel Rum Summit, from the West

90A. Western Safari *J. McIntosh, J.Shand, Atieeq Auda November 1994.*
A classic traditional Bedouin Route and possibly the easiest and most direct way to the top of Jebel Rum. About 1½km. Allow 3 hours from Wadi Rumman. P.D.
Follow Sabbah's route, then enter the huge hanging canyon by traversing N. above the cliff inside the canyon's entrance. Go up the canyon bed past water basins and continue for about 100m then scramble up the N side, to ledges. Gain them and go left, (a step of 3) passing a hollow with some inscriptions (possibly Thamudic) to eventually reach the upper edge of the big basin with a juniper tree high above the canyon entry cliff. From the back right side of the basin, the route trends right and back left up slabs, moving up a groove to a terrace, then left and straight up to the domes where a direct line is taken to the summit (a few cairns).
Descent: by this route, or via R.92.

90B. Western Safari,The English Way *A.Howard, D. Taylor April 15th 1996.*
A slightly more direct version of 90A, with a couple of exposed pitches of 3 on excellent black 'swiss cheese' rock to reach and climb the obvious crack that goes up to the big basin and juniper tree. About 1½km. Allow 3 hours from Wadi Rumman. P.D.
Approach: As 90A, moving on to the north wall of the canyon at the first side entrance after the water basins.
Descent: By 90A, or 92.

92. Sheikh Hamdan's Route It has been pointed out that there is a delicate and exposed little descent of 3m (3+) off a rounded ridge to reach easy rock just before the col under the summit. This is not marked on the topo (page 87), but it can be avoided by going right at the last 'flat area' to join 90A (see topos).

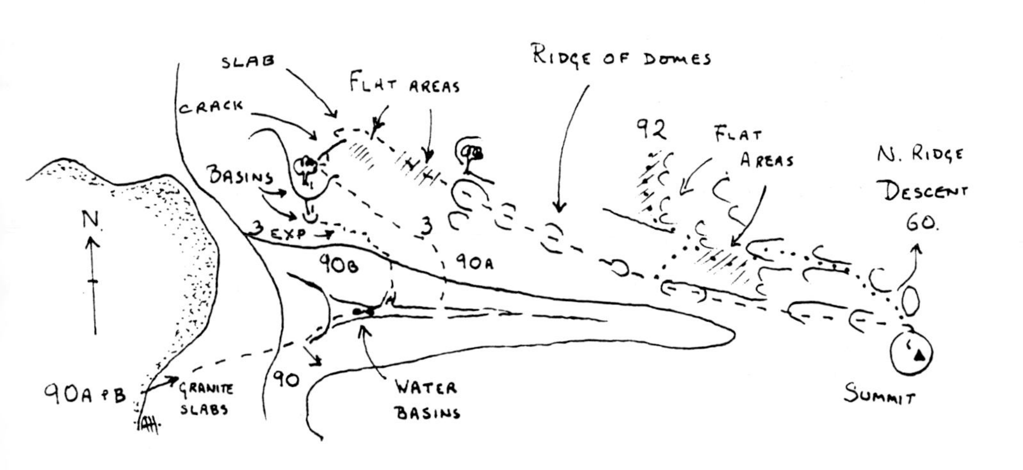

Jebel Rum Summit
Western Safari
Western Safari, The English Way

JEBEL UM ISHRIN MASSIF

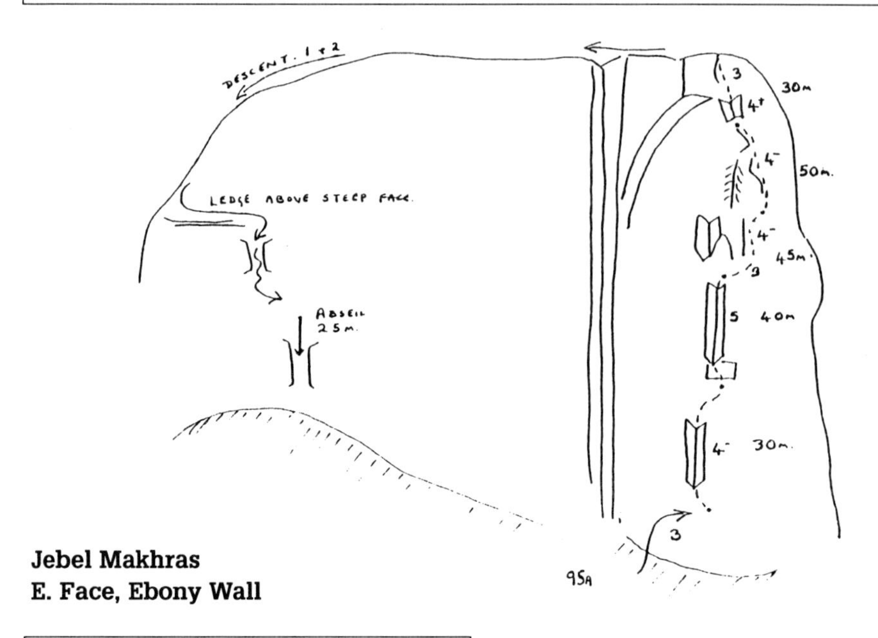

Jebel Makhras
E. Face, Ebony Wall

Jebel Makhras

95A. E. Face, Ebony Wall *C.Held, H. Mittermayr March 1993.*
A superb E face with inviting cracks and slabs. The route follows a line right of the obvious cracks in the centre of the big corner. Nice climbing on good rock. A.D. Sup. 200m.

Jebel Insjmareh

Pass N of Jebel um Ishrin, to the impressive NE Face on the second mountain E of the N end, with an obvious crack-corner line in the centre. Possibly also known as Jebel Reha.

95B. NE Face. The Schmuftlers *H.Mittermayr, C. Held 9th March 1993.*
Approach from the left and traverse a big ledge to the start of the climb (cairn and thread). Enjoyable climbing on good rock. T.D.Inf. 230m.

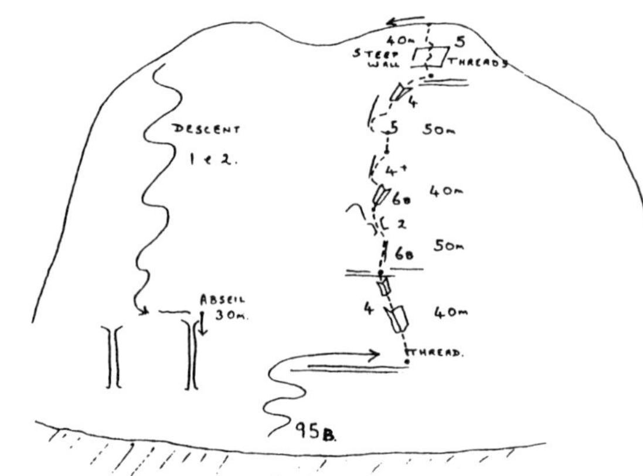

Jebel Insjmareh
The Schmuftlers

Jebel Hajaj. S. Summit

98A. Mohammed Musa's Route to Wadi um Ishrin *First reported ascent A. Howard, M.Shaw April 1994.*

A classic Bedouin crossing of this complex massif. Take plenty of abseil tape (and maybe a couple of pegs for emergencies). Approx 3km from Rum to Wadi um Ishrin.

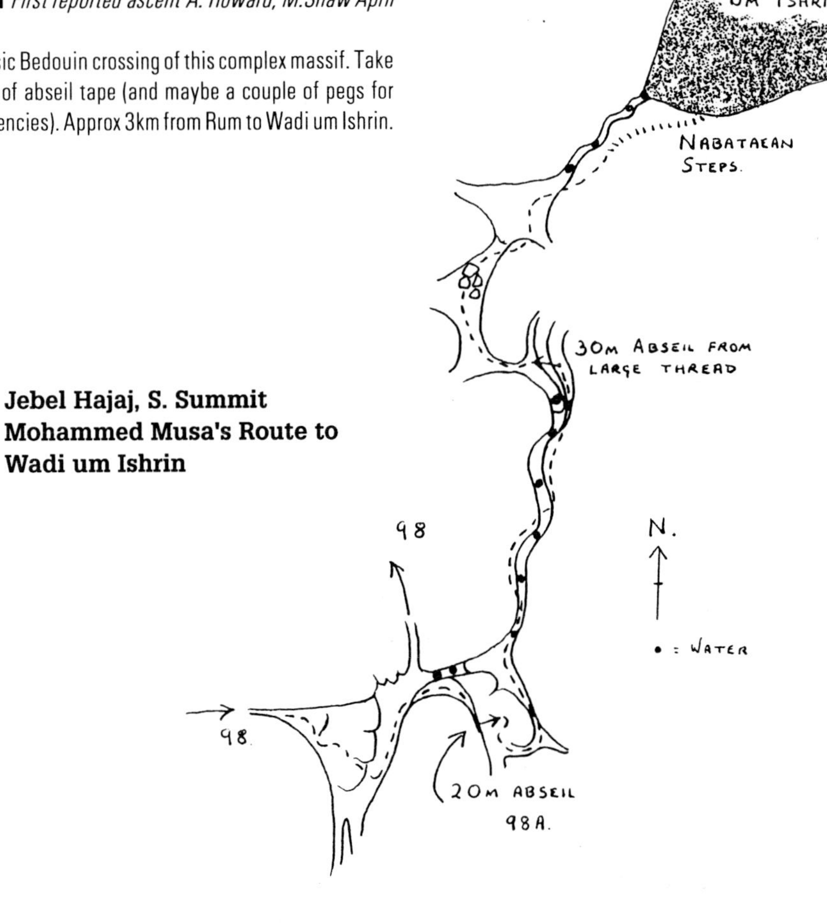

Jebel Hajaj, S. Summit
Mohammed Musa's Route to Wadi um Ishrin

P.D Sup. Allow 5 or 6 hours for the whole traverse. Follow Mohammed Musa's route (R.98) to the water holes just after the "very steep descent", in the very heart of the mountain. From here, the route traverses east on a ledge above the south side of the water hole, to an abseil point at its extremity. The way on is long and fascinating passing many pools, and although it follows the line of the canyon down to the NE and is inescapable, the easiest way is not always obvious. There is one more abseil from a huge thread (at the far end of a low ledge and not at first obvious) where the canyon level drops vertically and the final exit is down 2000 year old 'Nabataean steps' on the right (SE) side of the canyon (R101). To find them, take the right side out of the final sandy basin and contour along above the ravine and pools.

Return: Either arrange to be met in Wadi um Ishrin, or return by walking S. down the desert canyon on the E flank of Jebel um Ishrin (R101) then back to Rum by abseiling through Zernouk el Daber (R.123 & R.132), or by walking through Rakabat Canyon (R.130). Either way, allow another 3 hours.

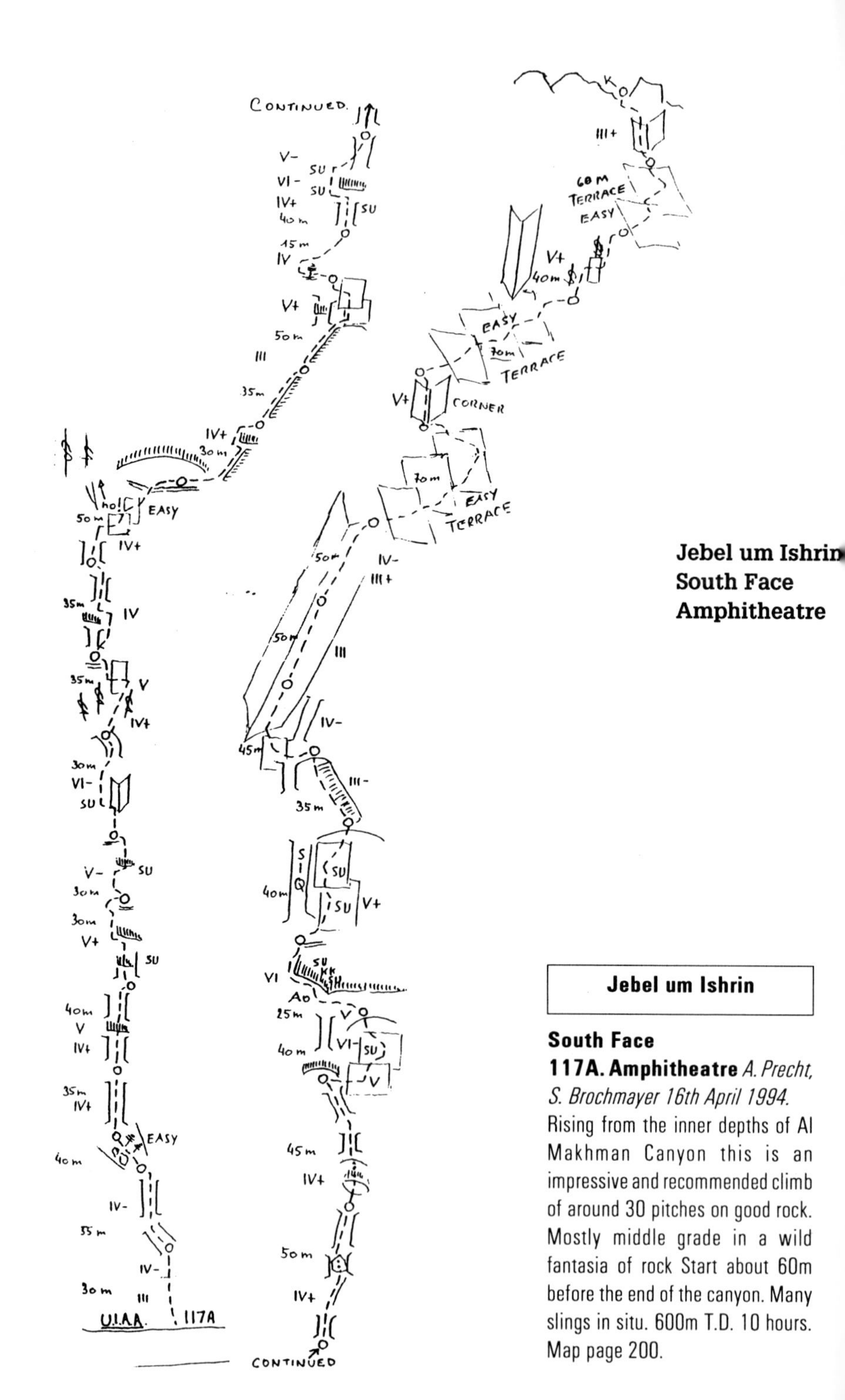

Jebel um Ishrin South Face Amphitheatre

Jebel um Ishrin

South Face

117A. Amphitheatre *A. Precht, S. Brochmayer 16th April 1994.*

Rising from the inner depths of Al Makhman Canyon this is an impressive and recommended climb of around 30 pitches on good rock. Mostly middle grade in a wild fantasia of rock Start about 60m before the end of the canyon. Many slings in situ. 600m T.D. 10 hours. Map page 200.

Jebel Kharazeh

North Face

Almost opposite the start of Amphitheatre, in the great chasm of Al Makhman is another long and serious route:

121A. Abraham *A. Precht, S. Brochmayer April 1994.*

Start left of Rock Fascination. A superlative tour on good rock. Many slings mark the route. 450m. E.D. 8 hours. Map page 200.

Jebel Kharazeh Abraham

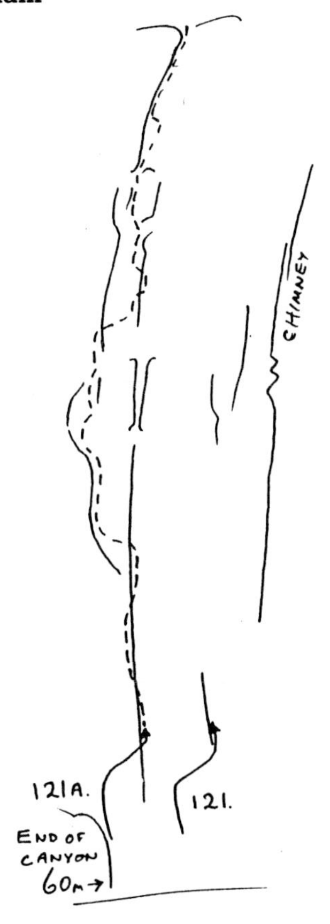

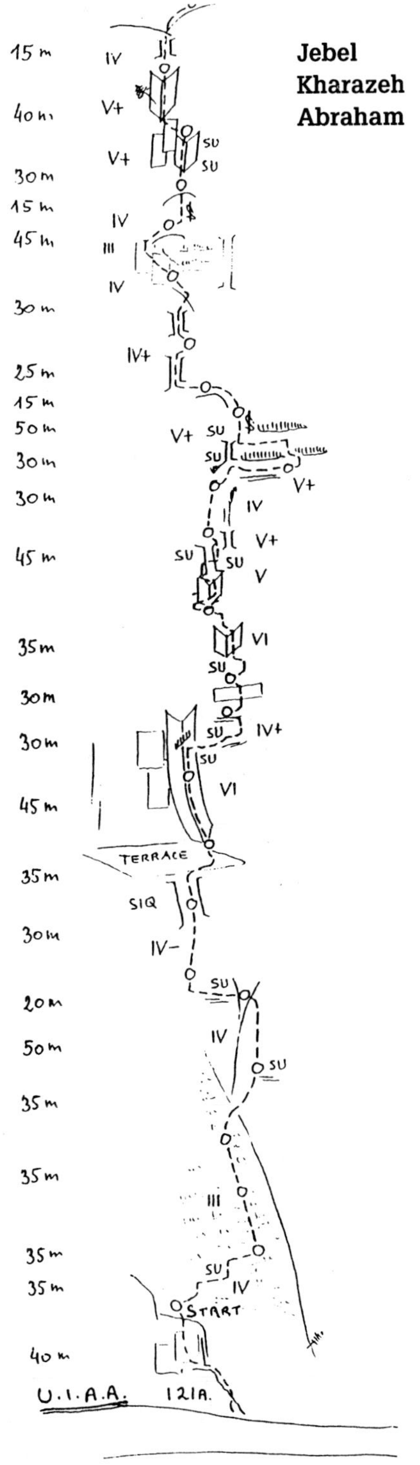

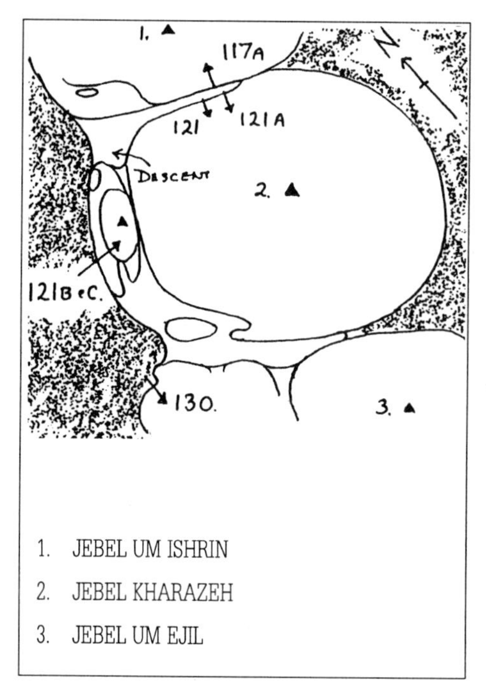

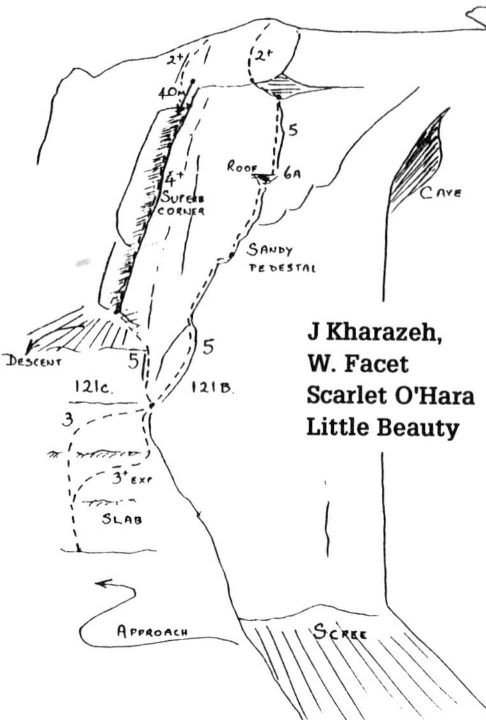

Jebel Kharazeh, W. Facet

Directly below the W Face of Kharazeh between the mighty gashes of Makhman and Kharazeh canyons is a subsidiary summit discernible from the Rest House. This gives two climbs:

Approach: Up Goat's Gully (see R.130) then left (N) across Kharazeh Canyon just above the cliff where it drops into the desert, and up screes to below the wall with a hanging cave on its right. Scramble left up easy rocks to a platform below slabs.

121B. Scarlet O' Hara *M. Shaw, A. Howard, D. Taylor 19th April 1994.*
A slabby start leads to an exposed upper wall and a good hanging crack to the left of the cave. 120m. 3+/5/6A/3.

121C. Little Beauty *A. Howard, D. Taylor, M.Shaw 24th April 1994.*
A slabby start leads to the hidden upper wall and an impressive corner crack. 120m 3/5/4+/3.
Descent: For both routes, from the summit descend the final pitch to an excellent thread above the cracks of Little Beauty. Abseil (40m) and scramble down right then left, to the starting platform.

Jebel um Ejil, S.W. Face

50m right of Little Gem and at the top right of the boulders in the entrance to the Hanging Garden, is a broken corner rising from a recess:

135A. Rescuer's Route *A. Howard, M. Shaw, D. Taylor 4th April 1994.*
Direct up the corner to a pedestal. 40m. 5.
Descent: By abseil. (The first ascent was followed by the rescue of two walkers stuck half-way down the abseil from Rakabat to Kharazeh Canyon with neither guidebook nor ropes, nor the ability to climb back up!)

Jebel um Ejil, S. Summit, North Domes

North West Towers

138. Point Alexandre This tower identifies the area (map page 111)

138A. The Full Monte *Geoff Hornby, Susie Sammut, Peter Bishop 31st March 1994.*

The obvious tower above Point Alexandre. A sandy crux is followed by better, easier climbing 200m. 5+/4+/5/3+/4/3+.

Descent: Down last pitch, then down the big gully with 2 abseils near the bottom.

138B. The Artful Dodger *Steve and Marie Bissel 31st March 1994.*

The route climbs the crack and pocketed wall above, to a belay, then up the undercut wall. 35m 5/6A.

Approach: Enter the narrow canyon between R.138 and R.138A leading towards Wadi um Ishrin. Just past the narrows is a flake crack on the left.

Descend: Down left, and down R.138.

Jebel um Ejil, West Face

The Crack in the Back

Jebel um Ejil, West Face

141A. Deviant Finish *M. Podd, B. Woodley April 1993.*

"Extends the pleasure for Franco-phobes"! From, R.5, traverse right (5) to belay, then up a left-facing corner (6A) to the left end of the ledge leading to the abseils.

141B. The Crack in the Back *A. Howard, D. Taylor 16th April 1993.*

A short and pleasant trip on mushrooms! 3/3/3/1/2. 160m. 1-1½ hours.

Approach: Through Rakabat Canyon until 30m before the scree ramp heading up to 'The Beauty'.The crack which gives the line of the route rises up through the mushrooms right of the big hanging wall.

Descent: Down the S Ridge from the platform with a few moves of 2 to the left, to the continuation ridge, finishing either left into the 'Hanging Garden' or down slabs on the right to reach Rakabat Canyon just N of 'the cross-roads'. ¾ hour.

Jebel um Ejil, N.E. Face

144A. Pooh Corner *Geoff Hornby, Susie Sammut 14th October 1995.*

A better version of R.144, starting 50m to its right at a shallow corner and groove system climbed in 4 pitches to join R.144. 5+ then easier. 120m to R.144.

Descent: By 2 abseils.

Route Locations Jebel Um Ishrin Massif South Summits

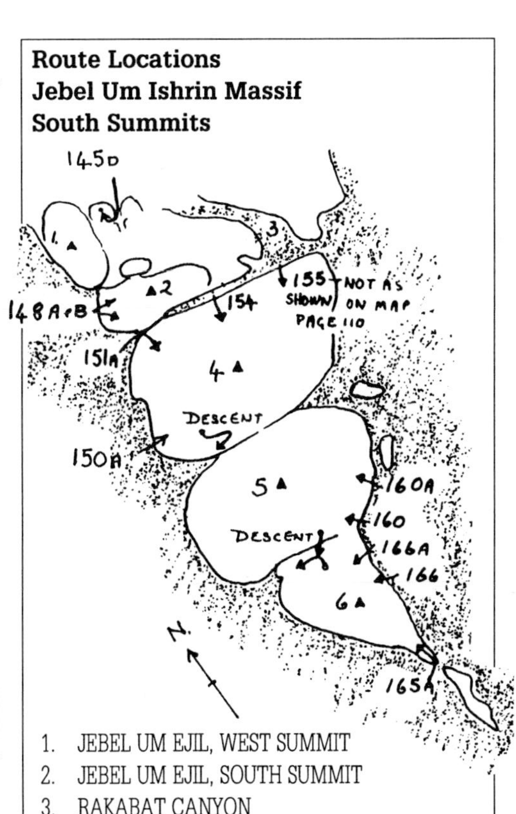

1. JEBEL UM EJIL, WEST SUMMIT
2. JEBEL UM EJIL, SOUTH SUMMIT
3. RAKABAT CANYON
4. NORTH NASSRANI
5. SOUTH NASSRANI
6. DRAIF AL MURAGH

Jebel um Ejil, S. Summit, N. Domes
Juniper Gulch

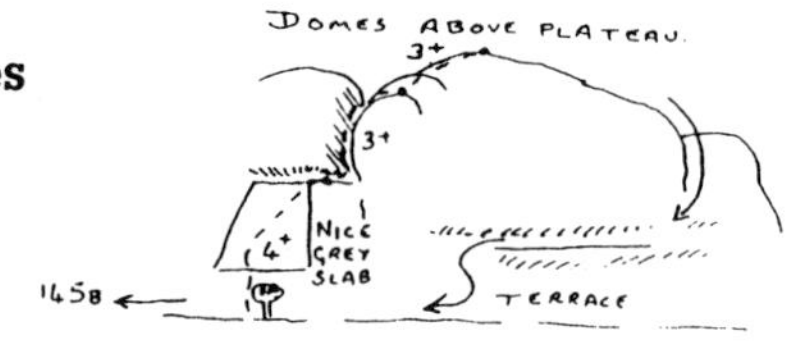

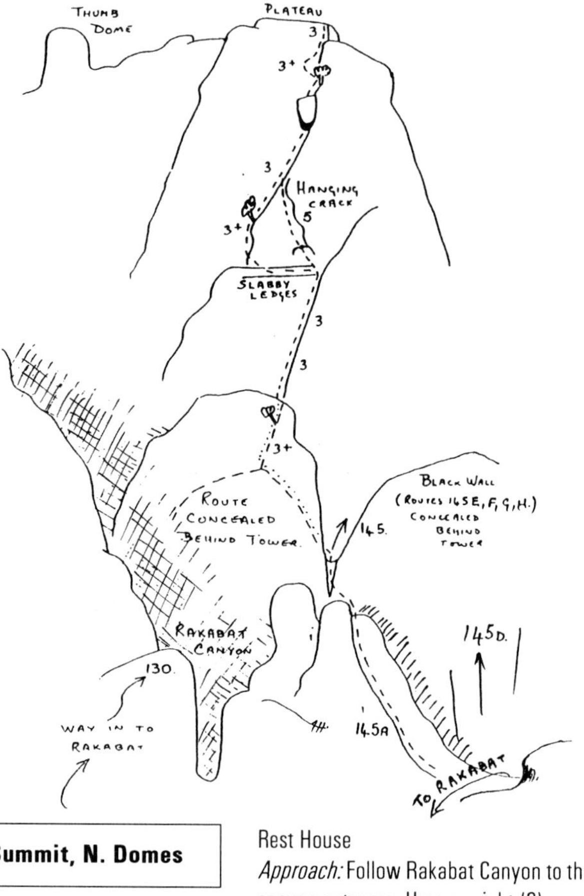

Jebel um Ejil, S. Summit, N. Domes

145A. N.W.Face. Juniper Gulch *A. Howard, D. Taylor 27th April 1993.*

Hanging Crack Variation, *M. Shaw, A. Howard April 1994.*

A very pleasant scramble up cracks and chimneys with juniper trees on the shady NW side of the mountain, to a large plateau which connects by an easy terrace to routes 145, 147 and 148. Above is a slightly harder but equally enjoyable optional finish onto the North Dome, or an easy finish onto Thumb Dome (145B).

A nice day out, on good rock throughout with approximately 300m of climbing. A.D. 2 1/2-3 hours from Rest House

Approach: Follow Rakabat Canyon to the col above the canyon entrance. Here go right (S) up an easy ridge of slabs as R.145 to enter a siq. Once inside go left at the 'cross-roads' and up to a saddle (ahead is a difficult descent into Rakabat Canyon).

From the col a wide chimney with a dead juniper at 10m marks the start of the route.

Descent: From the domes, go S, then down W and down short chimneys to a long red sandy ledge with overhangs above and below. The big terrace that leads to the plateau is underneath. Traverse N for 100m (2) along this ledge until it is possible to descend to the terrace and return to the plateau. Descend the route to Rakabat. 1-1 1/2 hours.

145B. Thumb Dome *A. Howard, M. Shaw April 1994.*
The 'thumb-shaped tower' seen above the entrance to Rakabat Canyon (page 112) can be reached easily from the big terrace of Juniper Gulch. Simply walk E, cross a siq then up slabs (2) following a crack and a corridor before scrambling onto the Dome on the right.

145C. This dome can also be reached by following Rakabat Canyon (R. 130) to the junction just before the pass. Then go S, up siqs through a cave to more siqs and slabs to reach the domes. (*McIntosh and Shand November 1994).*

The Black Wall

Just inside the entrance to Juniper Gulch is an exquisite little wall of sensually pocketed rock with opportunities for a few excellent single pitch climbs, four of which have been done. Protection is sparse and as a consequence routes 145E, F and G were climbed on top rope. Any other routes made here should be done this way - or better still, led - rather than defiling the crag with bolts .

Direct approach: It is possible to reach the Black Wall via a pleasant little climb which conjures up some unexpected entertainment.

145D. Houdini *A. Howard, D. Taylor April 9th 1996.*
Enjoyable, with a curious second pitch. 3/5/5 (or 6A/3/3. 150m $1^1/_2$ hours. Maps pages 201 and 202.

Approach as R.130 until just before the saddle above the ravine marking the entrance to Rakabat Canyon. At this point, just 50m to the south, is a ridge of rock split by a crack at the bottom with a nice looking slab forming the headwall of its distinctive square top. This top is the top of the Black Wall and the route finishes on it. The Black Wall climbs are on the opposite (south) side.

The other approach to the Black Wall is:
Siq Approach: Up Juniper Gulch (as 145A) to enter a siq above Rakabat Canyon. The siq descends to a 'crossroads.' Looking back, on its left (W) side, a south facing 20m black wall forms a little summit. The large platform at its foot is easily gained by a short scramble and there is a large shady boulder to escape under from the afternoon sun!

Reach the top via 145E, or by scrambling round the left side .

For top-roping the Black Wall climbs two ropes are useful, one to form a huge sling fastened to threads and friends on the opposite (Houdini) side of the tower, the other for the top rope and lower-off, if required.

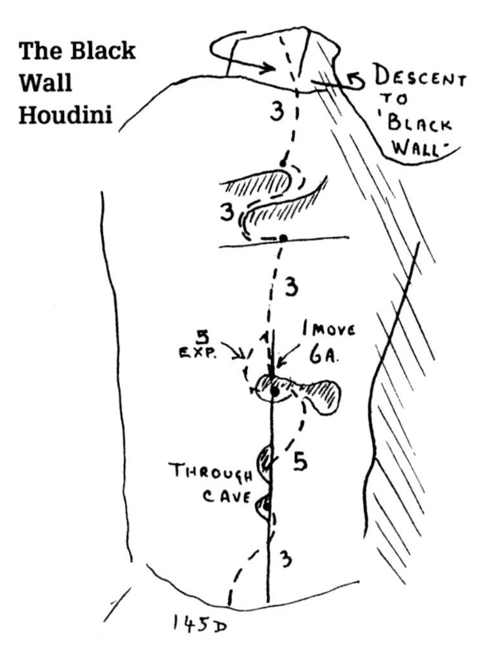

The Black Wall
Love at First Feel
A Touch too Much
For Those about to Rock
Back in Black

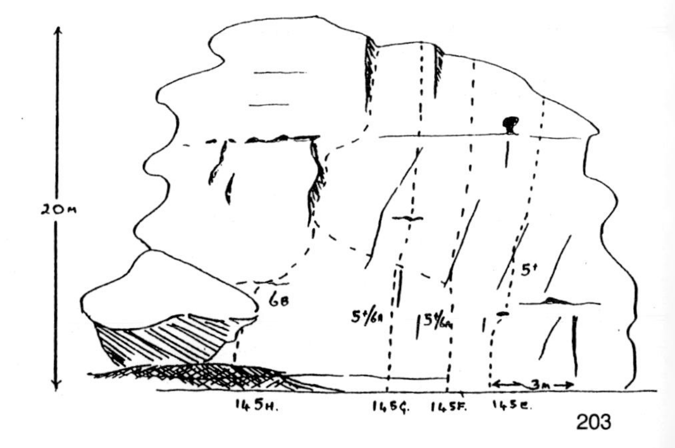

Black Wall map topo pages 202 and 203.

145E. Love at First Feel *A. Howard, M. Shaw, D. Taylor April 28th 1995.*

Small holes and cracks, just protectable with wires. 5+.

145F. A Touch too Much *A. Howard, M. Shaw, D. Taylor April 28th 1995.*

Sensual climbing on finger pockets. 6A.

145G. For Those about to Rock *M.Shaw, A.Howard, D. Taylor April 28th 1995*

More delectable finger insertions. Finish straight up, or go left to the corner. 6A.

145H. Back in Black *A. Howard April 9th 1996*

A delightful fingery traverse to gain the corner. 6B.

Jebel um Ejil, S. Summit

West Face

148A. Six Hundred und Eins *A. Precht, S. Brochmayer April 1994.*

Albert Precht's 601st new route! A good climb, trending slightly right, up the centre of the face, rising up from R.148 at the end of its first pitch. Interesting route finding on good rock. 200m. T.D. Map page 201.

148B. Costa Brava *Sabbah Atieeq, Rosa Povedano, Toti Vales January 4th 1995.*

A wandering route also sharing the first pitch of R.148 but then trending right across the lower wall to a ledge on the right arête, then up the concealed S. Face. 400m. Map page 201.

Jebel um Ejil, S. Summit, West Face
Six Hundred und Eins, Costa Brava

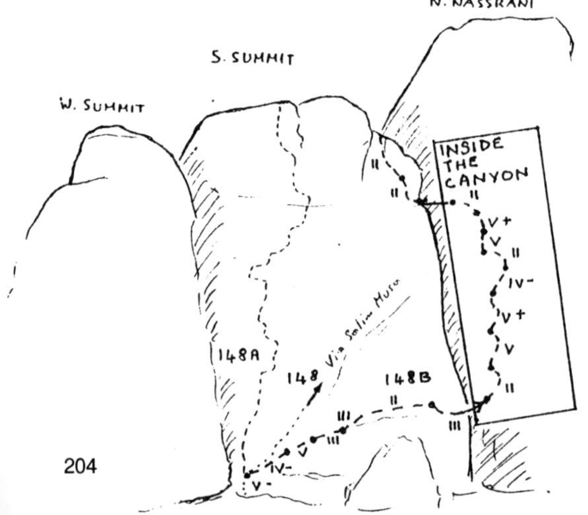

Descent: for both routes is as R.148 descent.

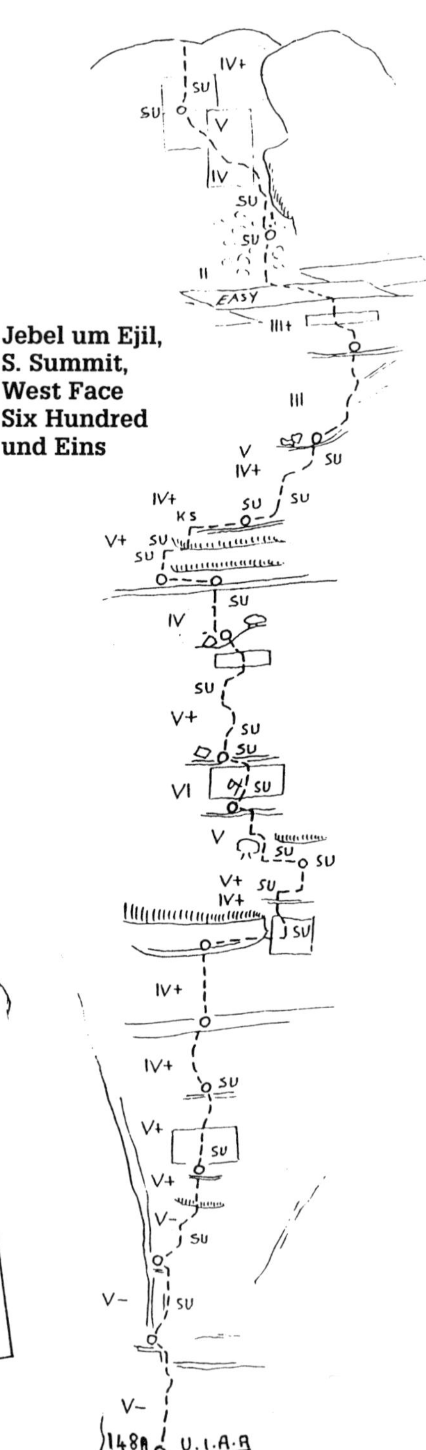

Jebel um Ejil,
S. Summit,
West Face
Six Hundred
und Eins

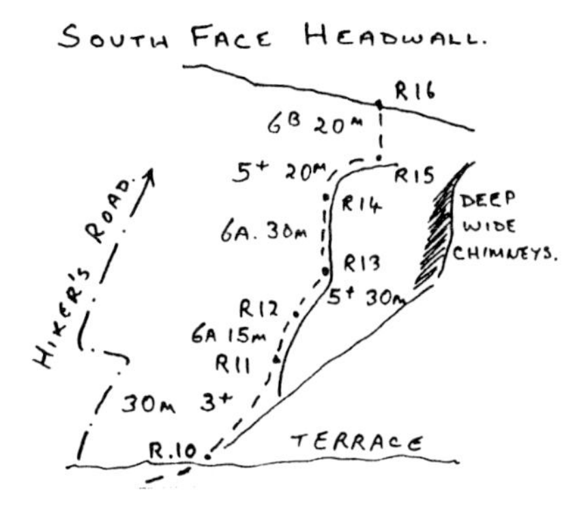

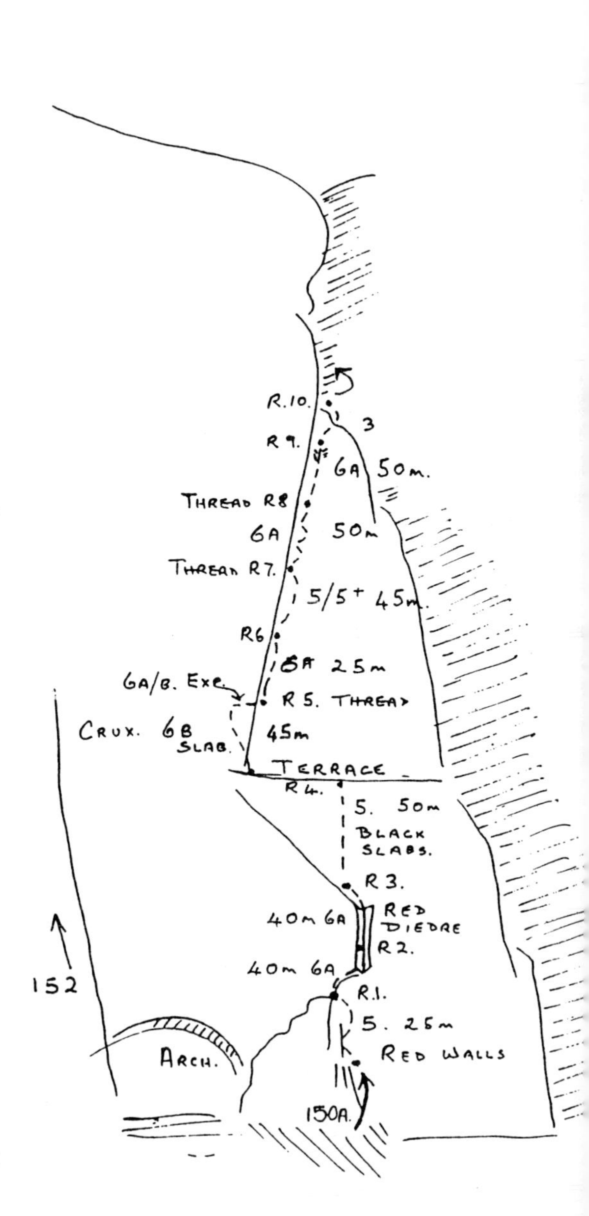

North Nassrani

150A. Tea on the Moon *O. Cantet, B. Martel, I. & E. Ratouis 12th May 1993 to Hiker's road. Completed 17th May 1993 with Sabbah Eid (the first Bedouin ascent of Nassrani).*

Mostly very good rock except for 3 or 4 sandy metres at the start of pitch 7. The climb provides a variety of climbing through slabs, diedres and walls. The red diedre identifying the second and third pitches is superb and the traverse of pitch 5 is "emotionally committing" and particularly difficult for climbers less than 1.7m in height. At that point, the rock is good on the black slabs and red overhang - do not try to climb in the sandy yellow crack which is always on the left. The line of cracks of the third part is obvious, to the right of Hiker's Road. Protection is good and needs a full rack of Friends and stoppers and many slings. (The last pitch of slabs (6B) can be avoided.) 350m (500m to the domes) T.D. Sup.6 hours to reach Hiker's Road and another 2 hours to the summit. Map page 201.

Approach & Descent: as the Hikers's Road. The Red Diedre of pitch 3 can be clearly seen. Start under a red overhang formed by red slabs and a leaning pillar.

North Nassrani, North West Pillar
Sabbah's Homeland

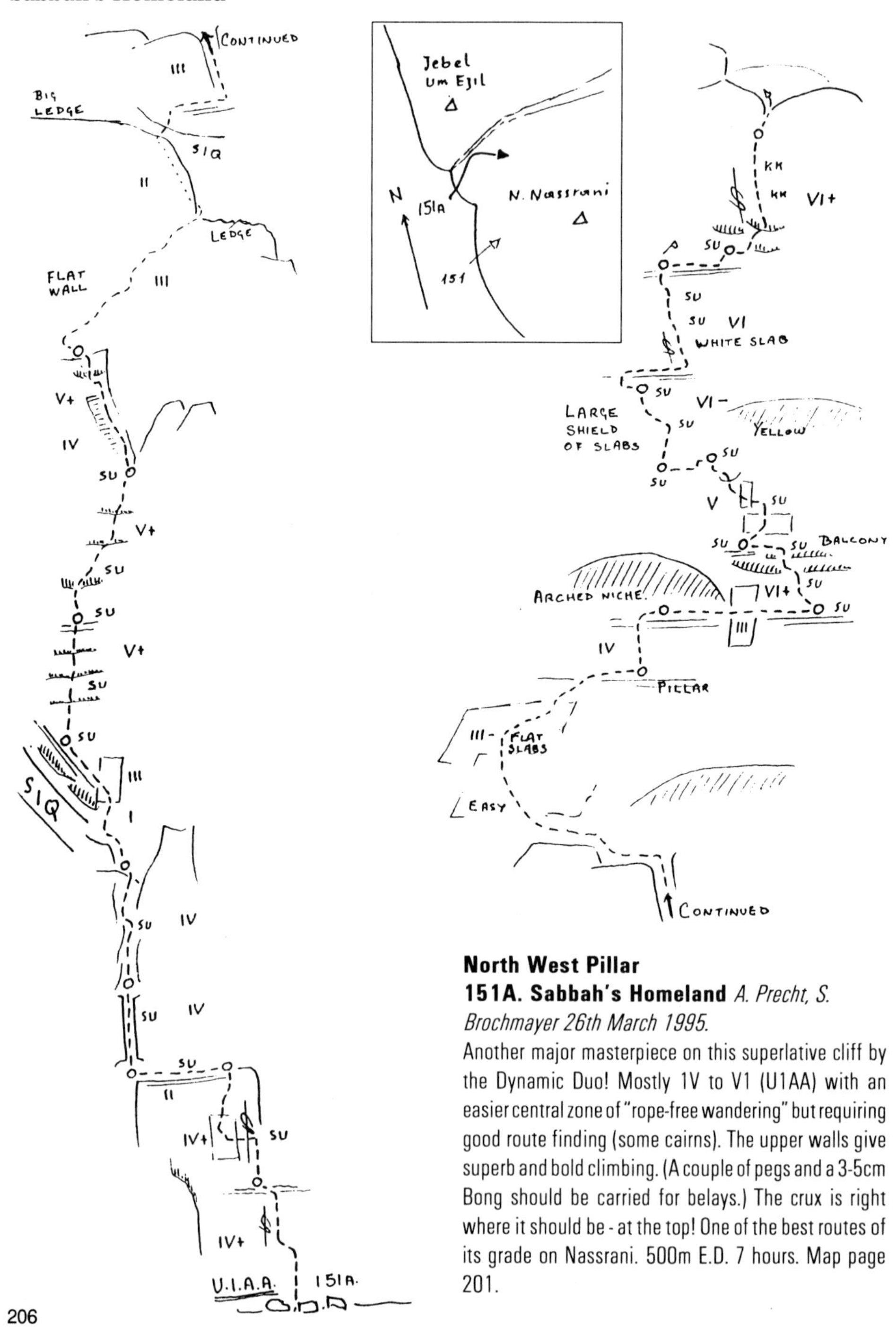

North West Pillar
151A. Sabbah's Homeland *A. Precht, S. Brochmayer 26th March 1995.*

Another major masterpiece on this superlative cliff by the Dynamic Duo! Mostly 1V to V1 (U1AA) with an easier central zone of "rope-free wandering" but requiring good route finding (some cairns). The upper walls give superb and bold climbing. (A couple of pegs and a 3-5cm Bong should be carried for belays.) The crux is right where it should be - at the top! One of the best routes of its grade on Nassrani. 500m E.D. 7 hours. Map page 201.

South Nassrani

South Face

160A. Die Sichl *A. Precht, S. Brochmayer 25th March 1995.*

Steep and challenging climbing on good rock through the mushrooms and overlaps to the summit cracks. 450m. E.D. 8 hours. Map page 201.

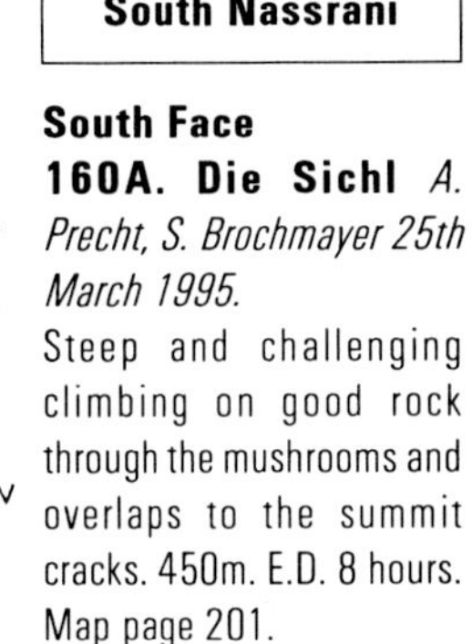

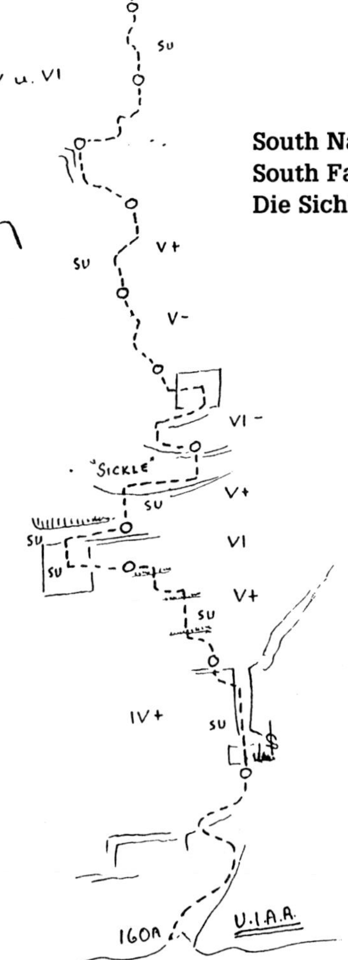

South Nassrani
South Face
Die Sichl

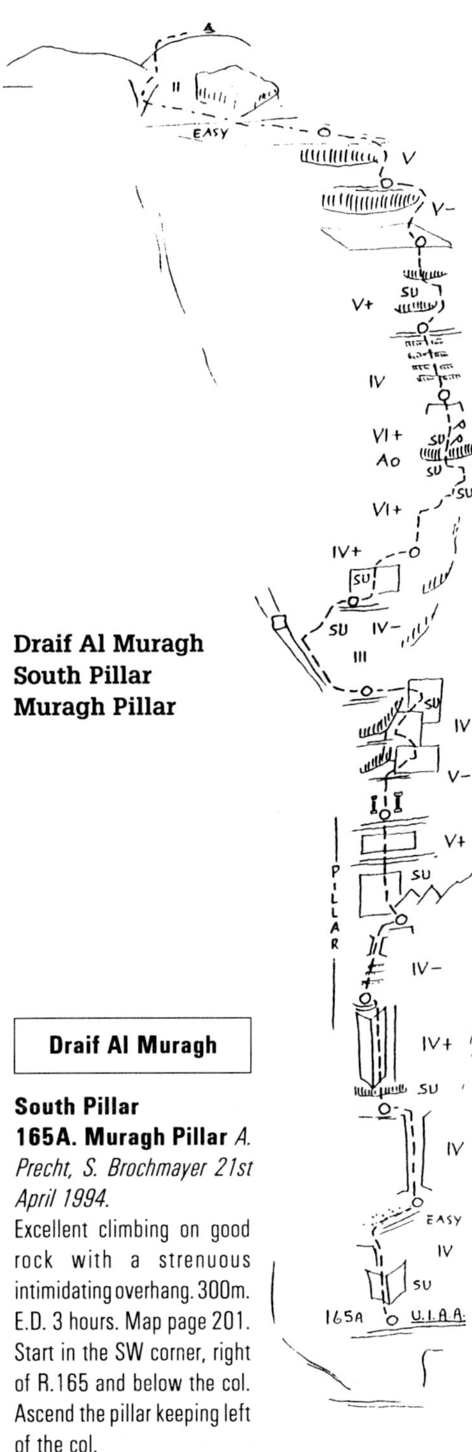

Draif Al Muragh
South Pillar
Muragh Pillar

Draif Al Muragh

South Pillar

165A. Muragh Pillar *A. Precht, S. Brochmayer 21st April 1994.*

Excellent climbing on good rock with a strenuous intimidating overhang. 300m. E.D. 3 hours. Map page 201. Start in the SW corner, right of R.165 and below the col. Ascend the pillar keeping left of the col.

166A. East Corner *A. Precht, S.Brochmayer 26th March 1995.*

Starts just right of R.166. Beautiful climbing on good rock with two difficult pitches (UIAA. V11) up the initial corner, then easier climbing above to the col below the S Ridge of Nassrani. 300m. E.D. 3 hours. Map page 201.

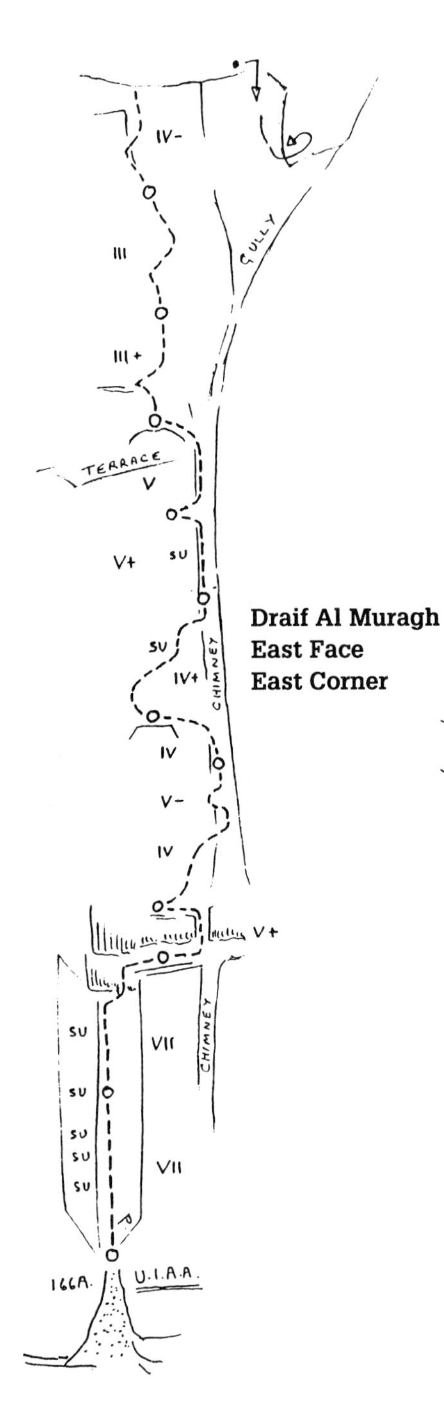

Draif Al Muragh East Face East Corner

El K'Seir (The Castle)

This peak is west of Jebel al Raqa, at the SE end of Wadi um Ishrin (map pg. 91)

S.W. Face

One line has been climbed to date, others are obvious and there are some very large boulders at the bottom of the face which provide entertainment.

172A. First, But Nice *E.G. Delaage, T. Renault April 1994.*

The route ascends the black wall left of the typical corner line giving nice climbing on good rock. 200m. D.

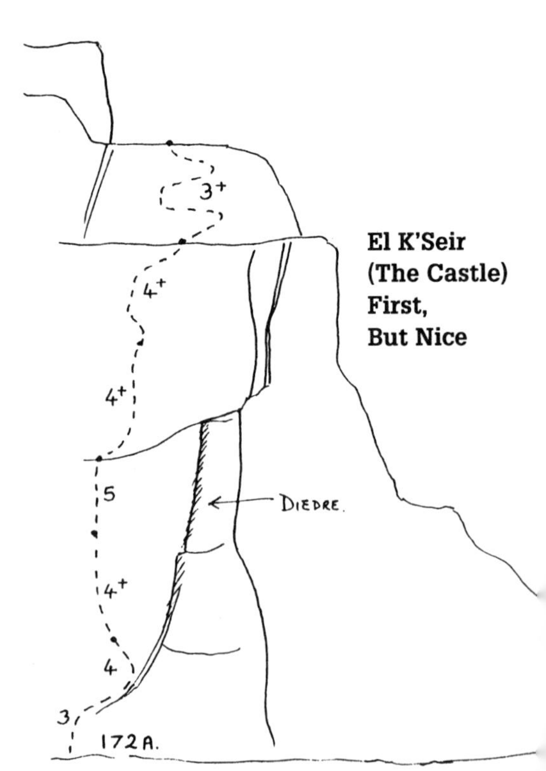

El K'Seir (The Castle) First, But Nice

BARRAH CANYON AREA

Jebel Barrah

174. Hunter's Slabs The vertical height gain is 500m, not 300m!

177. The Black Iris There is an easier Bedouin way over this ridge. No details.

Jebel Barrah The East Pillar, The Pillar of Ata Abu Rabeh

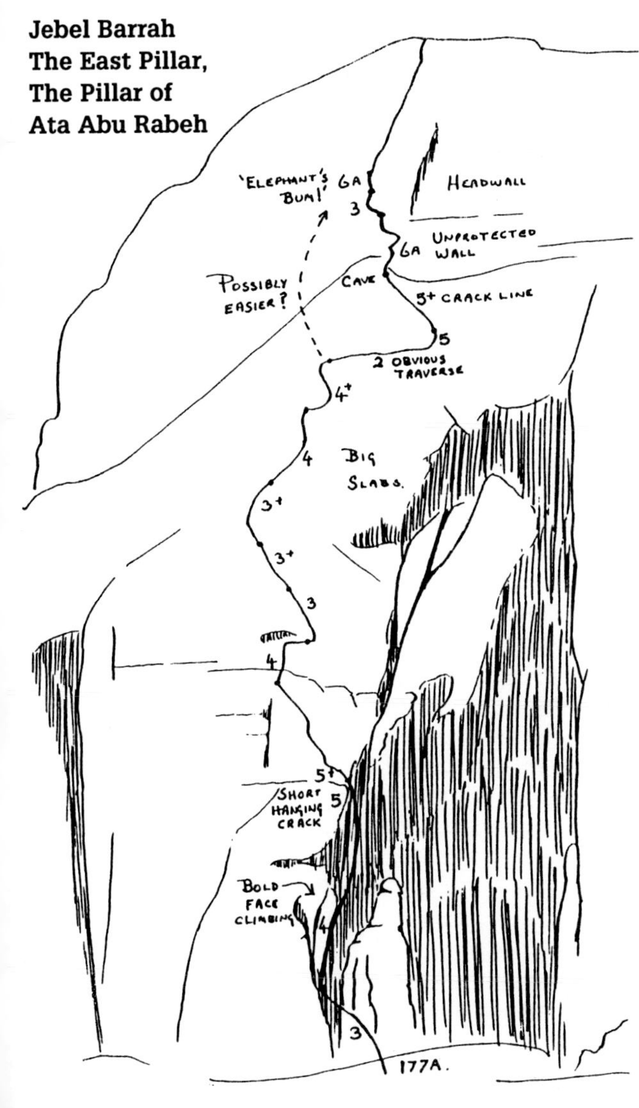

The East Pillar

177A. The Pillar of Ata Abu Rabeh *G. Hornby, S. Sammut 8th April 1994.*

This excellent climb is typical of Rum's big slabs - long, exposed and crossed by bulges and walls with inevitably complex route finding making a committing day out. The upper pillar crux is English E3 5b, with almost half a rope of exposure.

Combined with the descent of Hunter's Slabs it provides a memorable round trip. 550m. T.D.

The line taken, though complex, was always the easiest. Crucial features are:

(a) from the lower ramp go out left onto slabs (3/3+), then right and left to the crest.

(b) (4+/5) The pillar is cut by a siq. Gain its right wall. Rise across this to a short steep crack, to regain the crest.

(c) Continue through the bulge and pad up slabs.

(d) (4/5/6A) At the steepening, go right to a crack which leads up left. Up this until a protectionless wall (6A) blows your mind! (Maybe easier out left up steep slabs?)

(e) (5/4/4/3/) Up to a hollow, then a steep corner to a traverse left to a right slanting groove and to the top.

Approach: By 4-wheel drive to the foot of the pillar in Rad al Beidah (map pg. 135)

Descent: Down R.174.

Disi Rocks

186 A,B,&C. These short climbs have been put up by Wilfried Colonna and friends on the little cliff just S.of the railway-crossing on the road from Rum to Disi. No details.

Jebel Hiswa, West Summit

South Face

Two routes have been reported on the S side of a dome which is reported as being on the N side of the desert track to Disi, N of Barrah Canyon.Unfortunately the precise location is not clear from the first ascentionist's map so I include brief notes only:
On the right side is:

187A. South Crack *A.Stari, F.Kroll 17th March 1994.*
A pedestal and wall (4) leads to an impressive summit chimney and corner. 5/5+ A1/6A. 150m. T.D. 3 hours.
Descent: 1 abseil then down to the east then down to the SE with 1 more abseil.

Left of the above route is:

187B. Desert Relax *A.Stari, F. Kroll 18th March 1994.*
Start left of a white chimney and well right of a tower. Continue more or less directly up cracks and chimneys to the top 5/4+/4/5+/2. D.
Descent: 4 abseils down the route, the last down the white chimney. Perfect equipped piste. 1 hour.

East Summit

187C. A Bedouin route is reported up the east side of this top.

Rad Al Beidah

189. The new super crack project The project is still being worked by Wilfried Colonna and friends. The huge awe-inspiring E facing corner has now been climbed (7A), and a finish is planned up the headwall.

190A. To the right (S) of the entrance to Abu Iglakhat Canyon is a hanging 'Cenotaph Corner' climbed by Wilfried Colonna and friends (6C). No details.

Barrah Canyon

197A. Hala Bek *R. Bolle, H. Gargitter 26th February 1995.*
A two pitch route on a wall near R.197. Precise location not certain. 6A+/6A+.
Descent: Reverse the upper part (1 abseil) then left into a chimney, making a final abseil from a tree near the bottom.

Before entering the N end of Barrah Canyon, the outside NE Face well left of the entrance has an excellent black wall above a long leftward ramp.

202A. Salad-A-Din *T. Nonis, G. Hornby 28th February 1995.*
Good sustained climbing up the prominent crack and corner on the left, above the left end of the ramp. 200m. 5+/6A/5+/6A/6A.
Descent: By 4 equipped abseils.
There are more possibilities on the black wall to its right.

Next, back inside the canyon again,

206A. Suleiman's Ridge *Steve Kennedy, Andy Nelson 15th November 1994.*
Between R.206 and R.207 is a large ravine visible on the map (pg. 144). The route climbs the obvious slabby ridge on the right side of the ravine and should not be confused with a parallel ridge on its right. 300m. D.

Barrah Canyon
Salad-A-Din

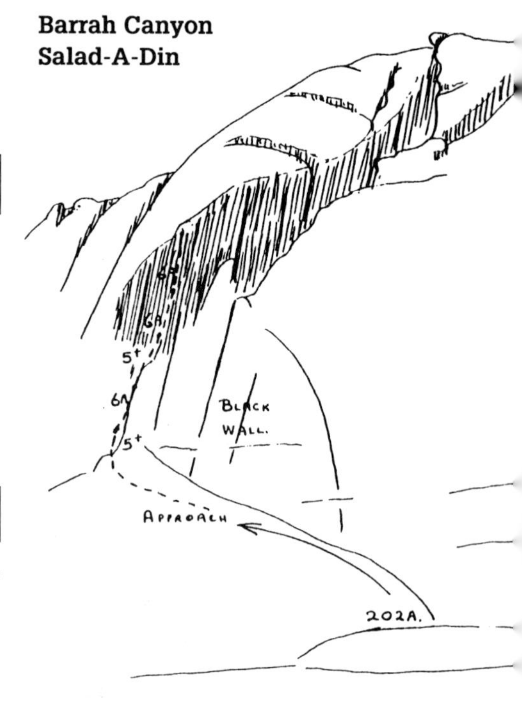

Up the corner right of the ridge-foot (4), to large platform then up the black wall and groove on the right of the bulging wall (5). Continue pleasantly up the slabby ridge (3 & 4).

Descent: Reverse the upper part (1 abseil) then left into a chimney, making a final abseil from a tree near the bottom.

Three single-pitch climbs have been added near to Merlin's Wand by five Swiss climbers. *21-27th October 1993:*

210A. Sido The short crack line just left of R210. 15m 5+.

210B. Tronche de Cake The black wall on its left. 35m 7A.

210C Mongolita et son Tuba The roofed corner 30m to the right of Merlin's wand. 25m 6A.

Descents: By abseil (equipped).

Five hundred metres S of Sundown (R.213) two routes are reported in a small siq. Precise location not known. *C& P Faivre, 30th April 1994.*

216A. Amstel The chimney line. 4/4/4/4+.

216B. Jamais sans mon Livre Traverse right from the above route to the corner crack. 4+/5+/6A.

Descent: 2 Abseils down 216B to the pedestal at its foot.

Much further south, up the canyon is the big west face of Abu Judaidah. In its centre is a very obvious crack heading for the summit, so far attempted in vain. Its first pitch is:

217A. The Start of the Beginning *T. Nonis, G. Hornby 2nd. March 1995.*

Possibly climbed before using aid. 40m. 6B+ (5.10c).

Directly opposite is:

217B. The Consolation Prize *T. Nonis, G. Hornby 2nd March 1995.*

The black water-worn crack on perfect rock. 25m 6A. (5.9)

Descent: There is a lower- off left of the top.

Barrah, South Canyon

At the right end of the wall right of R.218 is an obvious corner marking two single-pitch climbs. (Grades not known). *C. Hainz, H. Gargitter 27th February 1995.*

218A. Schoarf Unterwegs The corner 50m.

218B. Hala Hala The wall just round the right arête. 25m.

Seifan Kebir

West Face

219A. A Night At The Opera *T. Nonis, A&S Sammut, G.Hornby 17th February 1995.*

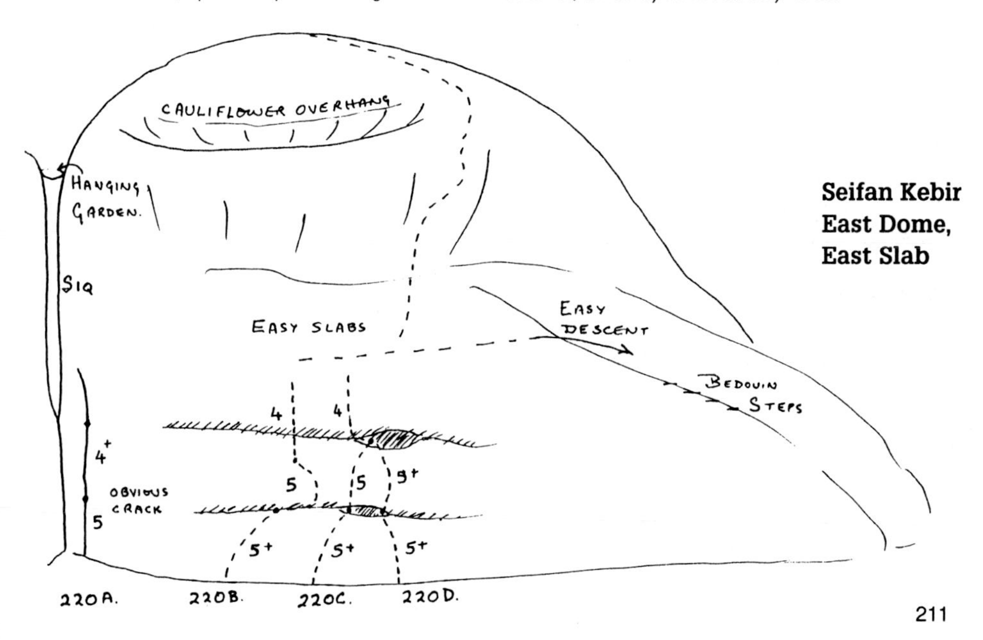

Seifan Kebir East Dome, East Slab

Ascends the buttress left of the summit, following slabs left of the N facing side wall in the middle of the west face. Not sustained, and sometimes loose. 350m T.D. Inf.

Descent: Down the SW Ridge to a huge square block, then a 40m abseil to the west. 2 more abseils (30m, 50m) then down to the big terrace crossing the W. Face below the headwall. Go N past the prow and down slabs in a gully line to the top of the first 5+ pitch. Abseil, then easily down the ridge to the N (long enough to cause a night out in T-shirts after a late start on the first ascent, hence the name!).

East Dome, East Slab

The following four very enjoyable routes are on a very beautiful slab reached by driving across the Disi flats past the N end of Seifan Kebir after which it may be necessary to walk the last 400m to the foot of the slab. (if you only have 2-wheel drive!). *G.Hornby, A, S. & M. Sammut and P. Bishop 3rd April 1994.* Topos page 211.

From left to right, beginning with the obvious crack right of the left edge of the slab, they are as follows :

220A. Maltese Falcon 100m 5/4+.

220B. Simply Red 100m 5+/5/4.

220C. Songlines 100m 5+/5/4

220D. Border Patrol 100m 5+/5+/4.

Any of the above routes can be continued to the summit 150m above, on easy slabs passing right of the overhangs near the top.

Descent: is easy with some Bedouin steps on the right of the slab.

Jebel Um's Daiat of Seifan, S. Summit

West Face

220E. The Good, the Bad, the Ugly *G. Hornby, S. Sammut 12th October 1995.*

The wall is seamed with cracks. This route takes one of them, up the left side of the main face, left of the top. After an initial long pitch of 5 the route relents to a direct line of 4 and 3 giving pleasant climbing. 180m A.D.Sup.

Descent: Down easily left of the route (looking out), crossing the route to a hidden abseil to the ground.

Jebel um Harag

This large peak is two kilometres S of Jebel Abu Judaidah (map pg. 135). It contains a massive Nabataean/Bedouin dam in its E side (in the siq visible on the map), the little valley at its entrance being a very pleasant area. This siq can be followed entertainingly for quite a way, and rumour has it that it's possible to go all the way through the mountain to the W. side!

Despite the size of this peak, only one new route has been climbed here to date:

222A. Sweaty Betty *T. Nonis, G.Hornby 26th. Feb 1995*

A nice mountain climb,not difficult but sometimes on poor rock. Predominantly 4 and 4+ with several short

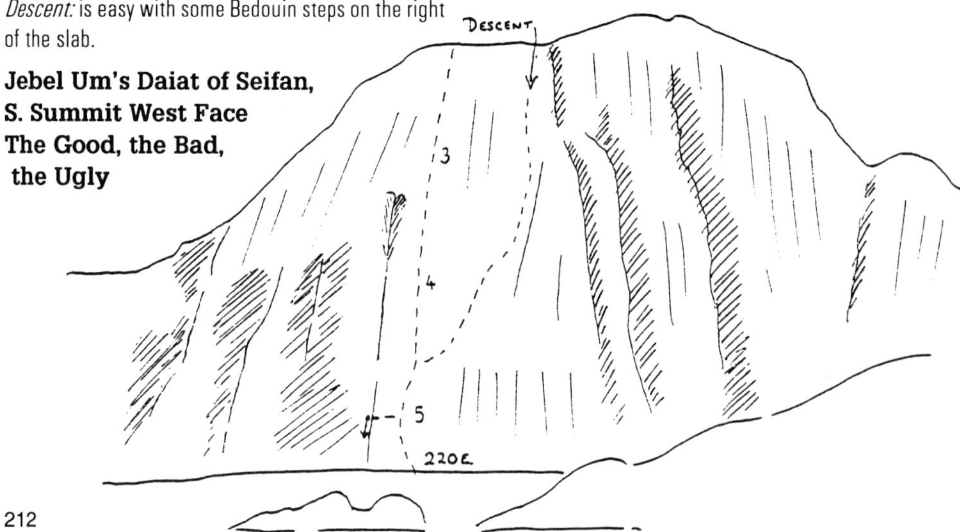

Jebel Um's Daiat of Seifan, S. Summit West Face The Good, the Bad, the Ugly

sections of 5+ in the lower cracks. 400m. T.D.Inf. 3 hours.

Descent: Down the route with one long abseil, then down a deep chimney in the lower section (5+). 5 hours.

200metres to the right of Sweaty Betty at the entrance to a very narrow siq is :

222B. Big Al Anfus *T. Nonis, A.Sammut 25th Feb 1995*

The crack and corner in the right wall. 25m. 6A (5.9)

Jebel um Tuleiha

This mountain is east of, and opposite Jebel um Harag, (map pg 135), from where the following route is obvious:

West Face

222D. Darkness on the Edge of Town *G.Hornby, A.& S.Sammut, T.Nonis 20th Feb 1995*

A lovely mountain climb with some short, hard cruxes, providing a great day out. 400m. D.

Climbs slabs below and left of the N facing side wall in the middle of the face, with several steps of 5 and 5+ moving left into corners.

Descent: Along the ridge and down the back to ultimately descend the huge sand slope left (NE) of the mountain.

Jebel um Tuleiha
West Face
Darkness on the Edge of Town

KHAZALI, BURDAH AND THE SOUTH

Khazali

223B. East Face A route has been climbed to the summit from the inner end of the N Canyon, up the East face by Sabbah Eid. No details, but he says the inscriptions in the canyon are coded messages identifying the route to hidden treasure on the top, so he goes up there whenever he's short of money!

Jebel Khush Khashah, N.E. Dome
North East Face
A Red Guitar, 3 Chords and The Truth

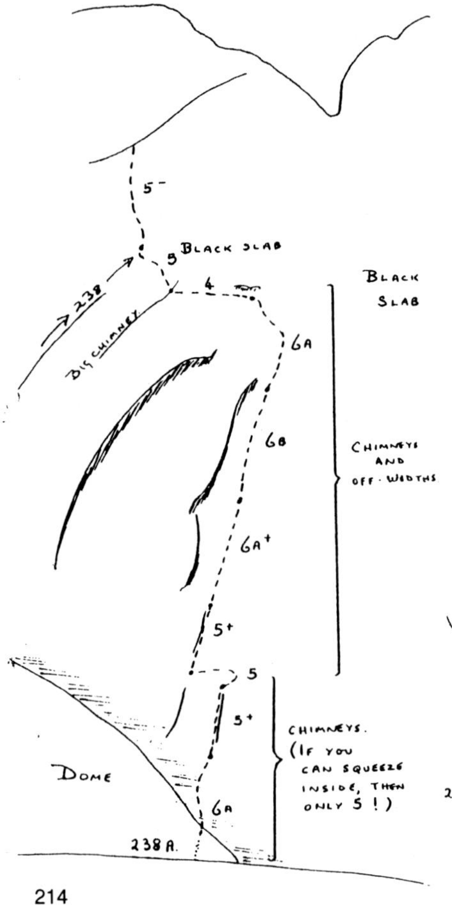

Jebel Khush Khashah, N.E. Dome

North East Face

238A. A Red Guitar,3 Chords and The Truth *T. Nonis, G. Hornby 3rd March 1995.*
Excellent crack climbing in the deep groove right of Purple Haze. Hendrix freaks will realise the affinity of route names! There is one bulge of poor rock but the route is predominantly superb water-worn off- widths. Carry the usual rack and 3 size 4 cams. 300m. T.D. Sup.
Descent: see R.238.

A route was also looked at to the left of R.238 without finding anything worthwhile.

Jebel Ikhnaisser

North Summit, N. Face

243A. Walking the Plank *M Shaw, A Howard, D. Taylor 2nd April 1994.*
Enjoyable and varied climbing commencing with a strenuous corner crack and finishing by an exposed traverse, then easily to the domes of the N. Summit. 250m D. Sup. 2½ hours.
Descent: From the N Summit plateau, cross a shallow

Jebel Ikhnaisser
North Summit, N. Face
Walking the Plank

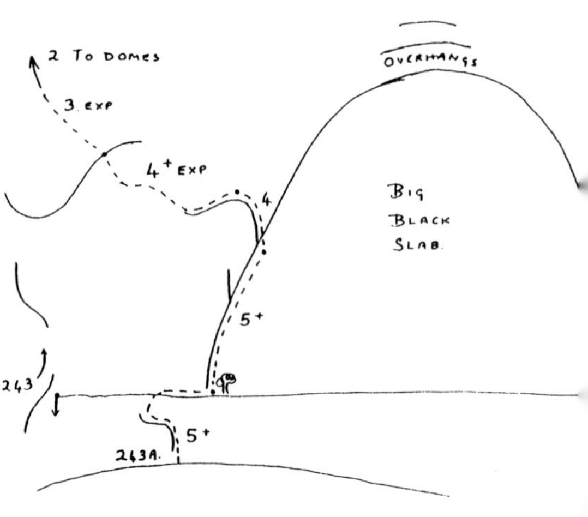

siq and contour west then south on a big ledge with a couple of awkward steps to the col at the top of the ramp and parallel cracks of R.240. Down this to the desert, then a 10 minute walk back to the start. 1 hour.

South East Face

243B. Trois Pignons *I. Poupinel, N. Maleway, B. Peronne, J. Robbe 16th April 1994.*

A nice, easy line with good protection and generally on good rock. 200m. P. D.

Ascend the wall to the right of a dam below a siq, then up (3, 3+) towards a roof and right (3) to the col below the headwall of R.240. Here, the easier right hand option of that route can be taken to the summit (3).

Descent: By R.240

Jebel Abu Khsheibah

West Face

The "left-hand crack" has now had its first pitch climbed:

245. Freedom as a Concept *P. Bishop, G. Hornby, S. Sammut 6th April 1994.*

The immaculate black corner 30m 6A.

Jebel um Hamata

This little top is at the NE end of the domes of Abu Khsheibah, (map pg.156).

North East Face

249A. Abu Sultan *Thierry Renault, Abu Sultan April 1994.*

Climb the right hand of two parallel cracks in the middle of the wall. Steep climbing but some poor rock. 120m 6A/5+/3.

Descent: Scramble down to the ledges at the top of pitch 2, then two abseils.

Jebel um Hamata
North East Face
Abu Sultan

3
5
5+ UGLY PASSAGE IN BLACK ROCK
5+
6A+ SANDY
NUMEROUS CRACKS
249A.

The left side of this little wall presents numerous cracks and possibilities.

Just N of here on the opposite side of a regularly used 4-wheel drive track from Burdah to Rum is a cluster of small domes, two of which have been climbed:

Bedouin Point 1165m

249B. East Face *M. Faiman, T.Behm 9th April 1994.*

A wandering line up the middle of the face; right, left (sandy, 4), right, then left and right again. Mostly 1 and 2. F.

Descent: The same way.

1. BEDOUIN POINT
2. JEBEL AEIDA
3. UNCLIMBED POINT
4. JEBEL UM HAMATA
5. BURDAH

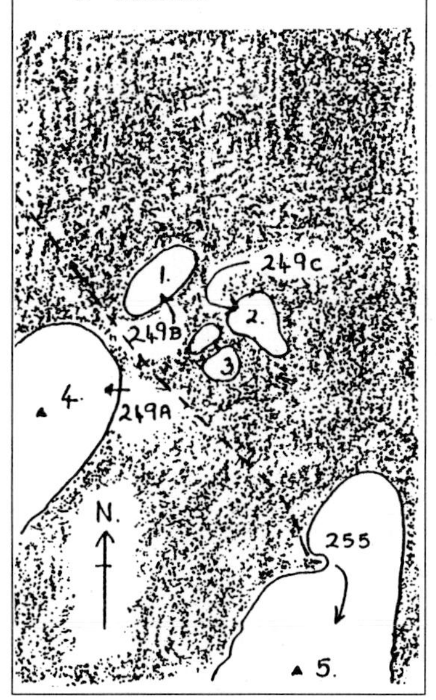

East of here is the Unclimbed Point (1140m) and, to its north,

Jebel Aeida 1110m

West Face

249C. Two Friends and the Desert *T. Behm, M. Faiman 9th April 1994*

A very beautiful little climb in a black and yellow corner with parallel finger cracks ending directly at the top. Good rock and protection (1 peg in situ). 100m. 5+/5-/5-. Map page 215.

Descent: Go down towards the north then right to a slab leading to an overhang. Climb down left and down a 20m chimney to the desert.

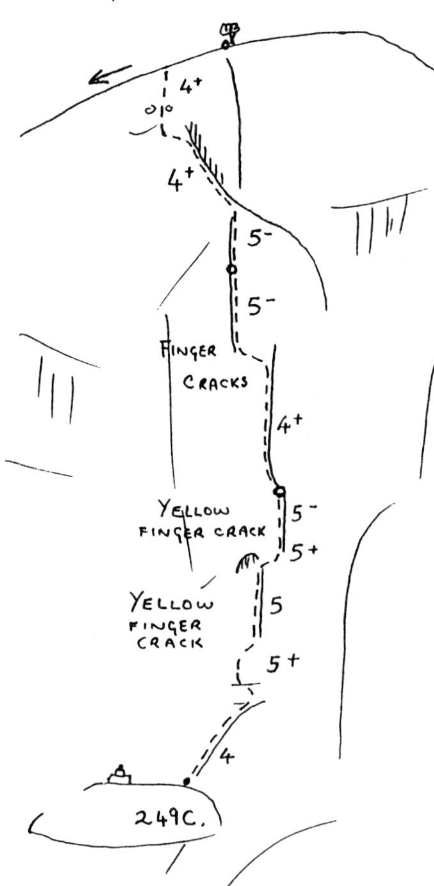

Jebel Aeida, West Face
Two Friends and the Desert

Immediately east of the north end of Jebel Abu Khsheibah (map pg. 156) is:

Jebel Dug'ranji

(Also known as Jebel um Saisiban el Januub.)

The following route is at the S end of the mountain. *Approach:* As R.250. The route will be seen on the left when entering the concealed desert basin N. of Jebel Um S'Daiat.

250A. S.E.Diedre, The Gorgon *(Probable first ascent of this summit) A. Howard, M. Shaw, D.Taylor 8th. April 1994.*

Named after the corals in the desert at the foot of the climb, the route ascends the attractive steep diedre which starts from a rock basin above a smooth slab. To its right is a chasm with a rock bridge. Enjoyable and varied climbing, 200 metres, then a long and easy scramble N to the top. D. 2-3 hours.

Descent: Go back a short way to the S, then left to domes below the E side of the summit . Go N on these to a black plateau, and continue N to an abseil from threads on the left side of a crack down a 40m vertical wall to a ravine. Cross the ravine onto its N side and continue along the NE edge of the mountain. Descend a groove to a hidden abseil (20m) into a corridor on the E wall. Descend this moving right (E) at half-way and down (3) onto a ramp of slabs which go all the way to the bottom. 1 hour, then a 15 minute walk S to the start of the climb.

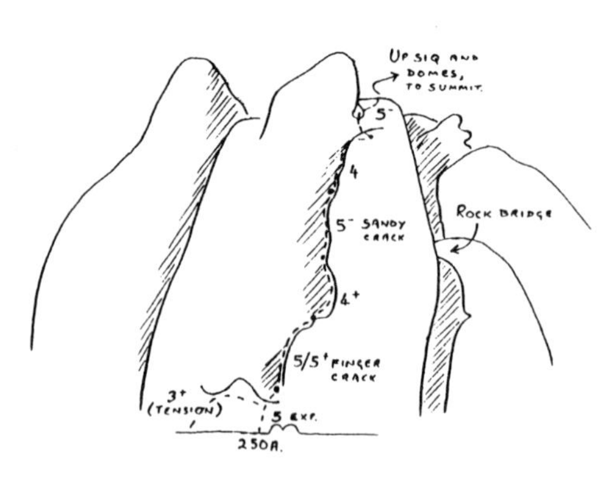

Jebel Dug'ranji
S.E. Diedre, The Gorgon

Jebel Farata Shaib

Four routes have been climbed at the N end of this peak. *Approach:* Down Khor el Ajram, then S between Um Saisiban and Um Hamata, (map pg. 156) where the parallel cracks of the next route become obvious.

254A. Macho Man and the Granny *A.Howard, D.Taylor, M.Shaw, Atieeq Auda 11th April 1994.*
Easy and direct climbing in a beautiful location with an excellent slab finish and a continuous choice of two lines. The highest top which is to the S is reached up a short wall (10m, 4+). 250m A.D. 1½-2 hours.
Descent: From the high top, go E, for 20m to a thread. Abseil 20m into the siq. Return to the wall above the route. Abseil 50m from a thread then down an easy slab and wall. Traverse right (3) to reach the route and descend this avoiding the first pitch by scrambling down left. 1 hour.
Alternatively, from the foot of the second abseil, follow ledges to a deep siq on the east side of the dome, then down with one short abseil at the bottom, to make a nice round- trip.

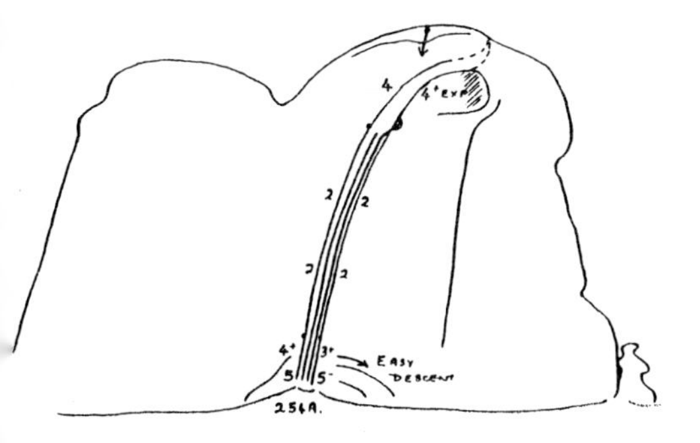

Jebel Farata Shaib
Macho Man and the Granny

To the left of 'Macho Man' is the northern nose of the mountain, around which are three routes:

254B. Lagavallin *Andy Nelson 9th November 1994.*
Straight up the nose and the cracks above to bulges and slabs. 100m 4+/4+.

254C. Balvenie *Stephen Kennedy, Andy Nelson 9th November 1994.*
Start 150m left of the nose at a flake crack corner out of a red ramp. Follow the crack then left through a small roof into a gully. 120m 4/4/4+.

254D. Mr Bean *D. Ritchie, N. Marshall 9th November 1994.*
50m left of the previous route is another clean flake crack. Climb it! 120m 4/4/3.
Descent: All three routes descend by a big spur and chimney on the west of the nose.

Burdah

East Face

256A. Tareeq Atieeq *Atieeq Auda, D. Taylor, A. Howard 1st May 1993.*
A companion line to Original Route and perhaps marginally harder, starting up a groove 20m to the left, then directly up a thin crack line in the slabs until forced to join Original Route by a siq. 250m. A.D. 1-1½ hours to the bridge. Maps page 218 and 219.

Next come more orange offerings on the sun-kissed slopes:

256B. Surfin' Satsumas *S. & M. Bissell 4th April 1994.*
Well right of R.256 just before the east face starts to drop back into a bay is a flake crack capped by a distinctive leftward arching overhang. Ascend the crack to the overhang (crux) then easy to the terrace. 70m 3/5+/6A/3. Map and topo page 219.
Descent: Go right (N) following shoulders then down a gully. (3).

259A. Marmalade Skies *S & M. Bissel, M. Sammut, P. Bishop 3rd April 1994.*
Yet another variation on R.258, this time peeling left from Orange Sunshine. 300m. D. Sup. Map page 218. From two-thirds up R258 traverse left into an amphitheatre and climb a series of pitches up the left edge to the terrace.
The above line can be gained independently from the left by either of two parallel crack-groove lines gained by trending right from the start of R.261 in the scree basin. These are:

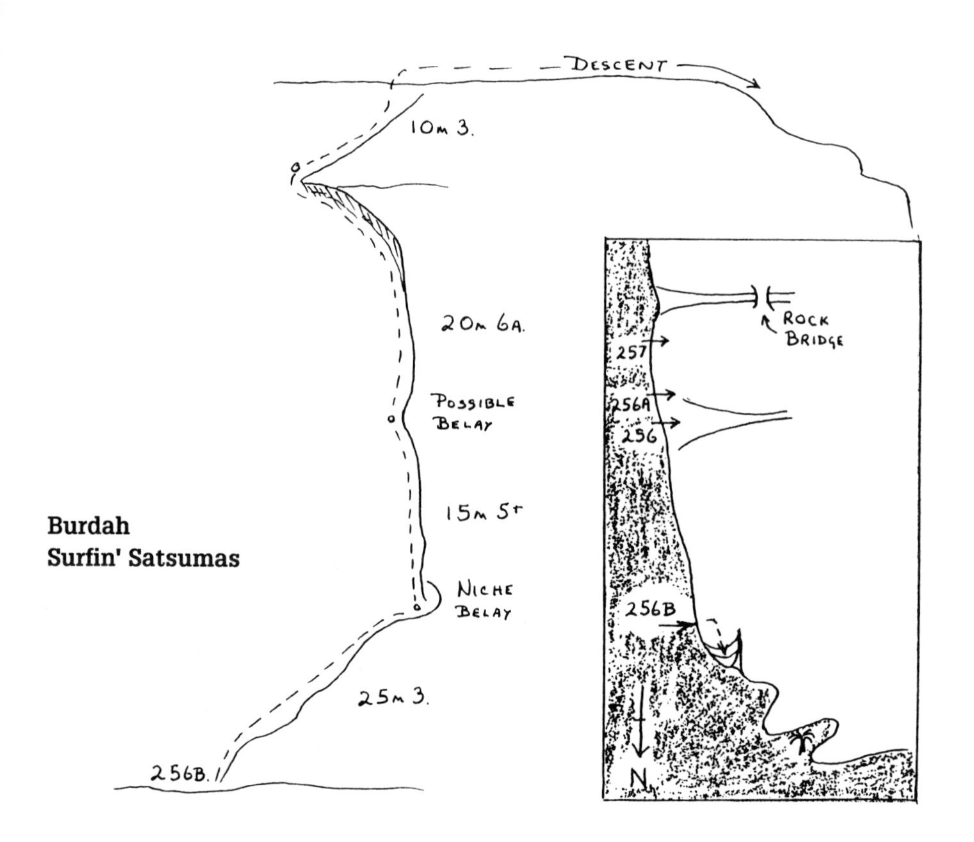

Burdah
Surfin' Satsumas

260A. The Golden Shred (Left-Hand) *G. Hornby, P. Ramsden 15th October 1995 200m D. Sup.* Map page 218.

260B. The Golden Shred (Right-Hand) *D. Hornby, P. Ramsden 15th October 1995 200m D.Sup.* Map page 218.

Also starting at R.261 is:

260C. Red Admiral *Andy Nelson, Neil Marshall November 1994.*
Take Tangerine Dream to the terrace, or variations to its left. At the terrace, move left to a prominent pure corner with a crack up the black wall going straight up to a yellow roof. Climb this for 150m (6A, 6B, 6B), the last pitch going left from a thinning crack to a flake. Pass the roof and continue up an easy blocky gully to the top 350m. T.D. Map page 218.

261A. Nectarine Nightmare *G. Hornby, S. Sammut, P. Bishop 4th April 1994.*
Takes a parallel line to R.261, up slabs well left of the scree-basin, finishing on the summit. Not sustained but several tough and loose pitches on the headwall. 350m T.D. Inf. Map page 218.
Start at the base of the obvious white drainage streak then pad up the slabs with a touch of insecurity (3,4) and up an unavoidable short wall (5+) to eventually arrive at the terrace. Above is an excellent groove (6A) below a yellow roof then left and up through loose grooves and pillars (5), "living-death" (maybe avoidable further left?), then more easily to the top.

Further left again one finds oneself behind a big sand dune,

Burdah, East Face Slabs

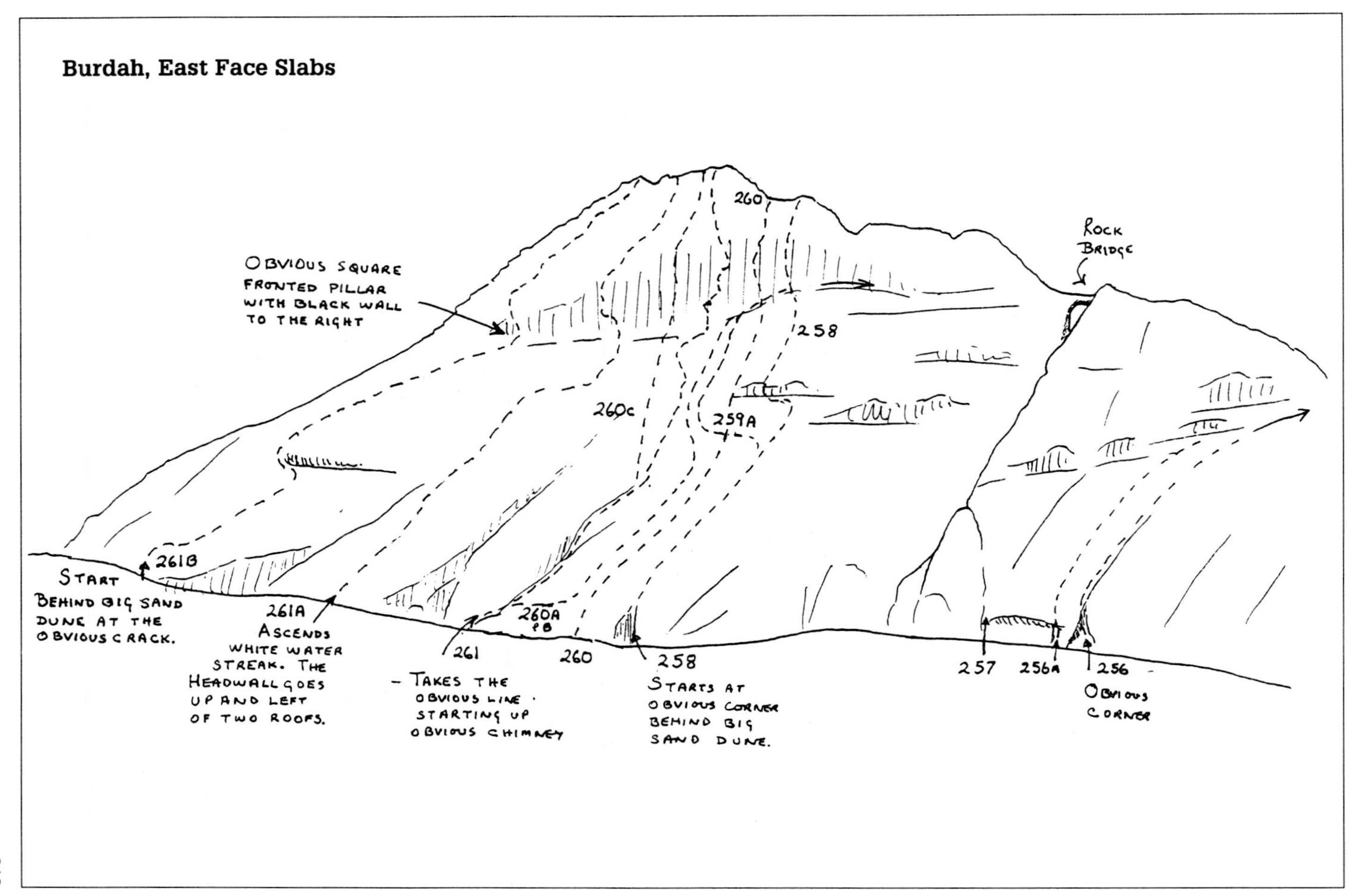

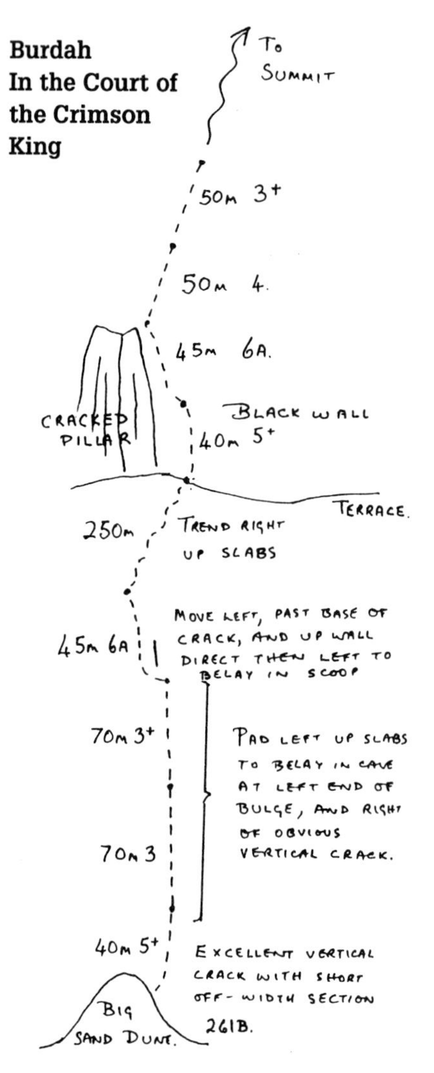

261B. In the Court of the Crimson King

A.& S. Sammut 3rd April 1994.

The best of this team's Burdah slab routes, and though not sustained it has several tough pitches. Start behind the dune at the excellent vertical off-width. T.D. 350 m. Map page 218.

Burdah South Summit 1464m

261C. South East Face *G. Hornby, S. Sammut 11th October 1995.*

A long route with little to recommend it, up easy angled slabs to below the steep headwall, avoided by trending right then back left above it. The crux is hard and loose. The rest is easy. Nice view from the top! 300m D. inf.

Massif of Jebel Suweibit

This is a very remote and quiet area just 5km north of the border with Saudi Arabia, with a few semi-nomadic Bedouin camps dotted around the desert landscape. (As the old border used to be north of here, some of the Bedouin carry Saudi passports and move across the border quite regularly.)

Approach: Drive down the Aqaba track until just SE of Jebel el Qattar (map pg. 6) from here cross dunes S, and SW though the domes of Um Sammen and along the E side of the large dome marked 1250m (map pg. 178). This is Al Giddar (The Pan). The Suweibit group will be seen to the S. (map pg. 177). Drive round its W side, then S to reach the next route. (A distance of about 24 K - allow 1 hour.)

Jebel Suweibit Gharbia

South Face

271A. The Haj *(Possible first ascent of this summit)*

A.Howard, M.Shaw, D.Taylor 23rd April 1995.

A stunning black pyramidal wall with an intimidating series of cracks up the centre of the lower face and an amazing diagonal line across the superb upper slab. A unique climb in a great setting. 280m T.D.inf 4-5 hours. Carry the usual rack of gear including at least one set of size 2-4 cams and some 5mm cord for the thread. Map and topo page 221.

Descent: Scramble E down the slabby ridge to a hidden abseil (20m) onto a pillar on the S face. (Here, it may be possible to abseil down the W side of the pillar onto scree and so directly to the gully head.) Now, go E down mushrooms then abseil (20m) into a chimney and scramble down returning W to the gully head.

At the top of the gully go behind big boulders, then a long walk east along a terrace (some short descents), then left to a 20m abseil down the nose. Left again through a passage and down to the edge of a steep chimney. Abseil into it (15m) and scramble to the desert. 1½ hours.

Jebel Suweibit Gharbia, South Face, The Haj

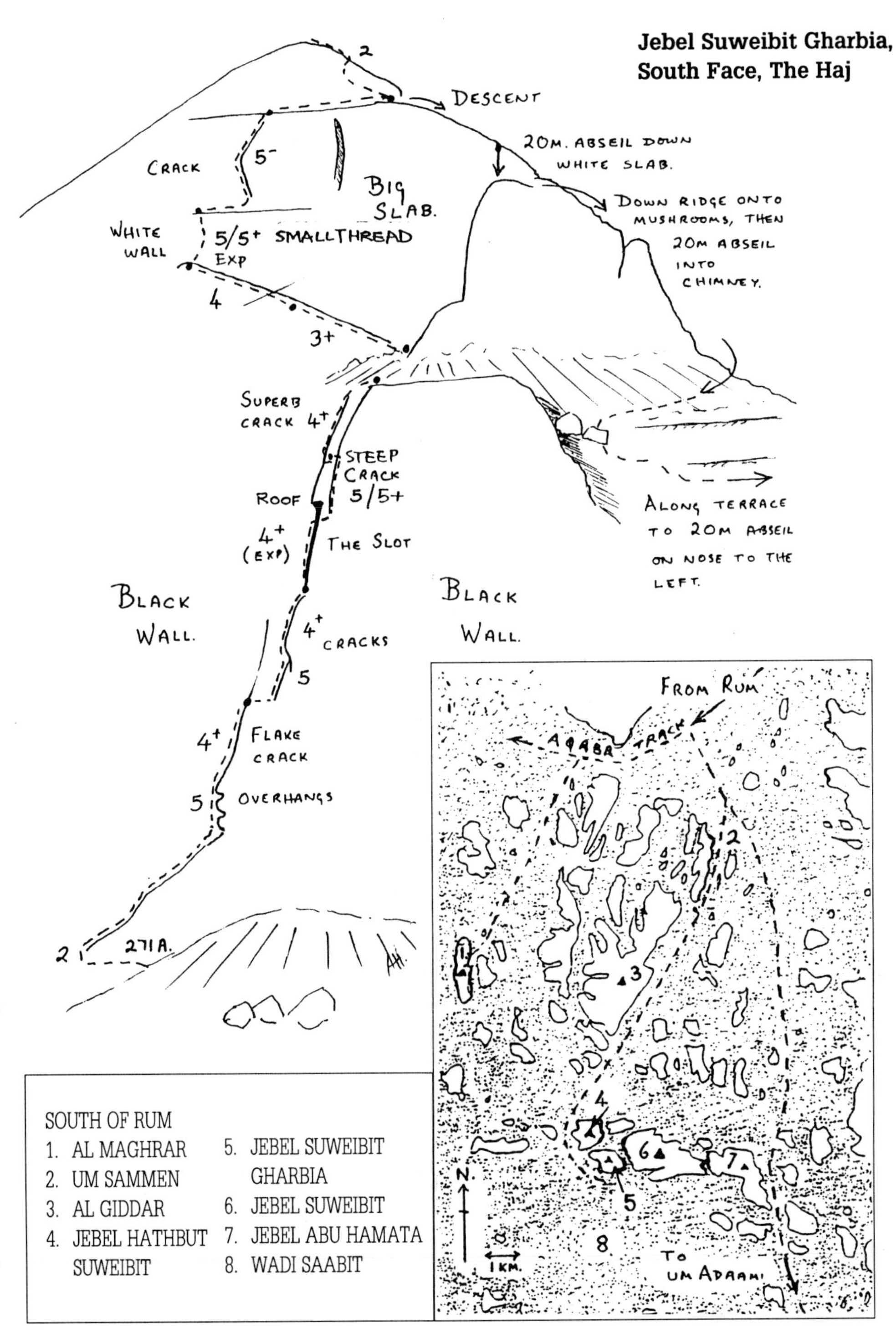

DESCENT
20M. ABSEIL DOWN WHITE SLAB.
DOWN RIDGE ONTO MUSHROOMS, THEN 20M ABSEIL INTO CHIMNEY.
CRACK
5-
BIG SLAB.
WHITE WALL
5/5+ SMALLTHREAD
EXP
4
3+
SUPERB CRACK 4+
STEEP CRACK 5/5+
ROOF
4+ (EXP)
THE SLOT
ALONG TERRACE TO 20M ABSEIL ON NOSE TO THE LEFT.
BLACK WALL.
BLACK WALL.
4+ CRACKS
5
4+ FLAKE CRACK
5 OVERHANGS
2
271A.
FROM RUM
AQABA TRACK
N.
1KM.
8
TO UM ADAAMI
SOUTH OF RUM
1. AL MAGHRAR
2. UM SAMMEN
3. AL GIDDAR
4. JEBEL HATHBUT SUWEIBIT
5. JEBEL SUWEIBIT GHARBIA
6. JEBEL SUWEIBIT
7. JEBEL ABU HAMATA
8. WADI SAABIT

Just N of the above summit, is:

Jebel Hathbut Suweibit

The east side of this small peak is reached by driving into the canyon which splits this group of peaks. A prominent bottom-less SE diedre will be seen just above the 'cross-roads'.

271B. Barefoot Groove *M.Shaw, D.Taylor, A.Howard, Atieeq Auda 20th April 1995.*
The obvious black groove is gained by cracks rising from the mouth of a gully, after passing an awkward (4+) section of mushrooms: 200m. A.D. inf. 1-1½ hours.
Descent: Go first N, then NW down slabs. 15 mins.

Anyone spending a day in this area will discover many more possibilities, some obvious, some in hidden canyons. Have fun!

Jebel Hathbut Suweibit
Barefoot Groove

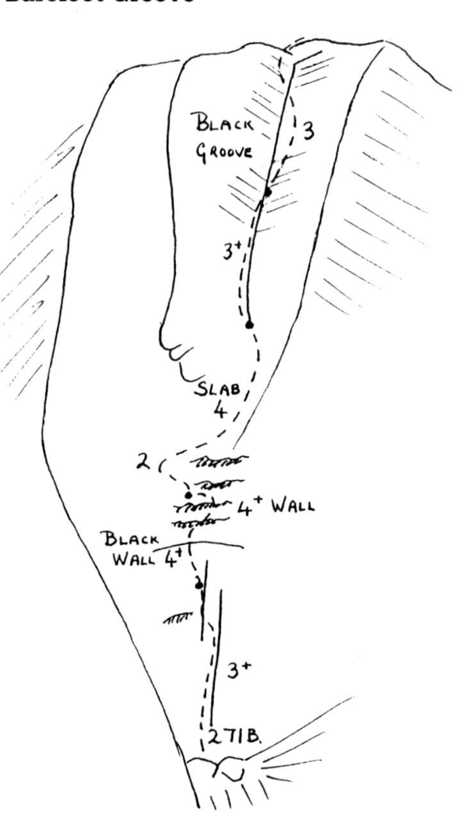

GRADED LIST OF ROUTES

The following list has been broken down into graded sections to give an idea of the number of routes available in each grade and in each area. The routes in each section are NOT in graded order but are listed as they appear in the book, including those in the 1996 New Routes supplement. The grading is the modern French system.

Whilst all climbs in this book should be worth doing unless stated otherwise, the best have been given 'star' status, from one star to three stars. This signifies ascending order of quality based on recommendations by the first ascent team and favourable comments from other climbers. The very best three-star routes are mostly of a nature unique to Wadi Rum. This should make the choice of a first route or final objective easier for visiting climbers whatever their standard. If you have any comment on star quality please leave your suggestions in the New Routes book at the Rest House.

E.D.

Jebel Rum Massif

Jebel um Ishrin Massif

Barrah Canyon Area

E.D.Sup

Jebel Rum Massif

Jebel um Ishrin Massif

Massif of Khush Khashah & Khazali

SHORT CLIMBS

These climbs are routes of 200m maximum length, frequently shorter and sometimes only single pitch. They are graded using the French system and listed area by area, as they appear in the book. Like the longer routes, the better climbs are given one to three stars in ascending order of quality. In general they have easy access and descents (often with fixed abseil pistes) and are in easily accessible areas. They are consequently less serious than most of the other routes in this book. However few have any fixed protection so a traditional 'rack' of chocks and cams will normally be needed and, in some cases, abseil slings. Anyone expecting a safe bolt protected sports climb will be disappointed! This is not what Wadi Rum is about: it's a 'wilderness area' - lets keep it that way!

Jebel Rum Massif

Jebel um Ishrin Massif

Barrah Canyon Area

Massif of Khush Khashah and Khazali

The Domes of Abu Khsheibah

Burdah

INDEX OF ROUTES

INDEX OF MAIN SUMMITS AND CANYONS

GLOSSARY OF CLIMBING TERMS

English	French	German	Italian
Abseil	Rappel	Abseilen	Discesa a corda doppia
Arch	Arc	Felsbrücke	Arco
Arete	Arête	Kante	Spigolo
Barrier	Barriere	Felsstufe	Barriera
Basin	Bassin	Becken	Bacino
Belay	Relais	Standplatz	Punto di sosta
Boulder	Roche	Block	Sassisho
Bolt	Spit	Bohrhaken	Spit
Bridge	Pont	Brücke	Ponte
Buttress	Contrefort	Rücken	Pilastro
Cairn	Cairn	Steinmann	Ometto
Canyon	Canyon	Schlucht	Gola
Cave	Grotte	Höhle	Grotta
Chimney	Cheminée	Kamin	Camino
Chocks	Coinceurs	Klemmkeile	Nuts
Chockstone	Bloc coince	Klemmblock	Masso incastrato
Cirque	Cirque	Talabschluss	Circo
Cleft	Cheminée très large	Weiter Kamin	Camino, largo da spaccata
Cliff	Falaise	Klippe	Falesia
Col	Col	Pass	Colle
Corner	Diedre	Verschneidung	Diedro
Crack	Fissure	Riss	Fessura
Crisps	Craquant	Kleingrissig	Piccolo appiglio
Crux	Passage clef	Schlüsselstelle	Passaggio chiave
Curve	Courbe	Gebogen	Curva
Dangerous	Dangereux	Gefährlich	Pericoloso
Diedre	Diedre	Verschneidung	Diedro
Difficult	Difficile	Schwierig	Difficile
Dihedral	Diedre	Verschneidung	Diedro
Dome	Dome	Dom	Cupola
Down	Vers le bas	Hinunter	Verso il basso
Drill	Drille	Bohrer	Foro
Edge	Arête	Kante	Spigolo
Exposed	Expose	Ausgesetet	Esposto
Fissure	Fissure	Riss	Fessura
Flake	Ecaille	Schuppe	Scaglia
Friction	Friction	Reibung	Aderenza
Gap	Brèche	Lücke	Forcella
Groove	Couloir étroit	Rinne	Canale stretto
Gully	Couloir	Couloir	Canalone

Headwall	Paroi	Gipfelwand	Parete
Inscription	Inscription	Inschrift	Graffito
In-situ	En place	Eingerichtet	In sito
Intimidating	Impressionant	Beeindruckend	Impressionante
Jamming crack	Fissure à coincement de mains	Handriss	Fessura per incastro della-mano
Layback	Dülfer	Piazen	Fessura alla dulfer
Ledge	Vire	Band	Cengia
Left	Gauche	Links	Sinistra
Loose	Friable	Brüchig	Friabile
Mushrooms - (of rock)	Champignons (de roc)	Felspilze	Fungo (di roccia)
Nuts	Coinceurs	Klemmkeile	Nuts
Obvious	Evident	Offensichlicht	Evidente
Overhang	Surplomb	Uberhang	Strapiombo
Peak	Pic	Gipfel	Picco
Peg	Piton	Haken	Chiodo
Pillar	Pilier	Pfeiler	Pilastro
Pitch	Longueurs de corde	Seillange	Lunghezza di corda
Plateau	Plateau	Plateau	Pianoro
Platform	Large vire	Absatz	Gradone
Polished	Lisse	Glatt	Levigato
Protection	Assurence	Sicherung	Sicurezza
Rake	Vire diagonale	Rampe	Cengia diagonale
Rappel	Rappel	Abseilen	Discesa a corda doppia
Ravine	Ravin	Relspalte	Gola
Rib	Cote	Rippe	Costa
Ridge	Arête	Grat	Cresta
Right	Droite	Rechts	Destra
Roof	Toit	Dach	Tetto
Saddle	Col	Sattel	Sella
Scramble	Escalade facile	Leichtes klettern	Arampicata facile
Scree	Eboulis	Geroll	Pietraia
Serious	Serieuse	Ernsthaft	Serio
Shoulder	Eperon	Schulter	Spalla
Siq (canyon)	Canyon	Schlucht	Canyon
Slab	Dalles	Platte	Lastra
Slings	Sangles	Schlingen	Fettuccia
Smooth	Lisse	Glatt	Liscio
Spur	Eperon	Pfeiler	Sperone
Steep	Raide	Steil	Rapido
Strenuous	Penible	Anstrengend	Faticoso
Summit	Sommet	Gipfel	Cima
Sustained	Soutenir	Anhaltend	Difficolta sostenuta

Tape (web)	Sangle	Schlauchband	Fettuccia
Thread	Enfiler	Sanduhr	Clessidra
Tor	Pointe	Türmchen	Punta
Tower	Tour	Turm	Torre
Traverse	Traversee	Quergang	Traversata
Tree	Arbre	Baum	Albero
Up	En haut	Hinauf	Su
Vertical	Vertical	Senkrecht	Verticale
Walk	Marche	Gehen	Camminata
Wall	Mur	Wand	Parete

الإهداء

نهدي هذا الكتاب الى أهالي
قرية رم عرفاناً لما أبدوه من حسن
الضيافة والصداقة. وكذلك لاظهارهم
الطرق البدويّة المؤدية الى الجبال
فليباركهم الله وليحفظ بلادهم.

المؤلفان
توني هوارد
ديانا تايلور

١٩٩٣

Text printed by St Edmundsbury Press,
Blenheim Industrial Park, Newmarket Road, Bury St Edmunds, Suffolk